Love and Violence

Marriage as Metaphor for the Relationship between YHWH and Israel in the Prophetic Books

Gerlinde Baumann

Translated by Linda M. Maloney

A Michael Glazier Book

LITURGICAL PRESS
Collegeville, Minnesota

www.litpress.org

A Michael Glazier Book published by the Liturgical Press

Cover design by David Manahan, O.S.B. Photo from Art Today, Inc.

Originally published as *Liebe und Gewalt. Die Ehe als Metapher für das Verhältnis JHWH–Israel in den Prophetenbüchern* by the Verlag Katholisches Bibelwerk GmbH, Stuttgart, SBS 185 (2000).

Scriptural quotations are based upon the New Revised Standard Version. Those altered in light of the author's German version are marked with **.

1 2 3 4 5 6 7 8

Library of Congress Cataloging-in-Publication Data

Baumann, Gerlinde, 1962–
[Liebe und Gewalt. English]
Love and violence : marriage as metaphor for the relationship between YHWH and Israel in the prophetic books / Gerlinde Baumann ; translated by Linda M. Maloney.
p. cm.
"A Michael Glazier book."
Includes bibliographical references and index.
ISBN 0-8146-5147-X (alk. paper)
1. Bible. O.T. Prophets—Feminist criticism. 2. Marriage—Biblical teaching. 3. Metaphor in the Bible. I. Title.

BS1505.6.M3B3813 2003
224'.064—dc21 2003047608

To my sister
Kirsten Baumann

Contents

Part III. Summary and Conclusion

Foreword

My interest in the unwieldy topic of the metaphors of marriage in the prophetic books began with my study of the book of Nahum, inspired by Elke Seifert's work,[1] in which she treated Nah 3:4-7 among many other texts. This relatively unknown prophet, with his image of God as rapist of the city of Nineveh, personified as a woman, seemed to me so scandalous that I wanted to shed more light on the backgrounds of that passage in the text. I began to craft my own route of access to Nahum and his image of God, problematic in other facets as well.[2] Since then I have concentrated my research on Nah 1:2-8. In my opinion this text attempts to embed this Nahum text describing God's violent behavior, which even in Old Testament times was experienced as repellent, in a broader theological horizon and thus to relativize it to some extent.

From the beginning, then, the center of my interest in the prophetic imagery of marriage was not YHWH the "loving husband." Moreover, as my investigation proceeded I doubted more and more whether the aspect of "the love of YHWH" for Israel was very important to the metaphoric complex itself. More strongly in the foreground, as the vocabulary selection in the texts reveals, was YHWH's punishment of Israel, or Jerusalem. Is the complex of metaphors of sexual violence really inseparable from the prophetic marriage imagery? That is one of the initial questions in this study. If the answer is "yes," the problem of how to deal today with such metaphors, and with such a God-image, is all the more acute.

I would like to add some personal reflections. Working with this topic was not easy. In the two years in which I wrote this book I have come to

[1] Elke Seifert, *Tochter und Vater im Alten Testament. Eine ideologiekritische Untersuchung zur Verfügungsgewalt von Vätern über ihre Töchter* (Neukirchen-Vluyn: Neukirchener Verlag, 1997).

[2] A first fruit of this encounter can be found in the *Kompendium Feministische Bibelauslegung*, completed several years ago. The essay is cited here as Baumann 1999a, since in the spring of 1999 the *Kompendium* was already in its second edition. (An English publication is in preparation through Wm. B. Eerdmans, Grand Rapids.)

realize more and more what kind of personal demands are posed by an engagement with violence. It has not left me—and it certainly has not left others—untouched. I had to struggle continually to distance myself from the violence in the texts. One reason for this is that violence is not restricted to these biblical texts. A glance at the present reality, of women especially, makes it obvious that there is no reason to set ourselves apart, in our "civilized perspective," from the supposedly raw morals and violent behavior found in ancient Israel. Although I live in what is in many respects a position of privilege, as an academic in the Federal Republic of Germany, I find myself exposed every day to various forms of violence, either potential or actual: beginning with physical threats at particular times and in particular places, continuing with subtle forms of misogyny and contempt for women in a wide variety of contexts, and not ending with the structural violence against women that persists in legal ordinances and institutional customs. Not without reason are new initiatives to combat "violence against women" emerging. In German society in the last few years there has been a growing awareness of the existence of violence in families. This awareness finds expression also, unfortunately, in salacious media treatment, especially of sexual violence against girls. In the process, violence against adult women and violence within marriage are often overlooked—and yet marriage is the relationship in which it is easiest for violent men to make women their victims: "The more you trust in a man, the more risky it is for your health: sexual relationships without illusion."[3] Alberto Godenzi gives that title to a chapter in his evaluation of a sociological study on the theme of sexual violence based on telephone interviews conducted in Switzerland in 1988. He expands on this: "A woman is more vulnerable to a man when she is in a one-to-one relationship with him. The man is a great deal more certain of his victim. It is obvious that these theses apply especially to marriage." In Germany the situation is not very different from that in Switzerland. The Brockhaus encyclopedia, a source that deserves to be regarded without a great deal of suspicion, states that, according to a poll conducted by Allensbach, rape occurs in every fifth marriage.[4] I doubt that this is different in the United States.

Alongside this face of present reality there are still other facets of violence against women: fantasies in the heads of hordes of people, over-

[3] This and the following quotation are from Alberto Godenzi, *Bieder, brutal. Frauen und Männer sprechen über sexuelle Gewalt* (2nd ed. Zürich: Unionsverlag, 1991) 135, 138. Elke Seifert (1997) drew my attention to this study; she quotes it frequently.

[4] *Brockhaus. Die Enzyklopädie in vierundzwanzig Bänden* (20th ed. Leipzig and Mannheim: F. A. Brockhaus, 1996–) 17 [1998] 172.

whelmingly of the male gender. In the "male fantasies" included in a study now almost twenty years old, Klaus Theweleit sketched a panorama of what literary men expressed about women at the beginning of the last century.[5] This certainly led to a greater degree of awareness about such thoughts on violence—but it is questionable whether it brought about a reduced "production" of such images.

I would like to add some remarks on the occasion of the American publication of this study. German and American societies are similar in many respects, but there are some differences. For one thing, the discussion of "domestic violence" in the United States began much earlier than in Germany and is far more extensively developed. On the other hand, personal experiences of violence in the context of war are still very vivid in broad segments of the civilian population of the "old continent," even almost sixty years after the end of the Second World War. I myself am the granddaughter and daughter of people who, as civilians in and after the World War, experienced in their own skin the various forms of military violence: bomber raids, hunger, misery, expatriation, occupation, the threat of rape, and so on. The fact that such experiences were still alive in my immediate context certainly impelled me, more than many other women exegetes, to focus sharply on the consequences of military conflict for women as the background of the prophetic marriage imagery.

In the context of scholarship, too, I see this study as a "cross-cultural" project. My close work with the original Hebrew text, as well as the search for an understanding of the text against its own historical background are due to my shaping in the context of German theological scholarship. It is true that I have not made a close examination of the details of the process by which the texts originated. That has to do with the way the study began and with the time available to me. On the other hand, I have attempted to take the text seriously in its canonical end-form, as we now have it. The fact that I do so is due not only to hermeneutical and feminist-theological considerations, but also to the influence on me of English-language scholarship. This mixture has resulted in a theology that considers the statements and metaphors of a text both in their historical context and in their effects on people today. I hope that this "crossing of boundaries" will be positively received in the United States as well, and I wish that this project

[5] Klaus Theweleit, *Männerphantasien.* 2 vols. (Frankfurt: Roter Stern, 1977–78). English: *Male Fantasies.* Translated by Stephen Conway in collaboration with Erica Carter and Chris Turner. Foreword by Barbara Ehrenreich. 2 vols. (Minneapolis: University of Minnesota Press, 1987–89), vol. 1.

may find imitators and advance the conversation between the scholarly contexts of the "old" and "new" worlds.

Three years have passed since the German publication of this book. During that time some additional works have appeared on the prophetic marriage imagery, including a number of my own pieces on individual topics. To the extent that I have learned from the researches of other exegetes, I have referred to them in the Notes.

I owe thanks to a whole group of people who supported me in the production of the German edition. But at this point my thanks go above all to Linda M. Maloney. She has worked with this unwieldy material, detected some minor and (yes, unfortunately!) major mistakes in the German publication and corrected them, sought out many English translations of German titles, and lent her wonderful style to the whole work. No one else has read this book as carefully as she has. I am lucky to have had her as a companion on the "second pilgrimage" through the stony thought-paths of the prophetic marriage imagery!

Gerlinde Baumann
Marburg, February 2003

Introduction

The texts containing prophetic marriage imagery[1] that we have to consider besides Nah 3:4-7 include Hosea 1–3; Jeremiah 2–3; Ezekiel 16 and 23; Isaiah 40–66; Lamentations 1; Micah 1; and Malachi 2. Here YHWH and Israel or Jerusalem are presented metaphorically as "husband" and "wife." In Chapter Three (B) I will give reasons for the way I have defined the semantic field of prophetic marriage imagery and the choice of texts that results.

The concept of "marriage imagery" is not really satisfying as a description of the phenomenon in question, but since it has become customary usage among scholars I have adopted it. It allows for a clarification of the problem that is the subject of this work, namely the tension between the image of marriage that emerges in the texts, shaped by its Old Testament context, and an understanding of marriage that has developed within the realities of modern Western cultures. That tension has to be taken into account at all times within this study. Even the language in which the marriage imagery is projected in the prophetic books is essentially different from that of its present-day audience. Let me offer a few examples:

A central term in the prophetic marriage imagery is the Hebrew word for "harlotry," or "prostitution," which here and there is used as equivalent to "adultery." According to Old Testament law codes, the penalty for adultery was death. Today, while it is true that many people regard adultery as "immoral" behavior, it is no longer a punishable offense in law. In older exegetical literature the "shameless behavior" of the "harlot" is regarded as "unchastity," words that are no longer part of the active vocabulary of most people. Even in newer contributions to scholarship the behavior of the "woman" Israel/Jerusalem is frequently called "infidelity." That word, at least, is certainly in active use today, but not only to describe "straying"

[1] Since there is no English word directly corresponding to the German collective term "Metaphorik," I will generally translate it as "imagery," but occasionally with other expressions that preserve the emphasis on its metaphoric character.—Tr.

from a relationship. The German word "Untreue" (infidelity) is indeed at home in many different contexts—for example, in the world of finance, where it designates punishable misuse of invested funds. We may conclude that the interpretation of marriage imagery in particular is highly contextualized, shaped in essential ways by the circumstances out of which the usage arises. In language and culture the Old Testament is fundamentally different from present-day life in Western Europe or North America. Misunderstandings in the interpretation of these texts are almost pre-programmed.

Tensions also arise in connection with the God-image in the prophetic marriage metaphors. Our ideas about what God should and should not do, what means "he" has at "his" disposal and which ones are hard for present-day people to stomach are different from those of the people of Old Testament times. The version of God in which "he" is presented, in connection with the prophetic marriage imagery, as a sexually violent male is just one of many problematic sides of the biblical God-image.[2] Meanwhile feminist exegetes, among whom I count myself, have investigated the role of the "women" Israel and Jerusalem in the prophetic marriage imagery, together with its implications for readers. However, very little has been said about the God-image in the texts. Even in works like that of Walter Dietrich and Christian Link on the "dark sides of God" or Manfred Görg's study of the "un-holy God" the problem of the divine rapist is set aside or minimized.[3] This book is moving across a theologically difficult field.

In order that this project may have a successful outcome I have preceded the text-studies proper, in Part II, with an introductory Part I, which gives some overarching explanations of various themes that are important for understanding the prophetic marriage imagery. First I offer an overview of a selection of the studies already presented on this theme (I.1.). Prophetic marriage imagery, as the name indicates, consists of images

[2] This is clear from works like those of Walter Dietrich and Christian Link (*Die dunklen Seiten Gottes. Vol. 1: Willkür und Gewalt; Vol. 2: Allmacht und Ohnmacht* [Neukirchen-Vluyn: Neukirchener Verlag, 1995/2000]) or Manfred Görg (*Der un-heile Gott. Die Bibel im Bann der Gewalt* [Düsseldorf: Patmos, 1995]).

[3] Dietrich and Link write (1:95) of the "jealous God" in Hos 2:18: "'Lord': this attribute is applied [in Hos 2:18] to Baal, not YHWH. In the one-to-one relationship with Israel, YHWH is (sic!) not the husband as lord, but simply 'the man.' Feminist ears should not hear wrong notes here. . . . The accent, however, lies . . . on the partnership between God and the people, which excludes self-glorification on the one side and subservience on the other." It is puzzling how Dietrich and Link support their interpretation, with its distinction between the attribute בעל in the sense of a loving husband (YHWH) and a powerful husband-lord (the competing Baal). The OT understanding of marriage, at any rate (see Chapter Three below), was unaware of such a distinction in its picture of the husband.

conveyed in words. These can be understood in many ways. Here I want to furnish my readers with a concept of metaphors that has a theoretical basis, a concept that is basic to contemporary discussions (I.2.). I will discuss some hermeneutical problems in dealing with metaphors and will attempt to distinguish between "explanation" of texts from their own context and "interpretation" in the present context. This is an endeavor to allow the texts themselves to speak out of their own metaphoric background, and also to be accountable to a present-day frame of reference. In our investigation of the texts the two cannot be kept completely apart, but an attempt at distinction can contribute to greater clarity in the exegesis. In a third step (I.3.) I will stake out the semantic field of the prophetic marriage imagery and thus the field of the texts to be examined. Here we must discuss a number of terms that present some difficulties for the translator. This will be followed by a definition of the relationship between the marriage imagery and the Old Testament metaphor that is most closely related to it: YHWH's "covenant" with Israel (I.4.). In a section on the ancient Near Eastern background for the metaphoric world of the prophetic marriage imagery (I.5.) I will ask whether there are sources in that world that can make it easier for us to understand these texts in their time and context.

In Part II of the book, then, I will turn to the texts in what at the present state of research appears to be their chronological sequence: Hosea, Jeremiah, Ezekiel, Lamentations, Isaiah, and the Twelve Prophets, exclusive of Hosea. I will deal with the book of Lamentations, the only non-prophetic book in this study, in an excursus: because of its brevity there is no need for chapter divisions in this case. As indicated above, considerable parts of the study will be devoted to an explication of the texts themselves. After an overview of the marriage imagery in the book in question (A), there will be an investigation of the semantic field of marriage and sexual violence in the book in connection with related Old Testament passages (B, C). Then follows a shift to the level of feminist interpretation of the texts, which in many places is critical in nature (D). The critique is concentrated on individual passages in the texts. Consequently, this study will first ask what other metaphors, besides that of marriage, are present in the particular literary context of this imagery, that is, in the field of female metaphors and God-image(s) in this individual biblical book (E). Are there perhaps some metaphors present that correct the marriage imagery or counter it in such a way that it may appear in a different light? At the end of each chapter I will offer a summary of the results of the investigation of the individual book (F), in which the findings of the previously separate "explanatory" and "interpretive" steps can be brought together.

I will deviate from this division of the chapters only in the case of the short book of Lamentations and the book of the Twelve Prophets (II.10). Since the book of the Twelve is already divided into individual writings a further subdivision would burden the chapter with a number of very short sections, something to be avoided.

A third and final section will draw conclusions from the study. After a review of the results of the textual studies I will emphasize the necessity of reflective and critical reading. There is still an urgent need for research on the God-image. A look to the future will consider, among other things, the question whether there can be counter-texts or "compensatory texts" for these, with the help of which the problematic biblical passages containing the prophetic marriage imagery can be more adequately interpreted.

Part I

The Prophetic Marriage Imagery: Research and Background

Chapter One

Overview of Recent Scholarly Discussion and Definition of the Author's Position

A. Preliminary remark

Prophetic marriage metaphors have been the object of theological research in a number of ways.[1] In Old Testament exegesis the examination of God-imagery is frequently the context for a confrontation with these marriage metaphors.[2] The female metaphorical personae, in their individual

[1] They have also been important in several different ways in dogmatic theology. There is a very trenchant example in Karl Barth: "Man is primarily and properly Yahweh, and woman primarily and properly Israel. . . . That is why we have to do here with God's word concerning man, so that we cannot deviate on either side from what is said. We note that Old Testament prophecy everywhere presupposes the sin of man, Israel's apostasy, and therefore the Law and judgment of God, but also and more particularly the faithfulness of God. It thus speaks in the light of the shattering of the original on the side of man. It speaks of the covenant broken by Israel, and therefore of the unfaithful wife who has forfeited her rights and dignity. But in contrast it also speaks of the kindness and mercy of the Husband whom she has left and injured, but who does not abandon her. . . . We must be clear that they [the Old Testament poets—*GB*] were not just speaking symbolically or allegorically; they were speaking directly and concretely of man and woman and their relationship" (Karl Barth, *Die Kirchliche Dogmatik*. 4 vols. in 13 [Zollikon/Zürich: Evangelischer Verlag, 1939–67]. III/2: *Die Lehre von der Schöpfung* 358–59; English: *Church Dogmatics*. 4 vols. in 12. Authorized translation by G.T. Thompson. [London: T & T Clark, 1936–63] 297–98. I am grateful to Helga Kuhlmann for this reference. I cannot undertake a discussion of Barth's conception of the relationship of the sexes with reference to YHWH's relationship to Israel at this point, but I would like to refer to the critique by J. Christine Janowski of the significance of gender differences in Barth ("Zur paradigmatischen Bedeutung der Geschlechterdifferenz in K. Barths 'Kirchlicher Dogmatik,'" in Helga Kuhlmann, ed., *Und drinnen waltet die züchtige Hausfrau. Zur Ethik der Geschlechterdifferenz* [Gütersloh: Chr. Kaiser, 1995] 140–86). She deals with the connection to the marriage of YHWH and Israel especially on pp. 165–68.

[2] This can be illustrated, for example, in Stephen Bitter's work on the history of exegesis (*Die Ehe des Propheten Hosea. Eine auslegungsgeschichtliche Untersuchung* [Göttingen: Vandenhoeck & Ruprecht, 1975]) with regard to Hosea 1–3. The overwhelming majority of interpreters, as becomes clear, are interested in how God can command, or personally enter into, a marriage with a "prostitute." The moral offensiveness of this is regarded as the core problem in the text (thus Bitter's brief summary on pp. 181–82).

character and problematic, are scarcely visible. Since the 1980s there has been a clear shift in exegetical treatment of the prophetic marriage metaphors. Whereas in older (non-feminist) works the subject was most commonly discussed under the topic of "God's love,"[3] the foreground is now occupied by the aspect of violence against the "wife" in the marital relationship (with reference to concrete women's experiences), as well as by the pornographizing of the imagery.

In what follows I will present several recent contributions to the theme, in the order of their publication. My selection makes no claim to comprehensiveness. The focus is on studies that treat not only the texts, but the *complex of metaphors* they use. Feminist contributions to research are richly represented, for their determined adoption of a new angle of vision has given the strongest impulse to the discussion. As my survey has shown, there are very few studies of prophetic marriage metaphors in recent exegetical discussions outside the branch devoted to feminist research.

The beginning of feminist exegetical treatment of prophetic marriage metaphors coincides with the first efforts at feminist scholarly exegesis. Consequently, some of the older contributions treated a number of themes together, without clear differentiation. Later there was a sharper distinction drawn, particularly among three thematic complexes: individual texts (primarily Hosea and Ezekiel), themes ("whoredom" or the problem of violence against women), or the manner of presentation within the texts (pornography).[4]

B. Several earlier approaches

The beginning of feminist exegetes' engagement with prophetic marriage metaphors is marked by the publication of Letty Russell's *Feminist*

[3] Here we may mention, for example, Joseph Ziegler, *Die Liebe Gottes bei den Propheten. Ein Beitrag zur alttestamentlichen Theologie* (Münster: Aschendorffsche Verlagsbuchhandlung, 1930). Athalya Brenner remarks critically of the focus of previous exegetes: "A metaphor for a wayward people who deserve their fate, a 'true-life' situation utilized for religious instruction: that was the critical consensus before feminist Bible critics started to problematize the husband/wife image" (*The Intercourse of Knowledge. On Gendering Desire and 'Sexuality' in the Hebrew Bible* [Leiden and New York: Brill, 1997]). Another new work that treats this categorization under the topic of the love of God is that of Brigitte Seifert, *Metaphorisches Reden von Gott im Hoseabuch* (Göttingen: Vandenhoeck & Ruprecht, 1996).

[4] For work on Hosea, for example, Yvonne Sherwood, *The Prostitute and the Prophet. Hosea's Marriage in Literary-Theoretical Perspective* (Sheffield: Sheffield Academic Press, 1996) 265–86; Marie-Theres Wacker, *Figurationen des Weiblichen im Hosea-Buch* (Freiburg: Herder, 1996) 129–37; or Rut Törnkvist, *The Use and Abuse of Female Sexual Imagery in the Book of Hosea. A Feminist Critical Approach to Hos 1–3* (Uppsala: Academia Ubsaliensis, 1998) 63–72 offer surveys of feminist exegetical research on the prophetic use of marriage metaphors.

Interpretation of the Bible in 1985.[5] This volume contains two studies that treat the theme either directly or indirectly.[6] T. Drorah Setel studies the depiction of the "woman" Israel in the book of Hosea.[7] From the perspective of a present-day feminist who has been sensitized to the phenomenon of pornography she proposes four analytical categories, through which she attempts to discover whether there is pornography in Hosea. These categories comprise the features, functions, definitions, and causes of pornography. In what follows I will describe those categories in some detail, because they have been taken up repeatedly in later feminist discussions.[8]

Setel cites as the features of pornography that female sexuality is depicted as negative in contrast to male sexuality, that women are degraded and publicly humiliated, and that female sexuality is portrayed as an object of male possession and male control. The representation of women as analogous to "nature" also falls within this category. As the function of pornography Setel points to the maintenance of male domination through the denial or misnaming of female experience. Within this type of pornographic discourse she includes the representation of female objectification as universal truth and not as something that has developed over time and therefore can be changed. From the same perspective, power relationships are concealed: it is widely assumed that pornography is only about sexuality, not about domination. She finds that another function of pornography is the failure to distinguish between the terms prostitute, harlot, and whore. Setel asserts as common to feminist definitions of pornography the fact that it is intended to reinforce male dominance. In this setting masculinity is demonstrated by the exercise of power and superiority. Such an image of masculinity easily evokes corresponding behavior and is meant to prevent women from achieving greater autonomy.

With respect to the interpretation of the Old Testament term for "harlotry," or "whoring," Setel differentiates the verb זנה and its derivatives. In today's parlance "harlots," "prostitutes," and "whores" are not the same thing, and within the Old Testament we should also distinguish among these different groups of women. Whereas a prostitute uses her sexuality

[5] Letty M. Russell, ed., *Feminist Interpretation of the Bible* (Philadelphia: Westminster, 1985); German translation 1989.

[6] Directly: T. Drorah Setel, "Prophets and Pornography: Female Sexual Imagery in Hosea," 86–95; indirectly Susan Brooks Thistlethwaite, "Every Two Minutes: Abused Women and Feminist Biblical Interpretation," 96–110.

[7] Setel, "Prophets and Pornography," especially 90–94.

[8] For example, by Athalya Brenner, "On Prophetic Propaganda and the Politics of 'Love': The Case of Jeremiah," in eadem, ed., *A Feminist Companion to the Latter Prophets* (Sheffield: Sheffield Academic Press, 1995) 256–74.

to earn her living, a harlot is a woman who is not subject to any controlling male. For Setel, a "whore" is a woman who is the object of male control and degradation.[9] Setel and other feminist exegetes following her see the "harlot" (זונה) Gomer in Hosea not as a professional prostitute, but as a woman who lives promiscuously or maintains sexual relationships outside of her marriage. The depiction of the wife as harlot makes female sexuality not only an object, but a symbol of evil.[10] Because this and the other criteria for pornography given above are fulfilled, Setel designates the depiction of the "woman" Israel in Hosea as pornography.

Phyllis Bird has considered the theme of "whoredom" in the Old Testament on several occasions.[11] She works with narrative texts in which prostitutes are the heroes—but after their brief appearance these women disappear again into obscurity in Israel's history.[12] Bird affirms that the meaning of זנה in the Old Testament varies and often remains unclear. On the whole, however, it is true that "*znh* is not used for incest or other prohibited relationships, such as homosexual relations or bestiality. It focuses on the absence of a marriage bond between otherwise acceptable partners."[13] In addition, Bird considers the different legal positions of men and women in ancient Israel when she sketches the field of meaning of זנה: "As a general term for extramarital sexual intercourse, *znh* is limited in its primary usage to female subjects, since it is only for women that marriage is the primary determinant of legal status and obligation."[14] She also refers to the patriarchal double standard: the ambivalent attitude toward זונות—es-

[9] Setel, "Prophets and Pornography," 87–88. Setel distinguishes (87–88) three words for women who are often called "whores" in contemporary American everyday language. (Such terms are not so readily translated into German.) We should also consider the fact that for a long time now certain terms, like "whore," have not been merely put-downs for women, even those who are not prostitutes. For more than a decade the word has served, in Germany and elsewhere, as a self-description used by prostitutes who give it a positive connotation. This again makes clear how important it is, today as in the past, to take account of the context within which we interpret words. For the theme of "harlotry" and the root זנה see also below, Chapter 3 C i, with further literature on the topic.

[10] Setel, "Prophets and Pornography," 94.

[11] Phyllis Bird, "The Harlot as Heroine: Narrative Art and Social Presupposition in Three Old Testament Texts," *Semeia* 46 (1989) 119–39 (1989a); eadem, "'To Play the Harlot': An Inquiry into an Old Testament Metaphor," in Peggy L. Day, ed., *Gender and Difference in Ancient Israel* (Minneapolis: Fortress, 1989) 75–94 (1989b). Both essays are reprinted in Bird's collection, *Missing Persons and Mistaken Identities. Women and Gender in Ancient Israel* (Minneapolis: Fortress, 1997).

[12] Bird, "The Harlot as Heroine"; she studies Tamar in Genesis 38, Rahab in Joshua 2, and the women in 1 Kings 3:16-27.

[13] Bird, "'To Play the Harlot,'" 90 n. 13.

[14] Ibid. 77.

pecially in its metaphorical usage—can be adequately interpreted against that background alone.[15]

Fokkelien van Dijk-Hemmes, whose focus was literary-critical in its orientation, studied prophetic marriage metaphors in two Old Testament texts. First, in an investigation of the gender of the speaker in Hosea 2 in comparison to the Song of Songs, she determined that in Hosea it is only the "I" perspective of the "man" (Hosea or YHWH) that speaks, while the woman is condemned to silence.[16] The text does not reflect the relationship between the sexes, but rather proposes its own version of gender roles. The woman is depicted as someone completely dependent on a man. Van Dijk-Hemmes offers as a contrast a picture of a woman's relationships in which she does not appear as passive.

On the basis of this study, van Dijk-Hemmes later turned her attention to Ezekiel 23.[17] She expands her analysis with the aid of Carol Newsom's thesis on the way metaphors function,[18] but also refers back to the categories of pornography that Setel had proposed (see above)[19] and embeds them in the hermeneutical schema that she developed in cooperation with Athalya Brenner.[20]

[15] Ibid. 79: "The anomaly of the prostitute as a tolerated specialist in an activity prohibited to every other woman is a particular feature of patriarchal society, representing an accommodation to the conflicting desires of men for exclusive control of their wives' sexuality (and hence offspring) and, at the same time, for sexual access to other women. The greater the inaccessibility of women in the society as a result of restrictions on the wife and unmarried nubile woman, the greater the need for an institutionally legitimized 'other woman.' The prostitute is that 'other woman,' tolerated but stigmatized, desired but ostracized."

[16] Fokkelien van Dijk-Hemmes, "The Imagination of Power and the Power of Imagination. An Intertextual Analysis of Two Biblical Love Songs: The Song of Songs and Hosea 2," *JSOT* 44 (1989) 75–88. She offers a summary of her own work in Athalya Brenner and Fokkelien van Dijk-Hemmes, eds., *On Gendering Texts. Female and Male Voices in the Hebrew Bible* (Leiden and New York: Brill, 1993) 167–68; Marie-Theres Wacker, *Figuration des Weiblichen* (1996) 134–37; 321–33 also discusses this essay.

[17] Van Dijk-Hemmes, "The Metaphorization of Woman in Prophetic Speech: An Analysis of Ezekiel XXIII," *VT* 43 (1993) 162–70; lightly edited and reprinted in Brenner and van Dijk-Hemmes, *On Gendering Texts* (1993) 167–76.

[18] Carol A. Newsom, "A Maker of Metaphors: Ezekiel's Oracles against Tyre," in James L. Mays and Paul J. Achtemeier, eds., *Interpreting the Prophets* (Philadelphia: Fortress, 1987) 188–99.

[19] In doing so she emphasizes especially the first two, characteristics and function.

[20] See Brenner and van Dijk-Hemmes, *On Gendering Texts* (1993); for the methodological and hermeneutical introduction see especially 1–32. In this proposal Brenner and van Dijk-Hemmes look for Old Testament texts that, despite male authorship, articulate the voices and traditions of women. Such "F-texts," which they distinguish from the "M-texts" marked by a male perspective, reflect the widest possible variety of women's experiences. The cultural model on which Brenner and van Dijk-Hemmes base their work presumes that in Old Testament times there could have been a women's culture that differed from the dominant male culture. This thesis is supported

In Ezekiel 23 the women in the text are made "whores," which is intended to shock the audience.[21] The text's portrayal of the women is filled with tension: on the one hand the "whoring" of the "women," Samaria and Jerusalem, is depicted as something that has happened to them, that they have passively suffered.[22] On the other hand, they are found guilty for having caused their own abuse.[23] But not only that: according to the text's portrayal, they are still enjoying it.[24] Such a depiction of female sexuality contains a crass misnaming of female experience,[25] and according to Setel's categories it must be regarded as pornographic.[26] According to van Dijk-Hemmes the text's portrayal of female and male sexuality offers different opportunities for male and female identification. Both sexes can identify with female Israel, but only men have an "escape" from this proffered identification: they can recognize their situation also in that of the wounded and revenge-seeking husband, who is in the right. This opportunity for identification is not open to women. In this way the metaphorization of women in Ezekiel 23 "performs first and foremost a violent speech act which is even more offensive than the Hosean version: it simultaneously shapes and distorts women's (sexual) experience."[27]

One of the first thorough textual studies on female imagery focusing on *one* prophetic book was undertaken by Julie Galambush. She concentrated on the Jerusalem imagery in the book of Ezekiel. After an introduction containing a section on metaphoric theory she presents a brief overview of marriage imagery in all the prophetic books, and then investigates Jerusalem as "woman," first in Ezekiel 16 and 23, and then in the rest of the book of Ezekiel. Her conclusions lie on several levels.[28] In the marriage imagery in Ezekiel 16 and 23 the relationship between YHWH and Jerusalem is shown to be one in which the "whorish" wife does not fulfill her obligation to marital subordination and fidelity. This gives the husband, YHWH,

---

by ethnological theories. Such a "marginal" women's culture, despite its partial independence, agrees for the most part with the dominant male culture because it exists within the latter. Against this theoretical background Brenner and van Dijk-Hemmes investigate especially the prophetic texts that make use of marriage metaphors.

[21] Ibid. 172.

[22] Ibid.

[23] Ibid. 173.

[24] Ibid. 174.

[25] Ibid. 173–74; van Dijk-Hemmes uses this expression (p. 173).

[26] Ibid. 175.

[27] Ibid. 176.

[28] Julie Galambush, *Jerusalem in the Book of Ezekiel. The City as Yahweh's Wife* (Atlanta: Scholars, 1992), especially 159–63.

every reason for a strong and violent reaction. In this way the actual destruction of Jerusalem can be seen as a deed of YHWH carried out as a consequence of his humiliation. Galambush then develops a comparison of Ezekiel's marriage imagery in chs. 16 and 23 with other feminine titles of Jerusalem: in other parts of the book as well the choice of terms from the field of female sexuality for the "woman" Jerusalem serves to depict the city as soiled and polluted in a way that only women can be portrayed. The "female" character of the city is maintained in Ezekiel 40–48 when the restored city is described in typical female roles as nourishing, fruitful, and the property of her "husband." In addition, there are also parallels at the symbolic level between the "woman" and the Temple. Both can be "polluted" in their interior places, sexually or in the Temple precincts. Both types of pollution result in YHWH's being shamed. He can only free himself from this shame by punishing the "woman." This fact makes it possible to regard the destruction of Jerusalem as an action that restores YHWH's strength and honor.

The drawback of this imagery is not only its pornographic character, as described above by Setel. Galambush sees in the presentation of female imagery in Ezekiel still other tendencies that she describes as controlling and fetishistic. The "woman" Jerusalem, who by the end of the book is completely under divine-male control, becomes a stony replacement for YHWH's previous unfaithful wife.

Andreas Weider has also investigated prophetic marriage imagery, concentrating on Hosea 1–3 and its influence on the book of Jeremiah. Weider is indebted to the traditional forms of the historical-critical method and does not adopt a critical perspective toward prophetic marriage imagery. He seamlessly reproduces the course of prophetic polemic against the "woman" Israel and sometimes adds to it through his own evaluation.[29] Weider repeats Hosea's argumentation and its altered form in Jeremiah. He accepts the dating of Hosea before Jeremiah from previous research,[30] as well as the topoi that Hosea's development of the marriage imagery is biographically motivated and that the "harlotries" refer to fertility cults. At the end of his work he describes the "divine marriage metaphor" in Hosea 1–3 and in Jeremiah under five aspects, differently ordered in Jeremiah and Hosea. Weider

[29] Andreas Weider, *Ehemetaphorik in prophetischer Verkündigung. Hos 1–3 und seine Wirkungsgeschichte im Jeremiabuch. Ein Beitrag zum alttestamentlichen Gottes-Bild* (Würzburg: Echter, 1993). An example from Hosea 2: "However, the attitude of the accused is incorrigible. She persists hard-headedly on her chosen way" (p. 200).

[30] Wacker, *Figurationen des Weiblichen* 5–20, also looks at the theses of older and newer research on Hosea.

describes the order in Jeremiah as "salvation-historical" in contrast to the "empirical" order in Hosea.[31] The aspects are "leading out of Egypt (= first great proof of love)," "desert period (= period of young love)," the "gift of the land and the land's gifts (= bridal gifts)," "Israel's 'harlotry' (= adultery)," and "failure to recognize YHWH (= grounds for separation)."[32]

Athalya Brenner concentrates her studies of the prophetic marriage imagery on the book of Jeremiah. She, too, follows Setel's categories for pornography in her first essay,[33] although she places more stress on the complex contexts, both social and psychological, that shape how pornography produces its effects. Brenner focuses especially on Jeremiah 2; 3:1-3; 5:7-8, and passages from Jeremiah 20 and 31. Her orientation is to the final text. She first develops how the "woman" Israel/Jerusalem is animalized in Jer 2:23-28, her sexuality presented as something driven by nothing but lust.[34] The purpose of the passages in Jeremiah is to shock the "woman" Israel/Jerusalem, and so also the audience, using the imagery to effect a change in attitude, so that the people will be ashamed and be transformed into a well-behaved partner pleasing to God. For Brenner a comparison with *The Story of O,* a sado-masochistic novel by Pauline Réage, plays a crucial role. Ultimately, in a constellation of relationships much like that in Jeremiah, the woman as person and subject is to be broken and subjected to male control and access. In Jeremiah the "woman," first made into an "animal," is to be lifted up and, through re-education, accommodated to divine-male demands. Brenner sees two possible ways for women to read this: either they must subject themselves to this construction of the sexes, placing female sexuality under male control, or else they must resist this "religious pornography." However, the latter can only partially succeed, since the imagery works at a level that prevents any complete avoidance of it.

In another article[35] Brenner develops the thesis that the texts of the prophetic marriage imagery are not only pornography, but also propa-

[31] Weider, *Ehemetaphorik* 205, 207.

[32] Ibid. 213–14, in tabular form.

[33] Athalya Brenner, "On Prophetic Propaganda and the Politics of 'Love': The Case of Jeremiah," in eadem, ed., *A Feminist Companion to the Latter Prophets* (Sheffield: Sheffield Academic Press, 1995) 256–74.

[34] Nelly Stienstra, *YHWH is the Husband of His People. Analysis of a Biblical Metaphor with Special Reference to Translation* (Kampen: Pharos, 1993) 164 n. 43, exercises a strongly polemical critique of Brenner's interpretation of Jeremiah 1. She disputes, among other things, that in Jeremiah 2 the "woman" Israel/Jerusalem is equated with a wild ass.

[35] "Pornoprophetics Revisited: Some Additional Reflexions," *JSOT* 70 (1996) 63–86, as re-edited in Athalya Brenner, *The Intercourse of Knowledge. On Gendering Desire and 'Sexuality' in the Hebrew Bible* (Leiden and New York: Brill, 1997) 153–74.

ganda. Comparing a catalogue of criteria for modern propaganda with the corresponding biblical text, she discovers that both employ similar techniques. In addition, Brenner engages again with critical voices that question whether the prophetic texts employing marriage imagery are really pornography. Differently from the Song of Songs, where the fantasies of the speakers are not attached to hierarchically ordered gender roles, in Hosea, Jeremiah, and Ezekiel gender asymmetry and stereotypical presentation play an important role. Therefore, and because of the use of violence in the relationship between the sexes, Brenner concludes that these are pornographic, not erotic texts.

Nelly Stienstra approaches the prophetic marriage imagery in three ways,[36] shedding light on it from the perspectives of exegesis, linguistic theory of metaphors, and translation criticism. She focuses her textual work on Hosea. In addition, she treats marriage in the Old Testament and, in summary fashion, the texts of the other prophets that employ marriage metaphors, as well as pre-Hoseanic Old Testament traditions.[37] In accordance with her basic theory of metaphors[38] she compares the "donor field" of each of the metaphors she discovers with its "recipient field," and attempts to determine the unspoken ideas that lie behind each of the metaphors. This results in a line of development for prophetic marriage imagery. Ezekiel 23 constitutes an exception; here Stienstra finds a degenerate form of the metaphor that no longer has anything to do with concrete marital relationships.[39] Stienstra asserts that our completely different understanding of marriage today creates a problem in transferring and comprehending the marriage metaphors.[40] Her suggestion for a solution to the problem is that today's readers should make greater effort to place themselves, mentally, within the world of ancient Israel and its metaphors.[41]

Renita J. Weems' work also focuses on the way metaphors produce their effects. However, in her reflections on prophetic marriage imagery she gives special attention to the network of religious, political, and social dis-

[36] Stienstra, *YHWH is the Husband* (1993).

[37] It is somewhat offputting that Stienstra at times only refers to older literature for her longitudinal studies, and that she offers no translation for texts outside Hosea (see ibid. 129 n. 6).

[38] Stienstra bases her work on that of George Lakoff and Mark Johnson (*Metaphors We Live By* [Chicago: University of Chicago Press, 1980]), among others.

[39] Stienstra, *YHWH is the Husband* 161, 186.

[40] Ibid. 188: ". . . we have to admit that at this moment in history, the marriage metaphor does not mean to people what it used to mean." Stienstra's portrayal of marital relationships—both in Old Testament times and today—is decidedly different from that of feminist theologians. She makes no mention of the problems of domestic and social violence against women that motivated feminists to criticize prophetic marriage imagery.

[41] Ibid. 189–90.

courses. These three fields of meaning are inseparably overlaid upon one another. Relationships of dominance and structural inequality between men and women therefore have a powerful influence on the interpretation and reception of biblical marriage metaphors. Weems devotes her work to the prophetic marriage imagery in Hosea, Jeremiah, and Ezekiel. She works with the final text, without translating major chunks of material or attempting a detailed investigation of them. Her explanations of the ways in which marriage imagery produces its effects are in close accord with a posited discourse situation.[42] A hierarchic and even violent aspect is inherent in the marital relationship between YHWH and Israel/Jerusalem, even more so than in other possible metaphors of relationship drawn from the world of ancient Israel.[43] Important for her are possible influences of these texts on the idea of God,[44] but also the effect on the audience's self-image: the primary goal of the marriage imagery is to evoke a feeling of shame in the hearers in order to achieve a change in their behavior. The marriage imagery is problematic because of its consequences for our present-day images of relationships—including, according to Weems, the association of romance with rape.[45] Weems' hermeneutical conclusions indicate that the prophetic marriage imagery can have fatal consequences, especially for the victims of sexual violence—primarily through their affirmation that violence can bring about a "healing" of the relationship. Therefore in dealing with prophetic marriage imagery we should keep in mind that it is one of a great many attempts to image God and God's relationships with human beings.

Two German-language books published in 1996 deal, at least in part, with prophetic marriage imagery. Brigitte Seifert investigates the God-metaphors in Hosea. Her work has two emphases. First she undertakes a

[42] I question whether this view is sustainable, from a historical perspective, since a major share of the effects produced by marriage imagery is traceable to the written version.

[43] Weems here refers to George B. Caird (*The Language and Imagery of the Bible* [Philadelphia: Westminster, 1980] 177), accepting, with slight modification, his listing of five areas of human life as the principal models for biblical metaphors of the relationship between YHWH and Israel. For Weems these are the constellations of judge-accused, parent-child, master-slave, king-vassal, and husband-wife (Renita J. Weems, *Battered Love. Marriage, Sex, and Violence in the Hebrew Prophets* [Minneapolis: Fortress, 1995] 16). Weems had already demonstrated in a 1989 essay on Gomer in the book of Hosea that sexual violence is an inseparable part of the marriage imagery ("Gomer: Victim of Violence or Victim of Metaphor?" *Semeia* 47 [1989] 87–104, especially 91–93).

[44] "The point of the marriage metaphor . . . is to justify the violence and punishment the subordinate endures and to exonerate the dominant partner from any appearance of being unjust" (*Battered Love* 19).

[45] Weems elaborates on this especially in the fourth chapter of her book (ibid. 84–104).

tour of theories of metaphor, with a look especially at older initiatives,[46] emphasizing theological metaphors and comparisons as well as the relationship among metaphors for divine revelation. Although Seifert adopts interaction theory, she does not ask the (hermeneutical) question about how to deal with differences between the historical-social situation and connotations of metaphors in Old Testament times and today. Hence she does not take a critical view of the image-content of the marriage metaphors.[47] Instead, Seifert is interested in the claims of metaphors to truth and revelatory character, which she associates with historical proof. In the exegetical part of her work the prophetic marriage imagery is treated under the heading "love betrayed," together with other metaphors for God ("threatened ruin," "experience of care," "inconceivable mercy"). After a minute analysis and historical embedding of the texts, Seifert comes to the conclusion that Hosea's marriage imagery simultaneously expresses God's closeness and intimacy with human beings on the one hand, and God's distance and unavailability on the other. The anthropomorphic depiction of YHWH that is conveyed by the marriage imagery is relativized and transcended in Hos 11:9.

Martin Schulz-Rauch's book, which also appeared in 1996, is similar to Weider's in investigating certain themes in the book of Hosea and their reception in Jeremiah. He concentrates on Baal, the retrospectives on history, and the metaphors of marriage and prostitution. Schulz-Rauch uses the historical-critical method and adheres closely to the texts. Essays in metaphor theory are not part of his work, nor does he display any awareness of a problem. He differentiates, within the terminology of "marriage and prostitution metaphors,"[48] between metaphor and analogy, which in turn can constitute a similitude or a comparison.[49] In his conclusion he as-

[46] Brigitte Seifert, *Metaphorisches Reden von Gott im Hoseabuch* (Göttingen: Vandenhoeck & Ruprecht, 1996). She uses Paul Ricoeur (33–37), but not Lakoff and Johnson (1980), who are especially important for American exegetes.

[47] Seifert does observe, with regard to the "public shaming of the adulteress" in Hos 2:12, that this "idea of standing naked in the pillory . . . is much more hideous than the thought of no longer harvesting wool and flax" (*Metaphorisches Reden* 107). Later, however, she comes to a different evaluation of the prophetic marriage imagery as a whole: "As regards the woman in the metaphor we must probably rediscover the value and worth a human being acquires through the experience of being loved in spite of failure. Under this aspect the marriage metaphor loses its discriminatory character toward women" (ibid. 138).

[48] Martin Schulz-Rauch, *Hosea und Jeremia. Zur Wirkungsgeschichte des Hoseabuches* (Stuttgart: Calwer, 1996) 151.

[49] The attempt at differentiation is found on pp. 152–53 and 175. There is no reference to secondary literature, which is regrettable since, for example, Hans-Peter Müller, *Vergleich und Metapher im Hohenlied* (Fribourg: Universitätsverlag; Göttingen: Vandenhoeck & Ruprecht, 1984) 12–13 refers to Song 1:15; 4:1; 5:12, where comparison and metaphor can indeed mean the same thing.

serts that Jeremiah very probably follows Hosea in his formulation of marriage imagery, modifying it at some points: "Jeremiah's use of this model of discourse [marriage imagery—*GB*] differs from that of his predecessor in two particular ways: The younger prophet makes no use at all of the form of the marriage similitude, adopting instead only the form of the marriage comparison. In addition, Jeremiah makes a more consistent effort than Hosea to make it impossible to draw conclusions about YHWH's role as husband with Israel as his wife."[50]

Yvonne Sherwood's work appeared in the same year. She focuses especially on Hosea 1–3, the literary figures who appear there, and their mutual relationships, as well as the reception of these aspects of the text in secondary literature. The textual "problems" often observed in Hosea, that is, statements that at first glance make no sense, she addresses with the aid of literary theory. "Reader-response criticism" appears here alongside semiotic analysis and a deconstructivist investigation; feminist exegetical initiatives are also considered. Sherwood is mainly concerned to examine the text and its secondary reception from a variety of perspectives.[51] Introductions to the various ways of reading take up a relatively large amount of space, and work with the biblical text is correspondingly restricted. At the end Sherwood classifies Hosea 1–3 as a text showing amazing kinship to works of postmodern authors: both are in part fragmentary, are characterized by interruptions, leap backward and forward in their action, and contain audience insult as one of their elements.[52]

Another English book on prophetic marriage imagery was presented in 1996 by Raymond C. Ortlund, Jr.[53] This author considers himself an evangelical Christian and directs his remarks to a broader audience than biblical specialists. He was inspired to write his book by reading Stienstra's work.[54] Ortlund surveys the entire Bible in his portrayal of "whoredom" in Israel/Jerusalem's marriage with YHWH. His starting point is the Old Testament's understanding of marriage, which he develops from Gen 2:23-24 and describes as monogamous. From that starting point he takes up the texts of the Pentateuch that speak of Israel's "whoring after other gods" (Exod 34:11-16; Lev 17:7; 20:4-6; Num 15:38-40; Deut 31:16; Judg 2:16-

[50] *Hosea und Jeremia* 194.

[51] Yvonne Sherwood, *The Prostitute and the Prophet. Hosea's Marriage in Literary-Theoretical Perspective* (Sheffield: Sheffield Academic Press, 1996). This impression is confirmed by the jacket text, where the book is recommended both as a contribution to research on Hosea 1–3 and as an introduction to modern biblical exegesis.

[52] Ibid., especially 328–29.

[53] *Whoredom. God's Unfaithful Wife in Biblical Theology* (Grand Rapids: Eerdmans, 1996).

[54] Ibid. 8.

17; 8:27, 33). "It is significant that the clearest marital images early in the story of the covenant people are Israel's whoredom and Yahweh's jealousy in return. From the beginning, the marriage was strained. That tension will break out into open conflict in the prophetic literature."[55] Ortlund's remarks on the prophetic texts are mainly comments on individual verses, following a rough chronology.[56] His perspective on the texts is shaped by his view that the purpose of the prophetic marriage imagery is first revealed in the New Testament: it is only the "spiritual sense," in which the Church takes its place as the bride of Christ, that resolves the problem of the Old Testament texts.[57] Human marriage is an image of divine love for the church. For Ortlund a direct consequence of this is that pre- and extramarital sex and homosexual partnerships are to be condemned,[58] and that feminist critique of the prophetic marriage metaphors must be rejected.[59]

Marie-Theres Wacker, on the other hand, works with the female imagery in Hosea 1–3 from a feminist perspective. She adheres closely to the texts, making use in her book of a wide methodological repertoire. After an introduction on the history of research she sketches the structure of Hosea 1–3, again with reference to the work of feminist exegetes. Texts from Hosea 4–13 give an overview of the further redaction of the imagery already used in Hosea 1–3. Works on the history of textual origins and development and in the field of the history of religions make it possible for us to show that Hosea 1–3 is a text that contains older elements but in its present form was composed in the post-exilic period. "The history of the origins of the book of Hosea as a whole cannot be reduced to a linear schema; it should rather be described as a continuing process of discussion in which the feminine always remains central, and yet experiences contrary evaluations and functionalizations (from a male perspective)."[60] The female imagery that is used is "not well suited as a basis for the construction of utopias,"[61] and the

[55] Ibid. 45.

[56] Some of his ordering does not correspond to the current state of historical-critical research, for example when he dates Isa 57:3 to the pre-exilic period (ibid. 80 n. 10).

[57] Ibid. 136–37.

[58] Ibid. 172–73.

[59] Ibid. 177–85. Ortlund discusses passages from Athalya Brenner and Fokkelien van Dijk-Hemmes's 1993 book *On Gendering Texts*. According to him, feminist criticism can only be applied to these texts because it is marked by a false hermeneutics (*Whoredom* 181–83). On the other hand, Ortlund regards criticism of violence against women to be absolutely necessary (182).

[60] Marie-Theres Wacker, *Figurationen des Weiblichen* 329.

[61] Ibid. 330.

relationship "between the divine and the feminine seems profoundly problematic, 'love' only determinable *e negativo*."[62]

Important insights into the texts containing prophetic marriage imagery are found also in the work of Elke Seifert, although she covers a much larger field. The focus of her study is the relationship between daughters and fathers in Old Testament texts, in which the daughter is at her father's disposal and subject to his coercive power. After an introduction that describes the previous (and not very plentiful) research in this field and proposes a hermeneutic, Seifert offers a systematic investigation of the numerous Old Testament texts on the daughter-father relationship. Historical questions about the background of the texts are not central; rather, the author critiques the texts, from a feminist perspective, in terms of their patterns of thought and argumentation. By bringing the Old Testament texts into dialogue with social-scientific and other works on the sexual abuse of girls and women she uncovers descriptions of sexual violence or structures of violence toward women and female personifications at many points in the Old Testament texts. In this context Seifert also investigates the texts about "daughter Zion" and other metaphoric "women" in the prophetic books.[63] She clearly indicates that these are male projections of femininity.[64] Images of God are also analyzed: in the texts containing the prophetic marriage imagery God frequently appears in the role of rapist.[65] I will refer to Seifert's work especially in the sections on feminist critique.[66]

Rut Törnkvist's work covers a much smaller field: she studies Hosea 1–3. Her interest centers on the female sexual imagery in those chapters and especially the image of YHWH as husband and lover in contrast to the

[62] Ibid. 328.

[63] Elke Seifert, *Tochter und Vater im Alten Testament. Eine ideologiekritische Untersuchung zur Verfügungsgewalt von Vätern über ihre Töchter* (Neukirchen-Vluyn: Neukirchener Verlag, 1997) 251–98.

[64] Ibid. 250, on the presentation of "daughter Zion": "By means of the metaphoric 'text worlds' conceptions of femininity are produced and these conceptions advance . . . patriarchal interests." On Ezek 16:23 she writes: "They [the images—*GB*] contain male fantasies that for the most part are misogynistic and defamatory of female sexuality."

[65] Ibid. 308–309.

[66] In addition to the above book, I will refer to two other contributions by this author: Renate Jost and Elke Seifert, "Das Buch Ezechiel," in Luise Schottroff and Marie-Theres Wacker, eds., *Kompendium Feministische Bibelauslegung* (2nd ed. Gütersloh: Gütersloher Verlagshaus, 1999) 278–90, and Elke Seifert, "Tochter und Vater im Alten Testament oder: Die Notwendigkeit einer Ideologiekritik an patriarchalen Rollenklischees im Ersten Testament," in Ulrike Eichler and Ilse Müllner, eds., *Sexuelle Gewalt gegen Mädchen und Frauen als Thema der feministischen Theologie* (Gütersloh: Chr. Kaiser, 1999) 76–98.

image of the land or the people as wife/woman.[67] Törnkvist begins her study with some remarks on feminist literary criticism and metaphor theory, adapting the notion of conceptional metaphors from Lakoff and Johnson.[68] For Törnkvist, a gendered perspective is important for the reception of secondary literature and for work on the biblical text.[69] She orients her exegetical work in terms of Mieke Bal's narratology, that is, consideration of the gender of the persons appearing in the text as well as that of the readers is taken more strongly into account. In addition, the social and legal conditions in ancient Israel play an important role in the explication of the backgrounds of the texts, as does an investigation of the root זנה ("whoring") in the Old Testament. Törnkvist proposes the thesis that Hosea's marriage imagery is probably to be understood against the background of a threatened civil war. The group within the population that represents the opposition to Hosea is to be defamed as "foreigners," as social and sexual deviants and abusers of the norms. The majority of readers are to be persuaded that this group is in the wrong. The "right" position is Hosea's. To that extent Hosea 1–3 is to be read as a text that makes use of the assignment of sexual roles for religious and political purposes.[70]

C. Evaluation

Let me conclude this overview with a short summary of what has already been treated by scholars and where there is still need for research:

We already have a series of works on individual biblical texts containing prophetic marriage imagery. The focus has been especially on Hosea 1–3.[71] Thus far there is no study that considers all the texts containing prophetic marriage imagery.[72] When a number of texts are treated there is

[67] Thus formulated by Törnkvist, *Use and Abuse* 17. For comment on Törnkvist's work when still in manuscript form see Sherwood, *The Prostitute and the Prophet* (1996) 266 n. 46.

[68] For more on this, see below in Chapter 2 K.

[69] For the discussion of "gender" as socially-constructed sex see, e.g., Regine Gildemeister, "Die soziale Konstruktion von Geschlechtlichkeit," in Ilona Ostner and Klaus Lichtblau, eds., *Feministische Vernunftkritik. Ansätze und Traditionen* (Frankfurt and New York: Campus, 1992) 200–39.

[70] Törnkvist, *Use and Abuse* 173.

[71] Hosea is the principal subject of the studies by Setel (1989), Bird (1989b), van Dijk-Hemmes (1989), Weider (1993), Stienstra (1993), B. Seifert (1996), Schulz-Rauch (1996), Sherwood (1996), Wacker (1996), and Törnkvist (1998). Jeremiah is treated especially by Brenner (1995, 1996). Ezekiel is analyzed by Galambush (1992) and van Dijk-Hemmes (1993).

[72] Weems (1995) treats Hosea, Jeremiah, and Ezekiel, and so is the author who has thus far drawn the longest bow. However, her work is not text-analytical; she takes up the texts in a secondary step after problematizing the imagery.

always one that is clearly the focus of interest.[73] Most of the studies do not have primarily historical-critical interest in the text; they work with the endtext,[74] or else the text itself is not the subject of the investigation; the focus is on possible receptions and interpretations.[75] Some studies focus on the root word זנה in order better to categorize the designation of "woman" Israel/Jerusalem as a "whore."[76]

Some studies are prefixed by theories of metaphor.[77] Following this, especially in feminist-exegetical works, are critiques of the content of the imagery. The problematic aspects are seen to be the hierarchy inherent in the Old Testament marriage relationship, the one-sided dependence of the woman on the man, and especially male violence as a legitimate means of disciplining the wife, with its possibly fatal consequences as a model for current marital relationships.

In light of what we have seen of the selection thus presented, what has long been lacking is a study of the book of Isaiah,[78] as well as a study that will consider the whole field of prophetic marriage imagery, starting from the biblical texts. The latter is what I propose to offer in this book. However, within this framework I cannot enter in detail into the problems of each individual text or investigate the layering in a number of texts. My efforts will focus on giving a survey of the texts and the main points of concentration in each, placing them within their respective contexts in Old Testament theology and applying feminist-critical reflection.

D. Violence against women as depicted in the Old Testament: Hermeneutical guidelines for this study

In feminist discussion there has been a good deal of reflection on the connection between biblical texts and the experiences of today's women. There are a great many different approaches, depending on the textual basis and the methodological and hermeneutical choices of the author.

[73] Thus with Galambush (1992: Ezekiel), Weider (1993: Hosea 1–3; Jeremiah 2), Stienstra (1993: Hosea 1–3), Schulz-Rauch (1996: Hosea 1–3; Jeremiah 2).

[74] Here we should mention, for example, Galambush (1992), Ortlund (1996), and Elke Seifert (1997).

[75] This is true for Setel (1989), van Dijk-Hemmes (1989 and 1993), Brenner (1995 and 1996), Weems (1995), and Sherwood (1996).

[76] Thus, for example, Bird (1989a, 1989b) and Törnkvist (1998) 95–115. Cf. also below, Chapter 3 C i.

[77] These considerations are found in the work of Galambush (1992), Stienstra (1993), Weems (1995), B. Seifert (1996), and Törnkvist (1998).

[78] However, Beate Schmidtgen has worked on this theme, as noted above (*Die Stadt als Frau im Buch Jesaja*. Dissertation in typescript. Basel, 2001).

Here I would like to bring together some thoughts that may make it possible for us to develop a hermeneutics that is especially applicable to the texts containing marriage imagery.[79]

Fundamental to feminist research in this field is the observation that the relations between the sexes play a constitutive role, both as regards the reconstruction of a historical background for understanding and with respect to a contemporary reading and understanding of the texts. Men and women are, for the most part, not portrayed in Old Testament texts as equals. There are obvious hierarchies, especially in the realm of marriage. Power relationships play a crucial role. Women are primarily regarded as possessions of their fathers and later of their husbands.[80] They have no right of disposition over themselves.[81] Added to this is another, equally serious difference between ancient Israelite and current thinking that affects especially the worth assigned to female sexuality.[82] While at present self-determination regarding one's own sexuality is a postulate, at least in Western societies, so that legal consequences are attached to offenses against it, there was no, or almost no such thing in ancient Israel. An offense against the sexuality

[79] In the special field of (divine) violence against metaphorical "women" otherwise very productive initiatives such as those of Ulrike Bail (*Gegen das Schweigen klagen. Eine intertextuelle Studie zu den Klagepsalmen Ps 6 und Ps 55 und der Erzählung von der Vergewaltigung Tamars* [Gütersloh: Chr. Kaiser/Gütersloher Verlagshaus, 1998]) or Ilse Müllner (*Gewalt im Hause Davids: Die Erzählung von Tamar und Amnon (2 Sam 13,1-22)* [Freiburg: Herder, 1997]; eadem, "Sexuelle Gewalt im Alten Testament," in Eichler and Müllner, eds., *Sexuelle Gewalt gegen Mädchen und Frauen* 40–75), which focus on violence against concrete women, cannot be so profitably applied.

[80] This aspect is probably most responsible for the fact that marriage imagery serves to portray the relationship between YHWH and Israel; see below, Chapters 3 A and 4 C.

[81] Elke Seifert demonstrated this in *Tochter und Vater* (1997) for the relationship between daughters and their fathers in the Old Testament. She also makes it clear that according to the texts the fathers never exercise their right of disposition over their daughters in the sense of care or protection, but that the daughters [and to a certain degree the unmarried sons as well—*GB*] are called upon by their fathers to advance their own interests (*Tochter und Vater,* especially 51–128).

[82] Ilse Müllner summarizes: "The criterion of the woman's willingness, for us now as ever the most appropriate measure of sexual violence, is not central in the biblical texts, for three reasons . . . ." The reasons she adduces are that the texts, written from an androcentric perspective, refuse women the status of subjects (from a legal point of view as well), that women are not represented as active subjects of their own sexuality, and that social relationships in the OT world were given much greater weight than in our individualistic society. Hence social roles and "places" are much more sharply defined in the OT. (Müllner, "Sexuelle Gewalt," 47–49). For this theme cf. also F. Rachel Magdalene, "Ancient Near-Eastern Treaty-Curses and the Ultimate Texts of Terror: A Study of the Language of Divine Sexual Abuse in the Prophetic Corpus," in Athalya Brenner, ed., *A Feminist Companion to the Latter Prophets* (see n. 8 above), especially 338–41. We should also note that the understanding of sexuality in ancient Israel is a field of study in which there is still a great deal of work to be done—the cultural specifics have been far too little explored for us to be able to make accurate statements about them.

of a woman was not in itself a crime; criminal were only the offenses that touched the sexual right of disposition or possession of another man. Women who had left their families of origin and were not betrothed or married were accordingly without legal protection and could be mistreated in any way without the perpetrator's needing to fear any consequences.[83]

For prophetic marriage imagery we must further take into account that here, as is also sometimes the case today, the realms of sexuality and war overlap. Since the prophetic marriage imagery, historically speaking, was probably concerned with the exile, and thus also with war and similar conditions within which the women in a conquered land were frequently raped, it seems likely that in this instance both metaphor-complexes are joined. War can be expressed in a metaphor of rape, and vice versa.[84] Sexual or sexualized violence is done to Israel as a metaphorical woman: as a consequence of her "harlotry" she is either abandoned by her (ex-)lover YHWH to be raped (as in Ezek 16 and 23), or else YHWH himself is depicted as a sexual abuser (Jer 13:22, 26). This fate not only befalls Israel, but also other, foreign city-"women": Babylon in Isa 47:2-3 and Nineveh in Nah 3:5-7. The background for such imagery is found in the metaphor of the city as woman, very widespread in the ancient Near East; the Old Testament imagery is by no means unique in this respect. As F. Rachel Magdalene has described, from an Old Testament point of view it is not even remarkable that YHWH appears as a (sexual) abuser of "his" wife Israel/Jerusalem. This is perfectly consistent with the marriage metaphors: a husband had the right of control over his wife and could apply such punishments to her.[85] Similarly, he had no need to fear punishment for raping

[83] Here we can only refer to further literature on the complex legal regulations in the Old Testament; cf., for example, Athalya Brenner, "On Incest," in eadem, ed., *A Feminist Companion to Exodus and Deuteronomy* (Sheffield: Sheffield Academic Press, 1994) 113–38, and Carolyn Pressler, "Sexual Violence and Deuteronomic Law," in ibid. 102–12.

[84] The basis for this observation is the essay by Pamela Gordon and Harold C. Washington, "Rape as a Military Metaphor in the Hebrew Bible," in Brenner, ed., *A Feminist Companion to the Latter Prophets* 308–25. They refer here (313–14), among other things, to ענה II ("humiliate"). However, Ilse Müllner ("Sexuelle Gewalt," 46–47) emphasizes that the verb alone is not sufficient for an adequate naming of rape: "At no point is a single word sufficient to describe the act [of rape—*GB*]. Despite the brevity of the portrayal, which is repeatedly emphasized in a great many exegeses of biblical narratives, we must say that there are always a number of verbs describing the action . . . ."

[85] On the basis of the legal provisions in Deuteronomy it can be established that men could punish their wives drastically for adultery (Carolyn Pressler, "Sexual Violence," 111–12). However, Pressler makes an important point at the end of her description and evaluation of the Deuteronomic texts (p. 112): "These values and assumptions [that female sexuality is the property of men—*GB*] extend through and beyond the biblical text; they are not unfamiliar today."

foreign women in time of war.[86] Even in modern times rape committed during military conflict has only been punishable under the international law of war since the Geneva Convention of 1949. In actuality such actions are only punished in the rarest of cases.[87]

With these reflections I want to make it clear that in interpreting these texts one must make a very careful distinction between the original context, with its internal logic, and our present-day ways of thinking. Otherwise, as the examples collected by Elke Seifert show, the texts of the prophetic marriage imagery can easily be used to legitimate or possibly even to incite sexual violence by fathers against their daughters or husbands against their wives.[88] In addition, these texts also make use of thought models according to which women are to be regarded as morally degraded, and therefore ultimately responsible for what happens to them.[89]

It is important to hold up a critical point of view that insists on the full human dignity of women against the thought models and ideologies I have described—which are still to be found today. This involves a broader understanding of sexual violence, which does not begin with forcible sexual intercourse. Sexual violence is present wherever the following criteria are fulfilled:

> 1. A person is used by another as an object for the gratification of certain needs. These needs are either sexual in nature and/or they are non-sexual needs that are expressed in sexualized form (e.g., the desire to experience power, to degrade, to assert oneself, etc.). 2. For this purpose actions are imposed on the person or demanded of that person that are culturally associated with sexuality. Among these are not only actions such as, for example, the touching of sexual organs or sexual intercourse, but also those that in our society are associated in a broader sense with sexuality, as for example suggestive remarks, whistles, or nude photos. 3. These actions are carried out with the aid of differences in resources or power and against the will of the person.[90]

[86] Thus, among others, F. Rachel Magdalene, "Ancient Near-Eastern Treaty-Curses," 336–41.

[87] In very recent times the "International Criminal Tribunal for the Former Yugoslavia" (the Hague Tribunal) has made efforts to investigate and punish war crimes, including rape.

[88] Elke Seifert points to this danger (*Tochter und Vater* 318). Let me cite here only the statement of a husband who frequently raped his wife, quoted by Alberto Godenzi (*Bieder, brutal. Frauen und Männer sprechen über sexuelle Gewalt* [2nd ed. Zürich: Unionsverlag, 1991] 51): "When it comes over me, I speak to her. Yesterday I said: Now I need to hit you a couple more times so you'll know where God sits."

[89] Fokkelien van Dijk-Hemmes pointed out with regard to Ezekiel 16 ("The Metaphorization of Women" 173), even before Elke Seifert *(Tochter und Vater)* that we find here the model according to which women are responsible for their own abuse.

[90] Ulrike Brockhaus and Maren Kolshorn, *Sexuelle Gewalt gegen Mädchen und Jungen: Fakten, Theorien* (Frankfurt: Campus, 1993) 28 (quoted from Elke Seifert, *Tochter und Vater* 13).

This book will take a critical feminist perspective on the depictions of violence against women in the texts of the prophetic marriage imagery. However, the texts must also be tested to see whether, in addition to their problematic aspects, they contain starting points from which an understanding of women, gender roles, and marriage appropriate for today can be encouraged. In conclusion we will ask whether it is adequate to start with biblical "counter-texts" or to find other biblical images that make possible a counter-reading[91] against the degrading and violence-imbued view of (metaphorical) women.

[91] For the concept of "counter-reading" cf. the Hedwig-Jahnow-Forschungsprojekt's essay, "Feministische Hermeneutik und Erstes Testament," in Hedwig Jahnow et al., *Feministische Hermeneutik und Erstes Testament. Analysen und Interpretationen* (Stuttgart: Kohlhammer, 1994) 72–73: "'Counter-reading' means for us that we offer resistance against the strategies in the text that legitimate violence. The violence expressed in the texts should [and may!—*GB*] not be relativized in the process." Elements of the critique of violence or alternative God images in biblical texts should be set against the metaphors of violence. However, I would no longer go as far as this article, which I had a share in writing, when it speaks of a "liberating reading" of such texts. Nevertheless, it seems to me now as then both possible and meaningful to seek for biblical counter-voices, "objections" against the texts of violence. For the book of Isaiah see Gerlinde Baumann, "Prophetic Objections to YHWH as the Violent Husband of Israel: Reinterpretations of the Prophetic Marriage Metaphor in Second Isaiah (Isaiah 40–55)," in Athalya Brenner, ed., *Prophets and Daniel* (Sheffield: Sheffield Academic Press, 2001) 88–120, especially 99–110.

Chapter Two

Understanding the Imagery

A. Preliminary remark

The theme of this work is a way of speaking about YHWH and Israel/Jerusalem and their relationship to one another that I am calling "prophetic marriage imagery." This mode of discourse is called "prophetic" because, except for Lamentations, it appears exclusively in the Old Testament prophetic books. The concept of "marriage imagery," however, requires a lengthier explanation. In the first place it seems relatively clear that "marriage" refers to the legalized union between a man and a woman. In this section we will not attempt any further distinctions, such as could be made, for example, between particular legal or customary rules, or regarding monogamy and polygamy. In these aspects marriage in Old Testament times was remarkably different from a present-day Western-derived understanding. Whatever it is necessary to say on this subject will follow later, in Chapters 3 and 4.

At this point the concept of "imagery" (metaphors) must be set within a theoretical framework, for what a metaphor is, how it functions, and what further implications follow for its interpretation have all been discussed and argued in detail in the past decade. In this study I adopt the most broadly accepted theories, especially as found in English-language exegeses with a feminist-critical or literary-critical orientation. I will mention first of all the initiatives of Paul Ricoeur and of George Lakoff and Mark Johnson.[1] These initiatives have been taken up in feminist exegesis,

[1] Paul Ricoeur, "Stellung und Funktion der Metapher in der biblischen Sprache," in Paul Ricoeur and Eberhard Jüngel, *Metapher. Zur Hermeneutik religiöser Sprache* (Munich: Kaiser, 1974) 45–70; idem, "The Metaphorical Process as Cognition, Imagination, and Feeling," *Critical*

together with other possible theories, by, for example, Julie Galambush, Claudia Camp, Renita Weems, and Rut Törnkvist. In addition, Marjo C. A. Korpel, for example, has adopted these and other proposals for comparing Ugaritic and Old Testament metaphors for God.[2]

B. What is a metaphor?

The reflections on metaphor theory that are offered here are oriented to their possible application to Old Testament texts; it is not possible or desirable to present my own full-scale theory of metaphors. Let me begin with a definition of metaphor that is as adequate as possible to what we find in the texts. After that it seems appropriate to consider initiatives that study the way metaphors function, and not their genesis or historically specific conditions for their origin that can scarcely be applied to the ancient Near East. Also excluded from the discussion are proposals that are primarily founded on Aristotle's *Poetics* and represent so-called substitution theory, which assumes that in metaphors something is designated by a different word for which a more precise word could be substituted. In this way, to put it briefly, a metaphor appears as a stylistic figure that expresses, in poetic fashion, something that could be said just as well in conceptual language, and probably with more precision.[3] This is not the case with the prophetic marriage imagery, as also in many other instances of God-imagery. (See the extended discussion of this topic in section E below.)

More adequate in this respect are the newer theories, especially those founded on the work of Max Black as received by Paul Ricoeur, which describe the relationship between the designation and the thing designated as "interaction."[4] "What, then, is metaphor? It is an expansion of the denota-

Inquiry 5 (1978) 143–59; idem, *The Rule of Metaphor: Multi-Disciplinary Studies of the Creation of Meaning in Language* (London: Routledge and Kegan Paul, 1978); idem, "Die Metapher und das Hauptproblem der Hermeneutik," in Anselm Haverkamp, ed., *Theorie der Metapher* (2nd ed. Darmstadt: Wissenschaftliche Buchgesellschaft, 1996); George Lakoff and Mark Johnson, *Metaphors We Live By* (Chicago: University of Chicago Press, 1980). In my discussion of Ricoeur and Lakoff/Johnson I will also refer to the work of Gerhard Kurz, *Metapher, Allegorie, Symbol* (4th ed. Göttingen: Vandenhoeck & Ruprecht, 1997).

[2] Cf. Marjo Christina Annette Korpel, *A Rift in the Clouds. Ugaritic and Hebrew Descriptions of the Divine* (Münster: Ugarit-Verlag, 1990), especially 35–87.

[3] We may also doubt whether in the case of the OT we can speak of conceptual language at all; thus, e.g., Gerhard von Rad, *Weisheit in Israel* (Neukirchen-Vluyn: Neukirchener Verlag, 1970) 75–77.

[4] The initiative of Lakoff and Johnson, *Metaphors We Live By*, representing a much broader concept of metaphor, and its reception, for example, by Claudia Camp, "Metaphor in Feminist Biblical Interpretation: Theoretical Perspectives," *Semeia* 61 (1993) 3–36, will not be dealt with

tion by the transfer of 'labels' to new objects that resist this transfer."[5] In Ricoeur's linguistic-philosophical project the two elements of the metaphor are "tensively" related.[6] Ricoeur can even express this tension in the predication with the concept of impertinence: "Metaphor is an 'impertinent' predication, that is, one that offends against the ordinary criteria of appropriateness or pertinence in the application of predicates."[7] The new thing thus produced is creative and also effects an imaginative and reflective process in the readers (see section I below).[8]

C. The metaphor of marriage for the relationship between YHWH and Israel/Jerusalem

This means that in the case of the prophetic marriage imagery the content of the metaphor must be conceived more precisely and differently than it has been heretofore. This metaphor cannot simply present YHWH as husband and Israel/Jerusalem as wife. The tension and novelty in such a metaphor are relatively slight; it was fairly common in the ancient Near East to speak of a city as a "woman."[9] Nor is it at all unusual to find the God of Israel imaged in male roles. Rather, it seems that *"Israel as adulterous wife"* and the relationship of YHWH to this "wife" constitute the content and tension of the metaphor. The same can be demonstrated through word study: the root זנה is the most important indicator of the appearance of this metaphor. Therefore as regards the prophetic marriage imagery our attention should focus not only on the description of the two individual figures of YHWH and Israel/Jerusalem as husband and wife; the

at this point. Starting with prophetic marriage imagery, we will here focus on literary metaphors that (presumably) were created with intent. These are the object of Ricoeur's studies. The subject is not "everyday metaphors" that are used unconsciously and unintentionally. Nor can we here deal with poststructuralist criticism of concepts of metaphor as formulated by Camp, following Jacques Derrida and Chris Weedon ("Metaphor in Feminist Biblical Interpretation," 15–17, 28–30).

[5] Ricoeur, *Metapher* 52.

[6] Ibid. 48.

[7] Ricoeur, *The Rule of Metaphor.* The quoted material is from a preface to the German edition, not present in the English version: Paul Ricoeur, *Die lebendige Metapher. Übergänge* (2nd ed. Munich, 1991) vi.

[8] "The *new* pertinence or congruence proper to a meaningful metaphoric utterance proceeds from the kind of semantic proximity which suddenly obtains between terms in spite of their distance. Things or ideas which were remote appear now as close" ("The Metaphorical Process as Cognition, Imagination, and Feeling," 147); similarly *The Rule of Metaphor* 6: "Thus, resemblance itself must be understood as a tension between identity and difference in the predicative operation set in motion by semantic innovation."

[9] For additional discussion see below, Chapter 5.

events that occur within their relationship constitute a separate element of the metaphor.[10] What is "metaphorical" in the prophetic marriage imagery is the particular elaboration of Israel/Jerusalem as an unfaithful wife, and YHWH as a husband who, despite her failings, for the most part clings tenaciously to the marriage and the marital relationship itself.

D. Further terminological distinctions: "imagery" and "personification"

To this point I have been using several different terms without defining or distinguishing them from one another. When I speak of "imagery" [German: *Metaphorik*] as distinct from "metaphor" one should think of what Paul Ricoeur calls "root metaphor." He illustrates this with an example that I also have in view here: the God-imagery of the Old Testament.[11] Here I will use the concept of "imagery" in the sense of a root metaphor and call the individual parts of the metaphoric complex "metaphors." To use a different image, the marriage imagery constitutes a roof under which are collected various ideas/images that, depending on the circumstances, can also be located on a variety of different levels. First we should mention the images of YHWH as husband and Israel/Jerusalem as wife, with the foci already identified. Parallel to this, for example, is the image of YHWH as father and Jerusalem/Zion as daughter. These individual figures can also be called "personifications,"[12] because through them entities or substances are presented as persons that cannot be seen "concretely" as such.[13] Metaphors such as childhood (Ezekiel 16) or family (the sisters in Ezekiel 23) are then to be located on a still lower level.

[10] Janet M. Soskice points out, in her work on metaphors and religious language, that there are not always just two interacting poles or elements in metaphors; occasionally an element is not even named, but it is also possible that more than two elements are involved (Janet Martin Soskice, *Metaphor and Religious Language* [New York: Oxford University Press, 1985] 43, 49).

[11] "Certain metaphors appear that *collect* numerous partial metaphors, drawn from different areas of experience, and endow them with a kind of equal weight. These 'root' metaphors have a special ability to evoke a limitless number of possible interpretations on a more conceptual level. Thus they both *collect* and *diffuse*. They *collect* subordinate metaphors and *diffuse* new strands of thought" (*Metapher* 64).

[12] Apt here is what Gerhard Kurz says about personification: "We may say that (many) personifications rest on the reification of metaphoric meaning" (*Metapher, Allegorie* 58).

[13] I will occasionally use the term "concrete" in opposition to "metaphorical." My concern is that one should avoid denying that metaphors have their own reality, as happens if one speaks of non-metaphorical discourse (which can only be supposed to occur if one adopts a relatively narrow concept of metaphor, like that of Ricoeur) as "real" discourse.

E. God imagery as a special case

Paul Ricoeur explains the "semantic mechanism of the metaphor" in part by saying that one must "have grasped" a new meaning "on the ruins of the direct reference that corresponds to the normal lexical rules, in order to understand that this other meaning uncovers another dimension of reality and thus frees a new interpretation of the world and of ourselves."[14] This presupposes that there really is such a lexical meaning or, to put it another way, a direct reference.[15] Such is not the case with God-imagery: people use metaphors for God precisely because God is not visible and "concrete" in this sense.[16] Hence in God-imagery there is no tension between a "first reference" within the elements of the metaphor and a new, indirect reference. This may be one reason why God-metaphors are so powerful—and so hard to "correct" once they have achieved their powerful effect.

F. Another special case: sexual imagery

There are certain conditions that apply to metaphors in the realm of language concerning sexuality. As Athalya Brenner shows, in the Old Testament there is practically no non-metaphorical or non-euphemistic word or expression for the sexual organs.[17] This has consequences for imagery. Erotic and sexual imagery, we must conclude, function differently from the way imagery is used in other cases. Here we can observe, in the case of the Old Testament, some commonality with today: whereas "normally" something less well known is illustrated in terms of something that is more familiar, in the realm of sexual imagery something well known is illustrated

[14] Ricoeur, *Die lebendige Metapher* vi–vii.

[15] Ricoeur, "The Metaphorical Process" 153: "This suspension, however, is only the negative condition of a second-order reference, of an indirect reference built on the ruins of the direct reference."

[16] This description of God-imagery resembles the "absolute metaphor" that Hans Blumenberg speaks of, with reference to Emmanuel Kant: "Our 'absolute metaphor' appears here as a *transfer of reflection on an object of observation onto a completely different idea to which perhaps no observation can ever directly correspond*" (Blumenberg, *Paradigmen zu einer Metaphorologie* (Frankfurt: Suhrkamp, 1998) 12 (emphasis in original). Fruitful for my study is also a consequence of such considerations: "Hence absolute metaphors also have *histories*. They have histories in a more radical sense than do concepts, for the historical shifts in a metaphor bring to the fore the metakinetics of historical horizons of meaning and ways of seeing, within whose concepts they experience their modifications" (ibid. 13). I am indebted to Bernd Kuschnerus for the reference to Blumenberg and for other suggestions for this chapter.

[17] Athalya Brenner, *The Intercourse of Knowledge. On Gendering Desire and 'Sexuality' in the Hebrew Bible* (Leiden and New York: Brill, 1997) 33: ". . . biblical designations of human erogenous zones, primary and secondary and of both sexes, are in general euphemistic."

by something equally well known. The latter could, of course, theoretically be called "precision," but it really should not. The excitement in erotic or sexual imagery lies precisely in this: that there is only an *allusion* to the well-known body parts, which possibly would be considered obscene if referred to directly. This does no damage to the understanding of this imagery within a particular cultural context. But there can be problems when the allusions in the Old Testament must be understood out of a decidedly different context, such as that of today. This difficulty—which must be kept in mind when interpreting the text—is only one part of the whole field of problems presented by the interpretation of metaphors. In the next section I will explain why, in general, a stricter attachment to the context exists in this case.

G. Interaction as functional principle of the metaphor and its consequence: contextuality

As I have said above, I accept the point of view that the elements of a metaphor interact. This interaction begins when the elements of the metaphor, which previously had no connection to one another, are brought more closely together: "The metaphor is nothing other than the attachment of a known label with a given past to a new object, which first resists, and then succumbs to this transfer."[18] Ricoeur shifts the metaphor "into the vicinity of a calculated mistake;" "the literal falsehood is thus an element of the metaphoric truth." It is not agreed beforehand whether a metaphor will be accepted as meaningful or seen as inappropriate. Marjo Korpel illustrates this by comparing metaphors from the field of mountain imagery: whereas in English (and in this case also in German) it is normal to speak of the "foot" of the mountain, this precise metaphor does not exist in Hebrew; here, in contrast, a mountain can have a "head," "shoulders," a "torso," and so on.[19] Metaphors, we may conclude, are highly context-dependent constructions, because of the fragile and difficult relationship between their elements. Particular metaphors have meaning only in certain cultures and language contexts, and even there they do not last for all time. Many a common metaphor, especially from poetic language, coming to us from previous centuries meets today with incomprehension, something that can easily be demonstrated from old songbooks. The reason for this lies, among other things, in the changed contexts of human life: thus today agrarian metaphors (e.g., "death, the grim reaper") are much less often

[18] Ricoeur, *Metapher* 52–53 (partial citations).

[19] Korpel, *A Rift in the Clouds* 50.

created and harder to understand than they used to be, because farming no longer represents the life-context of most people.

This dependency on context also affects marriage imagery, which draws its power and significance from the realm of human life in community. The notion of marriage in ancient Israel and how this was seen as an adequate metaphorical counterpart to the relationship between YHWH and Israel/Jerusalem need no longer be equivalent to a present-day American or western European image of marriage and our current explorations of God-relationships. On the contrary: it is to be expected that in both areas shifts have occurred that cause the metaphor today to make a different statement from that of Old Testament times. Against the background of our different language, with our ideas about equality of rights in marriage and a post-Enlightenment understanding of religion, quite different connotations enter into marriage metaphors, and entirely different tensions appear in contrast to those that—presumably—existed in the days of the Old Testament.

H. "Explaining" and "interpreting" metaphors: the procedure in this study

The context-embeddedness of metaphors I have just explored suggests a two-layered procedure for the interpretation of prophetic marriage imagery. I therefore propose, following Ricoeur, a distinction between "explanation" and "interpretation."[20]

"Explanation" is concerned with the meaning of the metaphor, its immanent purpose. This book will attempt[21] to explore the "historical" meaning as an approach to the Old Testament meaning of the metaphors, which is simply to be brought out of the linguistic and life setting of that time.[22] First I will devote a brief analysis to a "key word" in prophetic marriage metaphors, the root זנה, as the constitutive element of the entire complex of imagery (in Chapter 3 below). Since this study must be limited to a

[20] Ricoeur, "Die Metapher und das Hauptproblem," 363.

[21] I am quite aware that there can be no neutral understanding of historical texts, because my own pre-understanding and current perspective always shape my interest in the text. Nevertheless, in this first interpretive step I will at least attempt to allow the OT texts to speak in and out of their own internal context.

[22] This may perhaps be related to a further statement of Ricoeur's ("Die Metapher und das Hauptproblem," 374), although presumably in making this statement he had in mind much smaller semantic units and probably was not considering religious texts: "The power of metaphors arises, within a poetic work, from their connection *primarily* with the other processes of the *lexis,* then with the 'fable,' which is the essence, the immanent 'sense' of the work, and third with the intentionality of the work as a whole. . . . In this sense the power of metaphors rests upon that of the whole poem."

short space, the further "explanation" will rest primarily on the context of each formulation of the imagery *within a particular book;* in this step of the investigation I will consider especially the *endtext* of the biblical book in question. Not only the corresponding Hebrew words will be considered, but also the "persons" and roles that appear in the imagery: YHWH, Israel/ Jerusalem, women and men.

In the "interpretation" (Part II, section D in each chapter) I will be more concerned with the aspect of meaning or significance, focusing on current interpretation in our own context. My authorities here will be those who have studied these texts with full awareness of the problems involved in interpreting metaphors. Most of these are feminist exegetes. At what point do they inject criticism in the interpretation of the texts? What seems to them to be problematic, and for what reasons? Does reading metaphors from today's (which today's?) perspective displace the meaning of the metaphors, possibly in a direction that runs contrary to the "meaning" explained previously?

I. The role of "feeling" in the interpretation of metaphors

As has become clear in this attempt to explain how metaphors function, understanding them is a very complex process. Paul Ricoeur points out that understanding metaphors proceeds on several levels, only one of them rational or cognitive. In addition, as he shows, there are the levels of "imagination" and "feeling."[23] In my interpretation of how we understand metaphors these imaginative and feeling aspects are intensified when it is a question of metaphors that strongly address our emotions. Prophetic marriage imagery is situated in precisely that area. It evokes experiences from our emotional life: it is about relationships between human beings and the longings and hopes, wounds and disappointments involved in those relationships, about jealousy and betrayal; it is about sexuality, begetting, conceiving, and birth, about the beginning of life and about death. It seems to

[23] Ricoeur, "The Metaphorical Process," especially 145–46, 154–49. Ricoeur explains these concepts as follows: (ibid. 151): ". . . the metaphorical sense is generated in the thickness of the imagining scene displayed by the verbal structure of the poem. Such is, to my mind, the functioning of the intuitive grasp of a predicative connection." Ricoeur deliberately distinguishes "feelings" from emotions (ibid. 155–56): "To the extent that in emotion we are, so to speak, under the spell of our body, we are delivered to mental states with little intentionality, as though in emotion we 'lived' our body in a more intense way." In contrast, he writes (ibid. 156) that "feeling is not contrary to thought. It is thought made ours" and "I claim that feeling as well as imagination are genuine components in the process described in an interaction theory of metaphor. They both *achieve* the semantic bearing of metaphor" (ibid. 155).

me that it is very, very difficult to achieve an internal distancing from these experiences, all of which have happened to most people in one way or another and are evoked in the contemplation of these metaphors, or to manage a cognitive control of what happens as we understand them.[24] Hence in the case of the prophetic marriage imagery there is particularly great danger that prior experiences—of whatever shape or form—will influence our understanding of the metaphors more sharply than in other cases. I will discuss the specific "dangers" in the next section.

J. The "reverse action" of imagery

In his theory of metaphor Paul Ricoeur emphasizes the power of metaphors to create something new, "to open a new possibility of existence."[25] Other works on metaphor have developed this aspect, which I would like to call the reverse action of metaphors, more strongly than Ricoeur did. This is true especially of metaphors that have become such matter-of-fact inhabitants of our linguistic storehouse that they are scarcely even recognized as metaphors any more. Korpel gives some examples in her treatment of this aspect of metaphors: following Max Black, she cites the example of the wolf, which through its interaction with the human within the context of metaphor has come to seem much more human than before. She continues: "The 'smiling sun' personifies the sun, but at the same time it makes people look sunnier. So if God is called 'Father,' the interaction-view of metaphor implies that in a way such an epithet may honour a father too, making him seem more god-like."[26]

In the case of prophetic marriage imagery this "reverse action" of the metaphor can, for example, take place in such a way that the images of women, men, God, and marriage are influenced by it even today. Because this imagery has become so matter-of-fact, and at the same time is so emotionally powerful, this reverse action is probably not evident to most of its recipients. A further reason why especially in the case of this imagery we may expect a strong reverse effect lies in the special nature of God-imagery, already discussed above. We humans have "nothing but" metaphors to use when we try to speak of God, and there is no "concrete"

[24] Julie Galambush writes cautiously: "Because the apprehension of metaphorical meaning involves, at a certain level, the assent of the reader, the effect of metaphor goes beyond the verbal" (*Jerusalem in the Book of Ezekiel. The City as Yahweh's Wife* (Atlanta: Scholars, 1992) 9.

[25] Ricoeur, *Metapher* 45 (and later in many other places), here with explicit reference to biblical language.

[26] Korpel, *A Rift in the Clouds* 71; she refers to Max Black, *Models and Metaphors* (Ithaca, N.Y.: Cornell University Press, 1962) 38–44.

divine corrective for the metaphors, even if they have outlived their usefulness or become problematic in some special way. This book will point primarily to two potentially problematic implications of the prophetic marriage imagery: the hierarchical image of the marital relationships, and the legitimacy of the use of violence for the "discipline" or "punishment" of an "unruly wife."

K. The "morality of metaphors" or: questions of dominance and authority

Metaphors are not only context-dependent in their origins and interpretation. They are, in addition, anything but disinterested products of thought that exist as neutral and value-free. This aspect of metaphors can be demonstrated especially in light of the work of George Lakoff and Mark Johnson. Their project rests primarily on linguistics and cognitive psychology. Metaphors, according to their thesis, strongly shape our thinking because they play a "conceptional" role even in our acquisition of language and in the development of thought. It is impossible to escape them and their effects.[27] Lakoff and Johnson's model is attractive for my study because it provides a starting point for demonstrating that worldviews are also built up on the basis of metaphors. Although these two scholars are thinking of much more elementary metaphors than the prophetic marriage imagery, I nevertheless think it will be possible to make fruitful use of their thinking in this field as well, and especially to the effect that when metaphors are used we should be attentive in the highest degree to the implications they bring with them. Gerhard Kurz applies this principle in the case of certain metaphors that are intended to—and do—"demolish" political opponents.[28] In light of what was said in the preceding section, we note that the reception of the prophetic marriage imagery demands the application of an especially high degree of critical awareness, because this imagery is not so much received on the cognitive level, nor does it have its primary effect there. Here a particular substance of thought—possibly not even part of the intention of the "inventor" of the imagery—is being conveyed: for example, alongside statements about God and God's people, these metaphors are passing on to their readers cultural stereotypes, such as those of "man" and "woman" and their socially-constructed "opposite" natures.

[27] Lakoff and Johnson, *Metaphors We Live By*. Their model can be criticized in that their emphasis on the early learning of metaphors and their interweaving in our language and thought seems to make any distanced reflection or separate analysis of them almost impossible.

[28] Kurz, *Metapher, Allegorie* 25.

When faced with these constructions, we must critically question whether they are still appropriate today, or indeed whose interest is served by maintaining such constructions. Metaphors can act as stabilizers of control for certain dominant groups. Metaphors, like discourses, can also be created and strengthened, kept alive or reduced to silence. In Part III of this book we will discuss the elements of the content of the prophetic marriage imagery in the Old Testament that ought to be questioned from this critical perspective.

Chapter Three

Marriage, Adultery, "Harlotry": The Vocabulary of the Prophetic Marriage Imagery

A. Marriage, adultery, and divorce in the Old Testament

The Old Testament has no fixed and delimited language for the legal side of marital relationships.[1] There is an essential connection between this and the fact that Hebrew has "no term for 'marriage' or 'to marry.' The expression 'A is the husband/wife of B' is sufficient identification of the man or woman as married."[2] For other actions or events in the marital realm words were used that in normal usage outside the context of marriage have other meanings. A man "marries" (בעל, "rules over," or לקח, "takes") a woman. In the other direction, it is never said in the Old Testament that a woman "takes" or marries a man. After the marriage the man is then the "husband" (בעל, "lord, ruler") of the woman. He alone can end the relationship, by "sending away" (שׁלח) or "casting off" (גרשׁ) his wife, or by issuing a "bill of divorce" (ספר כריתות). According to the Old Testament witness, divorce cannot be initiated by a woman.

If we are to get an adequate idea of what marriage meant in the Old Testament we must take the ancient Near Eastern context into account. The major difference between the idea of marriage then and now is that in the ancient Near East marriage was for the most part polygynous. To what degree the literary evidence of polygynous marriage in Old Testament texts allows us to draw conclusions about the actual occurrence of this way of life is difficult to say. The economic situation of the family was a key factor in the possibility that the marriage was polygynous. Because wives and children had a

[1] On this see Chapter 4 below.

[2] Josef Scharbert, art. "Ehe/Eherecht/Ehescheidung II. Altes Testament," *TRE* 9 (1982) 311–13, at 311. In what follows I am dependent on his article and that of Bernhard Lang, "Ehe I. Altes Testament," *NBL* 1 (Zürich, 1991) 475–78.

claim to maintenance from the *pater familias,* multiple marriage was only possible for economically well-to-do men. To that extent the depiction of men with multiple wives can also serve to emphasize their wealth.

Clearly more women than men "break" (נאף) their marriages (i.e., commit adultery) in Old Testament texts. The reason for this is that the conditions for adultery are different for the two sexes.[3] Here again the understanding of marriage as in principle polygynous forms the background: while a man can marry several women, a woman can only tie herself to one man. "Adultery for men is only intercourse with someone married to another, while for a married woman it is intercourse with another man."[4] In most cases adultery was punishable by death.

Also unlike today, in ancient Israel marriage was essentially a hierarchical relationship.[5] Nevertheless, in individual cases an egalitarian relationship of the two marital partners would have been possible. Essentially, marriage served to provide a framework for maintaining the (extended) family; blood bonds and economic relationships were thus regulated. "Loving" and "hating" in this context (thus, e.g., in Deut 21:15-17 and correspondingly in the Codex Hammurabi) were terms with legal connotations and not expressions of feeling.

We should mention one unique characteristic of the prophetic marriage imagery in contrast to the textual depiction of human marriages in the Old Testament: although it is not at all exceptional for sexual intercourse to be mentioned in the Old Testament (especially ידע, "know," with the man as subject and the woman as object), nothing is said of this in either a nega-

[3] Gale Yee explains why the accusation of adultery falls more frequently on women than on men in the Old Testament: "An implicit double standard existed in the public evaluation of a man who broke wedlock. Extramarital activity, which would have been inexcusable for the wife, was tolerated for the husband in many cases. A man was not punished for having sex unless an engaged or a married woman was involved *and* he was caught in the act (see Deut. 22:23-29). Engaging the services of prostitutes was acceptable (see Gen. 38:12-23; Josh. 2:1-7; 1 Kings 3:16-27). This double standard underscored the issues of honor and paternity that so characterized the ancient Israelite society, making the woman the primary offender in adulterous acts" ("Hosea," in Carol A. Newsom and Sharon H. Ringe, eds., *The Women's Bible Commentary* [Louisville: Westminster John Knox, 1992] 195–202, at 198).

[4] Scharbert, "Ehe/Eherecht/Ehescheidung," 312.

[5] It should only be noted that this "present-day" understanding of marriage is but a few decades old. As late as 1930 Joseph Ziegler (*Die Liebe Gottes bei den Propheten. Ein Beitrag zur alttestamentlichen Theologie* [Münster: Aschendorffsche Verlagsbuchhandlung, 1930] 84–85) could propose a picture of marriage in which it is not evident that he is distinguishing between his own time and that of ancient Israel: "As the man is lord of his wife as a consequence of the marital bond, so that his partner belongs to him and therefore must be obedient and at his service, so also Yahweh is the lord of Israel, which, by the power of the mutual covenant, belongs to Yahweh and therefore must obey and serve him."

tive or positive sense as regards the "couple" YHWH and Israel/Jerusalem.[6] This can be seen as an indication that marital imagery for the divine-human relationship does not encompass all possible aspects of a human marriage. It will become clear in what follows that in this imagery a selection has been made and a focus chosen.

B. The vocabulary of the prophetic marriage imagery

In the texts of the prophetic marriage imagery there is a cluster of terms that appear in other Old Testament texts in connection with marriage. On this basis we can rightly speak of "marriage imagery" or "marriage metaphors."

However, it is not "love" that serves as the key word in these texts. A much better indicator is the appearance of זנה, "whoring," or "harlotry," and its derivatives. In connection with זנה we often find נאף, the proper term for "adultery." This reference is one of the most important indications that this imagery really does describe a marriage between YHWH and Israel/Jerusalem. Besides זנה and נאף, the texts have other terms in common as well. The punishment of the "woman" is often illustrated in images that seem to be scenes of sexual violence—at least to present-day readers.[7] The "nakedness" (ערוה, מער, נבלת, שבל, or שול) of the "woman" is "uncovered" (גלה) so that all the onlookers can see (ראה) her "shame," "humiliation," or "disgrace" (קלון or חרפה). "Normal" marriage language is used in only a few texts.

Prophetic marriage imagery can be found in the following texts: Isa 1:21; 50:1; 54:1-6; 57:6-13; 62:4-5; Jer 2:1-3, 13; 4:1-31; 13:20-27; Lam 1:1-22; Ezekiel 16 and 23; Hos 2:1-23 [MT 2:4-25]; 9:1; Mic 1:6-7; Nah 3:4-7; Mal 2:10-16. In addition there are some texts that do not use the corresponding vocabulary and do not explicitly address or mention the "woman," but that clearly have the prophetic marriage imagery as background: for example, Isa 49:15-23; 51:17–52:2; Jeremiah 30–31; Mic 1:4; Zeph 3:14-17, and others.

A survey of the above texts reveals a kind of "history of the relationship" between YHWH and "his wife." In general terms it consists of five motifs:[8] First, there is a narrative of the marriage between YHWH and his

[6] This observation was made by Odil Hannes Steck ("Zion als Gelände und Gestalt. Überlegungen zur Wahrnehmung Jerusalems als Stadt und Frau im Alten Testament," *ZThK* 86 [1989] 261–81, at 275, with reference to Urs Winter, *Frau und Göttin. Exegetische und ikonographische Studien zum weiblichen Gottesbild im Alten Israel und dessen Umwelt* [Fribourg: Universitätsverlag; Göttingen: Vandenhoeck & Ruprecht, 1983] 632ff., 639).

[7] See Chapter 1 D above.

[8] I have already presented this outline and a detailed exposition in an earlier essay ("Connected by Marriage, Adultery and Violence: The Prophetic Marriage Metaphor in the Book of the Twelve and in the Major Prophets," *SBL Seminar Papers* [Atlanta: Scholars, 1999] 552–69).

"wife," as well as her "harlotry." Second, YHWH's reaction is described as the punishment of the "wife," often painted in scenes of sexual violence or as divorce from "her." Third, YHWH then also takes Zion/Jerusalem (or Judah) as a wife, and she, too, "whores" away from him. Fourth, she is also punished by him, or he considers divorce. Finally, in many texts a fifth motif announces, after the punishment or suffering of the "wife," that YHWH has forgiven her, put an end to her suffering, or restored her (as land or city).

Besides these motifs there are others within the field of prophetic marriage imagery in which, while a "woman" appears together with YHWH, she is not his "wife." Here we should mention, on the one hand, the texts that speak of the punishment of "foreign" "women" or "daughters." These texts also employ the vocabulary of sexual violence (Isaiah 47; Nah 3:4-7). On the other hand, we also find "daughter Zion/Jerusalem" or the "daughter of my people" (e.g., Jeremiah 4, 6, 8, 9, 14; Zech 2:6-13 [MT 2:10-17]; 9:9). These figures are more or less completely dependent on YHWH, as concrete daughters in ancient Israel were dependent on their fathers,[9] but these are not YHWH's wives.

Finally, there are also some terms within the field of prophetic marriage imagery that appear in only a few texts. These are בגד, "be unfaithful," טהר, "be pure/clean," טמא, "be impure/unclean," צהל, "whinny," עגב, "burn," כשף, "cleanse," זמה, "shameful deed," גלול and שקוץ, "idol," and תועבה, "horror, loathing." The fact that these are not mentioned in all the texts indicates that they represent a metaphorical field that is not meant to be emphasized in every case. They are clarified each time in the context in which they are used.

Now, after this overview, I would like to examine in more detail the most important Hebrew terms—or at any rate, those that are most difficult to translate with clear and precise meaning. These are "whoring" or "harlotry" (זנה) and the "uncovering" (גלה) of the "woman's" "nakedness[?]" (שול or שבל). In the studies of the texts in the individual prophetic books of the Old Testament we will then point out specific nuances of the terms within this spectrum of meaning.

[9] Fathers' power of disposition over their daughters in the Old Testament has been thoroughly investigated by Elke Seifert in her dissertation (*Tochter und Vater im Alten Testament. Eine ideologiekritische Untersuchung zur Verfügungsgewalt von Vätern über ihre Töchter* [Neukirchen-Vluyn: Neukirchener Verlag, 1997]). See Chapter 1 above.

C. Some terms in the prophetic marriage imagery and their implications

i. זנה, *"harlotry" or "whoring"*

The verb זנה, with its derivatives, זונה ("whore"), זנות, זנונים, and תזנות ("whoredom," "prostitution") appears at 138 places in the Old Testament, overwhelmingly in the prophetic texts. זנות, תזנות,[10] and זנונים are abstract plurals, with זנונים emphasizing the habitual nature of the activity.[11] Usually appearing as a *qal* feminine participle taken substantively, זונה designates the "whore" or "harlot." It is difficult to reproduce זנה adequately in German or English. In commentaries the זונה is often referred to as a "tart" or "whore" or "harlot" or adulteress, although it is seldom explained what we are to understand these to be. In addition, moral judgments are swiftly attached. Here I want to associate myself with Renate Jost, who chooses the German words for "whore" or "prostitute" to translate זונה, "since both, in contrast to 'harlot,' are at present used as a self-designation by [German] women who exercise that profession."[12] Unlike Jost, however, I find it important to expand the concept of "whore" and "whoring" for זונה or זנה. As I will explain further below, the meaning of זנה cannot be restricted to the practice of prostitution for the sake of earning one's living; it encompasses a broader spectrum.

In the *Theological Dictionary of the Old Testament,* Seth Erlandsson discusses the meanings of זנה and זונה; unfortunately he does not always clearly distinguish the levels and connotations of adultery, prostitution, "cultic prostitution," and worshiping foreign gods or the actions of a זונה within the "covenant relationship" between YHWH and Israel. Unlike the legal term נאף, זנה does not simply mean "commit adultery." How are these two roots to be distinguished from each other? One notable difference between זנה and נאף is that זנה is used almost exclusively for the actions of women or female personifications,[13] whereas נאף can also be committed

[10] The derivative תזנות appears only in Ezekiel, but there 22x.

[11] This is pointed out by Bruce K. Waltke and Michael P. O'Connor, *An Introduction to Biblical Hebrew Syntax* [Winona Lake: Eisenbrauns, 1990]) 121.

[12] Renate Jost, *Frauen, Männer und die Himmelskönigin. Exegetische Studien* (Gütersloh: Chr. Kaiser, 1995) 101 n. 8.

[13] Seth Erlandsson, art. זנה, *zānāh, TDOT* 4:99–104, especially 100–101. Erlandsson does not use "whore or harlot" differently, and "wantonness" is not clearly distinguished from them. [Translator's note: David E. Green, the translator of *TDOT* 4, uses the terms "harlot," "harlotry," and "prostitute" for the several German words cited here.] Moreover, Erlandsson does not indicate his own position with regard to the biblical texts; he simply describes them without acknowledging any distance from them. At one point the article even minimizes sexual violence: Erlandsson sketches the legal prescription regarding the forced marriage of a raped woman in Deut 22:28-29 (where the verbs תפש, "grasp, seize" and ענה II *piʿel,* "rape" leave no doubt that this is about rape)

by men.[14] In addition, זנה often takes on the metaphorical significance of worshiping foreign gods,[15] something not so frequently found in the case of נאף. Erlandsson names, as the criterion of differentiation between זנה and נאף, the fact that with נאף a "covenant relationship" (betrothal or marriage, also metaphorically) between the woman and the man is wounded, which need not be the case with זנה. However, he admits that זנה occasionally takes on a meaning that approaches that of the narrower נאף.[16] The reverse is not true; נאף remains the proper term for adultery.

Feminist exegetes have investigated the meaning of זנה from a number of different angles. I have already discussed T. Drorah Setel's theses on the translation of זנה.[17] Here let me examine several further nuances.

Phyllis Bird warns us to pay attention to the social background in our interpretations of זנה. She has determined that the meaning of the root differs in the Old Testament according to the context in which it is found, but in general it refers to a nonmarital relationship between two partners who are otherwise free to marry.[18] Bird further observes that זנה is more frequently used in reference to women than to men because marriage had far greater consequences for the legal status of women than for that of men.[19] Moreover, the patriarchal double standard of morality must be kept in view as background for the interpretation of זנה in the Old Testament.[20]

---

in these words: "When sexual intercourse is initiated before a marriage contract has been sealed and neither of the parties is already married, the man must marry the woman and may not divorce her" (p. 100). There were two exceptions, of which Erlandsson mentions only one, in Num 25:1 (ויחל העם לזנות, "the people began to play the harlot") with the grammatically masculine subject "Israel," and the Moabite women as object. Besides this, in Hos 5:3 there is an example with Ephraim, a masculine subject for זנה; cf. Marie-Theres Wacker, *Figurationen des Weiblichen im Hosea-Buch* (Freiburg: Herder, 1996) 159 and n. 56.

[14] For example in Exod 20:14, *par* Deut 5:18; Lev 20:10; Isa 57:3; Jer 5:7; 7:9; 9:2 [MT 9:1]; 23:10; 23:14; 29:23; Hos 4:2, 14; 7:4; Mal 3:5; Ps 50:18; Job 24:15, and in Prov 6:32.

[15] This is its meaning in Exod 34:15-16; Lev 17:7; 20:5-6; Num 15:39; Deut 31:16; Judg 2:17; 8:27, 33; Jer 2:20; 3:1, 3, 6, 8; 5:7; Ezek 6:9; 16:15-17; 20:30; Hos 1:2; 4:10, 12, 15, 18; 5:3; 9:1, and in 1 Chr 5:25; 2 Chr 21:11, 13.

[16] Erlandsson, זנה, 100.

[17] T. Drorah Setel, "Prophets and Pornography: Female Sexual Imagery in Hosea," in Letty M. Russell, ed., *Feminist Interpretation of the Bible* (Philadelphia: Westminster, 1985) 86–95, especially 87–88 (see Chapter 1 above).

[18] Phyllis Bird, "'To Play the Harlot': An Inquiry into an Old Testament Metaphor," in Peggy L. Day, ed., *Gender and Difference in Ancient Israel* (Minneapolis: Fortress, 1989) 75–94, at 90 n. 13. She thus excludes sodomy and homosexual relationships, which in any case are impermissible according to the legal texts.

[19] Ibid. 77.

[20] Ibid. 79: "The anomaly of the prostitute as a tolerated specialist in an activity prohibited to every other woman is a particular feature of patriarchal society, representing an accommodation

Hannelies Schulte treats another aspect of זנה. Looking at narrative texts (Judg 11:1-2; Josh 2:1-21; 6:22-23, 25; 1 Kings 3:16-27), she proposes the thesis that זונה only acquired the negative meaning "whore" or "prostitute" in the royal era, while originally זונה was a term stemming from the matrilineal family structure and referring to an independent woman. When this family structure died out in the royal era the expression זונה was taken over for the newly developed lifestyle of prostitutes.[21] This thesis was later adopted and reformulated by Rut Törnkvist. In her study she emphasizes that זנה, as a term from the realm of sexuality, may not be interpreted without regard for its ideological dimensions.[22] Against the patriarchal background of ancient Israel a word like זנה is more appropriate than a legal term like נאף for describing a whole spectrum of deviant behaviors of the "woman" Israel/Jerusalem. With results similar to Schulte's, Törnkvist discusses (in light of Judg 11:1 and 19:2) the implications of זנה for Israelite conceptions of marriage. While in earlier times the married pair lived with the wife's father (patrilocality), in later times they came more commonly to live with the husband's family (virilocality). The increasingly rare patrilocality became suspect; in a "normal" marriage the wife moved to the husband's family. The term זנה, originally employed for a wife living with her father, came more and more to embody the idea of socially deviant behavior, until finally it also included prostitution. "The זנה woman or wife is in turn interpreted as a dubious one, a single woman, a loose woman, and in the end when the traditions of patrilocal marriage have fallen into oblivion, a prostitute."[23]

Marie-Theres Wacker has concentrated still more on this last aspect. Especially in connection with the formula אשת זנונים ("wife of whoredom") in Hos 1:2, according to Wacker, the word refers to an "erotomaniac."[24] This

---

to the conflicting desires of men for exclusive control of their wives' sexuality (and hence offspring) and, at the same time, for sexual access to other women. The greater the inaccessibility of women in the society as a result of restrictions on the wife and unmarried nubile woman, the greater the need for an institutionally legitimized 'other woman.' The prostitute is that 'other woman,' tolerated but stigmatized, desired but ostracized."

[21] Hannelies Schulte, "Beobachtungen zum Begriff der Zônâ im Alten Testament," *ZAW* 104 (1992) 255–62, at 261–62.

[22] Rut Törnkvist devotes a long section in her work on Hosea to זנה (*The Use and Abuse of Female Sexual Imagery in the Book of Hosea. A Feminist Critical Approach to Hos 1–3.* [Uppsala: Academia Ubsaliensis, 1998] 95–115).

[23] Ibid. 114.

[24] The term "erotomaniac," like "nymphomaniac," is in my opinion not without its problems. It is not only that these words have a pejorative echo. Behind them lies the idea that there is an absolutely calculable "good" measure (not sharply delineated by cultural notions) of sexuality for women, beyond which we can diagnose a pathological condition of "hypersexuality"—thus the definition of "nymphomania" in the relevant German lexicon (Willibald Pschyrembel, *Klinisches Wörterbuch* [257th ed. Berlin and New York: de Gruyter, 1994] 1089).

is to make clear "that Hosea's wife is portrayed as a woman who seeks sexual liaisons with men on her own initiative, but not as a professional harlot who lives, or must live, from the sale of her body."[25] In that case we would find here evidence of the tendency to use זנה to describe deviant sexual behavior by women.

In summary, we may conclude that זנה primarily describes sexual activities outside of marriage, mainly by women. Adultery (נאף) can be an action within the spectrum described by זנה. The *qal* participle of the verb, זונה, designates any woman who lives her sexuality outside of marriage; she may do so in order to earn her livelihood. However, זונות are not only professional prostitutes, but all women who have sexual relations with men to whom they are not betrothed or married. As indicated above, I prefer to describe this with the English words "whoring" or "whore," or sometimes "harlotry" and "harlot."[26] Today these words are also frequently used to brand women's "deviant" behavior, and the same was true at particular periods in the history of ancient Israel. What is regarded as "deviant" depends in each case on the particular context and the interests of the authors.

We observe that זנה and its derivatives are frequently used in the prophetic marriage imagery in the Old Testament, where they usually refer to the worship of foreign gods. This is not always made especially clear by the addition of a phrase such as "after foreign gods." In a certain sense this use of זנה serves to sexualize false religious behavior in general. This meaning of זנה has become so matter-of-fact that the word attains the status of a fixed concept and is understood even outside the developed marriage imagery as describing behavior of the "woman" Israel/Jerusalem that is negatively evaluated in the texts.

ii. גלה*, "uncover"*

According to the universal understanding of scholars, גלה is a root with two meanings. It is not clear, however, whether there are two roots that can be strictly separated: thus the terminological compromise, "two meanings." Frequently suggested as fundamental meaning for both roots are on the one hand "lead away" (often into exile, the גולה), and on the other hand "uncover."[27] Of primary interest as regards the prophetic marriage imagery

[25] Wacker, *Figurationen des Weiblichen* 41.

[26] I am aware, and I regret, that in doing this I am in danger of falling into the clichés of a popular way of speaking, deserving of criticism, according to which all women who exercise their sexuality outside of fixed relationships are lumped together with professional prostitutes, but I see no alternative.

[27] Thus Claus Westermann and Rainer Albertz, art. "גלה, aufdecken," *THAT* 1[4] (1984) 418–26, at 419, and Hans-Jürgen Zobel, art. "גלה, *gālāh*," *TDOT* 2:476–88, at 477.

is the second meaning, "uncover." It appears in the *qal, nipʿal, piʿel, puʿal,* and *hitpaʿel,*[28] and "always describes the uncovering of something that is normally hidden."[29] It refers primarily "to the forbidden area of sex"[30] and especially to "uncovering the 'nakedness' [sexual organs] or what covers it."[31] גלה, "uncover," "lay bare" appears in seven places in the context of prophetic marriage imagery, always with a very concrete meaning and with an object. Where the object can be translated with assurance (ערוה, "nakedness," in Ezek 16:36-37; 23:10, 18, 29) or relative assurance (נבלת in Hos 2:12 and שבל in Isa 47:2), גלה relates to what is "laid bare" and not to what is taken away for that purpose. If this is in fact the case, we have a translation problem in two other passages: what is the relationship to this "uncovering" of the object שׁול, which is found with גלה in Nah 3:5 (and with חשׂף in Jer 13:22), and in fact with the further expression עַל־פניך, "over your face"? In addition, שׁול cannot be given a simple and straightforward translation. Among the meanings discussed are "genitals" and "skirt hem." If the former is accurate, the question arises how this עַל־פניך can be "laid bare" "over your face." In this section I will attempt first of all to clarify the possible translations of גלה, and then turn to the problems surrounding שׁבל/שׁול.

A review of the *nipʿal, piʿel,* and *puʿal* instances of גלה shows that the verb itself has no sexual connotations, and requires further definition to give it that meaning. For that purpose the mention of the object ערוה is enough to make גלה a term for sexual intercourse.[32] The expression גלה *piʿel* plus ערוה is found in the context of prohibition of sexual intercourse twenty-two times in Lev 18:6-19; 20:11, 17-21, and in Ezek 22:10,[33] always with a masculine subject and as something (not) to be done to a woman. In Leviticus 18 and 20, then, גלה with the object ערוה means the act of sexual intercourse.[34] Hans-Jürgen Zobel remarks, with respect to the meaning of all instances of גלה in the prophetic texts, that the word is used

[28] Westermann and Albertz, "גלה," 419.

[29] Ibid. 422.

[30] Ibid.

[31] Ibid.

[32] This was emphasized by Karl Elliger in his remarks on Leviticus 18: "The prohibition 'you shall not uncover the nakedness' may in fact be meant not only in the transferred, but also in the narrower and most limited sense of the word. It may be that there is no thought of marriage here at all, but all the more of any and every kind of sexual activity, such as can be evoked by common life in a confined group" ("Das Gesetz in Leviticus 18," *ZAW* 67 [1955] 1–25, at 8).

[33] Karl Elliger, *Leviticus* (Tübingen: J.C.B. Mohr, 1966) 238 n. 10; in Ezek 22:10 "their fathers' nakedness" refers to the fathers' wives.

[34] Herbert Niehr points out that this formulation is a euphemism (art. "עֶרְוָה, "*ʿārāh,*" *TDOT* 11:343–49, at 347).

in the context of images "for fornication, shame, and utmost insult."[35] In addition, we should note with Erhard Gerstenberger that even in the less specific uses of גלה with the object ערוה "looking at a person's nakedness . . . is always degrading for that person."[36] Therefore the uncovering of a person's nakedness, even without its being specifically interpreted as sexual intercourse or in connection with further violence, is to be regarded as an act of humiliation and as sexual violence in the broadest sense.

However, in some of the texts of the prophetic marriage imagery it is not so clear what meaning is attached to גלה; particularly questionable is Nah 3:5. Godfrey Driver has presented the thesis that the object of גלה, when it means "uncover," is always the thing that is laid bare or uncovered, and not the thing that is removed for the purpose of uncovering.[37] What should we think of this thesis? An investigation shows, first of all, that גלה *nipʿal/piʿel* can have a great variety of objects. The most frequent, especially in Leviticus 18 and 20, but also in prophetic texts, is "nakedness" or "shame" (ערוה). Besides this, however—contra Driver—there are also passages in which the current translations describe not the act of uncovering, but what is removed for the purpose. This can be designated grammatically as the difference between a direct object and a prepositional augmentation, that is, an indirect object. Thomas Podella remarks in this connection, citing Wolfgang Richter: ". . . clauses constructed with the verb גלה contain no doubled expression of objects, direct object + prepositional object,"[38] which is what we are led to expect by common translations of Nah 3:5 as "I will lift up your skirts (direct object) over your face (prepositional object)."

Can the thesis that גלה never appears in the Old Testament with two objects of different types be verified as regards גלה in the *qal, piʿel, puʿal,* and *nipʿal?* An investigation of the appearances of גלה reveals that this is not the case. Apart from Nah 3:5, גלה appears with a direct object and an ad-

[35] Zobel, "גלה, *gālāh*," 479.

[36] Erhard S. Gerstenberger, *Das dritte Buch Mose. Leviticus* (rev. ed. Göttingen: Vandenhoeck & Ruprecht, 1993) 226; emphatically also Athalya Brenner, *The Intercourse of Knowledge. On Gendering Desire and Sexuality in the Hebrew Bible* (Leiden and New York: Brill, 1997) 42.

[37] Godfrey R. Driver, "Isaiah 6:1 'His Train Filled the Temple,'" in Hans Goedicke, ed., *Near Eastern Studies in Honor of William Foxwell Albright* (Baltimore and London: Johns Hopkins University Press, 1971) 87–96, at 96: "Thus both subject and object of the verb [גלה] are always in the O.T. that which is uncovered or disclosed, never that which is removed so that something else may be uncovered or disclosed, even when the basic sense of the verb is obscured by an ellipse of the object with the active form or by the use of the passive form derived directly from it."

[38] Thomas Podella, *Das Lichtkleid JHWHs. Untersuchungen zur Gestalthaftigkeit Gottes im Alten Testament und seiner altorientalischen Umwelt* (Tübingen: J.C.B. Mohr [Paul Siebeck], 1996) 52.

ditional prepositional designation in Ezek 12:3 *(qal);* Amos 3:7 *(qal);* Ps 119:22 *(piʿel),* and Job 12:22 *(piʿel).* However, there is an additional reason to translate the expression שׁוּלַיִךְ עַל־פָּנָיִךְ differently from what Podella suggests: if both שׁוּלַיִךְ and עַל־פָּנָיִךְ are not understood as objects, the suffix on עַל־פָּנָיִךְ can only be regarded as a second determination of שׁוּלַיִךְ, which is already determined by a suffix, which is grammatically impossible.[39] Therefore we must assume that in Nah 3:5 גלה in fact can carry *both* an object *and* a prepositional expression. From this point we must further ask whether גלה can describe what is taken away in order to uncover something, or what is uncovered by the action.

In order to answer this question it will be helpful to know whether גלה is also construed with an indirect object in other Old Testament passages. For this purpose we must investigate further. We are concerned with the passages in which possibly—otherwise than in most appearances of גלה—there is mention not of what is uncovered (as direct object), but of what is taken away (as indirect object). Besides Jer 13:22 and Nah 3:5 this is the case also in Deut 22:30 [MT 23:1]; 27:20; Isa 22:8; 47:2; Job 41:5. Most of these texts are problematic to translate and should therefore be examined more closely, especially as regards the object they give for גלה.

In Deut 22:30; 27:20 the object of גלה *piʿel* is the father's "skirt" (כנף).[40] We find evidence of the root כנף in broad sections of the ancient Near East. In the Old Testament it is usually used for the wings of various kinds of beings: for example, in a prominent text also for the wings of the seraphim in Isa 6:2. However, besides this meaning כנף can also be used metaphorically

[39] Cf. GK §§125a and 127a. (English: *Gesenius' Hebrew grammar, as edited and enlarged by the late E. Kautzsch.* 15th impression, Index of Passages rev. and corr. by John B. Job [Oxford and New York: Clarendon Press, 1988]).

[40] For what follows see Ges[17] 353–54 (cf. English: *Gesenius' Hebrew and Chaldee Lexicon to the Old Testament Scriptures: Numerically Coded to Strong's Exhaustive Concordance, With an English Index of More Than 12,000 Entries.* Translated by Samuel Prideaux Tregelles [Grand Rapids: Baker Book House, c1979]); *HAL* 462–63 (cf. English: *The Hebrew and Aramaic Lexicon of the Old Testament,* subsequently revised by Walter Baumgartner and Johann Jakob Stamm, with assistance from Benedikt Hartmann . . . [et al.]. [1st English ed. Leiden and New York: Brill, 1994–2000]); A. S. van der Woude, art. "כנף, *kānāp,* Flügel," *THAT* I[4] (1984) 833–36; and Werner Dommershausen, art. "כנף, *kānāp,*" *TDOT* 7:229–31. Paul A. Kruger has presented a study of כנף and its symbolic meaning, especially in 1 Sam 15:27, in his "The Symbolic Significance of the Hem *(kanaf)* in 1 Samuel 15.27," in Walter T. Claassen, ed., *Text and Context. Old Testament and Semitic Studies for F. C. Fensham* (Sheffield: JSOT Press, 1988) 105–16. Here, as elsewhere in similar contexts (idem, "The Hem of the Garment in Marriage. The Meaning of the Symbolic Gesture in Ruth 3:9 and Ezek 16:8," *JNWSL* 12 [1984] 79–86; "Rites of Passage Relating to Marriage and Divorce in the Hebrew Bible," *JNWSL* 21 [1995] 69–81), he adduces Mesopotamian divorce documents in support of his thesis, as do a great many other scholars as well; on this see Chapter 5 below.

for the "border" or "hem" as "wing," thus as the "limit" of an object. Hence כנף appears in various contexts with reference to clothing, to describe the hem or corner or tassel of a garment; legal connotations may be present.[41] In Deut 22:30; 27:20 there is reference to a sexual and marital-legal act, as is evident from the context: "to uncover a man's garment means to interfere in his marriage."[42] In any case it is clear that in Deut 22:30; 27:20 גלה *piʿel* with כנף very clearly has an object that, in the form of the "skirt," describes something "taken away," and not, as in most other cases of גלה, what is uncovered.[43]

In Isa 47:2 the case is quite clear: the text here speaks of "uncovering" or "removing" (גלה *piʿel*) the "veil" (צמה) or the thigh (שוק). Especially interesting in this text is the next half-verse. In Isa 47:3b חשׂף *qal* is used parallel to גלה. חשׂף appears in nine places in the Old Testament. There are problems with the translation especially in Joel 1:7 (where it is used in a *figura etymologica* for "stripping the bark" from fig trees or vines) and Ps 29:9 (where it seems to describe the stripping of "shrubs"; however, the masculine substantive יער is used only here with the feminine plural). Separate treatment is otherwise given for the most part only to the occurrences in Isa 30:14 and Hag 2:16, for which the meaning "draw out" is suggested. Thus the word, in its roots and in their relationship, is not undisputed, as a glance at the lexicons will show:

> Ges[18] attributes the phenomenon to two distinct roots: חשׂף I corresponding to Akkadian *ḫasapu*, "uproot," and II corresponding to Akkadian *esepu*, meaning among other things "pour out a liquid," "decant."[44] Only the appearances of חשׂף in Isa 30:14 and Hag 2:16 are assigned to the second root. The first root is divided into two sub-meanings: on the one hand, "peel" (Joel 1:7 and Ps 29:9), and on the other hand "lay bare," "uncover," with the accusative of the thing or person. Ges[18] assigns Jer 13:26 and Isa 47:2 also to this meaning.
>
> The subdivision in *HAL* is different.[45] Here again two root words are supposed: root I from Ugaritic *ḥsp*, "dip water," "pour," and root II from the Arabic basic meaning *ḥašafa*, "hasten." While the second root is assigned only to Ps 29:9, together with the possible derivative חשׂיף, *HAL* attributes all the other occurrences to the first root. Its three meanings are given as "strip" (Joel 1:7), "lay bare" (the majority of occurrences, including Isa 47:2 and Jer 13:26), and "draw up" (Isa 30:14; Hag 2:16).

[41] This is true especially of Ruth 3:9 and Ezek 16:8, where covering with the corner of the garment expresses the act of marrying.

[42] Dommershausen, "כנף, *kānāp*," 231.

[43] So also van der Woude, "כנף, *kānāp*, Flügel," 835, and Dommershausen, "כנף, *kānāp*," 231.

[44] Ges[18] 405.

[45] *HAL* 345.

However, one constant runs through all these translation variants: חשׂף always stands with the accusative of the thing or person. An openness with regard to the object, as noted above in the case of גלה, is not apparent for חשׂף. Nowhere does חשׂף refer to what is taken away for the purpose of laying bare. Since in Isa 47:2-3 it is parallel to גלה, this can be seen as an indication that גלה in Nah 3:5 also describes the uncovering of the "shame," i.e., the genitals.

It is also important in this connection that the expression used in Nah 3:5 appears in Jer 13:26 as well—except that the verb is different; the Jeremiah text has חשׂף instead of גלה. Beyond this, גלה is also used in Jer 13:22 with an object, but here again with one that presents problems for the translator. שׁבל, "skirt," or something similar will be considered in more detail below as a term parallel to שׁוּל; in this passage the verse cannot be used to argue for a particular meaning of גלה.

Thus, starting from the meaning of חשׂף in Isa 47:2 and Jer 13:26 we may formulate the thesis that it is more probable as regards גלה in Nah 3:5 that the word describes the "laying bare" of a part of the body than that it refers to the "removal" of a covering.

For the last verse to be considered, Job 41:13a [MT 41:5a], we can only surmise that the object of גלה is something to be taken away for the purpose of laying bare. Here the object of גלה *pi'el* is a construct phrase: "the surface/upper part of his garment." In this passage from the second divine discourse Leviathan is being described in poetic terms. The second part of this verse is especially opaque, which is why an interpretation of the first part can only be made with reservation. It is especially regrettable that as regards Job 41:13, because of the unclarity of the second half of the verse, no clear translation of the object of גלה can be given, since this passage, with the combination of גלה + פנה, is the closest Old Testament parallel to the expression גלה + על פנה in Nah 3:5.

The investigation of גלה with various objects shows that Driver's thesis[46] is not accurate. There are, in fact, some passages in which גלה has with it, as object, the thing that is "taken away." This can be said with certainty of Deut 23:1; 27:20 with the object כנף, and for Isa 22:8 with the object מסך. With some probability what is referred to in Isa 47:2bα (צמה) and in Job 41:13 (פני לבושׁ) is what is "taken away." However, in some of the questionable passages it is possible that what is "uncovered" is also placed as an object of גלה: this is certainly the case in Isa 47:3 (ערוה) and probably also in Isa 47:2bβ (שׁבל) and in Jer 13:22 (שׁוּל).

[46] See the quotation above in n. 37.

Hence, against the background of its other uses in the Old Testament, גלה can have both a direct object (here what is "uncovered") and an indirect object (what is "taken away"). For Nah 3:5 in particular this means that our attention must now be directed to the meaning of the problematic noun שׁוּל.

iii. שׁבל/שׁוּל, *"nakedness" or "skirt hem"*

The word שׁוּל appears either in a cultic context or in connection with metaphors of sexual violence. There are only eleven instances in the Old Testament, with the forms always plural (or dual). For more than half, the meaning is not in doubt: in Exod 28:33, 34; 39:24, 25, 26 שׁוּלִים describes the lower border, the "hem" of the priest's so-called "robe of the ephod." Also in a cultic context is what is probably the best-known use of the word: in the vision in Isa 6:1 the שׁוּלִים of the enthroned YHWH fill the hall of the Temple. The remaining four instances, in Jer 13:22, 26; Lam 1:9, and Nah 3:5, use שׁוּל in depictions of sexual violence. In Jer 13:22 the prophet announces to the personified city of Jerusalem what will be imaginatively carried out in 13:26: because of the personified city's great sin, YHWH will "lift up" (v. 22: גלה *nipʿal*; v. 26: חשׂף) her שׁוּל. As a result, in v. 22 violence is done (חמס *nipʿal*) to her body, and in v. 26 her "shame" (קלון) is revealed (ראה *nipʿal*). The action in Lam 1:9 is also directed, in word and image, against Jerusalem: when "all who honored her" have seen (v. 8: ראה *qal*) her nakedness (ערוה) she groans and turns her face away; her uncleanness (טמא) klings to her שׁוּלִים. Driver's suggestion may be tested by this passage. His argumentation begins from the unclear meaning of the word שׁוּל,[47] and his impression is supported by the relevant lexicon articles. Driver founds his thesis on the connotations of the word in the LXX[48] and in Jerome, in Arabic, and in the Mishnah, all of which point to "hanging down" or "being slack."[49] Driver also supports the meaning he suggests, "extremities," with passages from the Pesharim and Targumim.[50] However, his translation is problematic when applied to Nah 3:5.

[47] The noun cannot be derived from any known Hebrew word; for the nominal form there is only a note by Hans Bauer and Pontus Leander (*Historische Grammatik der hebräischen Sprache des Alten Testaments* [Halle a.S.: Max Niemeyer, 1922; repr. Hildesheim: G. Olms, 1965] §61m): שׁוּל is said not to be among the nouns with a long middle vowel because the length of the vowel results from a middle consonant's having fallen out of the word **šubl*. Bauer and Leander refer to the hapax legomenon שׁבל (in Isa 47:2), although its meaning is no clearer than that of שׁוּל.

[48] LXX, for example, translates τὰ ὀπίσω σοῦ, "your back," "behind."

[49] Driver, "Isaiah 6:1," 88; *HAL* 1338 also points to the Arabic *sawlat* as slackness of the belly or other parts of the body.

[50] Driver, "Isaiah 6:1," 89.

The verse is in many ways similar to Jer 13:22: YHWH now lifts up Nineveh's שׁולים over her face and shows (ראה *hip'il*) the nations her "nakedness" (מער) and the kingdoms her "shame" (קלון). In this Jer 13:22 and Nah 3:5 are not only very similar: both also have the prepositional phrase על פניך, "over your face" as an addition to שׁול. This expression makes Driver's suggested interpretation of שׁולים as "genitals" very improbable—unless, of course, the whole expression על פניך שׁליך at this point is to be understood as deviating from the otherwise normal usage.

> Thus the difficulty in translating על פניך lies in the fact that the expression, as an additional qualification of the verb גלה, is really superfluous, or at any rate is difficult to locate syntactically. Podella combines the expression על פניך with שׁול and makes the whole phrase the direct object: "what hangs over your face."[51] It is also worth mentioning, as another possibility, that the Old Testament contains instances of the "prepositional phrase"[52] על פנים, referring to the whole person, and thus used in metaphorical expressions as *pars pro toto*. According to Horacio Simian-Yofre the combination of על פנים + the person means "'face to face with,' 'near,' in the physical or moral presence of someone."[53] There are, however, other connotations of the expression as well: for example, in Nah 2:2[MT 1], where the "person" in question is the "scatterer" or "destroyer" who advances against Judah: "In Gen 16:12 and Nah 2:2(1), the meaning is 'against' . . . ."[54] A. S. Van der Woude[55] remarks, regarding the expression על פנים: "Also in relation to persons *'al-p^ene* occasionally means 'at the expense of,' 'to the disadvantage of' (Gen 25:18; Deut 21:16; probably also Gen 16:12 . . .)."[56] In contrast, for the expression על פנים in the context of the prophetic marriage imagery Lyle Eslinger emphasizes for Jer 13:26 the metaphorical meaning: "The meaning of the prepositional phrase [על פנים—*GB*] is 'spitefully,' literally 'to your face.' The parallel, created by the identical pronominal dual suffixes, between the *šûl-ayik* and *pān-ayik* is an intentional humiliating pique. The only additional information provided by the prepositional phrase, therefore, is that uncovering the *šûl* is an act of spite."[57] We may note as common to all these suggestions that על נפים is a phrase that can express the idea that an action is being done against the corresponding "person."

[51] Podella, *Das Lichtkleid JHWHs* 52.

[52] This is the word used by Horacio Simian-Yofre (art. פָּנִים, *pānîm, TDOT* 11:589–615, at 607).

[53] Ibid. 612.

[54] Ibid.

[55] A. S. Van der Woude, art. פנים, *pānîm,* Angesicht, *THAT* II^3 (1984) 432–60, at 435.

[56] Ibid. 445.

[57] Lyle Eslinger, "The Infinite in a Finite Organical Perception (Isaiah VI 1-5)," *VT* 45 (1995) 145–73, at 154.

In his work on שׁוּל, Eslinger first addresses himself to Driver's 1971 essay. Driver had pointed to the lack of plausibility in the usual translation of שׁוּל as "train," asserting that such a translation was problematic because there are only rare indications in ancient Israel and in the ancient Near East that garments had trains.[58] Starting from this, Eslinger subjects the instances of שׁוּל to a closer examination, keeping his central focus on Isa 6:1. In doing so he also takes into account the metaphorical manner in which the word is used. Regarding שׁוּל in Jer 13:22, 26 and Nah 3:5 he comes to the conclusion that the reference is to the female genitalia.[59]

However, before we settle on a clear location for שׁוּל we must take into account the parallel use of שֹׁבֶל, "train" or something similar, in Isa 47:2. A. F. L. Beeston sees the word *sabil,* "public well" in Arabic as a parallel.[60] From that point of view he reconstructs the following meaning for Isa 47:2: Babylon, personified as a Chaldean lady, is degraded by being forced to work as a farm woman. She takes the mill and grinds grain, puts off her veil and draws water *at the well.* Of course, Beeston cannot explain the connection of v. 2 to v. 3, where there is a clear description of the uncovering of "shame." Because of the insecurity of the Arabic parallel—Beeston himself admits that there is no direct connection between שֹׁבֶל and *sabil*—and because of the lack of attention to the context of v. 3 this original thesis seems somewhat too speculative. But what does שֹׁבֶל mean, then? The origin and meaning of this *hapax legomenon* is uncertain, similar to the case of שׁוּל. That 1QIsa[a] has שוליך instead of שֹׁבֶל is an indication that at least at a later time the two words had similar meanings. At this point we should also engage one of Eslinger's observations. He points to the sexual undertone of "grinding," which arises on the one hand out of the similarity between the movement of the millstones against each other and the copulation of mammals and human beings[61] and on the other hand from the assonance of the "millstone" רחים with רחם, the "woman's womb" or "uterus."

A further argument for possibly translating שֹׁבֶל in Isa 47:2-3 as "genitals" is the usage elsewhere of the verb associated with it, חשׂף (see above). In the other passages with which we associate this meaning חשׂף always takes the accusative of the thing or the person.

It is not necessary, in order to solidify the thesis that the words שֹׁבֶל/שׁוּל can also describe sexual organs, to demonstrate that these words always refer to genitalia wherever they appear. That would take too little account

[58] Ibid. 145; Driver, "Isaiah 6:1," 87.

[59] Eslinger, "The Infinite," 153–55.

[60] A. F. L. Beeston, "Hebrew *Šibbolet* and *Šobel,*" *JSS* 24 (1979) 175–77, at 176.

[61] Eslinger, "The Infinite," 149–50.

of the character of sexual imagery in the Old Testament, as I have already said above (Chapter 1 F). Against the background of these observations we should not expect that the words used to describe genitalia in various cases are always used in a metaphorical sense every time they appear. As regards שׁוּל it is certainly possible that the word may be used in a non-metaphorical sense for the "hem" or the lower border of a garment, as is the case in Exod 28:33-34; 34:24, 25, 26. The word is appropriate as a metaphor for genitalia for two reasons: on the one hand, it describes something that is, in any case, hanging down, and on the other hand it is not unusual for the covering to refer to what it hides.[62] It is also entirely possible that שׁוּל in Jer 13:22, 26; Nah 3:5 and שֹׁבֶל in Isa 47:2 are to be understood as metaphors for female genitalia. It is equally possible that the word occasionally refers also to a covering or its removal.

[62] Eslinger, ibid. 152, observes this with regard to Jer 13:22: ". . . it is conceivable that we face here another euphemistic metonymic transference from the clothing to the principal body part it is aimed to cover . . . ."

Chapter Four

Theological Location of the Prophetic Marriage Imagery: *berit* as a Related Idea

A. Preliminary remark

The marriage metaphor for YHWH's relationship to Israel can be assigned to the group of anthropomorphic metaphors of relationship.[1] This group includes metaphors that attempt, with the aid of human relationships, to give a picture of the relationship of YHWH to his people Israel, his city Jerusalem, or to individual human beings. Besides marriage, the idea of "covenant" as metaphor[2] for the relationship of YHWH to Israel builds on an anthropomorphism. In what follows I will not speak of "covenant," but instead, following Gross, I will use the word *berit*.[3] *Berit* can be defined

[1] As mentioned above (Chapter 1, n. 43), Caird lists five areas of human life as principal models for biblical metaphors of the relationship between YHWH and Israel: "In the Bible the five metaphors in most common use to express God's relationship with his worshippers are king/subject, judge/litigant, husband/wife, father/child, master/servant" (George B. Caird, *The Language and Imagery of the Bible* [London: Duckworth; Philadelphia: Westminster, 1980] 177). This list, with minor variations, was adopted by Renita Weems in her *Battered Love. Marriage, Sex, and Violence in the Hebrew Prophets* (Minneapolis: Fortress, 1995) 16.

[2] *Berit* has scarcely been regarded as a metaphor by scholars heretofore, but cf. Sabine van den Eynde, "Daughters of Abraham!? On 'Covenant,' Women and Gender," LAUD Linguistic Agency, Series A. General and Theoretical Paper No. 472 (Essen, 1999) 2.

[3] Ernst Kutsch has written several times on the problems with this translation in German (*Verheissung und Gesetz. Untersuchungen zum sogenannten "Bund" im Alten Testament* [Berlin and New York: Walter de Gruyter, 1973] 174–206; *Neues Testament—neuer Bund? Eine Fehlübersetzung wird korrigiert* [Neukirchen-Vluyn: Neukirchener Verlag, 1978] 165–68; "Bund I. Altes Testament," *TRE* 7 [1981] 397–98). He points out that what is at issue here is a twofold relationship between promise and law, and not a "covenant" with the connotations this involves in German [or in English—Tr.], such as mutuality or equality of the partners. Critique and refinement of Kutsch's position are offered, for example, by Thomas Krüger (*Geschichtskonzepte im Ezechielbuch* [Berlin and New York: Walter de Gruyter, 1989] 103–105). Because of the undisputed differences between the implications of German "Bund" or English "covenant" and Hebrew ברית, in what follows I will speak of *berit*. For this circumlocution let me refer to the reasons given by

as ". . . elected, as opposed to natural, relationship of obligations under oath."[4] *Berit* and marriage stand side by side in a number of Old Testament texts.[5] Several terminological connections or overlaps between the two metaphors strengthen the relationship between them.

However, before this can be shown we must address three problems. First, it must be pointed out that there is no strictly circumscribed semantic field for marriage in the Old Testament.[6] Words for "marry" and the like have other connotations in other contexts.[7] Second, we will not delimit the semantic field of prophetic marriage imagery here; that has already been discussed in more detail above (Chapter 3 B). Finally, the concept of *berit* in the Old Testament is itself complex: There is not simply one "covenant," but a number of different notions or concepts of *berit* in the different parts of Old Testament tradition. These are in themselves quite varied.[8] The adaptation to the content and the context—dealing with Israel's experience of exile as an action of YHWH—suggests that in the prophetic books

---

Walter Gross (*Zukunft für Israel. Alttestamentliche Bundeskonzepte und die aktuelle Debatte um den Neuen Bund* [Stuttgart: Katholisches Bibelwerk, 1998] 10): ". . . a precise German translation appropriate (supposedly) to the particular context would conceal a circumstance that is of the highest importance for the present state of the question, namely that the texts often play with various meanings of *berit,* and would obscure the fact that the concrete meaning of the text is questionable."

[4] Thus Gordon Paul Hugenberger, *Marriage as Covenant. A Study of Biblical Law and Ethics Governing Marriage, Developed from the Perspective of Malachi* (Leiden: Brill, 1994) 11. He himself admits that the criterion of the oath is disputed (ibid. 11–12).

[5] Werner H. Schmidt (*Alttestamentlicher Glaube* [8th ed. Neukirchen-Vluyn: Neukirchener Verlag, 1996]) points out that "covenant" is "only one possible description among others for the relationship to God."

[6] On this see above in the first section of Chapter 3.

[7] We may adduce as an example here the "*terminus technicus* for marrying," which according to Horst Seebass is לקח (art. לקח, *lāqaḥ, TDOT* 8:16–21). In the context of relationships between men and women this word has yet another connotation: as we can tell from the context, it occasionally acquires the meaning "have sexual intercourse," with a male subject and a female object (Gen 34:2; 2 Sam 11:4). This level, too, is addressed in the prophetic marriage imagery. Even though the term לקח may not be directly used, in Ezek 16:8, for example, a sexual connotation to the expression "you became mine" is not completely out of the question. Concerning two other passages in which לקח can have sexual connotations Seebass writes: "Merely taking a woman . . . is a base act (Gen. 34:2). Subsequent marriage can rectify the situation, but is not compulsory. [How does Seebass envision a "rectifying" of the "situation" of rape through the marriage of the rape victim to the rapist?—*GB*] David, too, took Bathsheba before he was able to marry her (2 S. 11:4). In neither instance is force mentioned" (*TDOT* 8:19). By no means is this true. Genesis 34:2 not only says that Sichem "seized" (לקח) Dinah, but also that he did violence to her, or raped her; this is expressed with the term ענה II, which is also used elsewhere for rape.

[8] On this see, for example, Schmidt, *Alttestamentlicher Glaube* 161–66, and Gross, *Zukunft für Israel* 10, and elsewhere.

we should be especially on the alert for the Deuteronomic idea of *berit.*[9] There we will be most likely to find parallels to the marriage imagery.

B. Terminological parallels between *berit*- and marriage imagery

The linguistic fields of *berit*- and marriage terminology are connected at many points—not, however, in the realm of an *exclusive terminology of marriage,* the presence of which in the context of the notion of *berit* might establish a clarity of meaning, for such clarity does not exist in the Old Testament.[10]

However, there are terminological links between marriage and *berit* on another level. In this connection we should first mention the use of language in Hosea. The negatively reversed and altered so-called "covenant formula" (Hos 1:9) "you are not my people, and I am not your אהיה ("I am," as name of God according to Exod 3:14) corresponds to a formula that is obviously derived from it, but applied to marriage, in Hos 2:2 [MT 2:4]: "She is not my wife, and I am not her husband."

A very direct and explicit connection between the *berit*- and marriage relationships is drawn in Ezek 16:8. Here *berit* is used in the sense of a term for marrying.[11] But it is rather doubtful that this also refers to the *berit*-relationship of YHWH to Jerusalem, at least if one gives credence to Moshe Greenberg's statement that in Ezekiel there is such a relationship to Israel, but not to *Jerusalem.*[12]

There is no indication in Jeremiah that *berit* and the marriage relationship are terminologically connected. It is true that Jeremiah frequently

[9] For a summary of late-Deuteronomic notions of *berit* and their questions and problems see Gross, *Zukunft für Israel* 65.

[10] Thus Josef Scharbert, art. "Ehe/Eherecht/Ehescheidung II. Altes Testament," *TRE* 9 (1982) 311–13, at 311: "The Hebrew has no term for 'marriage' or 'marry.' The expression 'A is the husband/wife of B' suffices to describe a man or woman as married."

[11] On this Bernhard Lang remarks: "A conceptual view of [marriage] as covenant *(b*ᵉ*rīt)* finds an occasional echo (Prov 2:17; Mal 2:14), but only in Ezek 16:8 is it explained in terms of a vow made to the woman (apparently as a promise of support, protection, good treatment, etc.)," "Ehe I. Altes Testament," *NBL* 1 (Zürich, 1991) 475–76. Elaine J. Adler also points to Mal 2:14; Prov 2:17, and Ezek 16:8, but in none of these passages is it obvious that marriage is to be understood as analogous to the special relationship between YHWH and Israel; instead, *berit* is an indicator for the fact that this is a legal relationship. Adler, *The Background for the Metaphor of Covenant as Marriage in the Hebrew Bible.* Dissertation, University of California, Berkeley (Ann Arbor: University Microfilms, 1989) 412.

[12] Moshe Greenberg, "Ezekiel 16: A Panorama of Passion," in John H. Marks and Robert M. Good, eds., *Love & Death in the Ancient Near East. Essays in Honor of Marvin H. Pope* (Guilford, Conn.: Four Quarters, 1987) 143–50, at 147, shows that precisely with an eye to this verse, Ezek 16:8, there is nowhere a reference to a covenant relationship between YHWH and his city, Jerusalem: ". . . God entered into a covenant only with his people, never with the city (v. 8)."

speaks of *berit,* but this idea refers to the relationship of YHWH to the Israelites or the house of Israel. It does not describe the relationship to YHWH's "wife" Israel.

For Amos, Isaiah, and Micah, Werner H. Schmidt asserts, following Ludwig Köhler, that in these books, at least in part, there is no reference to covenant at all.[13] Thus it is not the case that there are terminological connections between *berit-* and marriage imagery in all the Old Testament prophets.

There are some clear linguistic parallels between marriage- and *berit*-imagery when the texts speak of "loving" (אהב and its derivatives). "Loving" is to be understood not so much as the expression of an emotion, but rather as the maintenance of loyalty and fidelity to an agreement. In Deut 5:10 and similar expressions אהב, "loving" is parallel to "keeping YHWH's commandments."[14] Apparently it was not a very long road from the "contract love" of a *berit*-relationship to "marital love." In the Pentateuch, however, according to Moshe Weinfeld, it was not traveled.[15] In the prophetic marriage imagery, as also in the terminology of Israel's infidelity toward YHWH,

> the verb used . . . for disloyalty is → זנה zānāh, "to play the harlot, to whore" (*ʾachare*, "after"). Furthermore, the formula expressing the covenantal relationship between God and Israel, "I will be your God, and you shall be my people" (Lev. 26:12; Dt. 29:12[13]; etc.) is a legal formula taken from the sphere of marriage, as attested in various legal documents from the ancient Near East (cf. Hos. 2:4[2]). The relationship of the vassal to his suzerain, and that of the wife to her husband, leave no place for

[13] Schmidt, *Alttestamentlicher Glaube* 163, with reference to Ludwig Köhler, "Alttestamentliche Theologie," *ThR* 7 (1935) 272–73. However, Isa 54:10 does, in fact, speak of a *berit.* There YHWH promises his "wife" Jerusalem that YHWH's *shalom berit* will not waver. But what notion of *berit* is present here is not clear from the context.

[14] Jan Bergman, Alfred Haldar, and Gerhard Wallis also point this out in their article, אהב, *ʾāhab, TDOT* 1:99–118. They point to keeping the commandments as love in Deuteronomistic perspective (p. 115) and the underlying "political concept of love" in Mari and in the Amarna correspondence (pp. 100–101). "Thus parenetically the Deuteronomist has attempted to connect the idea of God's love for his people, which had been attained by the prophets [Hosea?—*GB*], with the concept of their responsibility, which he presents under the figure of the obedience of a vassal king to the lord of the covenant" (p. 116). William L. Moran also points to the ancient Near Eastern backgrounds of "loving" God ("The Ancient Near Eastern Background of the Love of God in Deuteronomy," *CBQ* 25 [1963] 87) and thus arrives at a chronological ordering of the notion of love in Deuteronomy before Hosea: ". . . the deuteronomic love of service is older, probably as old or almost as old as the covenant itself. If so, and if the old sovereign-vassal terminology of love is as relevant as we think it is, then what a history lies behind the Christian test of true *agapē*—'If you love me, keep my commandments'!"

[15] Moshe Weinfeld, art. ברית, *bᵉrîṯ, TDOT* 2:278.

double loyalty, and therefore are perfect metaphors for loyalty in a monotheistic religion.[16]

The ideas of *berit* and of marriage are also present in the terminology of adultery in human relationships (נאף) and Israel's breaking of its *berit* with YHWH. David Noel Freedman and B. E. Willoughby offer as examples in this context Jer 9:2-3 [MT 1-2]; 29:23; Hos 7:1b, 4; Mal 3:5; Ps 50:18, and Job 24:14-15.[17] They summarize: "Analysis of its distribution [i. e., the instances of נאף in the Old Testament—*GB*] shows clearly that the term was shaped by the Priestly tradition to denote an offense against marital law. The prophets borrowed this terminology to describe offenses against the covenant between Yahweh as husband and Israel his wife."[18] However, *berit* and נאף do not appear together in any verse of the Old Testament; the term זנה with a broad scope of meaning is found, though, together with *berit*, in Deut 31:16.[19]

Hence it can be asserted that there are terminological connections between the Old Testament *berit* and the idea of marriage at many points, indicating the close association of these two concepts of relationship.

C. Content parallels between *berit*- and marriage imagery

There are some similarities between *berit*- and marriage imagery in the way the partners' relationships are described. This becomes clear when we compare the content of *berit*- and marriage metaphors. Fundamental to both is the hierarchical relationship of the two sides: ". . . the covenant is not a contract; that is, it is not an agreement between equals."[20] The same

[16] Ibid.

[17] David Noel Freedman and B. E. Willoughby, art. נאף, *nāʾap, TDOT* 9:116.

[18] Ibid. 114. The fact that Freedman and Willoughby's chronology places the prophetic tradition, including Hosea, in the period after the Priestly traditions shows that they accept a complex history of development for the prophetic books, extending far into the post-exilic period, although they give no further reasons or explanation for this. In addition, some passages in the article are simply unclear; for example, on p. 114: "The adulteress is not a piece of property whose deceased value must be compensated for but the wife of a man whose relationship with her has been profaned." Is this meant to indicate that marriage in the OT, despite the lack of any religious ceremony at the time of the marriage (cf. Scharbert, "Ehe/Eherecht/Ehescheidung," 312) has something "holy" attached to it?

[19] William D. Whitt ("The Divorce of Yahweh and Asherah in Hos 2,4-7.12ff.," *SJOT* 6 [1992] 41–42) posits that the connection between adultery and the relationship between Israel and YHWH was introduced into Hosea by the Deuteronomistic redactors. Against this, however, is the fact that the root זנה for Israel's behavior is found in Deuteronomy only in Deut 31:16, but much more frequently in Hosea, Jeremiah, and Ezekiel.

[20] Schmidt, *Alttestamentlicher Glaube* 162; similarly Kutsch, "Bund I. Altes Testament," 398–99. These definitions of relationships have also been described by Moshe Weinfeld in his

is true for ancient Israelite (patriarchal)[21] marriage, in which the husband had the right to control his wife.[22] Israel/Jerusalem and concrete women are, in both fields of imagery, those who have less power. Barbara Bozak offers an overview of the parallels between the situation of Israelite women and YHWH's "wife" in Jeremiah 30–31. These aspects are not precisely true of all texts of the prophetic marriage imagery, but they show how strong are the possible parallels between "woman" and women, i.e., between the relationships of covenant and marriage. Bozak lists seven aspects: "Woman" Israel and women combine dependency on and attachment to the partner, the intimate nature of their relationship with the partner, exclusivity in their ties to one husband, legal obligations in their relationship to the husband, suffering as a part of life (e.g., in childbirth), and both reflect social conditions (for example in regard to the possibility of cultic activity or responsible participation in certain public functions).[23]

Beyond these fundamental commonalities, we need to take note of some further parallels in these ideas. First, Elaine J. Adler points to the ways in which the partners are chosen:

> . . . even if the element of choice was somewhat limited for the prospective groom, it is an element that characterized marriage more than any other social institution, and more than any of the other personal metaphors used in the Bible, such as parenthood or kingship. Thus regarding the very important biblical doctrine of election, marriage provides the most appropriate mundane analogue.[24]

TDOT article on *berit:* "The original meaning of the Heb. *berith* . . . is not 'agreement or settlement between two parties,' as is commonly argued. *berith* implies first and foremost the notion of 'imposition,' 'liability,' or obligation . . . . Thus we find that the *berith* is commanded . . . which certainly cannot be said about a mutual agreement" (p. 255).

[21] Irmtraud Fischer ("Das Buch Jesaja. Das Buch der weiblichen Metaphern," in Luise Schottroff and Marie-Theres Wacker, eds., *Kompendium Feministische Bibelauslegung* [2nd ed. Gütersloh: Gütersloher Verlagshaus, 1999] 246–57, at 251) shows, regarding Isa 57:6-13, that this patriarchal framework itself is important for understanding the logic of the marriage imagery: "The sexually insatiable and therefore unfaithful wife, who—as the pinnacle of perversion of feminine 'decency'—buys her own lovers (57:8) is a logical consequence of the patriarchal ideal of marriage, which demands exclusive fidelity only of the wife, not of the husband. When the people as wife of God enter the picture, idolatry as apostasy from YHWH is consequently portrayed in the image of adultery." In my opinion this observation applies also to most of the other texts of the prophetic marriage imagery.

[22] Thus very clearly in Lang, "Ehe I. Altes Testament," 477.

[23] Barbara A. Bozak, *Life "Anew." A Literary-Theological Study of Jer. 30–31*. AnBib 122 (Rome: Biblical Institute Press, 1991) 157–64.

[24] Adler, *Background for the Metaphor of Covenant* 387.

Gary H. Hall mentions three further parallels.[25] The first refers to the fidelity in the relationship required of the weaker partner toward the stronger. Here we can draw a parallel between the formulation of the first commandment, closely tied to the *berit,* and marital fidelity. "The first commandment requires absolute fidelity, and the only comparable institution in Israel that required a similar fidelity was marriage."[26] However, what Hall leaves out of consideration in this remark is again the inequality of the partners that we have discussed above.[27] The stronger partner can impose expectations and demands on the weaker partner that are simply impossible in the other direction.

Second, as shown above, absolute loyalty of the weaker partner to the stronger can be expressed also in words of "loving," and infidelity in the image of "leaving" or "abandoning."[28] Moshe Weinfeld explains that expressions regarding the "love" for YHWH demanded of Israel have models in ancient Near Eastern contractual texts and therefore belong more in the realm of juridical speech than in that of the emotional language to which they would be assigned today.[29] "The exhortations in Deuteronomy to keep loyalty to God are very close in form and style to the exhortations in the political treaties. As has been shown by Moran, the concept of the 'love of God' in Deuteronomy actually expresses loyalty, and it is in this sense that 'love' occurs in the political documents of the ancient Near East."[30] We should add here, in light of the terminological parallels introduced above, that "whoring" (זנה) is the central term in marriage imagery for "leaving, abandoning."

Third, it is a fact that feelings of "jealousy" (קנא) can be aroused when the stronger partner doubts the loyalty of the weaker.[31] Thus YHWH is said

[25] Gary H. Hall, *The Marriage Metaphor of Jeremiah 2 and 3: A Study of Antecedents and Innovations in a Prophetic Metaphor.* Dissertation, Union Theological Seminary of Virginia (1980) 170.

[26] Ibid. At this point there is also a difference between the *berit-* and marriage imagery for the relationship of YHWH to Israel: while in the *berit* YHWH makes an exclusive commitment to Israel, in the framework of the prophetic marriage imagery he possesses—corresponding to the socially accepted institution of polygamy—as many as four wives (Ezekiel 16).

[27] Angelika Engelmann points out the unequal legal situation of husband and wife in the Deuteronomic marriage laws ("Deuteronomium. Recht und Gerechtigkeit für Frauen im Gesetz," in Luise Schottroff and Marie-Theres Wacker, eds., *Kompendium Feministische Bibelauslegung* 67–79, at 74).

[28] Besides the remarks above in this section, see Hall, *Marriage Metaphor* 170: "Further, loyalty is described as love (Ex. 20:6 and the Shema, Dt. 6:5; cf. 10:12; 11:1), and there are warnings against lusting after other gods (Ex. 34:14-15; Num. 15:39)."

[29] Weinfeld, "ברית, *bᵉrîṯ,*" *TDOT* 2:278.

[30] Ibid. 268.

[31] Hall, *Marriage Metaphor* 170: ". . . in the second commandment Israel was told that Yahweh was a jealous *(qanna)* God. The same root is used in Num. 5:14 of the jealous husband."

in the second commandment of the Decalogue (Exod 20:5; Deut 5:9) to be a "jealous (קנא) God," with emotions parallel to those of the husband in a human marriage in Num 5:14.[32] However, קנא is not used in the prophetic marriage imagery. This aspect, then, despite what Hall postulates,[33] does not enter the picture here as a parallel between *berit*- and marriage imagery.

The commonalities in terminology and content between *berit*- and marriage imagery make it clear that neither refers to egalitarian relationships, but always to those between unequals. The stronger partner chooses the weaker. Loyalty and exclusive fidelity in the relationship are demanded of the weaker toward the stronger, but the reverse is not true. "Love" can furnish a linguistic framework for both relationships, but without having primarily emotional connotations.

D. The relationship between *berit*- and marriage imagery

What indications do we have about how *berit*- and marriage imagery can be related to each other? Renita Weems emphasizes that, unlike other metaphors, the marriage imagery makes it possible for us to appreciate different sides of YHWH: ". . . the marriage metaphor enables the reader to recognize the more passionate and compassionate side of YHWH."[34] This, of course, presumes a transformation in the image of God through which a more personal devotion and greater closeness to God can and should be expressed. The question is whether such a thing was thinkable in the monarchical period in Israel, or whether such a relationship is not more reflective of conditions in the post-exilic period.

Observations suggesting that the idea of *berit* is not in every respect appropriate for a new definition of the relationship between YHWH and Israel after the exile can also be seen as moving in the direction of a post-exilic situating of the marriage imagery. In the Deuteronomic/Deuteronomistic version that idea did, in fact, offer an explanation for the events of the past, which could be seen as "Israel's" breaking the *berit,* with corresponding punishment by YHWH as a consequence. But this interpretation is hard pressed to offer a starting point for a positive new definition of the relationship between YHWH and Israel after the exile.[35] In addition, the metaphor, on the one hand, lacks the persuasive power of a concrete, that is,

[32] Weinfeld, "ברית, *bᵉrîṯ,*" 278.

[33] Hall, *Marriage Metaphor* 170.

[34] Weems, "Gomer: Victim of Violence or Victim of Metaphor?" *Semeia* 47 (1989) 99.

[35] Gross, *Zukunft für Israel* 26, formulates this as regards the Sinai pericope, which contains three problems for the post-exilic period:

- Because the role of Moses as intercessor cannot be repeated, the project points backward.

historically visible model. On the other hand, there is no perspective in which to restore the relationship. As a result of the breaching of the covenant the land of Israel has been largely destroyed. In contrast, the prophetic books themselves offered a possibility for linking with the metaphor of marriage. Under certain circumstances, and with good will on both sides, at least in the human sphere a wrecked relationship can be begun anew.

Can we propose a relationship between *berit*- and marriage imagery that would have them following one another over a period of time? Here we can discuss such a possibility only in general terms, since the dating of the individual texts is problematic, and there is no consensus among scholars about chronology or layering at many points. First, however, we can note that the *berit* idea does not appear at all in some prophets.[36] A *berit* between YHWH and Israel/Jerusalem is completely absent from Isaiah, Amos, and Micah, and in Hosea it appears only once, without any relationship to the prophetic marriage imagery. This suggests the conclusion that the marriage imagery appeared chronologically *before* the *berit* idea.[37] This would contradict the notion that, as Hall supposes, Hosea's marriage metaphors are only another way of speaking about the *berit*.[38]

In attempting to establish a time line for these ideas, of course, we must keep in mind that in the realm of relational metaphors as a whole we can observe no tendency toward either unity or system. This is true not only of *berit*- and marriage imagery, but also of parent-child imagery as we find it, for example, in Hosea. Here, alongside a mixed imagery of marriage and covenant in Hosea 1–3, in Hosea 11 "Ephraim" is related to YHWH as child to mother or father.

We may say in summary that the different metaphors of relationship each have their own field of connotations and their own possibilities for expansion. They are not mutually interchangeable, but have their individual

---

- The people do nothing. They take no responsibility for their own failure; they neither contribute anything to the reversal nor change themselves; they do not agree again to the *berit* in Exod 34:27; instead, it is imposed on them.
- YHWH, too, does not relate to Israel's guilt; he only regrets his decision to punish.

The first problem is taken care of in the subsequent period through the fact that the role of Moses is not taken up again in the same way. The second and third problems are dealt with in later reconceptions of *berit*.

[36] This observation by Ludwig Köhler ("Alttestamentliche Theologie," 272–73) is reiterated by Werner H. Schmidt (*Alttestamentlicher Glaube* 163).

[37] This can be posited especially if—as most scholars believe—Hosea is to be regarded as the "inventor" or first exemplar of the prophetic marriage imagery.

[38] Hall, *Marriage Metaphor* 23: "In Hosea, marriage is another term for the covenant and includes obedience."

implications. Therefore the *berit*- and marriage imagery can scarcely be arranged in a chronological relationship. It is more appropriate to regard them as similar and sometimes contemporary phenomena, and not to suppose that one replaces the other. Apparently these metaphors were not perceived as competing or contradictory. The YHWH-image of the *berit*-relationship to Israel implies more distance than does that of the "husband" in the prophetic marriage imagery.

Chapter Five

Ancient Near Eastern Ideas as Background for Prophetic Marriage Imagery

Scholars have in the past looked for ancient Near Eastern ideas in the background of two aspects of the prophetic marriage imagery: the image of the "city as woman/wife," and the punishment of stripping naked and/or sexual violence directed against a "city-woman/wife" or against concrete wives. The hope is that by referring to the ancient Near Eastern environment we may develop a background for the prophetic marriage imagery that casts some light on it that the Old Testament does not provide. In addition, it is often the case that only a comparison with ancient Near Eastern parallel texts brings out the special implications of the Old Testament formulations.

A. The ancient Near Eastern background of the idea of the "city as woman/wife" in the prophetic marriage imagery

The background for the Old Testament idea of the city as woman has been studied for quite some time, especially in light of the "daughter Zion" texts.[1] There is consensus on some theses among Old Testament scholars. Christl Maier summarizes these:

[1] Odil Hannes Steck ("Zion als Gelände und Gestalt. Überlegungen zur Wahrnehmung Jerusalems als Stadt und Frau im Alten Testament," *ZThK* 86 [1989] 263) remarks in this regard: "In fact, not only as regards categories of interpretation but especially in view of the religious- and tradition-historical backgrounds of this feature of Jerusalem [he is referring to Jerusalem as woman—*GB*] we are speaking of a difficult field that has by no means been thoroughly worked through." In saying this he apparently ignores the two fundamental articles on this theme by Aloysius Fitzgerald in the 1970s ("The Mythological Background for the Presentation of Jerusalem as a Queen and False Worship as Adultery in the OT," *CBQ* 34 [1972] 403–16; idem, "*BTWLT* and *BT* as Titles for Capital Cities," *CBQ* 37 [1975] 167–83).

> The female personification of the city that is found in Zech 9:9; Isa 1:8; Jer 4:30-31; 6:22-26, and in other places in the Hebrew Bible is, in terms of religious history, usually traced to the West Semitic tradition of a city goddess and consort of the city's protecting god; she also bears titles like "mother," "daughter," and "virgin." In the Attic heartland Athena was sung by Homer and Hesiod as the virgin daughter of Zeus, closely tied in with the fate of the city of Athens. It is true that an identification of goddess and city is only evident from the Hellenistic period onward in cities of Asia Minor and Phoenicia. It appears on coins bearing a woman's head wearing a crown of walls and towers and inscribed with the name of the city. A statue from Antioch by Eutychides dated ca. 300 B.C.E. depicts the city goddess wearing a flowing gown and bearing the same so-called city-wall crown. In the East, in Mesopotamia, the cities were grammatically masculine, but from Sumer we have so-called city laments from the end of the third millennium in which a goddess bewails the destruction of sanctuary and city. These are ritual texts recited at the rebuilding of capital cities like Sumer, Ur, and Nippur. The Sumerian tradition was carried on in the first millennium in stylized litanies of lament. There are signs that the West Semitic tradition was received even in the East in the neo-Assyrian period, to the extent that in the seventh century B.C.E. royal women appear as representatives of the capital cities. Thus the consort of Ashurbanipal appears on a relief wearing the city-wall crown. . . .[2]

It is quite possible that these ancient Near Eastern ideas underly the image of Jerusalem/Zion as "city-woman." However, that does not mean that the same has been shown for Israel/Jerusalem as YHWH's *"wife,"* since the question of the marital relationship of these two has been given relatively little attention in discussions of ancient Near Eastern backgrounds. "City-women" and "wife-women" have in common functions corresponding to women's roles in society. Maier mentions, for the role of mother, especially "providing the populace a place to live, an orderly way of life for heterogeneous population groups, and protection against external aggression."[3] The city as daughter, in contrast, corresponds more to the role of one who is protected by YHWH and subject to his control.[4] Thus there are some differences between "daughter Zion" and ideas that are to be expected in marriage imagery. Odil Hannes Steck has summarized them under three points:

[2] Christl Maier, "Die Klage der Tochter Zion. Ein Beitrag zur Weiblichkeitsmetaphorik im Jeremiabuch," *BThZ* 15 (1998) 176–89.

[3] Ibid. 186.

[4] Ibid. Steck, "Zion als Gelände und Gestalt," 272–73 mentions similar aspects.

> First: The [OT] texts do not know of city goddesses, and Zion, in relation to YHWH, is not a goddess, but, seen as a person, she is the city whom the one God takes to wife. Second: as Winter has rightly emphasized, there is an absence of features that would make Jerusalem equal to YHWH in this relationship. Third: as Winter has also pointed out, there are no erotic metaphors for the relationship.[5]

Considering the special connection existing between the metaphors of Israel/Jerusalem as "city-woman" and as "wife" of YHWH, by no means all the ancient Near Eastern parallels have thus far been examined. Here we must be content to observe that further research is necessary.

B. The ancient Near Eastern background of the punishment of the "woman/wife" in the prophetic marriage imagery

For some time there has been discussion of whether certain ancient Near Eastern texts can be seen as parallels to YHWH's punishment of his adulterous "wife" Israel/Jerusalem. These are the Old Testament passages in which YHWH's "wife" has her skirt lifted over her face, so that her genitals are exposed. This, or something similar, is found in Hos 2:10 [MT 2:12]; Jer 13:22, 26; Ezek 16:36-37; 23:10, 18, 29; Lam 1:8-9. It is not YHWH's wife, but an enemy power personified as female who is the victim in Isa 47:2-3 and Nah 3:5-6. In the past, texts from two areas have been adduced as material for comparison with this imagery. Attention has been directed, on the one hand, to rules of law applied to the behavior of concrete married women and the legal consequences (i), and on the other hand to prescriptions from ancient Near Eastern vassal treaties, especially the cursing formulae by which the greater power threatens drastic consequences to the vassal should there be a breach of the contract (ii). Here we will both review the previous studies and pose some critical questions.

i. Punishment of concrete women

Parallel texts from Babylon and Nuzi have played a particularly important part in research on this question. Curt Kuhl introduced them as early

[5] Steck, "Zion als Gelände und Gestalt," 275. Steck refers to Urs Winter, *Frau und Göttin. Exegetische und ikonographische Studien zum weiblichen Gottesbild im Alten Israel und dessen Umwelt* (Fribourg: Universitätsverlag; Göttingen: Vandenhoeck & Ruprecht, 1983) 632ff., 639. Irmtraud Fischer, "Das Buch Jesaja. Das Buch der weiblichen Metaphern," in Luise Schottroff and Marie-Theres Wacker, eds., *Kompendium Feministische Bibelauslegung* (2nd ed. Gütersloh: Gütersloher Verlagshaus, 1999) 251–52, also points out the absence of goddess-aspects in the "city-woman."

as 1934[6] in connection with the prophetic marriage imagery in Hosea. Since researchers even today are still referring to Kuhl,[7] we need to pay close attention to his essay here. Kuhl collects material from legal documents from the Sumerian to the neo-Babylonian periods. What is interesting in our context is the ancient Babylonian distinction between the legal consequences of a divorce: these were gravely different, depending on whether the divorce was sought by the man or the woman. While a man received a money penalty, a woman had to expect that her life and limb would be affected, and the death penalty was not out of the question.[8] In a marriage contract from Ḫana[9] the wife is threatened that if she should seek a divorce she must "go forth naked." In a man's testamentary disposition it is commanded that his widow, should she remarry, will have her garment taken from her and she will be led out "naked."[10]

Several things should be said about the texts in question. The ancient Babylonian legal prescriptions cited by Kuhl are characterized by the imposition of especially stiff and drastic conventional punishments. More or less at the same time, for example, in §§141-42 of the Codex Hammurabi there are clearly "more liberal" legal regulations.[11] The texts from Nuzi and Ḫana, like those that will be mentioned below from Emar, do not come from the Babylonian heartland, but from the very independent middle-Euphrates cultural region. The origin of these texts is dated to periods that in general were characterized by especially harsh legal ordinances for men as well as for women. The texts treated here come from a context dominated by property relationships of a very independent nature. This is indicated in part by the fact that the adjective *eriššī* means not only "go forth naked," as Kuhl translates, but also "be without means."[12] Thus

[6] Curt Kuhl, "Neue Dokumente zum Verständnis von Hosea 2,14-15," *ZAW* 52 (1934) 102–109.

[7] Thus, for example, Shalom M. Paul ("Biblical Analogues to Middle Assyrian Law," in Edwin B. Firmage et al., eds., *Religion and Law: Biblical-Judaic and Islamic Perspectives* [Winona Lake: Eisenbrauns, 1990] 344); like other authors, however, he does not take into account that the Nuzi texts Kuhl cited did not refer to adultery, but to a wife's desire for a divorce or the remarriage of a widow. For this see the reference below to the work of John Huehnergard, "Biblical Notes on Some New Akkadian Texts from Emar (Syria)," *CBQ* 47 (1985) 428–34, who takes into account other texts besides those treated by Kuhl.

[8] Kuhl's text shows as possible legal consequences that the woman might be bound and thrown into the river, her hair cut off and she sold for money, or she might be thrown from a tower ("Neue Dokumente," 104).

[9] Text and translation in ibid. 105.

[10] Text and translation in ibid. 105–106.

[11] Cf. *Codex Hammurabi: textus primigenius*. Authored by E. Bergmann (3rd ed. Rome: Biblical Institute Press, 1953).

[12] See *AHw* 241. Von Soden distinguishes two meanings: in one, used together with *alākum*, *eriššī* means "(go) in nakedness," and in the other it means "be without means."

it cannot be clearly determined whether the stripping of the woman is the foremost part of the punishment. As John Huehnergard, whose interpretation of the texts will be discussed below, writes, the securing of the family property is the primary goal of this regulation.

The studies of Henry McKeating and Anthony Phillips also rest on the texts from Ḫana and Nuzi.[13] We may agree with McKeating's observation that in all kinds of legal prescriptions we are always dealing with norms or ideal propositions; whether these drastic punishments were ever actually imposed is not clear.[14] McKeating assumes that the death penalty demanded in Deut 22:22 for adultery was probably never applied.[15] Instead, he proposes the thesis that there were alternative punishments in Israel. Following other studies, McKeating asserts:

> There is a group consisting of Hos. 2.5 (2.3) (cf. Hos. 2.12 [MT 2:10]), Jer. 13.22.26f., Ezek. 16.37-39, 23.29, and possibly Nah. 3.5, all of which refer, for the most part somewhat obliquely, to an alternative penalty for adultery, that of disgracing the woman by stripping her naked in public. The case for the use of this penalty is strengthened by the fact that it was almost ubiquitous in the ancient near east.[16]

McKeating thus advocates the thesis that the public stripping of the adulteress—sometimes in addition to divorce—was an alternative to capital punishment.[17]

Anthony Phillips rejects McKeating's thesis. He tries to make it clear that adultery in ancient Israel—otherwise than elsewhere in the ancient Near East—was not regarded as an offense in the private sphere, but as an offense against God, and was accordingly avenged publicly.[18] After presenting McKeating's thesis, he interprets the public stripping in a different fashion:

> But as elsewhere in the ancient Near East, where divorce was for adultery . . . before the husband pronounced the divorce formula, the wife was stripped naked (Hos. 2.3 [MT 2:5]. This was not simply to indicate that her husband was no longer under any obligation to clothe his wife, but to proclaim

[13] Henry McKeating, "Sanctions Against Adultery in Ancient Israelite Society. With Some Reflections on Methodology in the Study of OT Ethics," *JSOT* 11 (1979) 57–72; Anthony Phillips, "Another Look at Adultery," *JSOT* 20 (1981) 3–25.

[14] McKeating, "Sanctions Against Adultery," 69–70.

[15] Ibid. 57–61.

[16] Ibid. 61.

[17] Ibid. 62.

[18] Phillips, "Another Look at Adultery," 3, 19, and elsewhere.

> publicly the shameful reason for the divorce. The wife was no ordinary divorcee but had acted like a common prostitute and was to be treated as such.[19]

Somewhat later Phillips repeats his thesis that prostitutes in ancient Israel were punished for their behavior. In Ezekiel "Israel" receives the same treatment as a prostitute.[20] This assessment of the meaning of זנה ignores, however, the fact that the verb not only means "prostitute oneself" but could be used to defame women.[21] Apart from that it sheds no light on the proposition that, or how, a whole group of people could be subjected to punishment simply for the way they earn their living.[22] Raymond Westbrook has also offered a fundamental critique of McKeating's and Phillips's articles: "The above theory in all its variations suffers from the same weakness: it relies not on evidence from the facts but on their silence."[23]

Building on previous research, John Huehnergard studies not only the texts already treated by Kuhl, but five new findings of Late-Bronze-Era Akkadian texts from Emar in Syria containing testamentary orders: if a widow remarries she is to be deprived of the property of her first husband and leave his house naked. In Huehnergard's opinion this stripping has a humiliating aspect: its purpose, however, is primarily the protection of the property of the family or clan.

> While there is in all of these texts undoubtedly an element of humiliation intended in forcing an individual to leave the paternal estate naked, there is clearly also an economic motive: the individual, prohibited from taking even a stitch of clothing, is made to renounce, symbolically, any claim to the estate in question. The reason for this stipulation in the case of a widow who wishes to remarry is clear. . . . The stipulations of these contracts, then, are intended to keep the patriarch's property within his family.[24]

Huehnergard connects the Emar texts with the prophetic marriage imagery and especially the stripping in Hos 2:3 [MT 2:5]:

> The parallels not only illustrate what was apparently a widespread custom, but also suggest that the treatment of the wife in Hos 2:4-5 [and, we might

[19] Ibid. 16.

[20] Ibid. 16–17.

[21] See above, Chapter Three.

[22] This is more reminiscent of prejudices and condemnations familiar even today that attempt to marginalize particular groups in society and even to deny that they have any rights!

[23] Raymond Westbrook, "Adultery in Ancient Near Eastern Law," *RB* 97 (1990) 544.

[24] Huehnergard, "Biblical Notes," 432–33. Huehnergard relates these regulations to those on levirate marriage in Deut 25:5; in the latter case it is also easily imaginable that it primarily served the purpose of protecting the family property.

> add, in other texts of the prophetic marriage imagery as well—*GB*] was intended, in addition to shaming her, to emphasize her sudden lack of economic security.[25]

Although I have already indicated my general agreement with Huehnergard's evaluation of the focus of the texts on the aspect of protection of property, I still have doubts about one other point. These texts are not apt parallels to the prophetic marriage imagery in the Old Testament in the narrower sense, because they are not about adultery and its punishment. They deal either with a divorce initiated by the wife or with the remarriage of a widow. The first is most certainly not in view in the prophetic marriage imagery, and the latter is not treated in the Old Testament legal texts. We might ask, however, whether the "harlotry" (זנות) of the "woman/wife" Israel/Jerusalem, corresponding to the ancient Near Eastern parallels, was meant to express her own desire for a divorce, so that the stripping or uncovering could be regarded as a legal consequence. In any case, because of the only partial overlap between the Old Testament and ancient Near Eastern texts, Huehnergard's conclusion must be relativized: The economic decline expressed in the stripping of the woman may indeed play some role in the Old Testament prophetic marriage imagery. But more in the foreground is the intention to humiliate the woman and to frighten her away from a divorce that she might want to seek. To that extent the Old Testament texts have shifted the statement of these texts—if, that is, the ancient Near Eastern texts *here adduced* are really the normative documents against the background of which the prophetic marriage imagery is to be understood.

The work of Raymond Westbrook takes us further. He collects and compares ancient Near Eastern and Old Testament legal texts on adultery, including, among others, a text from Nippur concerning judgment on an adulterous woman.[26] In addition to the divorce requested in response by the husband, the woman is to undergo a punishment very similar to the stripping scenario described in the prophetic marriage imagery. Westbrook concludes from the punishment mentioned here to the meaning of the scenes in the prophetic texts:

> In these prophetic passages therefore, we see a metaphor drawn from everyday life of the husband exercising a right to divorce his adulterous wife and drive her from the matrimonial home penniless and possibly naked. Presumably he

[25] Ibid. 433–34. Huehnergard here refers to Kuhl's 1934 work and to Cyrus H. Gordon, "Hos 2:4-5 in the Light of New Semitic Inscriptions," *ZAW* 54 (1936) 277–80, and Elena Cassin, "Pouvoirs de la femme et structures familiales," *RA* 63 (1969) 121–48.

[26] Raymond Westbook, "Adultery in Ancient Near Eastern Law," *RB* 97 (1990) 559.

> could have claimed the ultimate penalty but chose not to do so, which suggests that, as McKeating has argued, divorce and humiliation may have been a more common punishment for adultery than the terse provisions of the codes would imply.[27]

At this point there seems to be relative certainty about the ancient Near Eastern parallels to the stripping scenes in the prophetic marriage imagery. However, a critical observation should be made about this text from Nippur also. The case described here is unique and has no parallels. A look at the whole text will make it clear that this concerns a crime going beyond adultery:

> (1) Eštar-ummī (2) daughter of Ilī-asû (3) did Irra-malik (4) take in marriage. (5) In the first place, (6) she burglarized his storeroom. (7) In the second place (8) in his oil jar (9) she made an opening and (10) covered it up with a cloth. (11) In the third (12) place, he caught her upon a man; (13) to the body of the man on the bed (14) he tied her (15) (and) carried her to the assembly. (16) The assembly, (17) because with a man upon her (18) she was caught, (19) his/her divorce money . . . (20) so (they) decided; (21) her pudenda (22) they shaved; (23) they bored her nose with an arrow (24) (and) to be led around the city (25) the king (26) gave her over. (27) It is a decision of the king. (28) Išme-Dagan-zimu (29) was deputy.[28]

Another approach to the ancient Near Eastern texts is also possible. Thomas Podella devotes a section of his work on the divine garment of light in the Old Testament and its environment to the symbolism of clothing and unclothing.[29] In the legal texts in Mesopotamian lawbooks

> . . . we encounter, with only one exception, no legal acts in which clothing plays a role. The exception is from the Middle-Assyrian lawbook, which deals in the so-called "mirror for women" (Table A) with the covering of women in public (§40-41). The object (sic!) of the regulation is not the wife of a citizen, but four different groups of women: the *esirtu* "concubine," *qadiltu* (= *qadištu*) "*Qadištu*-woman," *ḫarimtu* "whore" and *amtu* "slave woman." Of these women it is said in §40,58ff. that the slave woman and whore must go "uncovered" (66f. 68f.) in the marketplace, and if they infringe these regulations they may be seized by anyone. For the other two groups of women it is decreed that an *esirtu* may remain covered when she

[27] Ibid. 562.

[28] Text in Samuel Greengus, "A Textbook Case of Adultery in Ancient Mesopotamia," *HUCA* 40/41 (1969–70) 33–44, at 34–35.

[29] Thomas Podella, *Das Lichtkleid JHWHs. Untersuchungen zur Gestalthaftigkeit Gottes im Alten Testament und seiner altorientalischen Umwelt* (Tübingen: J.C.B. Mohr [Paul Siebeck], 1996) 41–82; pp. 41–54 are of particular interest here.

> is accompanying her mistress, and a *qadiltu* only if she is married (58-62). An unmarried *qadiltu* remains "uncovered" (63-65). Covering here, then, represents the women's social status, with differences between social groups furnishing a further criterion.[30]

It is true of Middle-Assyrian legal texts, however, that—like the other texts already mentioned—they contain unusually strict regulations in all areas, as a glance at the body of laws makes clear.

As he continues his work Podella considers the meaning of the hem or skirt of the garment in different legal contexts. On the "lifting" of the "skirt" he writes:

> As in the process of marrying, so also in the legal process of divorce the skirt plays an important role when a married man wishes to divorce. Alongside instances from Nuzi we should mention particularly an ancient Babylonian text from Sippar: CT 45,86. It contains the interview with a married couple before the local court of jurisdiction. To the question whether this woman is his wife the husband answers in the negative, while to the same question directed to her the woman responds "I love my husband." Lines 26-28 then describe the husband's reaction:
>
> "He was unwilling. He knotted her skirt together and cut it off."
>
> After what had previously been said it appears that the tearing off of the skirt symbolizes a change in the woman's status. It remains unclear whether at the same time this is meant to represent the breaking apart of the relationship of the pair—as, for example, a rent in the social fabric . . . . The rites of removing garments and going naked away also belong within the context of social processes of dissolution. . . . Again, in documents from Nuzi and in the context of testamentary dispositions we find the notion of "taking off a garment and going away naked." . . . [These texts are those mentioned above, from Kuhl—*GB*.] The simplest explanation of these symbolic actions seems, then, to be that a change in legal or social status, invisible in itself, is made publicly visible. The public gesture added to the abstract legal decree testifies to and conveys the accomplished change to the public. The symbolic legal action enacted on the garment/skirt visibly illustrates (for the public) the change that has taken place.[31]

In his remarks Podella places the accent strongly on the legal symbolism, that is, the making public of a change in the legal status of persons, especially in terms of their clothing.[32] However, it cannot be established

[30] Ibid. 45–46.

[31] Ibid. 47–48.

[32] Podella points this out also in his excursus on "Mantle- and Garment Symbolism in the Old Testament" (ibid. 51–53). The expression "symbolism" can, however, evoke false associations in

that anything of the sort was widespread in the ancient Near East. On the other hand, it is not out of the question that such symbolism may be helpful for the interpretation of the corresponding passages in the prophetic marriage imagery.

ii. Ancient Near Eastern treaty curses

The work of Delbert R. Hillers from 1964 is referenced even in recent studies. Hillers presents cursing passages from a variety of ancient Near Eastern treaty texts, arranges them according to content, and indicates links to Old Testament texts. His principal thesis is that a great many of YHWH's judgment sayings against Judah and Israel rest on such ancient Near Eastern treaty curses.[33]

Some of the aspects treated by Hillers have been given special attention by F. Rachel Magdalene with respect to the prophetic marriage imagery. From a feminist-critical perspective she investigates the imagery of sexual violence inherent in the prophetic marriage metaphors. First she presents the prophetic texts containing these marriage metaphors, discussing individual words and contexts. She then looks at the ancient Near Eastern backgrounds and the instances of these metaphors, also taking into account their location within a patriarchal social structure and world of images. In this connection she takes up Hillers' study and engages it critically.

> Hillers surveyed the types of treaty-curses. They came in all varieties of maledictions and included 18 in all. The most significant for our purposes follow:
>
> 1. the city or nation will become a prostitute;
> 2. the city or nation will be stripped like a prostitute, and
> 3. wives will be raped.[34]

---

this context. Delbert R. Hillers suggests that we speak of performative utterances rather than symbolism ("Rite: Ceremonies of Law and Treaty in the Ancient Near East," in Edwin B. Firmage et al., eds., *Religion and Law: Biblical-Judaic and Islamic Perspectives* [Winona Lake: Eisenbrauns, 1990] 359).

[33] Delbert R. Hillers, *Treaty-Curses and the Old Testament Prophets* (Rome: Pontifical Biblical Institute, 1964). John Huehnergard, whose work was discussed above, makes connections similar to Hillers'. He remarks regarding the text on the Aramaic Sefire stele: "The issue here is not adultery, of course, but the political faithlessness of the woman's husbands. But again the image invoked by the curse is not only one of humiliation, but also one of economic destitution" ("Biblical Notes," 434 n. 27).

[34] F. Rachel Magdalene, "Ancient Near-Eastern Treaty-Curses and the Ultimate Texts of Terror: A Study of the Language of Divine Sexual Abuse in the Prophetic Corpus," in Athalya Brenner,

With regard to this listing of the three aspects that appear in the prophetic marriage imagery Magdalene observes:

> With this knowledge, suddenly the ancient metaphor of the cities of Israel and Judah as prostitutes and wives being subject to sexual debasement at the hands of the sovereign God becomes alive for us. Hillers noted the connection of the second curse to Isa. 3.17; 47.1-4; Jer. 13.22, 26; Ezek. 16.37-38; 23.10; 29; Hos. 2,4-5 (Eng. 2.2-3), 11-12 (Eng. 9-10); and Nah. 3.5.[35]

Magdalene augments the parallels with additional Old Testament texts, including verses with rape imagery.[36] However, she does not critique Hillers' method or procedure; her interest is rather in following up on his work and expanding it through some observations of her own.

Marie-Theres Wacker, on the other hand, has posed some fundamental questions to Hillers. The parallels he draws between ancient Near Eastern treaty texts in which prostitution appears in connection with threats and the Old Testament polemic against "harlotry" (זנונים)

> . . . are, however, by no means persuasive. In particular this concerns the treaty between Assurnirari V of Assyria and Matiʾilu of Arpad (the one who breaks the treaty shall be made a harlot and his soldiers shall be [made] women) as well as the first Sefire text, which threatens the stripping of the women of whoever breaks the treaty. The comparison with the stripping of a harlot is, however, simply conjectured from the text.[37]

In fact, in light of Wacker's work some aspects of Hillers' and Magdalene's procedure must be called into question. On the one hand, Hillers' remarks on the treaty between Asarhaddon and the Mede chieftain rest on the translation by Donald J. Wiseman,[38] which, because of its unreliability, has since been replaced by several newer versions.[39] A further point of

ed., *A Feminist Companion to the Latter Prophets* (Sheffield: Sheffield Academic Press, 1995) 343–44; the corresponding passages in Hillers' work are at pp. 58–60, 63.

[35] Ibid. 345, with reference to Hillers, *Treaty-Curses* 67.

[36] Magdalene, "Ancient Near-Eastern Treaty-Curses," 345–46.

[37] Marie-Theres Wacker, *Figurationen des Weiblichen im Hosea-Buch* (Freiburg: Herder, 1996) 28 n. 117, with reference to Hillers, *Treaty-Curses* 58–59. Hillers himself offers two suggested reconstructions of the text and challenges, without detailed argumentation, the reconstruction by André Dupont-Sommer (*Les Inscriptions araméennes de Sfiré [Siècles I et II]. Extrait des Memoires présentés par diverse savants à l'Academie des Inscriptions et Belles Lettres* XV [Paris: Impr. nationale, 1958] 18, 58).

[38] Donald J. Wiseman, *The Vassal Treaties of Esarhaddon* (London: British School of Archaeology in Iraq, 1958).

[39] For example, the German translation by Rykle Borger, "Akkadische Staatsverträge," *TUAT* I/2. *Staatsverträge* (1983) 160–76. Here (p. 160) there is also reference to literature that corrects

criticism is that in the vassal treaties the threat of violence against women is anything but central. Here, as a glance at the texts shows, the potential treaty-breakers are threatened with every conceivable kind of evil; punishment of women takes up relatively little space and is not in a prominent position.

Beyond this, we must pose a question about method. Quite apart from textual problems, is it methodologically justifiable to regard Old Testament metaphors as faithful reflections of formulations in ancient Near Eastern treaty texts? Should we not instead suppose that the very different literary and historical contexts produce sharper deviations and shifts in meaning?[40] We should also add, with respect to Hillers' exposition, that research since the publication of his book has radically changed the view of YHWH's "covenant" relationship to Israel, as indicated in the previous chapter.[41] As a result neither Hillers' thesis nor his premises can be unreservedly regarded as valid. Since *berit* can no longer be translated one-to-one with "covenant," and thus be regarded always as describing a mutual contractual relationship, corresponding treaty texts no longer represent unqualified parallels to Old Testament texts.

Despite these reservations, we can derive something from these texts for understanding the prophetic marriage imagery: Threats of violence against women are here found within the framework of scenarios in which it is prophesied that a vassal, should he prove unfaithful, will be subjected to every kind of fearful punishment imaginable. The connotation is thus clearly negative. Rape of women in the ancient Near East is therefore no more to be regarded as part of "normal" life than are the other curses (including cannibalism and murder). In times of peace, as we can see from legal ordinances, rape was under certain circumstances a punishable offense. However, as we have noted above, the punishment for rape was limited by patriarchal social structures.[42] In case of war, deportation, or captivity,

---

Wiseman's translation. In the same volume (pp. 155–58) Borger also offers a new translation of the treaty of Assurnirari with Matiʾilu of Arpad that Wacker discussed above (*Figurationen des Weiblichen* 28 n. 117).

[40] This criticism, in modified form, can also be applied to the partly similar procedure of Hans Ulrich Steymans, who in his work (*Deuteronomium 28 und die adê zur Thronfolgeregelung Asarhaddons. Segen und Fluch im Alten Orient und in Israel* [Fribourg: Universitätsverlag; Göttingen: Vandenhoeck & Ruprecht, 1995) draws very close connections between Deuteronomy 28 and the curses in Asarhaddon's rules for succession to the throne.

[41] See above, at the beginning of Chapter Four.

[42] We have already pointed above (Chapter One D, and Chapter Three C.i) to the implications of differences from today's definitions that are grounded in the strongly patriarchal structures of ancient Near Eastern societies. Like adultery, rape was only punishable if some man's rights were

of course, it turns out that rape and many other crimes that were normally punishable were not regarded as such. This context deserves further examination.

iii. War, imprisonment, and deportation

Wartime actions appear as background for the prophetic marriage imagery in two ways: On the one hand, in the ancient Near East (and unfortunately today as well) rape of the women among the conquered people by the victorious soldiers is nothing unusual.[43] It would not be surprising, then, if the city personified as a woman in this imagery suffered the same fate as its inhabitants. This presumes that what is depicted in the metaphors refers to real events in wartime. Since the marriage imagery in the Old Testament served as a means for interpreting the event of the exile we can, in fact, presuppose a context of war and the resulting exile of the population.

Ancient Near Eastern parallels to the imagery of stripping can, in addition, be found illustrated in pictorial imagery of prisoners and deported persons. Especially among the Assyrians it was policy to deport whole sections of the population of conquered peoples or cities. At a minimum, cultural uprootedness and the destruction of the social fabric of the group in question resulted from deportation. In this context there are also iconographic examples that witness to the fact that deported persons or prisoners in many cases had to strip or be stripped: in a monumental relief depicting one of Shalmaneser III's campaigns against Phoenicia we see naked male captives.[44] Images of women who are lifting their skirts, presumably under duress, are found in the same cycle.[45] The "black obelisk"

violated by it. Harold C. Washington embeds the ancient Near Eastern view of violence against women in a broader cultural horizon ("Violence and the Construction of Gender in the Hebrew Bible: A New Historicistic Approach," *BInt* 5 [1997] 352). He speaks of ancient Israel and the ancient Near East as a "rape culture." "In rape cultures, sexual assault is viewed as a manly act and women are regarded as intrinsically rapable." The biblical understanding of rape, he says, is well illustrated by the so-called rape laws in Deut 22:23-29 (ibid. 353). "The laws do not in fact prohibit rape; they institutionalize it and confirm men's control over women. Rather than 'rape laws,' the rules of Deut. 22:23-29 are best classified as a subset of the general law of adultery preceding them in Deut. 22:22."

[43] On this see, for example, Pamela Gordon and Harold C. Washington, "Rape as a Military Metaphor in the Hebrew Bible," in Athalya Brenner, ed., *A Feminist Companion to the Latter Prophets* (Sheffield: Sheffield Academic Press, 1995) 308–25, especially 313–17.

[44] *ANEP* plate 358, lower register.

[45] *ANEP* plate 365. For the interpretation see below (Alfred Jeremias, *Das Alte Testament im Lichte des Alten Orients. Handbuch zur biblisch-orientalischen Altertumskunde* [3rd ed. Leipzig, 1916] 689; Helga Weippert, "Textilproduktion und Kleidung im vorhellenistischen Palästina," in

of Shalmaneser III depicts the subjection of King Jehu, in images and in writing; here we see the subjected king without a garment on his upper body. Again, scenes from a campaign of Shalmaneser III, this time against the Hittite fortress of Dabigi, are found on the bronze gate of Balawat. Here, in the lower register, are captured women making a gesture that is also interpreted as lifting the hems of their skirts; that, at any rate, is Alfred Jeremias's reading from the first half of the twentieth century.[46] This interpretation has also been adopted very recently by Helga Weippert.[47] She also connects the pictorial evidence with certain texts from the prophetic marriage imagery:

> Stripping appears not only as a mourning ritual, but also as an expression of shame. . . . The Assyrians therefore pictured women going into captivity as lifting their skirts (cf. Isa 47:2; Jer 13:22, 26). Even when defeated enemies are pictured prostrating themselves before the Assyrian great king without garments on their upper bodies (for example, on the "black obelisk" or in the relief showing the capture of the city of Lachish) it appears that this was understood as a "shameful" stripping.[48]

However, the stripping of captives cannot have been universal practice, since there are many depictions from similar contexts that show clothed people being led away.[49]

For an understanding of the implications of stripping in the ancient Near East it is useful to keep in mind the meaning of clothing and unclothing in that place and time. Helga Weippert has provided the substance of this discussion in her short essay. It can be easily illustrated by the ivory plate from Megiddo: It is

> an outstanding example of the difference in status expressed in clothing: The shame of the enemies [men, *GB*] led out in chains is expressed by their nakedness; the two armed soldiers wear only loincloths, the palace servants

Gisela Völger et al., eds., *Pracht und Geheimnis. Kleidung und Schmuck aus Palästina und Jordanien* [Köln: Rautenstrauch-Joest Museum der Stadt Köln, 1987] 141).

[46] Jeremias, *Das Alte Testament im Lichte des Alten Orients* 689: "The baring of the ankle and lifting of the front part of the skirt hem was required as a humiliation of women captured in war as part of the triumphal procession, as we see from a depiction on the bronze gates of Balawat, Plate 279. [Isaiah] 47:3 is an added citation that speaks of the same thing. The threats in Nah 3:5; Isa 20:4; Jer 13:22, 26; Ezek 23:29, as well as Mic 4:11 refer to this."

[47] Weippert, "Textilproduktion und Kleidung," 141.

[48] Ibid. 141, with an illustration of the scene from the "black obelisk."

[49] Thus, for example, the captured women on Ashurbanipal's palace relief in Nineveh, who are fully clothed (*ANEP,* Plate 167), or *ANEP,* Plates 205, 321, 349, 351-355, 447, all of which show clothed, captured men.

> have robes reaching to their ankles. The king and the two women standing before his throne are most extensively clothed. . . . Rank is expressed in the degree to which the body is covered; a lower social status corresponded to a body clothed only partially or not at all.[50]

We can say here, then, that stripping in the context of war and the captivity of people of both sexes is iconographically attested. The most probable interpretation that suggests itself is that this is an expression of a major diminution in social status.

C. Evaluation

From ancient Near Eastern witnesses from different times and contexts we can only sketch a fragmentary picture to provide a background against which to decipher the texts of the prophetic marriage imagery. The motif of the "city as woman/wife" has still been too little studied to permit more extensive conclusions at this point. It is clear, however, that the personification of a city as "woman" did not happen only in Israel.

The punitive passages in the prophetic marriage imagery have parallels in ancient Near Eastern texts on the rules governing adultery and divorce, and also in iconographic evidence of military actions and deportations. These present more numerous and clearer parallels to the Old Testament texts than the cursing formulae from vassal treaties. This does not exclude the possibility that the cursing formulae may also contribute to illuminating the background of the prophetic marriage imagery. In any case, a circle is closed: When the cursing passages of the treaty texts threaten the stripping of women as something that will happen to the city or the land, behind the texts themselves stands the concrete reality of the lives of women in time of war.[51] However, in war the fate of being stripped fell not only upon women, but on men as well.

[50] Weippert, "Textilproduktion und Kleidung," 140. The subject is the plate from Tel el-Mutesellim from the 14th/13th century B.C.E.; Weippert also provides an illustration.

[51] Feminist exegetes in particular have pointed this out: e. g., F. Rachel Magdalene, "Ancient Near-Eastern Treaty-Curses," 347, and Pamela Gordon and Harold C. Washington, "Rape as a Military Metaphor," 324–25.

Part II

Textual Studies

Chapter Six

Hosea: "Primal Text" of the Prophetic Marriage Imagery

A. Survey of marriage imagery in Hosea

There is much in favor of seeing Hosea 1–3* as the "primal text" of the prophetic marriage imagery.[1] It is, of course, difficult to place this writing historically, because Hosea in the opinion of scholars has been revised and augmented through a great many redactions.[2] Nevertheless, we may proceed on the assumption that the introduction of the imagery itself is traceable to Hosea or his contemporaries. Which additions were made at exactly what levels of redaction, however, cannot be determined with certainty in the present state of research. Marie-Theres Wacker proposes that there were revisions critical of Samaria, but possibly also to be seen as intra-Jewish critique. It is probable that in the post-exilic period there was a far-reaching revision of the writing;[3] in the process the texts in chs. 1–3 containing the marriage imagery were probably altered as well.[4]

The importance of the discourse about marriage and adultery for Hosea and the whole Book of the Twelve Prophets is underscored by its prominent

[1] Thus, e.g., Jörg Jeremias, *Der Prophet Hosea* (Göttingen: Vandenhoeck & Ruprecht, 1983).

[2] Marie-Theres Wacker, *Figurationen des Weiblichen im Hosea-Buch* (Freiburg: Herder, 1996) concentrates on Hosea 1–3. She also offers a broad selection and discussion of the scholarly literature.

[3] For the terminology "book" for the whole book of the Twelve Prophets and "writing" for its individual parts cf. Aaron Schart, *Die Entstehung des Zwölfprophetenbuchs. Neubearbeitungen von Amos im Rahmen schriftübergreifender Redaktionsprozesse* (Berlin and New York: Walter de Gruyter, 1998) v, with reference to James D. Nogalski, *Literary Precursors to the Book of the Twelve* (Berlin and New York: Walter de Gruyter, 1993) and *Redactional Processes in the Book of the Twelve* (Berlin and New York: Walter de Gruyter, 1993).

[4] For the history of origins especially of Hosea 1–3 cf. Wacker, *Figurationen des Weiblichen* 221–59. A precise sketch of the growth of the book in light of this proposition is, however, difficult, since too few connections between the individual redactional fragments are established.

positioning at the beginning of the book and by its length. In Hosea 1–3* the earthly marriage of the prophet with the "wife of whoredom," Gomer, is made an analogy for the marital relationship between YHWH and the land of Israel. The most important passages are Hos 1:2 and 2:2–3:5 [MT 2:4–3:5]:

1:2 And YHWH said to Hosea:
"Go, take for yourself a wife of whoredom and have children of whoredom,
for the land is altogether whorish, (and) it is forsaking YHWH."

. . .

2:2[5] "Bring suit against your mother, bring suit!
For she is not my wife, and I am not her husband.
And she will put away the whoring from her face
and the adultery from between her breasts,
3[5] or else I will strip her naked and expose her as in the day she was born,
and make her like the wilderness, (and make her) like parched land,
and let her die of thirst.

4[6] And upon her children I will have no pity,
because they are children of whoredom.
5[7] For their mother has played the whore, she who bore them has acted shamefully.
For she said, 'I will go after my lovers,
who give me my bread and my water,
my wool and my linen, my oil and my drink.'
6[8] Therefore, behold, your way is blocked with thorns.
And I will wall up her walls so that she cannot find her paths
7[9] so as to run after her lovers; [and] she does not overtake them.
And she will seek them and not find them.
Then she will say: 'I will go
and return to my first husband,
for it was better with me then than now.'
8[10] For she did not know that it was I who gave her
grain and wine and oil,
and who lavished upon her silver and gold—they squandered it for Baal.
9[11] Therefore I will turn back[6] and take back my grain in its time
and my wine in its season,

[5] In the MT this passage begins at 2:4.

[6] Wacker, *Figurationen des Weiblichen* 69, n. 2, points out that שׁוב with a finite verb can be understood adverbially as "again," but need not.

and I will take away my wool and my flax,[7]
with which she covers her nakedness.[8]
10[12] But now I will uncover her shame[9]
in the sight of her lovers,
and no one can rescue her out of my hand.
11[13] And I will put an end to all her mirth,
her festivals, her new moons, her sabbaths,
and all her feast days.
12[14] And I will lay waste her vine and her fig tree,
of which she said: 'These are my wages of whoredom,
which my lovers have given me.'
And I will make them a thicket,
and the beasts of the field will devour them.
13[15] And I will punish her for the festival days of the Baals,
to whom she offered incense.
And she decked herself with her ring and jewelry,
and she went after her lovers.
And she forgot me," says YHWH.
14[16] "Therefore, behold, I persuade[10] her
and lead her into the desert, and I will speak to her heart.
15[17] And from there I will give her her vineyards,
and make the valley of misery a portal of hope.
And there she will answer[11] as in the days of her youth,
and on the day when she came out of the land of Egypt.

16[18] And on that day it will be," says YHWH,
"(that) you call: 'My husband!'
And you will no longer call: 'My Lord!'[12]
17[19] And I will take the names of the Baals out of her mouth,
and their names shall be remembered no more.

[7] Renate Jost, "Von 'Huren' und 'Heiligen.' Ein sozialgeschichtlicher Beitrag," in Hedwig Jahnow et al., *Feministische Hermeneutik und Erstes Testament. Analysen und Interpretationen* (Stuttgart: Kohlhammer, 1994) 131 draws attention to the fact that this list, from the Lipit-Eshtar texts (translated by Heiner Lutzmann, "Aus den Gesetzen des Königs Lipit Eschtar von Isin," *TUAT* I/1. *Rechtsbücher* [Gütersloh: Gerd Mohn, 1982] 23–31, at 28), resembles the list of items a man must give to a prostitute with whom he has children, and to the children themselves.

[8] The infinitive is, from the temporal aspect, subordinate to the finite verbs; therefore here (differently from Wacker, *Figurationen des Weiblichen* 68) it should not be understood as imperfect, but as present.

[9] For the hapax legomenon נבלות, "shame," see below, section C.

[10] For more on this see below, section B.

[11] Wacker, *Figurationen des Weiblichen* 74, lists the possible translations for the difficult וענתה in this passage (Hos 2:15-22 [MT 17-24]) and evaluates them. She joins the majority of interpreters in reading it here as ענה I, "answer," in awareness of the fact that in OT times the other meanings would have been heard within the text as well.

[12] For the different connotations of בעל in Hosea see below, sections B and D.

18[20] And on that day I will make a *'berit'* with them,
with the beasts of the field and the birds of the air,
and the creeping things of the ground.
And I will abolish the bow, the sword, and the weapons of war from the earth,
and I will make them dwell in safety.
19[21] And I will betroth you to me forever,
and I will betroth you to me with righteousness and justice,
and in steadfast love and mercy.
20[22] And I will betroth you to me in faithfulness,
and you will know YHWH.
21[23] And on that day it will be: I will answer," says YHWH.
"I answer the heaven, and it will answer the earth.
22[24] And the earth answers the grain and the wine and the oil,
and they answer Jezreel.
23[25] And I will sow her for myself in the land,
and I will take pity on Lo-Ruhamah,
and I will say to Lo-Ammi: 'You are my people!'
and he says: 'My God!'"

3:1 And YHWH said to me:
"Go again, love a woman, the lover of a neighbor and an adulteress,
as YHWH loves the children of Israel,
and they have turned to other gods and loved raisin cakes."
2 And I bought her for fifteen (pieces) of silver
and a bushel of barley and a measure of barley.
3 And I said to her: "You shall remain many days for me,
not playing the whore and not going with a man,
and I will be to you (in the same way)."
4 For the children of Israel remain many days without king and without princes,
without sacrifices and without pillars,
without ephod and teraphim.
5 Then the children of Israel will return,
and they will seek YHWH, their God,
and David, their king;
they will turn in awe to YHWH and to his goodness,
until the end of days.**

It cannot be determined at every point in the text whether the subject is Hosea's marriage to Gomer or YHWH's marriage to Israel. Gale Yee formulates this in a positive sense: "The tragic human story of the prophet interconnects with the metaphorical tale of Yahweh and Israel, so that the two stories become essentially one. The prophet creates in this fusion the powerful marriage metaphor to articulate the special covenantal relationship between God and Israel."[13]

A thesis long dominant in scholarship holds that the notion of the land of Israel as YHWH's "wife" is to be interpreted against the background of a nature religion common to Semitic peoples "in which Baal, who gives rain and therefore fertility, was regarded as the husband and the rain-imbued land as the wife."[14] Against this argument Marie-Theres Wacker shows that there is no trace of corresponding deities in the Canaanite pantheon and no instance of such ideas in Hosea.[15]

On the other hand, it is not completely impossible that goddess concepts may have motivated the language about YHWH's "wife" in Hosea.[16] As Fokkelien van Dijk-Hemmes has shown, it is entirely probable that passages in Hosea may offer a literary opposition to possible goddess-worship in Israel.[17] However, probably nothing more than a form of "reflected mythology" can be found in the texts.[18] We also cannot exclude the possibility that Hos 2:2–3:5 is concerned with the ancient Near Eastern concept of the city goddess.[19] We can, for example, see an indication of this in the fact that the "lovers" (usually מאהבים), who appear elsewhere in the prophetic marriage imagery, in Hosea (2:3, 5, 8, 10, 12, 13 [MT 2:5, 7, 10, 12, 14, 15]; 9:10) always have the connotation of alien gods and not, e. g., foreign powers.[20] Certainly the "lovers" in Hos 2:13 [MT 15] and 9:10 are

[13] Gale A. Yee, "Hosea," in Carol A. Newsom and Sharon H. Ringe, eds., *The Women's Bible Commentary* (Louisville: Westminster John Knox, 1992) 199; for the covenantal relationship between YHWH and Israel see above, Chapter 4.

[14] Wacker, *Figurationen des Weiblichen* 317.

[15] Ibid. 318.

[16] William D. Whitt, "The Divorce of Yahweh and Asherah in Hos 2,4-7.12ff.," *SJOT* 6 (1992) 31–67, at 67 and frequently elsewhere, has offered an interpretation of YHWH's "wife" that goes far in this direction. He proposes as background for Hos 2:2-5, 10-15 [MT 2:4-7, 12-17] a scenario within which Hosea appears as a fanatical worshiper of YHWH who, nevertheless, is not yet marked by the deuteronomic/deuteronomistic worship of YHWH alone. According to him, in Hos 2:4 the prophet is not describing Israel as "mother," but rather the goddess Asherah. Wacker, *Figurationen des Weiblichen* 323, engages Whitt's thesis and refutes it on a number of points.

[17] Fokkelien van Dijk-Hemmes advocates this thesis in her article, "The Imagination of Power and the Power of Imagination. An Intertextual Analysis of Two Biblical Love Songs: The Song of Songs and Hosea 2," *JSOT* 44 (1989) 85: "These two Goddesses [Asherah and Astarte] who represent the mother and the woman-lover are possibly hidden behind the 'spirit of harlotry.' In other words, the woman who is attacked in Hosea 2 is not only the woman of harlotry Gomer/Israel, but also the Spirit by whom she is inspired: the Spirit of harlotry/the Goddess(es)."

[18] Thus Wacker, *Figurationen des Weiblichen* 323.

[19] Ibid. 323–25; on this see also above, Chapter 5, section A.

[20] It is true that Hosea also contains (later?) references to Assyria (9:3-6; 11:5; 14:4) and Egypt (11:5) with the undertone that these powers are false helpers; however, neither Assyria nor Egypt is a "lover."

directly connected to Baal, which makes an interpretation in terms of goddesses improbable at least in those passages.[21] In any case, behind Hos 2:8, 13 [MT 10, 15]; 3:1; 4:12; 7:16; 9:10; 10:1, 8; 11:2, 7; 13:1-2 stands the problem of how to deal with the worship of gods other than YHWH. However, whether this rests on a historical foundation or is to be seen as defamation of opponents can rightly be questioned, with Rut Törnkvist:

> Apart from the diffusion in terminology, the relevant term for sexual intercourse for cultic or religious purposes cannot be prostitution, and the participants are not "prostitutes" at all. What we have, rather, are designations for different cult personnel *(Qadištu, Naditu, Assinnu)* and they seem to be highly respectable. The *Naditu*-woman was protected from divorce or displacement by a second wife, even if she remained childless, and the *Assinnu* seems to be a prophetic type of cult personnel. Although we have evidence of ancient rituals of "sacred marriage," i. e., *hieros gamos,* and allusions to sexual activities within this ritual, it should be kept in mind that ritual "prostitution" and ritual intercourse represent quite different practices and should be kept apart.[22]

Thus it is questionable how this worship of alien gods appeared concretely, and whether it corresponded to the Old Testament depiction of it. Wacker refers here to, among others, the study by Othmar Keel and Christoph Uehlinger, according to which

> . . . the apparently polemical presentation of the situation in the book of Hosea cannot be accepted unreservedly as a description of the conditions, and certainly not as a reflection of the self-understanding of the "other side." On the other hand, the global theory of a "fertility cult," together with the mutually exclusive categories of ethics or history vs. "nature" (developed from the perspective of "ethical monotheism" or notions of "salvation history") in the text of the book of Hosea needs to be revisited. To put it another way, the opposition between "Canaanite religion" and "Hoseanic theology," in its diverse components, must be debated all over again.[23]

[21] Wacker, *Figurationen des Weiblichen* 255, suggests another interpretation: "But could it not be the case that the explicit identification of the 'lovers' with 'Baals' in Hos 2:15a [i. e., 13a] points to a change in usage in exilic-postexilic times such that the discourse about מאהבים came to be understood as thoroughly political, and that therefore the cultic meaning in Hos 2:4ff. [i.e., 2ff.] had to be secured, after the fact, by Hos 2:15a [i.e., 13a]?"

[22] Rut Törnkvist, *The Use and Abuse of Female Sexual Imagery in the Book of Hosea. A Feminist Critical Approach to Hos 1–3* (Uppsala: Academia Ubsaliensis, 1998) 172.

[23] Wacker, *Figurationen des Weiblichen* 16, with reference to Othmar Keel and Christoph Uehlinger, *Göttinnen, Götter und Gottessymbole. Neue Erkenntnisse zur Religionsgeschichte Kanaans und Israels aufgrund bislang unerschlossener ikonographischer Quellen* (4th ed.

That debate cannot be conducted here, but it seems to me appropriate, in light of these considerations, to maintain some skepticism toward descriptions of historical "models" for Israel's "whorish" behavior.

B. The use of metaphorical marriage terms in Hosea

From the very beginning of the book of Hosea the marriage of Hosea and Gomer is closely connected to the relationship between Israel and YHWH. According to the superscription, Hos 1:2 begins with YHWH's order to Hosea to take (לקח) an אשת זנונים and have ילדי זנונים, "for the land is utterly whorish (זנה תזנה) (and) far from following YHWH." In this verse alone words with the root זנה are used four times. The expressions אשת זנונים and ילדי זנונים are constructed with the abstract plural זנונים, which emphasizes habitual behavior.[24] This word form is used more frequently in Hosea than in any other biblical book, and usually in a construct phrase. It serves to emphasize that both the personified "wife/woman" Israel (1:2; 2:2, 4 [MT 4, 6]) and the people of Israel (4:12; 5:4) as a matter of habit, so to speak as "recidivists," turn away from YHWH. In Hosea זנה consists in seeking the fruitfulness or the gifts of the land from other deities (2:5b[7b]). The "spirit of whoredom" (רוח זנונים, 5:4) leads the Israelites no longer to know YHWH, or to go away from him (4:12; cf. 9:1), indeed to go to the "lovers" (מאהבים) who, according to 2:13[15]; 9:10 are closely related to the בעלים. Only marginally and by way of hints is זנה associated with its original sexual field of meaning.

In reference to "concrete" Israelites זנה is close to the juridical term נאף, "commit adultery," or its derivative נאפופים.[25] The hapax legomenon נאפופים is used in 2:2[4] in parallel to זנונים ("whoring") to describe the "adulterousness" of the "woman/wife" in the text. In 3:1 נאף is used without a parallel to זנה to characterize the woman/wife whom Hosea is to "love." In the other passages (4:2, 13, 14; 7:4) נאף refers to the behavior of concrete Israelites. Wacker interprets the fact that נאף with reference to Gomer or "woman/wife" Israel is used relatively late and infrequently by Hosea as showing that the reproach against the Israelites applies "at the same time, in retrospect, to Hosea's wife as well."[26] David Noel Freedman and B. E.

Freiburg, Basel, and Vienna: Herder, 1998). (English: *Gods, Goddesses, and Images of God in Ancient Israel*. Translated by Thomas H. Trapp [Minneapolis: Fortress, 1998].)

[24] Ibid. 40, following Yee, "Hosea," 197, and with reference to Bruce K. Waltke and Michael P. O'Connor, *An Introduction to Biblical Hebrew Syntax* (Winona Lake: Eisenbrauns, 1990) 121: the form emphasizes that it is a question of a "repeated series of actions/habitual behavior."

[25] On this see Wacker, *Figurationen des Weiblichen* 61–62.

[26] Ibid. 61.

Willoughby write of the use of נאף and זנה in Hosea: "Hosea's wife Gomer is an example of terminological interaction, for she is both an adulteress and a prostitute (Hos. 2:4[2]; 3:1-3)."[27]

In general, as regards discourse concerning adultery and prostitution or whoring in Hosea, we see that it occurs in a great variety of connections. The land[28] (1:2; 2:2[4]?), Hosea's wife Gomer (1:2; 2:2[4]?; 3:3), her children (1:2; 2:4[6]), and also the people (4:10-11) together with the priests (4:14), the daughters of the people (4:13), and the brides (4:13), thus Israel (4:15) or Ephraim (4:18; 5:3; 6:10) "whore" (זנה and its derivatives) in serving alien gods. (The priests also commit "a monstrous crime" [זמה] in Hos 6:9.) In short, the "spirit of whoredom" (רוח זנונים, 4:12; 5:4) lies on them all. Gomer/Israel (2:2[4]; 3:1), but also the Israelites, male and female (4:2, 13-14; 7:4) commit adultery (נאף). For this Israel receives its "wages," אתנן, which according to 2:12[14] consist in vineyards and fig trees from the "lovers."[29] There is a difference here from, for example, the use of the imagery in Ezekiel. There Jerusalem refuses to accept any pay (Ezek 16:31). On the contrary: she herself pays her lovers (Ezek 16:33-34).

In comparison with other Old Testament texts it may seem striking that Hosea does not speak of YHWH's love (אהב) toward grammatically-feminine Israel. It is true that YHWH loves Israel (3:1), or the Israelites (9:15; 14:4[5]), and quite definitely his "son Israel" (11:1). But it is not said that YHWH loves the "woman" who stands for the land or the people of Israel.[30] However, on closer examination we see that with one exception[31] the parallel texts in Jeremiah, Ezekiel, and Isaiah do not speak of YHWH's love for feminine Israel or Jerusalem either, even though these texts, in part,

[27] David Noel Freedman and B. E. Willoughby, art. נאף *nā'ap, TDOT* 9:115.

[28] Wacker, *Figurationen des Weiblichen* 243, points out that besides Hos 1:2d only Lev 19:29 speaks of the land's "whoring."

[29] Hosea 9:1 stands outside the prophetic marriage imagery as such. Here the grammatically masculine Israel received "a prostitute's pay" on all threshing floors when it "played the whore" by departing from its God. As a comparable passage we may mention Isa 23:17-18: here אתנן is used in neutral fashion in connection with the "song about the prostitute" in v. 16 with reference to the "aging prostitute," the "daughter of Tyre." Contrary to Deut 23:19, the "prostitute's wages" are here dedicated to YHWH or belong to him as something "holy"; this seems to be possible because Tyre is personified as a foreign woman.

[30] Because she starts with an understanding of "love" that is tied to content, Brigitte Seifert comes to a different estimation of the marital imagery in Hosea: "For these metaphors, like scarcely any others, are able to convey YHWH's passionate love, which leaves nothing untried in its effort to win Israel back. It shows guilt in its deepest dimension as a behavior by which YHWH is personally touched and betrayed. He thus appears as a God who, because of his love, can be wounded" (*Metaphorisches Reden von Gott im Hoseabuch* [Göttingen: Vandenhoeck & Ruprecht, 1996] 138).

[31] The exception is Jer 31:3, where Israel is addressed as a feminine singular "you."

contain a very intense discourse about the marital relationship between YHWH and Israel.[32] This is scarcely remarkable in ancient Israel, since marriage, as we have shown above,[33] was not so much a love- as an economic relationship.[34] "Love" is, of course, in play when it is a question of the relationship between the "woman" Israel and her "lovers" (מאהבים, Hos 2:5, 7, 10, 12, 13 [7, 9, 12, 14, 15]). That these relationships are by no means free of economic aspects, however, is obvious in Hos 2:5b[7b] and in the provision of goods to the "woman."

It is clear from the significant verb לקח in 1:2 that Hosea is speaking of a real marriage, as well as from the formula in 2:16[18], which points to that context: "My lord" or "my husband," as in 2:16[18], is a sufficient formula for marriage.[35] It is disputed whether, on the other hand, 2:2[4] is an echo of a divorce formula;[36] in that case we would expect to find verbs such as שׂנא, "hate," or שׁלח, "send away," "dismiss."[37] In Hos 2:19-20[21-22] YHWH's tie to Israel is put on a new basis through a "betrothal." The verb ארשׂ is used repeatedly here, as at no other point in the Old Testament. It otherwise appears in law texts to describe the legal status of a woman and the corresponding consequences in law, usually in cases of rape (thus in Exod 22:15; Deut 22:23, 25, 27). In the context of the prophetic marriage imagery Hosea is the only author who speaks of a betrothal.

That this betrothal should not (or not only) be regarded in a romantic and positive light is hinted by Hos 2:14[16]: The verb פתה, "deceive" or "prevail upon" contains clearly negative aspects; it can also mean

[32] We may note simply in passing that in any case YHWH in the OT shows preference for grammatically masculine love-objects. Of 29 passages in which the grammatical gender of who or what is loved (אהב) by YHWH is perceptible, "his" love is directed only twice to a feminine object: In Jer 31:3 to feminine Israel addressed as "you" (singular), and in Ps 33:5 to grammatically feminine "righteousness" (צדקה, but parallel to the masculine משפט). In all the other passages the love is directed to real men (Solomon, Abraham, the "fathers," or the Israelites), to Israel designated as masculine, or to masculine abstractions.

[33] See above, Chapter 3 A.

[34] So, for example, Renita Weems, "Gomer: Victim of Violence or Victim of Metaphor?" *Semeia* 47 (1989) 99–100.

[35] According to Josef Scharbert, "Ehe und Eheschliessung in der Rechtssprache des Pentateuch und beim Chronisten," in Georg Braulik, ed., *Studien zum Pentateuch. Walter Kornfeld zum 60. Geburtstag* (Freiburg, Basel, Vienna: Herder, 1977) 214–15. In the Elephantine texts the words "you are my Baal" are attested as a marriage formula, according to (among others) Marie-Theres Wacker, *Figurationen des Weiblichen* 80, n. 64.

[36] Against a "divorce formula" in Hos 2:2[4]: (among others) Wacker, *Figurationen des Weiblichen* 117, n. 77.

[37] Raymond Westbrook points this out ("Adultery in Ancient Near Eastern Law," *RB* 97 [1990] 578, with n. 122): "It [Hos 2:2{4}] is therefore a reference to the formula rather than the formula itself."

"dissemble" or "incite to foolishness."[38] Rudolf Mosis sees the important point in Hos 2:14[16] as occurring elsewhere: "Yahweh brings Israel back into the wilderness and speaks to her heart, making her into a *peṯî* (factitive piel); he leads Israel, who is now as stubbborn as a stubborn heifer (Hos. 4:16 [i. e., 14]) back into a condition in which she can be shaped and tutored."[39] From today's perspective we must at the very least raise critical questions about the extent to which such "formation and education" of a woman by a man is appropriate in a marital relationship. The rest of the sentence makes it clear that it is not merely a question of education, but also of persuasion: Here YHWH speaks to Israel's "heart" (דבר על לב). This expression can also be found in the Old Testament in the context of love affairs (the "classic" passage is Ruth 2:13), but in at least two of these passages the aspect of violence is not absent from what follows (Gen 34:3; Judg 19:3). To that extent Hosea's choice of words already hints at Israel's dire fate.

Besides the words from the field of prophetic marriage imagery that are used in Hosea, we can also note omissions from that spectrum of words: there is nothing at all about "magic" or "witchcraft" (כשף) or "neighing" (צהל), and "lechery" (זמה) is mentioned only in reference to the priests in Hos 6:9. As regards historical and chronological questions touching the origins or writing down of the prophetic marriage imagery in the books of the prophets, this could be regarded as an indication of a not yet highly differentiated use of this spectrum of language, one that is original and still concentrated on the principal lines of thought. The following specifics in the use of the prophetic marriage imagery in Hosea should be noted: The "woman/wife Israel" in the text, who can scarcely be distinguished from the wife Gomer, "whores" away from YHWH, that is, she turns to other gods. Her misdeed is thus given religious connotation. She is accused of adultery with her "lovers," for which she receives "prostitute's pay." This points on the one hand to a strong tie between her and YHWH that is impaired by her action, but on the other hand she is characterized by the payment as a professional prostitute.

However, it is not only the female personification "Israel" who is accused of reprehensible behavior. The concrete Israelites also, perhaps as a summary of all their other crimes, commit harlotry and adultery (especially in Hosea 4) and are "faithless" to YHWH (בגד; 5:7; 6:7). So also the masculine-personified Israel, or Ephraim, is the subject of harlotry, the re-

[38] Cf. the passages and their implications in Ges^{17} 666.

[39] Rudolf Mosis, art. פתה, *pth, TDOT* 12:172.

cipient of prostitute's pay (9:1), by which "he" defiles himself (טמא; 5:3; 6:10). The concrete Israelites bring shame on themselves (קלון; 4:7, 18) or become "filth" (שקוצים) like their lover-gods (9:10). All the words just mentioned are occasionally used in later texts of the prophetic marriage imagery in connection with the "woman" Israel/Jerusalem, as we will show in discussing those passages. Here we will propose the thesis that in Hosea the fields of reference ("Israel" as woman, as son, and the Israelites) still appear separately. In the further development of the prophetic marriage imagery this separation is abandoned. Later all bad activity centers in the text-"woman." Besides this, the boundaries between cultic-religious, clearly sexual, and social misbehavior become more porous. זנה becomes a term for any and every kind of action directed against YHWH and his commandments; it is not critical whether such actions are done by human beings or personifications.

However, specific to the feminine personification "Israel" is punishment exacted in images of sexual violence. We will examine this more closely in what follows.

C. Metaphors of sexual violence in Hosea

As the text continues, the expressions referring to Hosea's wife Gomer or to Israel as "harlot" are augmented by others. In Hos 2:2[4] the Israelites addressed by the text are supposed to initiate a legal plea against their "mother" Israel so that she will remove the "whoring" (זנונים) from her face and her "adultery" (נאפופים) from between her breasts. If not, she is threatened with divorce. Immediately afterward, in v. 3[5], comes the first threat of punishment, on two levels: On the one hand a female personification is menaced with stripping, but on the other hand the threat is against the land, which will experience the "stripping" as its plants parch and wither.[40] This indicates a close relationship between the "woman" and the land, which will need to be examined later.

After a speech concerning the role of the "lovers" of the text-"woman" and their gifts to her the text returns in vv. 9b-10[11b-12] to the metaphor of stripping. The "woman" is to be punished or threatened with having the gifts given her by YHWH taken away—whereupon she will stand naked.

The background of a scene in which a woman is stripped naked has already been described above.[41] The choice of words for "stripping" in Hosea is striking in comparison to other texts of the prophetic marriage imagery.

[40] This is Wacker's interpretation, *Figurationen des Weiblichen* 62–63, 258.

[41] See above, Chapter 5 B i.

Here גלה, mainly in the *piʿel*, is chosen much more frequently as the word for the "stripping" of the "woman." Only in Hos 2:3[5]; Ezek 16:39; 23:26 do we find פשט *hipʿil*, "take off," "unclothe." This verb is almost always used transitively with a double accusative of the person and the thing. Otherwise the objects removed are skin, pelt, clothing, and weapons. Only in Hos 2:3[5] and 1 Chr 10:9 is no such object mentioned. In Hos 2:3[5] the nakedness of the "woman" or the land is the purpose of the punishment. This double reference is probably also the explanation for the lack of an object: that would have put too much strain on the imagery, which otherwise is used more cautiously and less concretely by Hosea.[42] The case is clearly different in Ezekiel: Here there is copious detail and the narrative is expanded in several directions.

Hosea also uses the more common verb for "stripping" in the prophetic marriage imagery, גלה, but not, as usually elsewhere, in combination with ערוה, "shame," "nakedness." In Hos 2:10[12] it is associated with the object נבלות. There has been a long discussion among scholars about this *hapax legomenon*.[43] A derivation from נבל III ("fool"), which is sometimes suggested, is not persuasive; more probable is the derivation from נבל II, "treat with contempt," with a spectrum of meaning that at least in Nah 3:6 extends to the sphere of sexual violence.[44] Marie-Theres Wacker points out that through the combination of נבלות with the verb גלה the proximity of נבלות to ערוה and its meaning, "nakedness," "shame," suggests a similar meaning for נבלות and ערוה.[45] The use of גלה with ערוה, as we have indicated above,[46] describes sexual intercourse. In a context of threat and punishment like this one it most probably refers to sexual violence.

[42] I question whether here, as Hans-Walter Wolff suggests (*Dodekapropheton I. Hosea* [3rd ed. Neukirchen-Vluyn: Neukirchener Verlag, 1976] 40), the removal of the husband's obligations is expressed through the unclothing of the wife. It is not certain that the OT has this meaning for פשט anywhere else. In addition, it is not clear that a divorce of Israel from YHWH is really taking place here. Instead, it seems to me that in this instance, parallel to the examples in Isa 32:11b and Ezek 26:16 mentioned by Hans Schmoldt (art. פָּשַׁט, *pāšaṭ, TDOT* 12:130), the reference is to a mourning custom; this would also correspond better to the parching of the land.

[43] Wacker, *Figurationen des Weiblichen* 69, n. 5, describes the discussion.

[44] Saul M. Olyan, "'In the Sight of Her Lovers': On the Interpretation of *nablut* in Hos 2,12," *BZ* 36 (1992) 261, after a brief investigation of possible derivations and translations of נבלות, comes to the conclusion that the word can be translated and understood on at least four levels, including sexual violence. With reference to Olyan, Paul A. Kruger ("'I will hedge her way with thornbushes' (Hosea 2,8): Another Example of Literary Multiplicity?" *BZ* 43 [1999] 92–99) in a short article establishes four levels of understanding also in Hos 2:8 (social—that is, related to marriage, political, religio-mythological, and intertextual).

[45] Wacker, *Figurationen des Weiblichen* 69, n. 5.

[46] See above, Chapter 3 C ii.

We can only speculate on the reasons why precisely these metaphors of violence were chosen or created in Hosea. Three possibilities can be suggested: First, marital infidelity on the part of the wife was associated with threats of violent or economically life-imperiling reactions on the part of the husband. We may indeed fear that this combination was part of everyday life in an Israelite marriage if the wife did not conform to her role.[47] This kind of "sanctioning" must have had a kind of matter-of-fact quality. Otherwise it could not have been applied in this way as imagery that was intended to persuade its recipients of its message. The fact that this tailoring of the imagery not only *uses* gender roles but also *cements* them, even under changed social circumstances, may also have played a role.[48] A second reason that may be mentioned is the parallelism between the "stripping" of the land and of a woman. In Hosea "woman" and "land" of Israel are closely related, and apparently the metaphor of stripping could be applied to both, each in its own way.

Renita Weems points to a third aspect of Hosea's marriage imagery, showing that the use of metaphors of sexual violence in Hosea 2 is by no means accidental: on the contrary, from the point of view of the text structure, imagery, and internal argumentation those metaphors play an important role. Weems presents three functions for discourse about sexual violence in Hos 2:2-23[4-25]: This imagery underlines Hosea's will to "rescue" his (or YHWH's) marriage by all possible means. It connects reconciliation with the previous punishment, and it foregrounds the correspondence between the punishment of public stripping and the crime, the "vulgar" behavior of the text-"woman" (2:2[4]). Extending Weems's line of argument, we may say that imagery of sexual violence strengthens an aspect of the marriage imagery that was probably also key to the depiction of YHWH's relationship to Israel through such imagery: There is no other image of God that can express and at the same time make emotionally

[47] On this see Elke Seifert, *Tochter und Vater im Alten Testament. Eine ideologiekritische Untersuchung zur Verfügungsgewalt von Vätern über ihre Töchter* (Neukirchen-Vluyn: Neukirchener Verlag, 1997) 258: "If we relate Hosea 1–3 to women's experiences today it is completely clear that the words of the prophet can no longer be received in our present circumstances as a matter of course. The fundamental inequality of power between the husband/YHWH and the wife (and children) creates a structure of relationships that lays the foundation for violence in the family."

[48] Rut Törnkvist has also written about the changes that may have lain behind the shift in meaning of זנה in Hosea: "The patriarchal marriage (the wife living in her father's tribe) was at length superseded by the virilocal one (the wife living in her husband's tribe). The husband's authority over his wife and children was strengthened by the power shift from father's house to husband's house. The wife's social and sexual behaviour was circumscribed and restrained" (*Use and Abuse* 172).

comprehensible YHWH's closeness to Israel as well as his passion for Israel and his holding fast to "her," in spite of her failings.[49]

Hence imagery of sexual violence in Hosea can be regarded not only as something quasi-accidental within the field of marriage imagery, as if it were a biographical relic of the narrative of Hosea's unfaithful wife or the overreaction, accidentally transmitted, of a man under powerful stress. In the social conditions out of which Hosea drew his metaphors and on behalf of which he speaks, the metaphors of marriage could not function unless the exercise of any and every kind of violence by a husband as punishment for his wife was an immediate part of the context. This thesis is supported by the long subsequent history of this very aspect, and by the developments it experienced at the hands of Jeremiah and Ezekiel.

D. Feminist theological interpretations of Hosea's marriage imagery

From a feminist-theological point of view the symbolic mixing and tailoring of gender roles with and to the God-image constitutes a core problem of the marriage imagery. Marie-Theres Wacker makes the point sharply: "The opening chapters of the book depict the (troubled) relationship between YHWH and Israel literarily through the (likewise troubled) relationship of a husband to a (his) wife, thus setting up an antagonism between the sexes in which the wife is assigned the human and uniquely guilty part, while the husband is made the representative of God and the guiding analogue of religious discourse."[50] What scholars have largely neglected in all this is the fact that Israelite marriage was not a symmetrical, "egalitarian" relationship between two people; within patriarchal social structures "a woman belongs to a single man, and he can send her away (but not vice versa)."[51] On the basic linguistic level the problematic character of these texts is constituted by the two-facedness of the basic metaphors[52] of "prostitution" (זנה and its derivatives) and "marriage" (in the terminology "take a wife," לקח אשה).

Renita Weems draws out the whole problematic of the imagery of sexual violence as applied to God and to the relationship of YHWH to Israel. As we have already mentioned, she uses Hos 2:2-23[4-25] as an example to reveal a number of ways in which imagery of sexual violence functions in the context of the text and its wider imagery, as well as the tight inter-

[49] Weems, "Gomer," especially 95–99.

[50] Wacker, *Figurationen des Weiblichen* 27.

[51] Ibid. Cf. also above, Chapter 3 A.

[52] This is Wacker's expression, ibid. 28, and frequently elsewhere.

weaving of marriage imagery and sexual violence. According to Weems the metaphor of YHWH as "lord" within the marriage is fatal when the pictorial components dominate over what they are meant to indicate, that is, when God is no longer regarded as *like* a husband, but *as* a husband. "In this case, a risky metaphor gives rise to a risky deduction: here, to the extent that God's covenant with Israel is like a marriage between a man and a woman, then a husband's physical punishment against his wife is as warranted as God's punishment of Israel."[53]

Other problematic (sub)aspects of Hosea's marriage imagery from a feminist perspective are clarified by Fokkelien van Dijk-Hemmes in her intertextual reading, in which she confronts Hosea 2 with the love poetry of the Song of Songs. This comparison makes it possible to perceive the contours of Hosea's image of marriage and its structures more clearly. The text-"woman" in Hosea 2 and the concept of her relationship appear only as shaped by a particular masculine point of view. Marie-Theres Wacker summarizes this aspect as developed by van Dijk-Hemmes:

> Beginning with the role of the mother, with whom the speaker associates the children, although polemically, it [the concept of the woman's relationship] can be described as one of mother-right; starting from the role of the harlot we find the model of a sexually self-determinative woman, or at least one who organizes her own subsistence by the sale of her sexuality. This conflict becomes dramatic—here we may pointedly summarize van Dijk-Hemmes' analysis—when it is functionalized theologically: The model of androcratic, monogamous marriage stands for a relationship to God on the part of Israel that, from the point of view of the book of Hosea, corresponds to YHWH's will for Israel; the model of the woman who organizes her own life, by contrast, represents idolatry. In turn, such an organization also serves to evaluate the two ways of life, resulting especially in a radical devaluation of the role of the harlot.[54]

Van Dijk-Hemmes formulates the point of the text this way: "The woman who expresses her desire for her lover becomes in the Hosean context a harlot who, in a shameless way, goes after her lovers."[55]

There is no place in Hosea for a love song as expression of the woman's desire, such as we find in the Song of Songs: only Hosea/YHWH speaks, and He alone has the initiative: "Her song of desire has been distorted and

[53] Weems, "Gomer," 100.

[54] Thus Fokkelien van Dijk-Hemmes, "The Imagination of Power," as described by Wacker, *Figurationen des Weiblichen* 135.

[55] Van Dijk-Hemmes, "The Imagination of Power," 82.

then deafened by His song."[56] The text-"woman" becomes the object of his action, in Hos 2:23[25] of his "sowing."[57] One effect of the Hoseanic depiction of wifely love is, according to van Dijk-Hemmes, the establishment of the enormous importance of fatherhood and fatherly authority.[58]

Marie-Theres Wacker demonstrates that the critique being expressed today by feminist theologians against the Hoseanic thought models does not apply merely to some possible statements in an ancient text by referring to some ways the marriage imagery has been received in current theological work.[59] What is most striking in the examples she selects is the lack of attention to the fact that statements about God can only be found in analogies. Besides this, in present-day interpretations the problem of violence in the texts is usually ignored altogether.[60]

E. Marriage metaphors in the context of Hosea's religious imagery

Neither the image of YHWH as master within the marriage nor the metaphorical depiction of Israel as a "wife of whoredom" floats unattached within the imagery of the book of Hosea. Both metaphors are associated with others. Our purpose now is to ask what those other metaphors are, and whether their presence or position in the texts as a whole achieves a change in the meaning of the imagery for God, Israel, or the feminine.

First let us examine the multifaceted God-imagery in Hosea.[61] Besides the image of the husband, the best developed metaphors are those of YHWH as a parent of "Israel," as well as those in which YHWH intervenes in his creation in various ways and at various points or is depicted through the created world.[62]

Besides the facets of the "husband" metaphors already described, others are added in the further course of the book of Hosea. Thus YHWH courts

[56] Ibid. 86.

[57] Ibid. 84.

[58] Ibid. 85.

[59] Wacker, *Figurationen des Weiblichen* 123–26.

[60] Rut Törnkvist, *Use and Abuse* 170, shows that male interpreters unanimously ignore the ascription of gender roles.

[61] Brigitte Seifert investigates a selection of these God-images in her *Metaphorisches Reden von Gott im Hoseabuch*. However, I consider her conclusion—that in Hosea rejection is expressed in non-anthropomorphic and acceptance in anthropomorphic metaphors—inaccurate. One counterexample among several is the very positively-connoted tree metaphor at the conclusion of Hosea in 14:8-9.

[62] Other metaphors, e.g., YHWH as shepherd (13:5-8), sickness (5:12-13), or physician (6:1-2) are not considered further here because they are not so broadly developed as those mentioned above.

Israel (2:14-15[16]17) or reminisces almost nostalgically on their time together in the wilderness (9:10). The image of YHWH as "lord" or "master" in the marriage, into which the husband metamorphosizes in 2:16[18], is contradicted in 11:9: now YHWH no longer wants to be regarded as איש, but as אל: "While there [in 2:16] YHWH's 'wife' will address him as *'îšî,* 'my husband,' that is revoked in 11:9."[63] Wacker associates this retraction with the God-image developed in Hos 11:1-4. Here YHWH's love (11:1) and tender care (11:4) for the infant Israel are described. Martti Nissinen has collected parallels to this text from neo-Assyrian royal oracles: here, among other things, the goddess Ištar appears as the king's wet-nurse.[64] In addition, the divine activities in the text, when viewed in light of the stereotypical roles they contain, indicate that YHWH's activity is more motherly than fatherly.[65] Wacker evaluates the combination of 11:1-4 with 11:9, and 11:6, 8 with YHWH's wrath, as a text that describes the "struggle within God's own self, in which God's motherly side fights against the warlike-destructive side. Thus the text does not present YHWH in a pure female-motherly form, but rather a form of the divine with two aspects: wrath that is prepared to destroy, but also mercy."[66] Nevertheless, the image of YHWH as parent is distorted by the way it is used at the beginning of Hosea: depending on YHWH's evaluation of the behavior of the "mother" he either turns away from her children and refuses them any kind of protection or care—the name of the daughter, לא רוחמה ("no pity") can be so interpreted[67]—or else he turns back to his offspring. Thus if we take the book of Hosea as a whole YHWH appears as a *paterfamilias* who according to his own discretion provides for those attached to him the things they need for life, or else refuses them. Here we can observe a shift within the metaphors of relationship in the Bible: as a parent, even more clearly than in the marriage metaphor, YHWH is the one on whom Israel is completely dependent.

The image in Hosea of a God who intervenes in his creation is much more varied than the familial images. In this metaphorical field we find assembled a whole series of aspects. YHWH intervenes directly both in human

[63] Wacker, *Figurationen des Weiblichen* 308.

[64] Martti Nissinen, *Prophetie, Redaktion und Fortschreibung im Hoseabuch. Studien zum Werdegang eines Prophetenbuches im Lichte von Hos 4 und 11* (Neukirchen-Vluyn: Neukirchener Verlag; Kevelaer: Butzon & Bercker, 1991), especially 280–90.

[65] Thus Helen Schüngel-Straumann, "God as Mother in Hos 11," in Athalya Brenner, ed., *A Feminist Companion to the Latter Prophets* (Sheffield: Sheffield Academic Press, 1995) 194–218.

[66] *Figurationen des Weiblichen* 308.

[67] Elke Seifert, *Tochter und Vater* 254.

procreation and in the universe as the totality of extra-human nature. The latter is expressed, for example, in the harmony of the beasts produced by YHWH in 2:18[20], in YHWH's answering (2:21-22[23-24]) the land or causing it to be parched (4:3), and in the ephemeral images of Ephraim in 13:3. Here YHWH appears as sovereign over the whole creation; in 8:14 he is then called עשׂה, "creator." YHWH is like the sun or the dawn (6:3), images that surely contain some precipitate of notions about the solar deities of the ancient Near East.[68] At the end of the book of Hosea (14:7-8[8-9]) YHWH can even appear as a fruit-bearing tree, an image that has parallels in the goddess-iconography of Israel's surrounding environment.[69]

By contrast, in 9:11-16 YHWH intervenes directly in human procreation: from birth on, "backwards" through pregnancy and conception, human life is cut off from the very outset (9:11b). Even the children already born are killed (9:12-13, 16), and women are made sterile (9:14). Other "outbreaks of rage" on the part of YHWH that are carried out primarily against women can be found in judgment sayings: mothers dashed in pieces on top of their children in battle (10:14), and pregnant women ripped open, their children smashed to pieces (13:16[14:1]).

The multitude of images of the divine in Hosea is augmented by an equally great multitude of titles for "Israel" or "Ephraim." Israel is not only a "whorish" wife, but as Israel/Ephraim it is also a beloved infant and son of YHWH (11:1-4). This image also has its critical angles: at its very birth Israel behaves foolishly (13:13); it struggles even in the womb (12:3[4]); we might say it is no wonder that it is a difficult child for YHWH to deal with.[70]

Israel is also depicted in nature images: It is a luxuriant but ungrateful vine (10:1-2), a silly and senseless (7:11-12) or fearful (11:11) dove, a wild ass (8:9), and in several places a steer or heifer. This image accents stubbornness (4:16) or original good will and docility (10:11), but often also the struggles with the steer cult in Bethel (8:5-6; 10:5-6, 12). There

[68] Thomas Podella, *Das Lichtkleid JHWHs. Untersuchungen zur Gestalthaftigkeit Gottes im Alten Testament und seiner altorientalischen Umwelt* (Tübingen: J.C.B. Mohr [Paul Siebeck] 1996) 194.

[69] Wacker, *Figurationen des Weiblichen* 304, with reference to Silvia Schroer, "Die Zweiggöttin in Palästina/Israel. Von der Mittelbronze II B-Zeit bis zu Jesus Sirach," in Max Küchler and Christoph Uehlinger, eds., *Jerusalem. Texte-Bilder-Steine. Zum 100. Geburtstag von Hildi und Othmar Keel-Leu* (Fribourg: Universitätsverlag; Göttingen: Vandenhoeck & Ruprecht, 1987) 201–25, and to Othmar Keel, *Goddesses and Trees, New Moon and Yahweh. Ancient Near Eastern Art in the Hebrew Bible* (Sheffield: Sheffield Academic Press, 1998).

[70] Wacker, *Figurationen des Weiblichen* 308, paraphrases the image of Israel in Hosea 11 humorously as that of "a small or growing boy . . . whose parents are slaving to bring him up right."

are also images from the round of daily life: Israel/Ephraim is like a half-baked loaf of bread (7:4-8).

Thus Israel is portrayed not only as "wife," but in many other images as well. It is true that the feminine imagery for Israel occupies a significant space, but it is by no means without alternatives in Hosea. How does this look from the other side, from the feminine aspect? Here, too, there are other feminine "figures."[71] Besides Gomer, often confusedly mixed up with "Israel," there are also the daughter לא רוחמה (1:6), who is renamed רוחמה in 2:1, 23[3, 25]. She is not only the prophet's own daughter; together with her brother she represents the whole of Israel. Besides זונות, 4:14 also mentions קדשות, "handmaids of God," whom the text defames as cult prostitutes, thus disqualifying them for their cultic service.[72]

However, men as well as women are criticized by Hosea. Most prominent here are the priests (4:4-10) who worship false gods. The men addressed in the text are, in 4:11-14, made responsible for the fact that their daughters and daughters-in-law or brides "play the whore." Hosea 12:2-14[3-15] seeks in the story of "Jacob," one of the earliest "ancestors" of Israel, the reasons for Israel's current wicked behavior.

We may conclude that in Hosea the marriage imagery is not isolated at any point at which it is applied. YHWH is depicted not only in the image of the "lord of the marriage," but also as father and mother, the caring parent, but also the abandoning parent. He is lord over the whole world, his creation; this power of his is particularly demonstrated in his intervention in fruitfulness and procreation. In this light the fruit-bearing and hope-giving tree at the end of the writing is not entirely unexpected: YHWH can give shape to his power over Israel in a great many different ways. This Israel is not only a "wife of whoredom," but also a disobedient son, yet both are (also) loved by YHWH. Israel can also appear in the images of a variety of animals and plants, though here there is a statement being made about its stupidity or stubbornness. In Hosea's view these characteristics of Israel make it scarcely distinguishable from the flesh-and-blood men and women in Israel. Here, however, we must note that men are more likely to appear as those responsible for actions, while women suffer the corresponding fate.

[71] See also Marie-Theres Wacker, "Traces of the Goddess in the Book of Hosea," in Brenner, ed., *A Feminist Companion to the Latter Prophets* 219–41.

[72] Ibid. Wacker supposes (p. 305) "that *qedeshin* lived outside a patriarchal marital and familial structure." At this point in her book there is also a lengthier discussion of the concept; cf. also Renate Jost, "Von 'Huren' und 'Heiligen,'" 134–35.

F. Summary

As regards a development or re-accentuation of the metaphors in the course of the book of Hosea,[73] the following may be said: The marriage imagery that dominates chs. 1–3 is, on the one hand, placed within a broader frame of reference in the course of the book of Hosea by the application of other metaphoric fields; it is therefore not the "whole truth" about the relationship between YHWH and Israel, but rather exists within a fabric of images. On the other hand, it is clearly contradicted, especially in Hos 11:1-4, 9. YHWH is no longer only the father of the family who abandons his children, but also a concerned and caring parent; YHWH is no longer only the violent and abusive husband/lord of his "wife," but God. YHWH no longer only intervenes destructively in the fruitfulness of the land and its inhabitants, but causes his people to flourish and becomes for them a tree that fulfills their elemental needs (Hos 14:8[9]).

It may be that Hosea's redactors saw in this shifting of the field of metaphors a possibility for correcting the marriage imagery in chs. 1–3. In any case, the great number of alternative fields of imagery relativizes the significance of the marriage imagery in Hosea. The parent-child imagery may have been chosen because it was less affected by social changes than was marriage; children's dependence on their parents is more strongly conditioned by biology than by culture.

The redactors of Hosea made no attempt to eradicate the marriage imagery. There may have been a number of reasons for that—including the fact that it made it possible to contend with the imagery and worship of the goddess, or that the marriage imagery already had a subsequent history within the Old Testament that made it appear less productive to eliminate it from the text than to correct it by counter-images. This can be taken as an encouragement to confront the marriage imagery and its problems today as well, and also in our own time to seek for counter-images.

[73] Despite the process of growth that the book of Hosea may have experienced, as sketched, e.g., in Wacker, *Figurationen des Weiblichen* 221–59, it appears to all readers, after its completion, as a work that is usually read from beginning to end. It therefore seems plausible to me that correctives to the initial chapters were introduced in the later ones.

Chapter Seven

Jeremiah: YHWH's Marriages with Israel and Judah

A. Survey of marriage imagery in Jeremiah

Jeremiah is similar to Hosea in placing the passages containing marriage imagery at the very beginning of the book. Thus the reader's picturing of the relationship between YHWH and Israel is shaped from the very beginning by this theological concept. Even though, in comparison to the book as a whole, this imagery does not occupy many text passages, its position nevertheless sets up the framework within which the relationship of YHWH to Israel, Judah, and Jerusalem will be interpreted from the outset.[1]

Imagery of marriage, adultery, and sexual violence is, as Angela Bauer has demonstrated, embedded in a broad framework of feminine imagery in the book of Jeremiah.[2] The degree to which its meaning has been influenced by this is something we will have to explore below (section E). A substantial difference from Hosea is that Jeremiah lacks any biographical point of contact with the marriage imagery; according to Jer 16:2 YHWH expressly forbids this prophet to marry or beget offspring. This is to serve as a sign to Israel: in view of the fate that awaits Israel it would be vain to

[1] This is similar to the position of Siegfried Hermann, "Jeremia/Jeremiabuch," *TRE* 16 (1987) 580. Kathleen M. O'Connor describes the marriage imagery in Jer 2:1–4:4 as a "root metaphor" ("Jeremiah," in Carol A. Newsom and Sharon H. Ringe, eds., *The Women's Bible Commentary* [Louisville: Westminster John Knox, 1992] 170); in her essay written with A. R. Pete Diamond ("Unfaithful Passions: Coding Women Coding Men in Jeremiah 2–3 [4:2]," *BInt* 4 [1996] 289–91) she uses this same expression. See the latter article also for further literature that supports this and other positions on the evaluation of the marriage imagery in Jeremiah.

[2] Angela Bauer, "Das Buch Jeremia. Wenn kluge Klagefrauen und prophetische Pornographie den Weg ins Exil weisen," in Luise Schottroff and Marie-Theres Wacker, eds., *Kompendium Feministische Bibelauslegung* (2nd ed. Gütersloh: Gütersloher Verlagshaus, 1999) 258–66. For further details see Angela Bauer, *Gender in the Book of Jeremiah. A Feminist-Literary Reading* (New York: Peter Lang, 1999).

bring children into the world. Thus in the book of Jeremiah there is no text that, like the passages in Hosea, can be applied simultaneously to *a* concrete woman/wife *and* to a "text-woman"—especially since Jeremiah talks of more than one "wife" of YHWH.

The story of YHWH's love and marriage in Jeremiah is concentrated in the second and third chapters. However, it is not always clear with whom YHWH is connected in what kind of relationship: In Jeremiah 2–3 the number and gender of the addressee "Israel," or "Jerusalem" and "Judah," both of which are related in content to "Israel," shift back and forth. In Jeremiah 2 the "house of Israel" is mentioned as a collective (2:4, 26), but Israel also appears as a son (2:14). Jeremiah 3 then frequently speaks of the feminine "rebel" (משובה) Israel (3:6, 8, 11, 12) as well as the "faithless" (בגודה/בגדה) Judah (3:8, 11). The two appear together in 3:6-13 in the narrative of "Israel's" "divorce" from YHWH and what happens afterward.

The narrative of YHWH's "love" story in Jeremiah begins with YHWH's appeal to the "woman" Jerusalem, reminding her of her love and fidelity to him (2:2). Immediately afterward, beginning at 2:4, the word is directed to Israel as a whole, addressed in the second person plural. The Israelites are reproached with having turned to other gods than YHWH—even the priests, "those who handle the law" (תפשׂי התורה) and the prophets (2:8) have forsaken YHWH, the "fountain of living water" (2:13). In 2:14-15 the gender and number shift again: now a rhetorical question is addressed to "Israel" in the masculine singular. Beginning at 2:16b the address changes gender again: now it speaks in the feminine. It is laid upon the "woman" that she has abandoned her God. Then, beginning at v. 20, she is accused of having "sprawled and played the whore" (צעה זנה) "on every high hill and under every green tree"—an expression drawn from a deuteronomistic formula.[3] This is the first mention of זנה in Jeremiah. Israel, sown by YHWH as a noble plant, has thus degenerated (2:21); it cannot be purified by any means (2:22). Every attempt on the part of "Jerusalem" to turn away her guilt is useless (2:23). In v. 24 the number of the subject again shifts to the singular; in the comparison of the "woman" with the uncontrollable sexuality of a young camel or a wild ass the terms are in the third

[3] This formula is also used, with some slight variations, in Jer 3:6; 17:2; cf. Moshe Weinfeld, *Deuteronomy and the Deuteronomic School* (Oxford: Clarendon Press, 1972) 322. For the connection between Hos 4:13; Deut 12:2, and Ezek 6:13, cf. William L. Holladay, "'On every high hill and under every green tree,'" *VT* 11 (1961) 176. Holladay thinks that the formula originates with Hosea and was first adopted into Deut 12:2. In his "family tree" of the formula, then, the "third generation" appears as words of Jeremiah in Jer 2:20, Ezekiel, and others. He sees Jer 3:6, 13 and 17:2 as dependent on Jer 2:20.

person singular.[4] We may see in this part a reference back to the imagery of Israel as a plow heifer in v. 20a; that seems[5] to be how we should understand the image of the yoke and the bonds.[6] Verse 25 then ties the animal metaphors back to the "woman," who is once again directly addressed in the second person singular. After this verse, however, the number and gender change once more: as before in 2:4-13, so now the subject of the sentence is the "house of Israel." In v. 28, then, the great number of Judah's gods is mentioned, with Judah now masculine in gender. In vv. 29-31 Israel is again addressed collectively and in the second person plural, as the fruitlessness of YHWH's "attempts at formation" is described; this includes a short quotation of a speech by Israel in v. 31, in the first person plural. Verse 32 then, with an image of a young woman or bride in her adornments, spoken in the third person singular feminine, makes a transition to vv. 33-37, where again Israel/Judah/Jerusalem, without name, is directly addressed in the second person singular feminine.[7]

In comparison to Jeremiah 2, in Jer 3:1-13 expressions drawn from marriage imagery appear much more frequently:

> 1 If a man divorces[8] his wife and she goes from him and becomes another
> man's wife, will he return to her? Would not such a land be greatly pol-
> luted?[9] You have played the whore with many lovers; and (could) you return
> to me? says YHWH. 2 Look up to the bare heights, and see! Where have you
> not been raped?[10] By the waysides you have lain in wait for them like Arabs
> in the desert; you have polluted the land with your whoring and wickedness.

[4] See more on this below, section E.

[5] Thus also William L. Holladay, *Jeremiah 1. A Commentary on the Book of the Prophet Jeremiah, Chapters 1–25* (Philadelphia: Fortress, 1986) 97. He suspects that behind the image of the yoke is Israel's "covenant" with YHWH.

[6] The image of Ephraim as a trained heifer is also used in Hos 10:11-12.

[7] From a thematic point of view Jeremiah 2 can be regarded as a ring composition: The chapter is framed by 2:2, 31-34 in passages that apply love imagery in the narrower sense. Within this external frame, first the "woman's" "crime" is told (2:4-13, 26-28), and in the center is placed the discourse about the "whore" with images of degenerate or animalized sexuality (2:20-24). This overall structure emphasizes the evaluation of the "woman's" sexuality as animalistic, as well as how that evaluation has run amok in comparison to the description of the concrete misdeeds. To that extent it is understandable that Athalya Brenner has focused her critique on Jer 2:22-23, since the text itself locates its focal point in that passage (Athalya Brenner, "On Prophetic Propaganda and the Politics of 'Love': The Case of Jeremiah," in eadem, ed., *A Feminist Companion to the Latter Prophets* [Sheffield: Sheffield Academic Press, 1995] 262–64); see more on this in section E below.

[8] In this context שלח *piʿel* can be understood only as referring to divorce in the juridical sense.

[9] Holladay, *Jeremiah 1,* 113 points out that חנף (3:1, 2, 9) describes an extreme type of "pollution."

[10] Angela Bauer's reflections (formulated in light of Holladay, *Jeremiah 1,* 114) regarding the translation of שגל are persuasive. She writes: "The metaphor depicts sexual violence. שגל carries

3 Therefore the showers have been withheld, and the spring rain has not come. Yet you have the forehead of a whore, you refuse to be ashamed. 4 Have you not just now called to me, My Father, you are the friend of my youth! 5 Will he be angry for ever, will he be indignant to the end?[11] This is how you have spoken, and you have done all the evil; this is what you did.

6 YHWH said to me in the days of King Josiah: Have you seen what she did, that rebel, Israel? She went up on every high hill and under every green tree, and played the whore there. 7 And I said after she has done all this: She will return to me—but she did not return. And her sister, faithless Judah, saw it. 8 She saw that for all the adulteries of that rebel, Israel, I had sent her away with a decree of divorce. Yet her sister, faithless Judah, did not fear; she too went and played the whore. 9 And it was through all her whoring that she polluted the land, committing adultery with stone and tree. 10 Yet for all this her faithless one, her sister Judah, did not return to me with her whole heart, but only in pretense, says YHWH.

11 Then YHWH said to me: Rebel Israel has shown herself[12] more upright than faithless Judah. 12 Go, and proclaim these words towards the north, and say: Return, rebel Israel, says YHWH. I will not look darkly[13] at you, for I am merciful, says YHWH; I will not be angry[14] for ever. 13 Only acknowledge your guilt, that you have sinned against YHWH your God, and wandered aimlessly[15] to the strangers under every green tree, and you have not obeyed my voice, says YHWH.**

In Jer 3:1-13 the relationship between YHWH and Israel is associated more definitively than ever before with discourse about marriage and divorce.[16] The half-chapter can be divided into three sections, each with its own focus: In

---

the connotation of forced sexual intercourse. The Masoretes consider the verb obscene and consistently replace it with שׁכב, 'lie with.' In all four instances, where the word occurs in the Hebrew Bible (cf. Deut. 28:30; Isa. 13:16; Zech.. 14:2), שׁגל can be rendered 'rape.' In all cases the context is one of sexual violence. Woman is violated" (*Gender in the Book of Jeremiah* 50–51).

[11] Both verbs in this verse have a double meaning: נטר and שׁמר basically mean respectively "retain" and "keep watch," but often have "wrath" or "anger" as object, though the object need not be explicitly named.

[12] Here נפשׁ should be read in the sense of a personal or reflexive pronoun, as it often appears in legal contexts: cf. Horst Seebass, art. נפשׁ, *nepeš, TDOT* 9:510–12.

[13] The unusual expression נפל *hipʿil* with פנים appears in the OT only here and in Gen 4:5-6; in both places YHWH is the subject. From Gen 4:5-6 we can conclude to the meaning, since in v. 6 the text speaks of "lifting up the face," that is, turning toward, as the opposite of "falling of the face" in v. 5; cf. Horst Seebass, art. נפל, *nāpal, TDOT* 9:495–96; Ernst Jenni, *Die hebräische Präpositionen*. Vol. 1: *Die Präposition Beth* (Stuttgart: Kohlhammer, 1992) 248.

[14] For the translation see above at Jer 3:5.

[15] פזר *piʿel,* "scatter" can best be rendered in this unique context as "wander aimlessly."

[16] The text of Jer 3:1-20 is probably the product of a multilayered textual history, summarized as follows by Günther Wanke: vv. 1, 2-3a, 3b-5, 19-20 appear to be pre-exilic and therefore oldest; vv. 14-18 are latest (*Jeremia 1,1–25,14* [Zürich: Theologischer Verlag, 1995] 48).

vv. 1-5, after the reference to the impossibility of remarriage between a couple who have divorced (v. 1a), which is closely related to Deut 24:1-4, the text describes how the "wife," by "playing the whore," has put her marriage with YHWH in jeopardy.[17] In vv. 6-10 names are mentioned: Israel, the "rebel" (מְשֻׁבָה, 3, 6, 8, 11, 12) and her sister Judah, the "faithless" (בגודה/בגדה, 3, 7, 8, 10, 11), have polluted the land by their "whoring." Finally, vv. 11-13 weigh the guilt of these two "women" and present possibilities for repentance. YHWH is prepared to retract his anger (v. 12), but in 15:6 this offer is withdrawn. In the further course of ch. 3 the "sons" (of Israel, שׁוּבוּ בנים שׁובבים, 3:14, 22) are also called rebellious and are summoned to repent. Thus the use of שׁוב and its derivatives produces a close connection between the deeds of the feminine personification Judah/Israel and their consequences, and those of concrete Israelites. The "relational history" of YHWH and the textual "woman/wife" Israel/Judah/Jerusalem can be thoroughly drawn from the way שׁוב and its derivatives are used:[18] After her "whoring" in 2:35 the "wife" speculates on the possibility that YHWH's wrath will turn away from her. In 3:1 there is a clarification of the legal situation in which a husband cannot return to his ex-wife after divorce, even if she should turn back to him. This expresses the impossibility of a second chance for the marriage between YHWH and Israel after a divorce has been completed—at any rate if this marriage has to be subject to the rules for human marriages. Despite the behavior of the "wife," in 3:7 YHWH hopes for her return; 3:10 notes that this is in vain: Judah does not turn to YHWH wholeheartedly. After this, 3:12, 14 direct the appeal for repentance to the concrete Israelites; for the moment the consequences remain uncertain in the text.

In Jeremiah 2–3 the "woman Jerusalem" and the "house of Israel" or "Jacob" are closely connected, at least by rhetorical means. The misdeeds of concrete human beings are not exposed in metaphorical discourse, but presented through description. The accusations against the "woman" Jerusalem, in contrast, are as metaphorical as the woman herself. Images of "whoring," enriched with cultic overtones, stand alongside plant and animal metaphors that express, through contrast, the difference between the "good" condition of Israel "at the beginning" and the later loss of control over sexuality (2:23-24).

[17] Verse 3, similarly to Hosea, draws the consequences of the "wife's" action for the land/agriculture. However, in Hos 4:1-3 the punishment of the land through desiccation of the vegetation is only predicted, while in Jer 3:3 it is described as past fact.

[18] However, William McKane's thesis that "[t]he thread on which the different parts of the chapter [3] are strung is constituted by שׁוב and its derivatives" appears overdrawn (*Jeremiah. Introduction and Commentary on Jeremiah I–XXV* [Edinburgh: T & T Clark, 1986] 82).

How does this clearly depicted textual "woman" in Jeremiah 2–3* stand in relation to the female personifications that appear later in the book?

Beginning at Jer 4:1, "Israel" appears almost entirely in the masculine gender. Besides "him," Judah and Jerusalem and those who live in them are also mentioned. From 4:5 onward Judah and Jerusalem have local significance; this is made explicit for the "cities of Judah" in 4:16. The association of the "cities of Judah" with the "streets of Jerusalem" in *parallelismus membrorum* appears still more frequently in the course of the book of Jeremiah, namely in 7:17, 34; 11:6; 33:10; 44:17, 21. From Jeremiah 4 onward, to summarize, we find a different way of speaking about Israel or Judah than in Jer 3:6-13. Now the personification is not so thoroughly developed and the character of the entities as city or land is more clearly evident.

Other metaphorical female figures besides "Israel" and "Judah" from Jer 3:6-13 are the various "daughters" mentioned in the book. From 4:11 onward the text speaks of the "daughter of my people," from 4:31 onward of "daughter Zion." Later there are other daughter-figures as well.[19] Common to them all is that judgments are addressed to them.[20] The "women" Israel and Judah mentioned in 3:6-13 do not appear afterward. Only in ch. 13 is reference made to a textual "woman" who, at least according to the Septuagint, is given the name "Jerusalem."

The textual "women" to whom YHWH is "married" either have more than *one* name, or else there is more than one "woman/wife." We take as given here that YHWH, as a grammatically masculine figure in the context of ancient Israelite ideas, can only marry female figures. Excluded as "wives" on the metaphorical level in Jeremiah 2 are the grammatically masculine entities (all of them named and associated with YHWH) Israel (2:14-15) and Judah (2:28), as well as the "people" (2:31-32)[21] and the "daughters." Accordingly, the only eligible wives for YHWH in Jeremiah 2–3 are Jerusalem, "rebellious" Israel, and "faithless" Judah. In 3:1-5 YHWH's reflections regarding divorce—including the legal considerations touching remarriage (3:1)—are not referred to one of the named female figures. However, YHWH carries out a divorce only against "Israel" (3:8), and only she receives a direct statement, later, of forgiveness (3:12).

[19] See below, Section E.

[20] Thus Elke Seifert, *Tochter und Vater im Alten Testament. Eine ideologiekritische Untersuchung zur Verfügungsgewalt von Vätern über ihre Töchter* (Neukirchen-Vluyn: Neukirchener Verlag, 1997) 276.

[21] One exception for עם, which in the OT almost always has masculine gender, is Jer 8:5. The ambiguous formulation שׁבבה העם הזה with feminine verb-form, עם, and masculine demonstrative, is clarified by the *BHS* through a conjecture of the verb as masculine.

What, then, is charged against the "women" in the book of Jeremiah? This is first evident in terms of those with whom they "play the whore" against YHWH. The focus of the usage of זנה in Jeremiah lies on cultic misdeeds, that is, the worship of foreign deities.[22] It is also possible to see the "lovers" as other nations, but with a different emphasis, as in Ezekiel, who puts primary emphasis on the great powers. Jeremiah is more likely to refer to those states that, like Israel and Judah, are under threat from the Neo-babylonians, or have already been subdued by them. These smaller states will be destroyed, like the textual "women" (22:20), or must go forth as captives (22:22), and the "women" will be forgotten (30:14).

But let us return to the religious aspect of the "lovers." The break in the "gendering" of the metaphors, which is probably not present at this point, may in fact exist elsewhere: with the "foreign gods" whom Israel, according to Jeremiah and the Deuteronomists, follows. At the beginning of the book the rebellious textual "woman" Israel reveres other gods besides YHWH; some of these are named. In Jeremiah 2–3* the god is specifically Baal[23] (in 2:23). Throughout the rest of the book of Jeremiah, however, other names are mentioned, including feminine ones like "the queen of heaven" (7:16-20; 44:15-19, 25) or the "Asherah" (17:2). Still, it is not entirely clear who or what the book of Jeremiah wants us to understand by these. Renate Jost has devoted a thorough study to this question, considering, besides Jeremiah 7* and 44*, comparable ancient Near Eastern texts as well as the contemporary social and cultural situation in which the texts probably originated. She concludes that Astarte, Asherah, and even Ishtar were worshiped in Israel and Judah from early times. "Their various aspects—with Astarte embodying the warlike, Asherah the nourishing, and Ishtar primarily the astral function—blended to form the figure of the queen of heaven." Jost continues: "Before the Josianic reform she [the queen of heaven] was worshiped alongside YHWH in the Jerusalem Temple as a national goddess. Later she retained her influence at the level of local and familial religion, and thus survived the destruction of the Temple. The cult of goddesses with the title "queen of heaven" is nothing specific to Israel or Judah; it is found from Mesopotamia through Egypt (Isis) and into the western Mediterranean world during a period of more than

[22] See more on this in the next section.

[23] In the entirety of chs. 2 and 3, Baal appears in 2:8 and 3:14, but not in direct connection with the "wife." Instead, Baal is mentioned (2:8) in relationship to the prophets who serve Baal, and (3:14) with reference to YHWH, who, in place of "Baal," calls himself Baal, that is, "Lord" of the children of Israel. Baal otherwise appears in Jeremiah in 7:9; 9:14; 11:13, 17; 12:16; 19:5; 23:13, 27; 32:29, 35.

two and a half millennia as a syncretistic phenomenon displaying, despite differences, the same characteristics as those that can be discerned from the book of Jeremiah."[24]

What does this finding signify for the interpretation/behavior of the "wife" of YHWH in the book of Jeremiah? As long as the worship of the queen of heaven and Asherah is considered only in the context of individual chapters in a single book the picture appears relatively consistent. The "wife" Israel/Judah/Jerusalem is not explicitly named as worshiper of these two, but instead an "ungendered" or two-sexed Israel. The same consistency in gendering is apparent if we consider only Jeremiah 2–3* and focus on the foreign god Baal: The "wife" Israel/Judah/Jerusalem has a masculine "lover," namely Baal. The imagery becomes problematic, however, when the beginning of the book of Jeremiah is compared closely with other chapters later in the book: Then it appears that the "wife" will also "play the whore" with goddesses like the queen of heaven; she will begin an "affair" with a "woman." We can only suppose that the later expanders of the book of Jeremiah, working against the background of Israelite prohibition of homosexual relations (Lev 18:22; 20:13), did not harmonize Jeremiah's marriage imagery from the beginning of the book with the later texts. This would favor distinguishing the metaphorical "women" from each other and, for example, not associating the "daughter Zion" named from Jeremiah 4 onward too closely with the "wife" Jerusalem/Israel/Judah from Jeremiah 2–3.*

Thus the marriage imagery is not equally definitive in all parts of the book of Jeremiah. It is true that the book begins with such imagery and that it recurs in the course of the book's development. This is prominently the case in Jeremiah 30–31. Barbara A. Bozak has devoted a closer study to the feminine imagery in Jeremiah 30–31. She demonstrates that here we find projected the vision of a happy relationship between YHWH and Israel that will function just when, and only when, the "woman" accommodates herself to the ideal of a patriarchally-defined female role. This is true especially of her complete legal and economic dependency on the man, but also of her unconditional and exclusive fidelity to him, yet it does not make her his total possession, without a will of her own.[25] The vision of

[24] Renate Jost, *Frauen, Männer und die Himmelskönigin. Exegetische Studien* (Gütersloh: Chr. Kaiser, 1995) 236.

[25] Barbara A. Bozak, *Life "Anew." A Literary-Theological Study of Jer. 30–31* (Rome: Biblical Institute Press, 1991) 157–64. Bozak interprets the text and its feminine imagery in a differentiated manner against the background of ancient Israelite marriage. She arrives (p. 164) at a rather positive interpretation: "The portrayal of Israel according to feminine categories is an effective

Jeremiah 30–31 consists, on the level of relationships, in "Israel's" complete fulfillment of the feminine role, after which YHWH, as "husband," writes the Torah in her (from this point of view completely passive) heart and makes a new *berit* with her (Jer 31:31-34). This possible reference to the marriage imagery at the beginning of the book is as far as it goes, however; the textual "women" Israel/Judah/Jerusalem are not mentioned again. Instead, Israel is now, in Jer 31:4, 21, a "young woman" (בתולה).

B. The use of marriage terms in Jeremiah

From within the semantic field of prophetic marriage and adultery metaphors, the book of Jeremiah uses especially זנה, נאף, and אהב with their derivatives, as well as צהל and זמה. We also find the ממלכות ("kingdoms") mentioned by Nahum, as well as כשף ("practice magic"), but not in the context of marriage imagery. There is no use at all of the term for "harlot's wages," אתנן. We need to give some extended attention to זנה and its derivatives, and to נאף; the other words will be discussed at the point where they appear in context.

The verb זנה appears in Jer 2:20 and 3:6 in the deuteronomistic formula already mentioned above, "on every high hill and under every green tree." These two passages are the only ones in the Old Testament in which זנה is associated with this expression. It is significant for an interpretation of the meaning of זנה in these passages that the deuteronomistic formulation is also used in Jer 17:2. Here a concrete explanation follows: The sin of the children of Judah consists in their having had altars and Asherahs "beside (עַל) every green tree, and on the high hills." This strongly suggests that in Jer 2:20 and 3:6 also זנה is to be understood as referring to the worship of other deities.

---

means of alluding to the desired relationship with Yhwh. Israel is not a 'possession' of Yhwh any more than a woman is the property of her father or husband. There is obvious dependence on the male yet this dependence is not absolute. Love and intimacy determine the husband's deeds for his wife while at the same time she acts with responsibility and even a certain autonomy. Such a situation adequately reflects Israel's stance before Yhwh. She is dependent on him yet also responsible for what befalls her. She is free to act, be it according to or contrary to the ideal of intimacy and exclusivity, yet her happiness and freedom lie in living in conformity with her knowing herself dependent on Yhwh and loved by him. If the Exile was considered a punishment for the sins of the people, then Jer 30–31 sets out a blueprint for a life which, more in harmony with the ideal relationship, points to a new beginning." A more critical view of Jeremiah 31 is found in Athalya Brenner, "On Prophetic Propaganda," 266–67. She acknowledges that here, in contrast to other passages in Jeremiah, there is no pornography (ibid. 267). "Nevertheless, the female images conform to the pattern established earlier and complement it through the suggested reversal. They constitute an additional transference of male concern about legitimate, properly allocated gender roles to religious discourse."

In Jer 3:1 the "woman/wife" Israel/Judah/Jerusalem is accused of "playing the whore with many," in connection with YHWH's reflection on whether to divorce this "wife." In a rhetorical question whose content and wording are closely related to Deut 24:1-4 the text considers whether it is possible that such a woman, who "plays the whore" with many men, can return to her husband.[26] We can conclude from Jer 3:8 that this is not the case. Here the text uses the relevant terms for YHWH's divorce from "woman/wife Israel": "send away" (שׁלח *piʿel*)[27] and the handing over of the "decree of divorce" (ספר כריתות).[28] After this her sister, faithless Judah, is also accused of "playing the whore." Correspondingly, we may suspect, she will experience the same fate as "Israel" in 2:37: conquest of the land and exile of its people. In 3:11-13, however, YHWH offers "Israel" another chance to repent. To that extent the use of the divorce imagery for the relationship between YHWH and the "woman" Israel/Judah is at least ambivalent: after the juridical prelude (3:1), the situation is such that YHWH's plea for the return of Israel/Judah from the "north" (3:12, 18) makes little sense. One possible solution to the problem would be to regard Israel/Judah not as "women/wives" who have entered into a second *marriage* with another man; after all, 3:1 speaks of "playing the whore" with "many."[29] In consequence, YHWH has already carried out his divorce from "Israel," but apparently not yet from Judah. This can be historically verified, since here Judah/Jerusalem has not yet gone into exile. According to 3:11-13 there is still the possibility that this/these "wife/wives" can return to YHWH.

But let us return to זנה. The substantive זונה, constructed from the feminine participle, appears in Jer 3:3 in the phrase "forehead of a whore," מצח אשׁה זונה. In the use of this expression we can see a reference to "whoredom" (זנונים) in the sense of externally obvious signs in Hos 2:2 [MT 4]. In Jer 5:7 we find the word in the construct phrase בית זונה, "houses of prostitutes," into which the sons of Jerusalem are going.

Among the derivatives of זנה, only the denominative זנות[30] appears in Jeremiah, and not the abstract plural זנונים, emphasizing habitual behavior,

[26] For further discussion of the connections between Jer 3:1 and Deut 24:1-4 see, among others, Holladay, *Jeremiah 1,* 112–13.

[27] In this meaning, according to Frank-Lothar Hossfeld et al (art. שׁלח, *šālaḥ*, *ThWAT* 8:66), שׁלח *piʿel* appears also in Deut 21:14; 22:19, 29; 24:4; Isa 50:1.

[28] This construct phrase is also used in Deut 24:1, 3, and Isa 50:1.

[29] Below, in section E, we will discuss how the ambivalences in the marriage and divorce imagery in Jeremiah are to be evaluated.

[30] The designation of this word as denominative follows GK §86k; according to this, זנות is to be understood as constructed from זונה.

which is found so frequently in Hosea (1:2; 2:2, 4 [MT 4, 6]; 4:12; 5:4).[31] In Hos 4:11; 6:10 זנות is connected with drunkenness and impurity—differently from Jeremiah, where the expressions parallel to זנות are רעה, "wickedness," in 3:2, and adultery in 3:9; 13:27. But what do we understand by these actions of the textual "women"? In 3:9 the adultery of the sisters Judah and Israel is described with the verb נאף, and in 13:27 the derivative of נאף, נאפים, "adultery," is used for Jerusalem's behavior.[32] Here two other expressions belonging to the field of prophetic imagery for adultery are paralleled to זנות and נאפים, namely מצהלה, "neighing," in a construct phrase with זמה, "shamelessness." The combination of words, which appears only here in the Old Testament, is probably to be interpreted as unbridled sexual desire, and is negatively valued. "Neighing" appears in Jeremiah also in 8:16 and 50:11 in its literal meaning, with horses as its subject; 8:16 contains the sole instance of the substantive in the Old Testament in addition to 13:27. In 31:7 צהל, in metaphorical language, describes Israel's jubilation, but in 5:8 it refers to the sexual desire of the sons of Judah for the wives of their neighbors.[33] Correspondingly, in 13:27 צהל represents the actions of Jerusalem, but in *parallelismus membrorum* to נאפים and זנות. In translations of Jer 13:27 it is occasionally suggested that the expression מצהלה זמת should be translated "lasciviousness."[34] The "adultery" of the textual "women" in Jer 3:13* is thus designated as debauchery caused by sexual voluptuousness; we can gather from the context that what is meant here is the worship of foreign deities. In Jer 3:6; 13:27 the deuteronomic formula about "playing the whore" on hills and under trees is close to adultery.

The proper term for adultery, נאף, must now be considered as a verb. Its derivative, נאפים, which we have just discussed, emphasizes the aspect of what is continuous, habitual.[35] In Jeremiah, נאף appears as a verb, with the

[31] For the meaning of the nominal construction זנונים cf. Marie-Theres Wacker, *Figurationen des Weiblichen im Hosea-Buch* (Freiburg: Herder, 1996) 40, as well as Bruce K. Waltke and Michael P. O'Connor, *An Introduction to Biblical Hebrew Syntax* (Winona Lake: Eisenbrauns, 1990) 121; see also above, Chapter 6 B.

[32] The abstract plural נאפים appears elsewhere in the OT only in Ezek 23:43. It is possible that it is a construction analogous to זנונים, which likewise emphasizes something habitual; cf. the previous note.

[33] In this connection Martin Schulz-Rauch points to the robust coupling of a stallion in heat (sic!), to which the actions of the Jerusalem men are compared (*Hosea und Jeremia. Zur Wirkungsgeschichte des Hoseabuches* [Stuttgart: Calwer, 1996] 215). In any case, for him (and most other interpreters, whom he cites on the same page, n. 5) the image is one of sexual excitement.

[34] Thus the Luther Bible in the 1985 translation (German *Geilheit*); the *Einheitsübersetzung* has "lascivious neighing" (*geiles Wiehern*).

[35] On the different usage of the *qal* and *pi*ʿ*el* of נאף, Ernst Jenni summarizes: "The Qal is a single case and has its object in the singular; the Piʿel is habitual and has its object in the plural"

textual "women," only in passages we have already discussed: 3:8, 9 and 13:27. All three verses also use זנה. However, the two words do not stand in *parallelismus membrorum,* and so we should not conclude that their meanings completely overlap in Jeremiah. It is also striking in the case of נאף, in contrast to זנה, that it is much more frequently used with reference to concrete people—all grammatically masculine (in 5:7; 7:9; 9:2 [MT 1]; 23:10, 14; 29:23). The parallel but not equivalent use of נאף and זנה indicates that in Jeremiah's usage "adultery" is the more common term for the behavior of *concrete* Israelites. It is possible for נאף to describe actual adultery, as in Jer 29:23 and 5:7; 7:9. In 5:7 the worship of other gods can echo as well. Besides the passages already mentioned, the same reference is present in 23:10, 14 (cf. 23:13, prophesying by Baal).

In summary, we may say that the wildly excessive, positively animal sex drive of Israelites like the city "women," expressed with צהל, is the basis of their wrong behavior. This behavior is described as, among other things, זנה. In Jeremiah, זנה is used in combination with a deuteronomistic formula to refer to the worship of foreign gods. It primarily describes the actions of the city "women," but also those of human men. That the abstract plural זנונים, which designates habitual behavior, is not used is adequately explained by the fact that the habitual aspect is not emphasized, in order, in 3:11-13, to leave open the possibility of repentance for the "women." The difference between this and 13:27, where the abstract plural form of the verb נאפים *is* chosen, can be explained by the circumstance that in the context of the punishment of the city "woman" Jerusalem in 13:20-27 the accusation of ongoing adultery makes sense. At this point in the book of Jeremiah there is no more talk of the possibility of repentance.

Otherwise, נאף primarily describes the actions of men. In the usage of זנה and נאף we have sketched there is indication of a break in the image of "whorish" Israel/Judah/Jerusalem: YHWH's "wives" are feminine personifications who discredit themselves morally through their "whorish" and "adulterous" actions; but on the human side it is the men who perform just such actions. The acts of the textual "women" provoke YHWH to plan divorce. As regards Israel those plans are already in motion; as regards Judah, not yet. Despite the existing tension with legal regulations in the

(*Das hebräische Piʿel. Syntaktisch-semasiologische Untersuchung einer Verbalform im Alten Testament* [Zürich: EVZ-Verlag, 1968] 161). However, this difference is not a factor in the use of the word in the book of Jeremiah, since both *qal* and *piʿel* are used in both finite (*qal:* 3:9; *piʿel:* 3:8; 5:7; 29:23) and infinite forms (*qal* infinitive: 7:9; 23:14; *piʿel* participle, "adulterers": 9:2 [MT 1]; 23:10) in unspecific and shifting ways for human beings and for metaphorical women.

intra-human sphere, the possibility of a remarriage with the "women" is left open.[36]

C. Metaphors of sexual violence in Jeremiah

Jeremiah 3:2 is the first passage in the book of Jeremiah to use metaphors of sexual violence. YHWH accuses the "woman/wife," who only in the later course of the text is called "Israel" or "Judah," of being raped[37] on the heights. The corresponding verb שׁגל is in the *puʿal* and thus gives no indication of who the rapist is. In 3:1b, however, there is mention of the "woman's" many "lovers/boyfriends" (רעים) with whom she is supposed to have "played the whore." In the context they alone come into the picture as possible subjects of שׁגל in 3:2. Here, according to YHWH's statement, the "woman" experiences sexual violence from her "boyfriends," with whom she herself has sought sexual contact. These "friends" certainly include also the Baals mentioned in Jer 2:23, whom Jerusalem has gone after.

The most extended text in Jeremiah incorporating metaphors of sexual violence is Jer 13:20-27. It is preceded by two verses that make clear that the context is the anticipation of exile for the inhabitants of Judah, but that also contain echoes of the sexual imagery in vv. 20-27. Here let me make just a few remarks that are important for locating the context: Verse 18 refers to both the king and the גבירה, usually given as "queen mother." The latter is also mentioned in Isa 47:7, also in the broader context of imagery of sexual violence. Considered from the point of view of the magnitude of her power, she also has some similarities to personified Nineveh in Nah 3:4-7. In Jer 13:18 the גבירה and the king are presented with an image of their approaching fall from power that is very close to their real situation: The crowns will be stripped from their heads. The consequences for the land are briefly stated in v. 19: According to v. 19a there will be no one to open and close the towns of the Negeb. Nowhere else in the Old Testament is it said that "towns," and not city or town gates, are opened or closed, but both verbs, פתח and סגר, appear with YHWH's "opening" (Gen 29:31; 30:22) and "closing" (1 Sam 1:5-6) of the womb, רחם. For Jer 13:19a this means that

[36] Mary E. Shields summarizes, with respect to the tendencies of Jeremiah's marriage imagery in contrast to that of Hosea and Ezekiel: "Within the scope of the pre-exilic texts, however, Jer. 3:1–4:4 represents an intermediate step in the development of the negative metaphors, developing the imagery in terms harsher than those of Hosea, while not pushing to the extremes of Ezekiel" ("Circumcision of the Prostitute: Gender, Sexuality, and the Call to Repentance in Jeremiah 3:1–4:4," *BInt* 3 [1995] 61).

[37] For שׁגל in Jer 3:2 see also above at n. 10.

here sexual imagery is at least in the background; moreover, v. 19b also contains a verb that is used in connection with sexuality: גלה. Jeremiah 13:19b uses the *hopʿal,* which elsewhere[38] describes leading into exile, but in v. 22 the *nipʿal* of the verb describes the "lifting up" or "uncovering" of the "skirt" of the personified "woman" Jerusalem. If in v. 19 "Judah" is understood not as the people, but as the land, then גלה can be interpreted as "uncovering" in the sense of the removal of its (covering) inhabitants. There is a similar threat in Hos 2:9-10 [MT 11-12]: YHWH announces an intention to deprive the land, or the textual "woman," of her covering (כסה) garments, and to bare (גלה *piʿel*) her shame before her lovers.

In Jer 13:20-21 the coming of the enemies is announced and their identity is revealed: They are the previous "friends" or "allies" (אלופים) of Jerusalem. Jeremiah 3:4, quoting the textual "woman," had already entitled YHWH "friend of my youth"; in the same context, as already shown, the "shaming" (שׁגל) of this woman by her former "companions" or "neighbors" (רעים) was also described. In the parallels we can see, alongside the deliberate creation of a connection between Jeremiah 2–3* and 13*, an emphasizing of the treachery of the—supposed—"friends" and a pointing to the true friend of Israel/Judah/Jerusalem, namely YHWH. Another metaphor from the realm of sexuality is used in v. 21b to illustrate the coming crisis: Like a woman in labor, the textual "woman" will have to suffer (labor) pains.[39]

The question of guilt is then posed in v. 22 and fully answered, including a description of the punishment to be expected. The verse reads:

> And if you say in your heart: Why have these things come upon me? it is for the greatness of your iniquity that your skirts/shame/genitals are uncovered, and violence is done to your body.**

The short reason given for "Jerusalem's" future miserable fate is her great "iniquity." This iniquity (עון) of the textual "woman/women" has already been made concrete, for example, in Jer 3:13: They run after foreign gods. The deuteronomistic formula about "playing the whore under every green tree and on every high hill," which recurs in 13:27, is also partially cited in 3:13. The same accusation is found in 3:13 and in 11:20; in the latter the crime is additionally qualified as פרר את ברית, "breaking the *berit*."[40]

[38] Jer 40:1, 7; Esth 2:6; 1 Chr 9:1.

[39] The image of giving birth is used frequently in Jeremiah with this connotation: 4:19, 31; 6:24; 13:21b; 22:23; 30:6; 48:41; 49:22, 24; 50:43.

[40] Jeremiah 30:14-15 gives an explanation, based on guilt, similar to that in 13:22b for why YHWH has struck Israel: על רב עונך עצמו חטאתיך ("because your guilt is great, your sins are so numerous").

In the announcement of punishment that follows, the verb גלה, already used in v. 19 with a different meaning, but now in the *nipʿal,* is employed with the noun שׁול. The "skirts" or "shame/genitals" of the "woman" are to be uncovered. Part b of the verse declares the purpose of this action: Reference is made, in metaphorical language, to "violent acts" against the "heels." The *nipʿal* of חמס is a *hapax legomenon* and is interpreted both in Gesenius[18] and in HAL not as a passive of חמס *qal,* but instead is translated with reference to גלה *nipʿal.* Both lexica suggest "be bared" as the translation.[41] After long discussion, J. A. Emerton also votes for this meaning.[42] However, a translation of חמס *nipʿal* by analogy to גלה does not seem methodologically appropriate, since the meaning of גלה itself is not undisputed: It can scarcely be regarded as helpful to explain an uncertain verb like חמס in terms of another uncertain verb like גלה. Thus it is more intelligible to translate חמס as the passive of חמס *qal.* This possibility echoes in "endure violence" in HAL,[43] and is also suggested by Gesenius[17] with "be treated violently."[44] This is how, for example, Herbert Haag and William Holladay translate it; for Haag "Jer. 13:22 *(nipʿal)* . . . speaks of physical assault on a woman"[45] and Holladay says: "Here again it is clearly sexual violence that is meant: the imagery has shifted from the loss of the flock to ravishment, an image for invasion (compare 'those who come in' in v. 20, which may have a sexual connotation . . . ; the image will be resumed in v. 26."[46] Still, this translation requires a more refined explanation, since the object of חמס *nipʿal* here, in a literal interpretation, is "heels" (עקב). The translations in lexica and dictionaries for the most part presume that these "heels" in Jer 13:22—unique in the Old Testament—

[41] HAL 316; Ges[18] 366.

[42] J. A. Emerton, "The Meaning of the Verb *ḥāmās* in Jeremiah 13,22," in Volkmar Fritz et al., eds., *Prophet und Prophetenbuch. Festschrift für Otto Kaiser zum 65. Geburtstag* (Berlin and New York: Walter de Gruyter, 1989) 19–28, supposes that עקב, "heels," is to be understood literally and not metaphorically (pp. 19–21), although this remains only a premise. In his opinion the frequent translation of חמס *nipʿal* as "be treated violently" does not fit this meaning. Emerton then sets forth the proposals offered by a number of people for translating חמס *nipʿal* in Jer 13:22. "Fitting the context" is the principal criterion given for determining the meaning of חמס *nipʿal;* in addition, he supports his proof with ancient translations as well as a thesis of Torczyner (1918), who in turn refers to Prov 26:6; Lam 2:6; Job 15:33, where, he thinks, חמס *qal* means "lay bare" (pp. 22–23). Emerton himself reconsiders חמס *qal* in Lam 2:6 and Job 15:33 and concludes that in both places "lay bare" best fits the contexts; the same is true for him with the meaning in Jer 13:22, which he translates as "are laid bare" (p. 27). The passages listed by Emerton are differently interpreted, for example, by Herbert Haag (art. חמס, *ḥāmās, TDOT* 4:479–80).

[43] HAL 316.

[44] Ges[17] 241.

[45] Haag, art. חמס, *ḥāmās,* 479.

[46] Holladay, *Jeremiah 1,* 414.

are to be understood, in accordance with the use of רגלים, as a euphemism for "backside" or genitalia.[47] It is in the nature of sexual imagery[48] that the texts cannot be pinned down to a single meaning. However, as regards Jer 13:22 a metaphorical understanding is most probable: apart from considerations of possible layers within the text, in the final version of Jer 13:20-27 sexuality—including birth (13:21), sexual misdeeds (13:27), and sexual violence (13:26)—is discussed in metaphorical fashion in a number of verses.

Hence we may consider it not improbable that in Jer 13:22 as well, in the context of the punishment of Israel, sexual imagery is being applied, and that in this connection the text speaks of Israel's "genitals" (עקב) "suffering violence" (חמס *nip'al*). In doing so, with the use of חמס this text goes beyond a "scene of uncovering" like those found in texts from the ancient Near Eastern context.[49] Here we definitely have a rape scene.

Neither in the case of "uncovering" or of "rape" can we determine who is doing it: both verbs are in the *nip'al*. However, if the verse is read together with v. 26 and the *nip'al* understood as *passivum divinum,* in this passage—as also in Isaiah 47—YHWH would be represented as a perpetrator of sexual violence.

Jeremiah 13:23-25 returns to the question in v. 22a about the "woman's" guilt, now discussed against the background of possible repentance. Surprisingly, no word from the root שׁוב, so common in the description of the "history of the relationship" between YHWH and Israel in Jeremiah 2–3*, is used here. This indicates that in Jeremiah 13 YHWH's patience toward Jerusalem is finally at an end, and repentance is no longer possible. In v. 23 the impossibility of changing human skin color or the leopard's spots is used ironically as an image for the impossibility of a change in "Jerusalem's" behavior. A fate like that of chaff is decided upon for the city "woman" Israel—or the exiled people: They will be scattered by the wind in all directions.

In Jer 13:26, then, the theme of "Jerusalem's" punishment through acts of sexual violence, introduced in v. 22, is taken up again. The impossibility of repentance and the future scattering thus achieves an *inclusio.* In v. 26 YHWH appears explicitly as a perpetrator of sexual violence:

> I myself will lift up your skirts over your face, and your shame will be seen.

[47] Thus Ges[17] 613; HAL 526; Hans-Jürgen Zobel, art. עקב, *'qb, TDOT* 11:315–20.

[48] See above, Chapter 2 F.

[49] See above, Chapter 5 B.

Differently from v. 22 above, now YHWH himself is the one who lifts "Jerusalem's" skirts over her face. The expression is similar to that in v. 22, but here, besides the naming of the one doing the action, the verb גלה is replaced with חשׂף, and a purpose is given for the "uncovering," with the phrase על פניך. Part b of the verse also gives a purpose for the action: "Jerusalem's" shame (קלון) is to be made visible to all. Other prophetic texts also use קלון with sexual connotations;[50] thus in Hos 4:7, 18 with זנה, and also in Nah 3:5; in this verse again very similarly to Jer 13:26. Nahum 3:5, like Jer 13:26, uses ראה as the verb; the shame is "shown." However, differently from Jer 13:26, Nah 3:5 does not have ראה in the *nipʿal,* but in the *hipʿil,* as "let [the nations] look." Nahum 3:5 also mentions, as indirect object, the ממלכות, "kingdoms," to which the "nations" correspond in the *parallelismus membrorum,* and קלון corresponds to "shame" (מרעה). This can be seen as a further indication that in Jer 13:26 קלון also at the very least possesses sexual connotations.

Besides "shame," in this metaphorical text Jerusalem's sin is also made public; it is described in v. 27 in a number of different terms. With נאף and זנה central accusations against the textual "woman" from chs. 2–3 are resumed in a nominal sequence. The abstract plural נאפים, as we have already said, designates the "woman's" adultery as habitual behavior. In this way the impossibility of repentance, which is emphasized elsewhere in the text, is again accentuated. The second term in the series, מצהלה, goes back to the root צהל.[51] "Neighing" can be used of horses, but also of people. The derivative מצהלה otherwise appears only in Jer 8:16, with a connotation of destruction that is echoed in the cry of the war horses. Here in 13:27 מצהלה, like צלה in 5:8, is also meant to have a sexual connotation; it parallels a strong human sex drive with that of horses.

The third part of the first quarter-verse is the construct phrase, unique in the Old Testament, זמת זנות, "shameless prostitutions." There is a strong sexual connotation also in זמה, especially in Priestly contexts. In Lev 18:17; 19:29; 20:14 it is used to characterize "incest" as "depravity." Ezekiel also uses it frequently, primarily in connection with the narrative of YHWH's marriage to the textual "women" Jerusalem, Judah, and Samaria in chs. 16 and 23. In Ezek 16:43, 58, and in a different context in 22:11 it is parallel to the "abomination" term תועבה, and in 23:27, 29, 35, 44 it appears in combination with זנה or its derivatives. In *parallelismus membrorum* to זנה we find זמה also in Ezek 23:27, the closest syntactic parallel (with these two

[50] In Isa 22:18 and Jer 46:12 קלון occurs, but not in this context.

[51] This was analyzed above, in section B.

words together) to the construct phrase in Jer 13:27. Then follows the phrase "on the hills and in the countryside," a reference to the deuteronomic formula about "playing the harlot on every high hill and under every green tree." This again illuminates the cultic context of the "sin" of the city-"woman": It is all about the worship of foreign gods.

The last of the terms describing "Jerusalem's" acts tends in the same direction. שקוץ is also used frequently in contexts shaped by the Priestly tradition; in the singular and as a verb it appears in the purity laws of Leviticus, and in the plural, in Ezekiel, it primarily describes idols. Like זמה, so also שקוץ is often combined with תועבה (Ezek 5:11; 7:20; 11:18, 21), as noted above with regard to זמה. In Ezek 8:10; 20:7, 8 and 37:23 the parallel to שקוצים is גלול, "idol." But as these passages show, שקוצים is not used in Ezekiel in the context of marriage imagery—differently from Jer 13:27. In fact, Jeremiah otherwise uses שקוצים primarily with the meaning "idol(s)" (4:1; 7:30; 16:18; 32:34); in 16:18 it is parallel to תועבה. Hence שקוצים can be regarded as a summary term for what is unclean; it is used together with טמא in 2 Kgs 23:13; Jer 7:30; 32:3; Ezek 5:11; 20:7, 30, often with reference to cultic places defiled by idols or abominations. That this aspect of defilement is also present in שקוצים in Jer 13:27 is made explicit by part b of the verse, which laments the deficient "purification" of Jerusalem, designated by טהר as the counter to טמא. These two words, שקוצים and טהר, appear together otherwise only outside the prophetic marriage imagery in Ezek 37:23, before the "covenant formula": "Then they shall be my people, and I will be their GOD." That neither the "covenant formula"[52] nor an opportunity for repentance is found in Jer 13:27 once again indicates the impossibility, in Jer 13:20-27, that Jerusalem will avoid punishment.[53]

Besides the passages we have examined closely (Jer 3:2; 13:20-27) there are other passages in this book that use metaphors of violence against women: e.g., Jer 2:29-37; 4:30-31; 6:2, 23, 26; 8:19, 22; 15:5-9; 22:20-23; 30:12-17; 31:4, 21; 51:2, 47.[54] Here, however, there is no imagery of sexual violence, since the relevant terms are not mentioned; instead, here it is a matter of feminine imagery in the context of punishment or war against Israel/Judah/Jerusalem.

[52] The "covenant formula" appears in Jeremiah in other places; thus in 7:23; 11:4; 24:7; 30:22; 31:1, 33, 38. According to Rolf Rendtorff (*Die "Bundesformel": Eine exegetisch-theologische Untersuchung* [Stuttgart: Katholisches Bibelwerk, 1995] 35–41) other, expanded formulae are also included there.

[53] It is true that Jer 33:8 presents a "purification" of Jerusalem or Judah by YHWH as a possibility. But this part of the book, in any case, speaks of a "reversal of the situation."

[54] Some of these passages are discussed by Elke Seifert, *Tochter und Vater* 277–81.

Summarizing this section, we may say that in Jeremiah imagery of sexual violence is found primarily in two places: in 3:2 and in 13:20-27. In 3:2 and 13:22 no perpetrators are named, but they are probably meant to be those with whom the textual "woman" (Israel/Judah/Jerusalem) is in a marital or extramarital relationship within the imagery itself. The perpetrators are, so to speak, to be found within the narrowest circle of the family or friends. In 13:26 there seems to be no hesitation in depicting YHWH in imagery in which he displays the traits of a perpetrator of sexual violence.

In Jer 13:20-27 sexual violence appears as divine punishment of the "woman." She has incurred the guilt of "breaking the covenant," which on the basis of the terminology used is to be identified as worship of foreign gods. There is also Priestly terminology present: By doing קָלוֹן and שִׁקּוּצִים the "woman" has become unclean (טהר).[55] To that extent the book of Jeremiah brings together Priestly and deuteronomistic terminology when it is a question of describing the "sin" of YHWH's "wife." This sin consists in the worship of false gods, and it is so "habitualized" in this book that, at least in 13:20-27, it appears that the "woman" has no further opportunity to repent. But if we look at the book as a whole we see that later in Jeremiah, in chs. 30–31, there is the idea of another possibility for restoration; the scene in 13:20-27, then, is not the book's "last word." Still, as far as the possibility of repentance on the part of the "woman/women" is concerned it *is* the final word, for in Jeremiah 30–31 nothing more is said of either of the two "women," so that from this point of view no possibility for repentance is conceded to them.[56] Moreover, the change that happens in chs. 30–31 lies solely in YHWH's hands and is no longer dependent on the willingness of the Israelites to repent.

[55] Helmer Ringgren (art. טהר, *ṭāhar, TDOT* 5:294) emphasizes that ethical (im)purity as well as religio-cultic is intended.

[56] This is not contradicted by the fact that in 31:16-17 a link back to 2:25a is constructed, primarily with formal means, as Konrad Schmid observes (*Buchgestalten des Jeremiabuches. Untersuchungen zur Redaktions- und Rezeptionsgeschichte von Jer 30–33 im Kontext des Buches* [Neukirchen-Vluyn: Neukirchener Verlag, 1996] 136), following William L. Holladay (*Jeremiah 2. A Commentary on the Book of the Prophet Jeremiah, Chapter 26–52* [Philadelphia: Fortress, 1989] 188): "Thus 31:16 reaches far back to the beginning of the book of Jeremiah and gives lamenting Rachel the hearing that, following 2:25, was refused to the person addressed there in the second person singular feminine, as 31:18-22 shows." Jeremiah 30:12-17 and 31:4-5 "take account of the restoration of Jerusalem and Samaria, but not as the capital cities of two kingdoms—which would contradict the concept of a single, whole Israel—but as the restoration of the two most important places whose destruction was symbolic of the collapse of all Israel" (p. 147). Although Schmid discusses the identity of the "woman" in Jeremiah 30–31 in relation to Jeremiah 2–4, in my opinion he does not give enough consideration to the different naming, which is in itself an indication of the discontinuity of the figures.

D. Feminist theological interpretations of Jeremiah's marriage imagery

What we observed with regard to Hosea's use of marriage imagery is also true, in part, of Jeremiah. Here female sexuality is represented in a problematic way: It is altogether negative, because it is projected as adulterous and "whorish," for example in Jer 2:20 or 3:2. Male sexuality, in contrast, is criticized only in individual men (5:7-8), but its real-life character does not become the vehicle of imagery for divine punishment. Since male sexuality is present in YHWH, who uses it as sexual violence, it acquires on the one hand a strongly violent aspect, and on the other a positive connotation: it appears as the good and right kind of sexuality.

It is different with female sexuality: If the textual "woman" Israel lives out her sexuality according to her own will, it is regarded in an exclusively negative light (3:3, 6, etc.). Female sexuality is the sole image for breaking the *berit*. There is no independent female sexuality that is regarded positively in the book of Jeremiah. According to Jeremiah, there is no possibility of positive *action* for Israel unless "she" subjects "her" sexuality to male control, that is, by accommodating to the interwoven divine-male view of a "good" female sexuality.

Mary E. Shields has studied the particular implications of gender roles in the rhetoric of Jer 3:1–4:4.[57] As long as the text is concerned with criticizing the audience (presumably consisting primarily of men), in 3:1-18, it provokes by attributing to its subject-hearers the position of a "whore." But when positive behavior is sketched, those addressed are allowed to perceive themselves in what is in any case a more familiar role for them, as "good sons" of the primeval father (4:1-4).[58] The sole positive female role is that of Israel as inheriting daughter (3:19-21). Circumcision will be the sign of Israel's future *berit*—a sign that is uniquely tied to the male sex, even when, as here, it is transformed into a circumcision of the heart.[59] Shields' feminist critique focuses on two points: First, the imagery and address of many texts exclude any possibility for women to find positive

[57] Shields, "Circumcision of the Prostitute" (see n. 36 above). For further details see Mary E. Shields' dissertation, to be published in Spring 2004 in the JSOT Supplements Series (Sheffield Academic Press): *Circumscribing the Prostitute: The Rhetorics of Intertextuality, Metaphor, and Gender in Jeremiah 3.1–4.4*.

[58] Ibid. 67: "What gives the language of this image its potency, however, is the rhetorical strategy of addressing the male audience with the feminine form of address. Such a strategy asks men both to identify themselves as the promiscuous woman and to resist that identification. As husbands (present, past, or future), the 'natural' identification, and thus the subtle pressure, is to identify with the male voice, the righteous husband—God."

[59] Ibid. 71.

points of identification within them.[60] Second, the feminine roles proposed in the texts tie women to a single model: ". . . with regard to female behavior, this text, by virtue of its imagery, confines women (and myself as a female reader) to two roles—faithful wife/daughter. Any behavior taking women outside these roles identif[ies] them as prostitutes."[61]

Athalya Brenner has introduced another point of criticism against Jeremiah 2–3.[62] Here, differently from Hosea or Ezekiel, female sexuality is equated with that of an animal. The image of Israel's sister Judah, who "'whored' with stone and tree" (Jer 3:9), tends in the same direction.

Another problematic aspect of the depiction of Israel is that the female figure almost never has a word to speak—and when she does, it is only in supposed quotations that establish her compulsive pursuit of the Baals and make it clear that she lacks any sense of guilt (2:23, 25). The text speaks *about* her from an exclusively male perspective; her own voice, her own will, even as regards her "marriage" to YHWH, is not recorded.

Brenner asserts that in the book of Jeremiah, still more than in Hosea, we find an objectification of female sexuality and thus a pornographic depiction of that sexuality in the sense proposed by T. Drorah Setel.[63] Brenner confirms this hard judgment with reference to Jer 2:23-25:

> 23 How can you say, I am not defiled, I have not gone after the Baals? Look at your way in the valley; know what you have done—a restive young camel interlacing her tracks, 24 a wild she-ass at home in the wilderness, in the lust of her "throat" sniffing the wind! Her lust—who can restrain it? None who seek her need weary themselves; in her new moon they will find her.
> 25 Keep your feet from going unshod and your throat from thirst. But you said, It is hopeless, for I love strangers, and after them I will go.**

Brenner sees the objectification of female sexuality in the fact that here the young camel and the wild ass are used to depict personified Jerusalem as pure lust or wantonness. Through this portrayal female sexuality acquires connotations of animality and thus of abnormality.[64] Associations

[60] Ibid. 73: "Yet woman remains to a large extent excluded from subjectivity in this text, both through the shifts to the masculine address when the conditions and promises for repentance are offered, and through the use of the metaphor of circumcision as a symbol of loyalty to YHWH."

[61] Ibid.

[62] Athalya Brenner, "On Prophetic Propaganda" (see n. 2 above) 262–64.

[63] Ibid. Pages 265–66 refer to Setel, "Prophets and Pornography: Female Sexual Imagery in Hosea," in Letty M. Russell, ed., *Feminist Interpretations of the Bible* (Philadelphia: Westminster, 1985) 86–95.

[64] Brenner, "On Prophetic Propaganda," 262–64. Nelly Stienstra, *YHWH is the Husband of His People. Analysis of a Biblical Metaphor with Special Reference to Translation* (Kampen: Pharos, 1993) criticizes Brenner's equation of the "woman" Israel/Jerusalem with the young camel and

with sodomy are evoked, and Lev 20:15-16 forbids sodomy on penalty of death. Another interpretation suggested by the metaphors is that the sexuality of all female creatures is driven not by socially accepted feelings, but by pure physical lust. In contrast to this, male (here divine) sexuality appears as controlled, social, and thus human. In all this, as also in Hosea, the woman, or personification of the woman, cannot speak for herself. In this depiction female sexuality is animalized. Renita Weems has shown the connection of such a portrayal to the punishment scene in Jer 13:20-27. The message is: By the uncontrolled, quasi-animal expression of her sexuality the textual "woman" has made herself an animal; she has degraded herself. Public stripping or rape is then only a logical consequence of the woman's behavior; she deserves her fate.[65] That this connection is no mere fantasy can be established by looking at the commentaries; I cite only one of many possible examples, from Paul Volz's commentary on Jeremiah.[66] The title he gives the section on Jer 13:20-27 is "The whore Jerusalem suffers the fate of a whore." In what follows Volz does not, for example, apply the adjective "horrible" to the description of sexual violence, but instead to the "immorality" of the city-woman Jerusalem portrayed in v. 27. Such attitudes make clear how important it is to confront the texts of the prophetic marriage imagery critically, to investigate the imagery itself, and not to shift too quickly to the level of interpretation.

E. Marriage metaphors in the context of Jeremiah's religious imagery

We will consider the religious imagery in the book of Jeremiah here especially from the aspect of relationships among YHWH, "Israel" (etc.), and the prophet. Are there ties between the different relationships that could yield a broader frame of interpretation for the prophetic marriage imagery?

Female imagery is used throughout the book of Jeremiah. In the first place there are the textual "women" Israel/Judah/Jerusalem, already described in detail in section A. Then there are considerable numbers of passages throughout the book of Jeremiah that have recourse to women and women's lives for their imagery. We may mention, for example, the talk

wild ass (p. 164 n. 143); she sees no connection between the "woman" and the animals. In my opinion this thesis overlooks certain maneuvers in the text: see above, n. 7.

[65] Renita J. Weems, *Battered Love. Marriage, Sex, and Violence in the Hebrew Prophets* (Minneapolis: Fortress, 1995) 58.

[66] Paul Volz, *Der Prophet Jeremiah*. Unaltered reprint of the 2nd Leipzig ed. of 1928 (Hildesheim, et al.: G. Olms, 1983) 157–58.

about the writhing of a woman in labor,[67] which is used especially for the experience of deadly fear or overwhelming pain in a situation of complete helplessness in the hands of another. Angela Bauer points out that this metaphor is used exclusively with negative connotations; neither joy over the birth of a child or the newborn child itself is ever mentioned.[68] The texts about the "daughter my people"[69] and "daughter Zion"[70] are related to the proverbs about foreign peoples naming "daughter Egypt,"[71] "daughter Dibon,"[72] and "daughter Babylon,"[73] as well as the "daughters," that is, the daughter cities, of Rabbah.[74] The "young woman Israel" (בתולת ישׂראל) is called upon in Jer 31:4, 13 to rejoice instead of mourning. But real women also appear in the book of Jeremiah, primarily in connection with hunger, death, and war.[75] They serve as illustrations of the effects of the divine judgment. In addition, in Jeremiah's depiction women are responsible for performing service and worship for the queen of heaven in Jer 7:16-20; 44:15-25. As mourning women and skilled women they play an important role in 9:17-22 [MT 16-21]. In addition there are mother figures, such as the foremother Rachel, who in 31:15 weeps for her children, and Babylon as a mother who is shamed and disgraced (50:12). Human mothers appear, among other places, in 15:8-9; they will lose their children. But Jeremiah's own mother also appears in the "confessions": not only that YHWH saw Jeremiah in his mother's womb before his birth (1:5), in order to take hold of him already then; later Jeremiah himself speaks woe over his mother (15:10) because she bore him, and he curses the day of his birth (20:14-18).

It is very difficult to tease out the most important strands from this close, many-colored weaving of female metaphors in Jeremiah. Angela Bauer has proposed a thesis: She posits as one of these strands that female

[67] In Jer 4:19, 31; 6:24; 22:23; 30:6; 48:41; 49:22, 24; 50:43.

[68] Bauer, "Das Buch Jeremia," 268: "Significantly enough, however, what is absent from the birth metaphor in the book of Jeremiah is the newborn child. Thus the liminal experience of childbearing becomes an image of death, reduced to pain and the threat of death without the joy of new life."

[69] As בת עמי in Jer 4:11; 6:26; 8:11, 19, 21, 22; 9:2, 8 [MT 1, 7]; 14:17.

[70] She is found in Jer 4:31 and 6:2, 23.

[71] In Jer 46:11, 19, 24.

[72] Only in Jer 48:18.

[73] She appears in Jer 50:42 and 51:33.

[74] The last are mentioned in Jer 49:2-3. The intended effect of this rhetorical means is presumably to deprive the powers hostile to Israel of part of their threatening character.

[75] "Human" daughters are mentioned as eaten or to be eaten in Jer 3:24 and 5:17; 19:9; they are burned as sacrifices in 7:31; 32:35; they must learn dirges in 9:20; they starve in 11:22; 14:16; they either are not born at all or they die miserably in 16:2, 4; but they also increase in 29:6; they drink no wine in 35:8; they are led away as prisoners in 41:10; 48:46 (52:1); or they emigrate of their own accord in 43:6.

imagery and the concrete reality of women's lives contribute "to represent the literary-theological developments in the book, developments that extend from a call to repentance in view of the immediate prospect of death and destruction, through recollections in sorrow, to an eschatological vision of salvation in exile. The embodiment of their voices, their ravished bodies (and their occasional dances of joy) function as metonymy for the society as a whole."[76] Can we develop any additional theses regarding the function of female imagery in the book of Jeremiah?

As Bauer has shown, images from the lives of women bear overwhelmingly negative connotations. "The female is identified with judgment and punishment."[77] These negative connotations can be connected to the fate of the prophet. First, a parallel can be drawn between Jeremiah's actions, as described in the confessions, and the textual "woman" (Israel/Judah/Jerusalem). The description of the prophet's suffering precedes everything else: First Jeremiah, because of his prophetic office, suffers violence and pressure from his surroundings. Then follow depictions of the suffering of the textual "woman." After the personal portrayal of the prophet's suffering ends with the confession in 20:17-18, the portrayal of the suffering of the textual "woman" Israel etc. ends as well. After this only the female personifications of foreign powers must still suffer violence and misery.

In addition, a connection can be drawn between the suffering of the prophet and that of the concrete women in the book of Jeremiah. The starting point for this thesis is the observation that the suffering of Israel is depicted with striking frequency in images from the lives of concrete women, images whose focus is very strongly on powerlessness and vulnerability. We may suspect that here there is a connection between the suffering of women and the suffering of the prophet—as a literary fiction as well. The prophet is represented as so powerless and overwhelmed by YHWH that he can best see himself in the role of a woman. In respect to his own helplessness, Jeremiah's social location is similar to the social location of women in ancient Israel as it appears in the book of Jeremiah.[78] The

[76] Bauer, "Das Buch Jeremia," 268.

[77] Ibid. The rejoicing of bride and bridegroom can be adduced as an additional example (Jer 7:34; 16:9; 25:10). It is only mentioned when it must fall silent, as an expression of the people's suffering. Only after the establishment of the new *berit* does YHWH permit it to be uttered again (33:11).

[78] This is also demonstrated by Christl Maier, "Die Klage der Tochter Zion. Ein Beitrag zur Weiblichkeitsmetaphorik im Jeremiabuch," *BThZ* 15 (1998) 189: "The loss of function suffered by the city, which emerges in the laments in Jer 4:19-21 and 10:19-20, leads in the overall development of the book to an exchange of roles. Jeremiah assumes the role of the exemplary lamenter, and in the late text Jer 1:17-19 is even declared to be a fortified city, an iron pillar, and a bronze wall (1:18)."

prophet cannot adequately defend himself and is therefore exposed to violence and attacks—unless someone else takes his part. It appears that there were no social rules for prophets to that end, as there were for women in ancient Israel. In any case, Jeremiah is over long periods exposed to the attacks of his opponents and has no advocate or defender—except for YHWH, whose intervention on Jeremiah's behalf, however, is not evident. Perhaps these parallels between the fate of women and that of the prophet explain why the book of Jeremiah is so filled with descriptions of crisis and helplessness in terms of women's lives: On the one hand the life experiences are similar, and so, on the other hand, are their descriptions.

What Siegfried Hermann describes as the "fateful" or "inescapable" character of the relationship between Jeremiah and YHWH can be understood along these lines.[79] This relationship is reflected in that of YHWH to the textual "women" Israel/Judah/Jerusalem. The prophet and the "women" are chosen by YHWH in their youth (1:5-10/2:2), and both are perceived primarily in relationship to YHWH, a relationship that in both cases is characterized by sharp swings between depths and heights. For both, their ties to YHWH shape their whole lives, their joys and sorrows, and for both their "partner" YHWH is portrayed as dominant. Both, despite a variety of attempts at escape, are unable to end the relationship[80] on their own initiative.

We should consider, however, that the analogy between the relationship of YHWH to Jeremiah and that of YHWH to Israel in many texts also has its limitation: While the literary Jeremiah, especially in the confessions, struggles to obtain an explanation for why he, as a prophet, has to suffer so much, the misery of the "women" is primarily depicted as something they have brought upon themselves. They can avert it by "turning back" to YHWH, through an improvement in their behavior. Certainly this way out is not in view in every text. For example, in 2:23-24 the "whoring" of the "woman" is compared to the lust of a wild ass or a young camel. The image not only implies an animalizing of female sexuality but presents the "sex drive" of the "woman/women" as something given, biological, and unchangeable. The statement in 13:23 is to be understood similarly; there the impossibility of a change in the behavior of the "woman" "Jerusalem" is made clear by a comparison with the impossibility of changing the skin color of an Ethiopian or the pelt of a leopard. Here, then, there are parallels

[79] See Hermann, "Jeremia/Jeremiabuch," 580–81.

[80] The *berit* relationship between Israel and YHWH can be mentioned as a constellation of ties that is equally "inescapable"; on this see above, Chapter 4 C.

to Jeremiah's fate: for him there is also no way out, no possibility of changing his behavior.[81]

There is also a connection, not only in general between female imagery and the fate of the prophet, but especially between what the book of Jeremiah says about the mother and the prophet's relationship to YHWH. Jeremiah pursues a ריב ("legal case") against YHWH, or YHWH with him (12:1), and in spite of this his relationship to God remains intact, if we follow the "confessions," which always end with praise.[82] In contrast, Jeremiah blames his mother for his fate: the prophetic "woe" falls upon her (15:10), and this immediately after the catastrophe breaking over Jerusalem has been illustrated in the fate of the mothers (15:8-9). That mothers share the guilt especially of their sons is shown also by Jer 22:26; 50:12: in the former case Jehoiachin's mother is to share his fate by going into exile, and in the latter instance "mother" Babylon must be ashamed for her children, or her deeds.[83] In 31:15 the ancestral "mother" Rachel weeps for her children, who have perished in war and exile; YHWH can again comfort her only through the promise of restitution and the new *berit*. Mothers, we find, must share the guilt of their children, or they are especially burdened by the fact that they survive their children and thus are surrendered to an uncertain future.

But it is not only the mothers, it is all women who, in the book of Jeremiah, are examples illustrating the punishment of the unfaithful "woman/wife" Israel/Judah/Jerusalem. It is true, as we have already shown above (section B), that it is overwhelmingly the male Israelites whose misdeeds are named in the book of Jeremiah and designated as the reason for YHWH's punishment (e.g., in Jer 5:7-8; 8:8-9; 9:2-7 [MT 1-6]; 18:18-20). But it is women who must do penance for those deeds, or it is female personifications who, for the reasons given, are accused of "whoring." YHWH's punishment for the evil deeds of the men is carried out through both examples: while the textual "women" must suffer sexual violence as punishment, the real women are punished by seeing their children starve,

[81] Angela Bauer develops a feminist-theological counterproposal for the "women" and the female image projected through them. She argues that women should not be laden with a one-sided powerlessness and negativity, as in the book of Jeremiah. Instead, individual experiences of strength must be set in opposition to Jeremiah's perspective, so that positive experiences, resistance strategies, and utopias can be developed (Bauer, "Das Buch Jeremia," 268).

[82] Kathleen M. O'Connor, "Jeremiah," 174.

[83] In Jer 50:11 the misdeeds of the "children" acquire a sexual undertone through the mention of "neighing" (צהל). Above (section B) we have located צהל within the broader context of sexual imagery. In other passages in Jeremiah similar images of sexual misconduct are frequently used as examples standing for the misdeeds of the "children of Israel."

slaughtered so that the adults may survive, or killed in war. All that remain are mourning women and widows, whose fate appears perilous in the extreme. Thus at this point in the book of Jeremiah there is a break in the gendering of the imagery: While the crimes are illustrated through male examples, it is women who furnish the examples to illustrate the destruction of Israel as punishment.[84]

There is much to indicate that while in the book of Jeremiah the sins and failings of the male Israelites are named, at the same time, and in a subtle way, women are regarded as the truly guilty ones: over and over again they are required to furnish the imagery through which YHWH's punishment is seen to fall on them.

The imagery of sexual violence, especially in Jer 13:20-23, must be interpreted in this context. The punishment of the people in the image of a "woman" embedded in this framework is by no means unique—but the image of sexual violence is. Here the divine punishment is carried out in a particularly crass manner. Jeremiah 13:20-27 and 3:2 correspond in that both represent sexual violence as taking place outside a marital relationship—with "lovers" or an "ex-husband." If the image is reversed, then marriage appears to offer a certain protection against sexual violence. In this Jeremiah's marriage imagery differs from that in Hosea; there the scene of sexual violence took place explicitly *within* a marriage.

Overall, the relationship between earthly and human marriage, in the prophetic image, has experienced a transformation from Hosea to its reception in the book of Jeremiah. Nothing is said of Jeremiah's married life except that, in Jer 16:2, YHWH imposes on him a requirement that he be unmarried and childless. Thus the book of Jeremiah lacks the biographical point of contact, the prophet's marriage, that is present in Hosea. Consequently the marriage imagery in Jeremiah is in the process of becoming totally independent. It is used without any connection to real conditions, and therefore it can no longer be explained or excused, as is occasionally attempted with regard to Hosea, by supposing that it reflects "bad experiences" of the prophet in his marriage. Moreover: in Hosea we encounter statements about a woman or female figure that shift between a concrete woman and the textual "woman." In Jeremiah we find primarily the latter, particularly personified Jerusalem (who is partly interchangeable with Israel), and Judah as well. This "isolation" increases the danger that such sweeping statements about "the woman" or "the women" are withdrawn

[84] A. R. Pete Diamond and Kathleen O'Connor have pointed to the explanation of the suffering of the textual "women" by the misdeeds of the male Israelites ("Unfaithful Passions," 309).

from experience and from criticism. Such ideological statements apparently need no longer be verified or falsified with respect to real women. In addition, as prophetic statements they lay claim to high authority. Thus there is the threat that in Jeremiah a negative image of women will be established beyond criticism.

A further difference between Hosea's and Jeremiah's use of marriage imagery lies in the fact that, as we have already briefly indicated above, in Hosea sexual violence appears more clearly as a part of the marital relationship than in Jeremiah. This is true at the level of content: It is not clear whether in Jer 13:20-27 YHWH is still married to the "woman." But it is also true of the arrangement of texts within the book: In Hosea the violent passage in ch. 2 is integrated within the usage of the marriage imagery; in Jeremiah ten chapters intervene between the two. This may be an indication that in the book of Jeremiah marriage and sexual violence are not so closely related as in Hosea and, as we will see in more detail below, in Ezekiel.

Finally, let us look briefly at the major lines in the picture of God in the book of Jeremiah. The image of God and the theology of the book of Jeremiah have a strongly deuteronomistic flavor. Besides this theological focus, the image of God can also be considered from the point of view of how YHWH constructs, adopts, and shapes relationships to his people. Apart from the marriage imagery in the broadest sense, which also includes references to the "love in the wilderness time," imagery of violence is dominant. Jeremiah himself is, according to 20:7, the victim of YHWH's "seduction" (פתה) or "overpowering" (חזק).[85] YHWH brings a lawsuit (ריב) against his people and his prophet;[86] in the sphere and hierarchy of *berit* terminology this means that extreme measures will be taken: YHWH reveals himself as a violent God toward his people. He strikes them, murders and permits murder—until in the "book of consolation" all the destructive and divisive violence is turned into its opposite. The "wife" previously struck by YHWH (30:12-17) will now recover, the marriage will be restored, and the land and the people will be granted peace. Taking the book as a whole, we see that YHWH's attitude takes a sharp swing: It

[85] It seems to me doubtful that Jer 20:7 is about a *sexual* overpowering; contra Bauer, *Gender in the Book of Jeremiah* 114–15. In her translation Jeremiah is "raped" (חזק) by YHWH. That would be a unique translation for חזק. The verb certainly expresses a total overpowering by someone stronger; to that extent the reference here could be to "rape" in a metaphorical sense. But in the context חזק, without further qualification, does not have sexual connotations. Those connotations are only marginally present in פתה.

[86] Moshe Weinfeld, art. ברית, *b^erîṯ*, *TDOT* 2:276, shows that the prophets often expressed warnings about breaking the *berit* in the image of a lawsuit: e.g., Jer 2:4-37.

changes from a harsh, destructive judgment to the gift of undeserved, gracious love, from tearing down to building up, from pulling out to planting.

When this God-image is combined with the female imagery the result is a picture in which the scenes of violence in women's lives and YHWH's sexual violence against his "wife" are not events or attitudes directed only against women. The prophet himself as a (fictional literary) male individual,[87] and the male members of the people as well, taste YHWH's violence. On the other hand, destruction and powerlessness are chiefly illustrated in images drawn from women's lives, and YHWH's "wife" is punished with forms of sexual violence that are, by preference, applied to women. Nor does Jeremiah accuse YHWH for his violent behavior as pitilessly as he accuses his own mother for having borne him and exposed him to all this. We may conclude that the theological interpretation of Israel/Jerusalem's fate—exile—in Jeremiah ends in producing a violent image of God. God turns his violence against his prophet, but primarily against his people. The latter is personified as female and suffers "marital violence," but, beyond this, the sufferings of the Israelites are painted most frequently in images drawn from women's lives.

F. Summary

In the book of Jeremiah we observe an unequal application of male and female imagery. If the traits and behavior attributed to the different sexes are considered, it becomes clear that suffering is expressed in images of women's life experience. On the metaphorical level "guilt" belongs primarily to the "women" Israel/Judah/Jerusalem. When the picture is concrete, it is mainly the misdeeds of men that are named. These metaphors and this choice of imagery can be explained from the context out of which the book emerged: Women were those who, together with their children, were defenselessly handed over to the experiences of war and exile. At the same time mothers and their children were the guarantors of the nation's future. In major parts of the book of Jeremiah, however, that very future for the people is out of sight. To that extent it is not only demonstrable from the concrete context, but also argumentatively plausible, that the people, like Jeremiah, will no longer bring forth children, that births without

[87] The first person in Jeremiah is not always projected as male. Barbara Bakke Kaiser, "Poet as 'Female Impersonator': The Image of Daughter Zion as Speaker in Biblical Poems of Suffering," *JR* 67 (1987) 167, points out that this person occasionally appears as a "female impersonator," that is, takes the role of a woman for the purpose of increasing the tension. "In verses 19-26 and again at the end of verse 31, Jeremiah adopts the persona of a woman in childbirth to impel his audience to experience the intensity of the community's agony."

children are described, and that birth itself remains nothing but an image for terror and helplessness. Within the field of marriage imagery this should be compared to the metaphors of rape: violence is done to defenseless Jerusalem, in the image of the "woman," in a form that deeply damages both her identity and her future life.

However accurate such imagery may have been in its own time and in the framework of the message of the book of Jeremiah, it must be regarded as problematic from today's perspective, because in it not only are gender roles and gender destinies of that time sympathetically portrayed and drawn in detail, but gender roles are tailored and projected beyond that particular time. The matter is especially difficult where YHWH—presumably in retrospect and from a perspective that regards him as the only God—is depicted as the originator of sexual violence against his "wife" in Jeremiah 13. With respect to the attitudes of violence-prone men today, we may find here models for violence against women. Similarly, the metaphors can also furnish models for mechanisms such as transfer of guilt from the perpetrators to the victims ("blaming the victims"). It is possible for perpetrators of sexual violence to use such texts to legitimate their behavior as the proper punishment for a husband to administer in view of any and all failures on the part of his wife. Likewise, these texts can inspire the fiction that a marriage can be restored through the rape of the wife, or that there could be a "healing" of the relationship. The image of God is especially problematic: YHWH himself appears as a God who lives within damaged relationships, and he has forbidden his prophet to marry (16:1-2). If we consider the relationship behind the metaphors in itself, God and his prophet are two men who, in their imagined actions or fantasies, exercise excessive forms of violence primarily against women—two men who live without women, without a relationship, self-sufficient and alone. This is an imagery that makes it possible to survive the deep crisis of a society heavily burdened by war and deportation, but that in today's world can create new problems.

Chapter Eight

Ezekiel: Climax of the Marriage Imagery

A. Survey of marriage imagery in Ezekiel

Ezekiel also uses the prophetic marriage imagery to illustrate the relationship between YHWH and his people or his city. In a book composed during the period of the exile and probably redacted later, the voice of the prophet Ezekiel primarily projects speeches of YHWH and the prophet's visions. The language is Priestly, but integrates deuteronomic and deuteronomistic *theologoumena*. The different patterns of thinking are not placed haphazardly alongside one another, but are woven together into a homogeneous whole.

Differently from Hosea and Jeremiah, the book of Ezekiel does not begin with the prophetic marriage imagery. The word-field of the marriage imagery occurs extensively in Ezekiel 16 and 23, thus in the first part of the book (chs. 1–32), but in the center of the whole. The context in which these marriage metaphors occurs, as in Hosea and Jeremiah, is always one of judgment, but what is different in Ezekiel is that these pronouncements of judgment are found within closed narratives. In Ezekiel 16; 23 we find a much-expanded form of the Old Testament marriage imagery. Measured by the length of the texts, their consistency, their detail, and the richness of the metaphoric imagery, these chapters are unique within the Old Testament.[1]

In Ezekiel it is absolutely clear who is meant by YHWH's "wife." In Ezekiel 16 it is Jerusalem; terms from the marriage imagery are especially thick in vv. 8-43:

[1] Julie Galambush describes the criteria for the uniqueness of Ezekiel's marriage imagery (*Jerusalem in the Book of Ezekiel. The City as Yahweh's Wife* [Atlanta: Scholars, 1992] 78–88). She points especially to the style (length, coherence, detail), content (actions of the metaphoric "women" and their historical references), and placement in the book (in the center rather than at the beginning).

8 And I [YHWH] passed by you and looked on you, and see, your time, the time of love (had come). I spread the edge of my cloak over you, and covered your shame: I pledged myself to you and entered into a "covenant" with you, says the Lord YHWH. You became mine. 9 I bathed you with water and washed off the blood from you, and anointed you with oil. 10 I clothed you with embroidered cloth and with shoes of *tashash* (-leather); I bound you in fine linen and covered you with silk. 11 I adorned you with ornaments and gave you bracelets for your arms, a chain for your neck, 12 a ring for your nose, earrings for your ears, and a magnificent crown upon your head. 13 And you adorned yourself with gold and silver, while your clothing was of fine linen, silk, and embroidered cloth. You had choice flour and honey and oil for food. You grew exceedingly beautiful, fit to be a queen. 14 And your fame spread among the nations on account of your beauty, for it was perfect because of my splendor that I had bestowed on you, says the Lord YHWH.

15 And you trusted in your beauty, and played the whore because of your fame, and lavished your whorings on any and all who passed by. 16 And you took some of your garments, and made for yourself colorful shrines, and on them played the whore. [Not through the sign, and it does not happen.][2] 17 You also took your splendid jewels of gold and silver that I had given you, and made for yourself male images, and with them played the whore; 18 and you took your embroidered garments to cover them, and set my oil and my incense before them. 19 Also my bread that I gave you—I fed you with choice flour and oil and honey—you set it before them as a pleasing odor; and so it was, says the Lord YHWH. 20 And you took your sons and your daughters, whom you had borne to me, and these you sacrificed to them to be devoured. Were your whorings not enough? 21 And you slaughtered my children and gave them to them and let them pass by them.[3] 22 And (in) all your abominations and your whorings you did not remember the days of your youth, when you were naked and bare, flailing about in your blood.

23 And after all your wickedness—woe, woe to you! says the Lord YHWH—24 you built yourself a platform[4] and made yourself a lofty place

[2] This verse section is hard to understand. Walther Zimmerli (*Ezechiel 1–24* [Neukirchen-Vluyn: Neukirchener Verlag, 1969] 336) writes on this passage: "Thus far it has not been possible to give a satisfying explanation . . . of this textual element."

[3] It is rather improbable that behind this passage (and similar ones like Ezek 23:37) stand religious practices of child sacrifice. H. F. Fuhs (art. עָבַר, *ʿāḇar, TDOT* 10:408–25) points out that in Deut 18:10 עבר is found in the context of magical practices; in Ezekiel this can well be a metaphorical usage or a circumlocution for consecration of children to other deities.

[4] For attempts to explain the difficult גב see Christl Maier, "Jerusalem als Ehebrecherin in Ezechiel 16. Zur Verwendung und Funktion einer biblischen Metapher," in Hedwig Jahnow et al., *Feministische Hermeneutik und Erstes Testament. Analysen und Interpretationen* (Stuttgart et al.: Kohlhammer, 1994), 92–93: "As a concrete background to גב Otto Eißfeldt had already pointed in 1936 to lead plates found in Assyria in the rooms of two palace complexes, stemming from the

in every broad square; 25 at every turn in every road you built your lofty place and made an abominable thing of your beauty, spreading your legs to all those who pass by, and multiplying your whoring. 26 You played the whore with the sons of Egypt, your neighbors with the big penis, multiplying your whoring, to provoke me to anger. 27 And see, I have stretched out my hand against you, reduced your rations, and given you up to those who seize you: the daughters of the Philistines, who were ashamed of your lewd behavior. 28 You played the whore with the sons of Assyria, because you were insatiable; you played the whore with them, and still you were not satisfied. 29 And you multiplied your whoring into the land of merchants, Chaldea; and even with this you were not satisfied.

30 How was your heart so dried up, says the Lord YHWH, that you did all these things, the deeds of a powerful, sluttish woman? 31 You built your platform at every bend in every street, and you made your lofty place in every broad square! Yet you were not like a whore, because you scorned payment. 32 The adulterous wife takes in strangers instead of her husband. 33 Gifts are given to all whores; but you gave your gift to all your lovers, bribing them to come to you from all around for your whorings. 34 So you were different from other women in your whorings: no one solicited you to play the whore; and you gave payment, while no payment was given to you; you were different. 35 Therefore, O whore, hear the word of YHWH!

36 Thus says the Lord YHWH: Because your ore was poured out[5] and you uncovered your shame in your whoring with your lovers and with all the idols of your abomination, and because of the blood of your children that you gave to them, 37 therefore, see, all your lovers, to whom you were so pleasing, are gathered, and all those who loved you and all those who hated you; I will gather them against you from all around, and will uncover your shame to them. And they see your total shaming.[6] 38 And I will judge you as women who commit adultery and shed blood are judged, and hand you over to blood vengeance, wrath, and jealousy. 39 And I will deliver you into

middle of the 13th century B.C.E. They show a naked woman sitting with spread legs on a low platform built of bricks, with a man standing before her and performing sexual intercourse with her. . . . In my opinion the linking of an image without inscription and a biblical text is problematic, especially since the latter is at least 700 years later. That Eißfeldt's interpretation has been adopted in newer studies, usually without commentary, shows how little attention has heretofore been paid to the imagery in this chapter, and how quickly conclusions are drawn from what is said to what is 'meant.' The metaphors, in fact, conceal the concrete meaning of the structures, and permit only echoes of cultic activity." In Ezekiel the word appears otherwise (though probably with a different meaning) in the context of the chariots (1:18; 10:12) and in the Temple vision as a part of the altar (43:13).

[5] Walther Zimmerli (*Ezechiel 1–24*, 339) writes regarding the difficult expression הִשָּׁפֵךְ + נחשׁת: "No matter how uncertain the exact etymological explanation [especially of הִשָּׁפֵךְ], there can scarcely be any doubt that this represents a parallel to the subsequent ערותך."

[6] On this see below, section C.

their hands, and they shall throw down your platform and break down your
lofty places; they shall strip you of your clothes and take your beautiful objects and leave you lying there, naked and bare. 40 And they shall bring up
a mob against you, and they shall stone you and cut you to pieces with their
swords. 41 And they shall burn your houses with fire and execute judgments
on you in the sight of many women; and I will stop you from playing the
whore, and you shall also make no more payments. 42 And I will satisfy my
fury on you, until my jealousy shall turn away from you; I will be calm, and
will be angry no longer. 43 Because you have not remembered the days of
your youth, but have enraged me with all these things; therefore, I have
turned your ways back upon you, says the Lord YHWH, and you will no
longer commit lewdness and all your abominations.**

Beginning with v. 44 the attention shifts to Jerusalem's sisters, Samaria and Sodom, who are addressed later, in ch. 23. Only in Ezekiel is Sodom counted among the sisters. Probably Ezek 16:44-63 should be regarded as a redactional addition.[7] No terms from the marriage imagery are used in that part of the text.

Julie Galambush has described the chiastic structure of Ezek 16:1-43.[8] The external frame is made up of vv. 1-5 (A) and 35-43 (A'), with aspects of imminent death, nakedness, blood, and rejection. A second frame is constituted by vv. 6-8 (B), with YHWH passing by, and vv. 23-34 (B'), with strangers passing by. Jerusalem enters into a relationship with both of them. The innermost pair is made up of vv. 9-14 (C) and vv. 15-22 (C'). YHWH as the one passing by in vv. 9-14 washes Jerusalem clean of blood and clothes her as a sanctuary, while the strange gods in vv. 15-22 are provided with clothing and food by Jerusalem; Jerusalem even sacrifices her children for them. In this way sanctuary aspects take the central place in the text (C/C'). Alongside this stands the wounding of the marital relationship (B/B'), while in the outermost frame Jerusalem's beginning and end are foregrounded in alternating correspondences (A/A'): "bloody, naked, rejected, and dead or dying."[9]

[7] On this see Christl Maier, "Jerusalem als Ehebrecherin," 89: "The dissolution of the discourse form on the one hand, as well as the intensification of the content in comparison to the very similar Ezekiel 23 on the other, both indicate that Ezek 16:44-58 represents a later word on the same theme."

[8] Galambush, *Jerusalem in the Book of Ezekiel* 100–101.

[9] Ibid. 101. It is interesting that the whole of ch. 16 can be structured as a chiasm on the level of the final text. M. G. Swanepol does this, and this yields another focus: YHWH's steadfast love frames the chapter (vv. 3-14/59-63); further within, Jerusalem's sins are named (vv. 15-34/44-58), and YHWH's judgment stands at the center (vv. 35-43) (M. G. Swanepol, "Ezekiel 16: Abandoned Child, Bride Adorned or Unfaithful Wife?" in Philip R. Davies and David J. A. Clines,

In many places Ezekiel 23 seems to represent a double tradition of Ezekiel 16. The images are similar, and there are overlaps even in terminology. But there is a difference in the way the two chapters each place their individual focus. Ezekiel 16 tells the story of Jerusalem as a girl who can only survive after her birth thanks to YHWH's care and concern, but who later, having been taken "to wife" by YHWH, proves very ungrateful to him, showing her ingratitude by turning to other men. Ezekiel 16 consistently speaks *to* the "woman" Jerusalem. In Ezekiel 23 that is the case only in vv. 21-35; the rest of the chapter speaks in the third person *about* the "woman" or "women." Here, perhaps as a continuation of Ezek 16:44-52,[10] the story of two sisters is told; it begins when they are in early adulthood:

> 1 And the word of YHWH came to me: 2 Mortal, there were two women, the daughters of one mother. 3 And they played the whore in Egypt; they played the whore from their youth. Their breasts were rubbed there, and their young bosoms were squeezed. 4 And their names were: Oholah, the elder, and Oholibah, her sister. And they became mine, and they bore sons and daughters. And their names were Samaria-Oholah and Jerusalem-Oholibah.
>
> 5 And under me Oholah played the whore, and she lusted after her lovers, the Assyrians, who were drawing near, 6 purple-clad governors and prefects,[11] all of them desirable young men, mounted horsemen. 7 She bestowed her whorishness upon them, the choicest sons of Assyria, all of them. And with all those after whom she lusted, with all their idols she defiled herself. 8 She did not give up her whorings that she had practiced since Egypt; for in her youth they had lain with her and squeezed her young bosom and poured out their whorishness upon her. 9 Therefore I delivered her into the hands of her lovers, into the hands of the sons of Assyria, for whom she lusted. 10 They uncovered her shame; they seized her sons and her daughters; and they killed her with the sword. And the news (of it) came to the women, and judgment was executed upon her.
>
> 11 And her sister Oholibah saw this, yet she was more corrupt than the other in her lusting and in her whorings, which were worse than those of her sister. 12 She lusted after the sons of Assyria, governors and prefects, who drew near her, clothed in full armor, mounted horsemen, all of them desirable young men. 13 And I saw that she defiled herself; they both took (one

---

eds., *Among the Prophets: Language, Image, and Structure in the Prophetic Writings* [Sheffield: JSOT Press, 1993] 93). Here we can observe how through the redaction—and through the perspective of the exegetes—YHWH is shifted more strongly to the center of the text.

[10] Whether this really does follow on Ezek 16:44-52 is questionable, for reasons of redactional chronology (cf. Thomas Krüger, *Geschichtskonzepte im Ezechielbuch* [Berlin and New York: Walter de Gruyter, 1989] 523).

[11] This is Krüger's rendition (ibid. 185).

and) the same way. 14 But she carried her whorings further; she saw male
figures carved on the wall, images of the Chaldeans portrayed in vermilion,
15 with belts around their waists, with flowing turbans on their heads, all of
them looking like heroes—a picture of the sons of Babylon (and) Chaldea,
the land of their birth. 16 And when she saw them she lusted after them, and
sent messengers to them in Chaldea. 17 And the sons of Babylon came to
her, to enter the bed of love, and they defiled her with their whorishness; and
she defiled herself with them. And she turned from them. 18 And she carried on her whorings openly, and uncovered her shame, and I turned away
from her, as I had turned from her sister. 19 And she increased her whorings, remembering the days of her youth, when she played the whore in the
land of Egypt. 20 And she lusted after her "paramours,"[12] whose penises
were like those of donkeys, and whose emission was like that of stallions.

21 And you longed for the lewdness of your youth, when the Egyptians
squeezed your bosom "and"[13] the breasts of your youth. 22 Therefore, O
Oholibah, thus says the Lord YHWH: See, I will rouse against you your
lovers from whom you turned away, and I will bring them against you from
every side. 23 The sons of Babylon and all the Chaldeans, Pekod and Shoa
and Koa, and all the sons of Assyria with them, desirable young men, gov-
ernors and prefects all of them, heroes, famous men, all of them riding on
horses. 24 They shall come against you, a crowd of chariots and wagons
[and] with a host of peoples; they shall set themselves against you on every
side with buckler, shield, and helmet, and I will commit the judgment to
them, and they shall judge you according to their ordinances. 25 And I will
direct my indignation against you, and they will deal with you in fury. They
cut off your nose and your ears, and whatever is left of you shall fall by the
sword. They seize your sons and your daughters, and whatever is left of you
shall be devoured by fire. 26 They shall also strip you of your clothes and
take away your fine jewels. 27 And I will put an end to your lewdness [from
you] and your whoring brought from the land of Egypt. And you shall no
longer lift up your eyes to them, or remember Egypt any more.

28 For thus says the Lord YHWH: I will deliver you into the hands of those
who hate [you], into the hands of those from whom you turned away; 29 and
they shall deal with you in hatred, and take away all your possessions, and
leave you naked and bare. And your whorish shame shall be exposed, and your
lewdness and your whorings. 30 This has happened because of your whoring
after the nations, with whom you polluted yourself with their idols. 31 You
have gone the way of your sister; therefore I will give her cup into your hand.

32 Thus says the Lord YHWH: You shall drink your sister's cup, deep and
wide—you shall be scorned and derided—[a cup that] holds so much. 33 You

[12] The translation is uncertain, since otherwise פלגש only appears in the OT as a word for "concubines."

[13] למען is unclear at this point.

are filled with drunkenness and sorrow: a cup of horror and desolation is the
cup of your sister Samaria. 34 You shall drink it and drain it out, and gnaw its
shards, and tear out your breasts; for I have spoken, says the Lord YHWH.
35 Therefore thus says the Lord YHWH: Because you have forgotten me and
cast me behind your back, [therefore] bear your lewdness and your whorings.

36 And YHWH said to me: Mortal, will you judge Oholah and Oholibah?
Then declare to them their abominable deeds! 37 For they have committed
adultery, and blood is on their hands; [with] their idols they have committed
adultery; and they have even carried before them for food the children whom
they had borne to me.[14] 38 More than this they have done to me: they have
defiled my sanctuary on the same day and profaned my sabbaths. 39 And
when they had slaughtered their children for their idols, on the same day they
came into my sanctuary to profane it, and behold: This they did in the midst
of my house. 40 And still more: they sent for men to come from far away, to
whom a messenger was sent, and they came. And for them you bathed [your-
self], painted your eyes, and decked yourself with ornaments; 41 and you sat
on a stately couch, with a table spread before you on which you had placed
my incense and my oil. 42 And the sound of a sated multitude was around
her, for the crowd, many men, were brought in drunken from the wilderness.
And they put bracelets on her arms, and a beautiful crown upon her head.
43 Then I said: Adulteries for the ragged. Now they are whoring her whorishness.[15] 44 And they have gone to her as one goes to a whore. Thus they
went in to Oholah and to Oholibah, wanton women. 45 But righteous men
shall judge you by the law for adulteresses and women who shed blood, for
they are adulteresses and blood is on their hands. 46 For thus says the Lord
YHWH: Bring up an assembly against them, to mistreat and plunder them.
47 And the assembly shall stone them and with their swords they shall cut
them down; they shall kill their sons and their daughters, and burn up their
houses with fire. 48 And will I put an end to lewdness in the land, so that all
women may take warning and not commit lewdness as you have done.
49 And they shall repay you for your lewdness, and you shall bear the sins
of your idols; and you shall know that I am the Lord YHWH!**

The two sisters, Samaria and Jerusalem, daughters of one of the mothers who reject men (16:45), have yearned from their youth for intimate contact with many men. Among these men, however—in a special feature of Ezekiel's tailoring of the marriage imagery—we are to imagine not only other deities, but also foreign powers, which are named, and which function as lovers for Jerusalem and/or Samaria.[16] These include both the

[14] See n. 3 above.

[15] The text of this verse is difficult to understand.

[16] Here let me refer to an interesting observation by Thomas Krüger (*Geschichtskonzepte im Ezechielbuch* 186–87) with regard to certain words in Ezek 16:11. תחש, שש, and רקם also appear

allied power, Egypt, and the oppressor, Assyria, as well as Chaldea, i.e., Babylon. Characteristic of Ezekiel is an aspect of this depiction that was already present, in a somewhat different form, in Hosea and Jeremiah in the context of the marriage imagery: Reference is made to history, to the imaginary biographical background of the "woman," to establish a foundation for her determination to "play the whore."[17] This applies, on the one hand, to concrete historical references—differently, however, than in Hosea and Jeremiah. While those two make only passing reference to the wilderness time, Ezekiel introduces a great many "facts" and "persons"; these, however, do not yield any picture that can be equated in all its elements with the historical texts of the Old Testament. To that extent the text remains somewhat open in its references and cannot be reduced to a paraphrase of history. On the other hand, this biography in Ezekiel is also applied to a metaphorical level, again differently from Hosea and Jeremiah. In the latter two the wilderness period appears as an ideal honeymoon, while Ezekiel integrates this historical connection more strongly with the metaphor of the "woman" and builds it up to form a family history. "Her" parental origins (ch. 16) and the experiences of "her" youth (ch. 23) have already laid the foundations for what will later be manifested in "her" falling away from YHWH.[18]

As Thomas Krüger has shown, the two metaphorical "women," Oholah-Samaria and Oholibah-Jerusalem, are used to exemplify historical concepts. Besides Ezek 16:1-43 and 23:1-30, of great significance for these concepts are Ezek 5:1-17 and Ezekiel 20. Here let me summarize Krüger's

---

in Priestly language with reference to the construction of the sacred tent; according to Krüger we should ask whether this was already present in the tradition available to Ezekiel and intentionally alluded to here: "Then the juxtaposition of Jerusalem's 'history of origins' and 'history of sin' in Ezek 16:1-43 could possibly be based on the confrontation between two models of 'Jerusalem': Jerusalem as Temple city vs. Jerusalem as royal city! The text would then be located within the discussion—which, *mutatis mutandis,* is already evident in the book of Hosea—about the function and significance of Jerusalem as capital city for Israel as a nation. In the negative judgment on the monarchy as a falling away from a 'theocratic' (not 'hierocratic'!) Temple-oriented model of Jerusalem, this would agree with the 'constitutional project' of the [book of Ezekiel]." This could offer an explanation for the fact that only in the book of Ezekiel do the "lovers" connote foreign powers.

[17] So also Maier, "Jerusalem als Ehebrecherin," 89, and Elke Seifert, *Tochter und Vater im Alten Testament. Eine ideologiekritische Untersuchung zur Verfügungsgewalt von Vätern über ihre Töchter* (Neukirchen-Vluyn: Neukirchener Verlag, 1997) 259.

[18] It may well be that a relationship between YHWH and Jerusalem is already doomed to failure at a still more fundamental level: Galambush shows that the "women," through reference to the "blood" of the child in Ezekiel 16 and to premarital sexual contact in Ezekiel 23, are characterized as unclean from the very start, which makes impossible any joining with YHWH, the Holy One (Galambush, *Jerusalem in the Book of Ezekiel* 111, n. 57).

most important results, insofar as they relate to the prophetic marriage imagery in Ezekiel 16 and 23.[19]

Ezekiel 16 and 23 develop a historical conception with three basic features. These chapters present a sketch that "describes, or rather announces the restoration of the relationship between YHWH and Jerusalem, Jerusalem's culpable resistance, and the removal of the resistance through the exercise of divine judgment."[20] This concept is described within the scheme of cause and effect, a frame defined by rights and decrees. The proof of guilt, the judgment, and its application are all named. The guilt consists in joining with foreign great powers (Egypt, Assyria, Babylon/Chaldea), worshiping their gods (גלולים), and the loss or sacrifice of sons and daughters.[21] Jerusalem can never make satisfaction for such a great sin. Because YHWH's tie to Jerusalem in Ezekiel 16 and 23 is not represented as mythical-indissoluble, but rather, in the image of the orphan child and the marriage, as in principle limited in time and subject to abrogation, the dissolution of the tie by YHWH after Jerusalem's enormous misdeeds is the logical consequence of her behavior.

In Ezekiel 23 Jerusalem's guilt is intensified in comparison to ch. 16. Again and again it is emphasized that she has learned nothing from the bad example of her "sister."[22] In addition, the text points out how ignorantly Jerusalem has behaved in the face of YHWH's attempts to "avoid legal action."[23] We should add that what is at stake in 16:33, 34, 41 is not Jerusalem's guilt, but rather the absurdity of her behavior in paying the "whore's wages" (אתנן) to her lovers.

In Ezekiel the fate of Jerusalem differs from that of Israel-Samaria. This is particularly in focus in Ezekiel 20. While at the end of ch. 20 the restoration of the "house of Israel" after the judgment is announced, Ezek 23:5-10 opens no such perspective any longer. Of course, the historical experience of the Northern Kingdom speaks in favor of the depiction in Ezekiel 20: even after 722 and the collapse of Israel, the complete end of the land and its inhabitants had not yet come.

Here, going beyond Krüger's work, we should introduce some further characteristics of the prophetic marriage imagery in Ezekiel. In ch. 20, just discussed, and in ch. 22 we find, framed by the chapters containing the

[19] Krüger, *Geschichtskonzepte im Ezechielbuch,* especially 139–95.

[20] Ibid. 163.

[21] Ibid. 177–78.

[22] This topos is found in Ezek 23:5-10, 13, 18b, but also in Jer 3:6-13, although the relationship of these two texts is not entirely clear; cf. ibid. 156, with the notes there.

[23] Ibid. 155, 163.

marriage imagery, some elements of content that resemble those in Ezekiel 16; 23. But unlike those chapters, in Ezekiel 20; 22 the same accusations are made without picturing Samaria or Jerusalem as metaphorical "women." Here, for the most part, the Israelites are addressed directly and without imagery. We can see a similar juxtaposition of metaphorical and non-metaphorical discourse on the sins of Israel/Jerusalem in Jeremiah as well.[24] But only in Ezekiel are the reproaches directed at the "women" qualified by words with the root טמא. Elsewhere in the prophetic marriage imagery the immediate consequence of "harlotry" or "whoring" is not described as "defilement."

To summarize what we have said thus far, the special tailoring of the marriage imagery in Ezekiel enables it to fulfill a series of functions that are not expressed in this way in Hosea and Jeremiah. First, YHWH's relationship to Israel and Jerusalem can appear, against Ezekiel's exilic background, as something contingent and subject to dissolution.[25] Unique to Ezekiel, in contrast to the version of the prophetic marriage imagery in Hosea and Jeremiah, is that here Jerusalem and Samaria have already had premarital sexual contacts. This formulation of the imagery causes them to appear as "polluted," so that from the very beginning a relationship between them and YHWH is laden with serious difficulties.[26] That the "lovers" are now the major powers and not only deities adds a political dimension to the religio-cultic one. This expansion of the imagery could already be observed in Jeremiah. In addition, the "lovers" can be seen as both attractive and dangerous, something that could also be said of treaties with the major powers. The frame of the imagery is being expanded: parents, the two sisters, and children take us far beyond the marriage imagery and present the panorama of a family. In this way, on the one hand, a greater affinity with experience and the real world is achieved, as Krüger observes.[27] On the other hand, this move also makes it possible to describe the misbehavior of the "woman/women" in a greater variety of ways.

However, we should also point to the "flip side" of this detailed development and expansion of the imagery in Ezekiel. In many places the im-

[24] See above, Chapter 7 C.

[25] Thus Krüger, *Geschichtskonzepte im Ezechielbuch* 163, and frequently.

[26] Thus Galambush, *Jerusalem in the Book of Ezekiel* 111, n. 57: "Though the claim of primal infidelity is inconsistent with the story in chap 16 of Jerusalem's foundling youth, it is entirely consistent with the implication of the story of chap 16 that Jerusalem was bad from the start. The charge that Israel was disobedient from the beginning is also made in the recitation of the exodus story in Ezekiel 20, in which Israel is said to have refused to 'abandon the idols of Egypt'; that is, Israel's disobedience antedates even the exodus."

[27] Krüger, *Geschichtskonzepte im Ezechielbuch* 198.

agery is so strongly influenced by its historical background that sometimes it is hard to understand *as imagery*. This is the case, for example, with the differences in historical origin of Jerusalem and Israel: Jerusalem as a young woman in Egypt does not correspond to the other descriptions of the history of YHWH with that city in the Old Testament: "The metaphoric context of the texts is completely exploded in the concrete proclamations of punishment,"[28] as we will see in more detail below. Galambush points out the same thing.[29] More important for her, however, is presenting the problem of the female metaphor "woman" (in her terminology, as "vehicle") for Jerusalem/Samaria (as "tenor") in the form it takes in Ezekiel:

> Given Ezekiel's sensitivity to the symbolic connection between the womb of Yahweh's wife and the inner sanctum of Yahweh's temple, his graphic depiction of a Jerusalem polluted from within by unclean blood has disastrous implications. At the level of the vehicle, Yahweh's wife is unclean in both her behavior (adultery) and her substance. Intercourse, the penetration of her unclean body, would be an abomination, even if performed by a (merely) clean male; such contact between the Holy One and a bloody woman would be unthinkable. At the level of the tenor, the implications are equally severe. If the sanctuary has become the locus of unclean blood, it is impossible for the Holy to remain within it.[30]

This is an appropriate observation as regards the position and tendency of the marriage imagery in Ezekiel: Differently than in Hosea and Jeremiah, the concern in Ezekiel is not to bring a people to repentance; its destruction is already determined and carried out. That destruction must be understood as a justified condemnation on Jerusalem, and for that purpose Ezekiel has fundamentally reshaped the existing imagery.[31]

Another feature of the reformulation of the imagery is the rupture at the end, when suddenly, at the end of the chapter, statements are directed to concrete, real women. We will return to that subject at the end of this chapter.

[28] Ibid. 179–80, with examples; see further below, section C.

[29] Galambush, *Jerusalem in the Book of Ezekiel* 114.

[30] Ibid. 104, in the context of the study of Ezekiel 16.

[31] On this see Galambush (ibid. 86–87): "The earlier prophets use the figure of the unfaithful woman to set the stage for their prophecy; appearing at the beginning of Hosea and Jeremiah, the metaphor provides an effective introduction to the themes of the people's depravity and of Yahweh's desire for their repentance. In Ezekiel's case, the metaphor is employed only after the time for pleading has passed. . . . Rather than urging her repentance, Ezekiel recounts Jerusalem's abominations in order to pronounce her sentence."

B. The use of marriage terms in Ezekiel

Like the prophetic books we have already examined, the book of Ezekiel has its own foci in its use of the marriage imagery. These are evident in the choice and frequency of the terms.

Of all the books in the Old Testament, Ezekiel has the most examples of words from the root זנה, primarily in chs. 16 and 23. Outside those two chapters, only 6:9 uses the verb, and 43:7, 9 the abstract זנות, in connection with the worship of foreign gods. A further special feature is the construction תזנות: All nineteen Old Testament instances of this word for "whoredom" are in Ezekiel, and exclusively in chs. 16 and 23. The word is constructed with the preformative ת- and has the same meaning as the other form of the abstract plural of זנה, זנות.[32]

In Ezekiel, זנה is found primarily in two contexts: On the one hand it refers to the worship of foreign gods, but on the other hand—and this is unique in the Old Testament—it can refer to making treaties with foreign powers. A close relationship with other, more powerful nations made it probable that their gods would also be worshiped in the land of Israel. To that extent the two connotations of זנה in Ezekiel are not strictly separable. The uniqueness lies precisely in the connection: The "women" do not choose their "lovers" for cultic-religious motives, as in Hosea and Jeremiah; they primarily enter into political alliances.

Jerusalem's (or Oholibah's) "partners" are the Egyptians (16:26; 23:3, 19, 21, 27) and the Assyrians (16:28; 23:12), but Jerusalem's desire also extends to Babylonians (16:29; 23:14-17). Egypt (23:3, 8) and Assyria (23:5, 7, 9) are also mentioned as lovers of Oholah (or Samaria). These, too, are the powers who partially carry out the sentence pronounced on the "woman."[33]

Besides the "lovers" in the Ezekiel texts using the prophetic marriage imagery there are other figures with whom the "woman" "pollutes" herself.[34] The terms used have religious connotations. Two words for foreign gods that are used most frequently by Ezekiel, of all the Old Testament books, are used in some places to designate the deities of Jerusalem's or Samaria's other "men." גלול is a contemptuous word[35] for "idols." It appears primarily in Ezekiel, and only here is it used within the context of the prophetic marriage imagery. In most passages in Ezekiel it refers to the

[32] On this cf. GK §85r.

[33] For more on this see below, section C.

[34] For the context of pollution see the following pages in this section.

[35] Krüger, *Geschichtskonzepte im Ezechielbuch* 178, translates it as "pieces of shit."

"idols" worshiped by concrete Israelites instead of YHWH. In 23:7, 30 it stands for the gods worshiped by the "lovers," whom Jerusalem/Samaria also adore as a consequence of their extramarital relationship. In 23:37 this is intensified still more: Now the גלולים are in fact those with whom Samaria and Jerusalem have committed adultery (נאף). This could mean that in this passage the distinction between the foreign powers as "lovers" and the gods has been abandoned. However, the verse could also be interpreted to mean that the term נאף is reserved for the behavior of the "women" with *gods*.[36]

Parallel to גלול as an expression for foreign gods, Ezekiel also uses שקוץ. The two words, גלול and שקוץ, appear together in Ezek 20:7, 8; 37:23. The contemptuous term שקוץ, which translates to something like "what is abominable," is not used by Ezekiel in the context of the prophetic marriage imagery.[37] However, it does appear in this context in Jer 13:27.[38] The word is found in the same context in Nah 3:6, but there it must mean something other than "idols," since personified Nineveh is threatened with being *pelted* with שקוצים.

In Ezekiel there is an additional term, תועבה ("abomination, abhorrence") that is often found with גלול as well as שקוץ. Only in Ezekiel does תועבה appear in the context of the prophetic marriage imagery. About a third of the Old Testament instances of תועבה are found in Ezekiel, and a fourth of those in ch. 16 alone. It offers a summary evaluation of the falling away of the Israelites from YHWH as "abomination," usually in the plural.[39] In the context of the prophetic marriage imagery this "abomination" is always tied, through suffixes, to the "women." Besides 2 Kings 21:22, תועבה is found with גלול in Ezek 6:9; 14:6; 18:12, and in a construct phrase with גלול in 16:36. Besides 2 Kings 23:13 and Jer 16:18, תועבה is combined with שקוץ in Ezek 5:11; 7:20; 11:18, 21. This indicates a certain affinity of the three words or ideas, with the combination of גלול or שקוץ with תועבה especially frequent, within the Old Testament, in Ezekiel. Through the choice of three different terms at once Ezekiel underscores his extremely negative evaluation of the Israelites' worship of strange

[36] See further on this subject at the end of this section.

[37] In Jer 4:1 YHWH demands that (grammatically masculine!) Israel remove the שקוצים from before his face and return to him.

[38] This is similar to the usage in Hos 9:10, where the lovers of the concrete Israelites are called שקוצים.

[39] It is precisely the plural that can "designate Israel's, or individual Israelites' sinful falling away . . . from YHWH as such, or refer in summary to individual sins previously mentioned under the heading of 'abomination'" (Horst-Dietrich Preuss, art. תועבה, *toʿēḇāh, ThWAT* 8:580–92).

gods. At the same time this gives foundation, on the religio-cultic level, to the negative evaluation of the behavior of the metaphorical "women."

Another evaluation of the woman's "whoring" is found in the term זמה, "depravity" or "lewdness." At least half of the Old Testament instances of this word[40] are in the book of Ezekiel, and primarily in the context of the prophetic marriage imagery.[41] זמה is a strong expression that already in its application in Lev 20:14 describes wrong behavior that is to be punished with death. Both in Lev 19:29 and in Ezek 23:27, 29, 35, 44 זמה is placed alongside forms of זנה.[42] In addition, זמה appears in Ezek 16:43, 58; 22:11 with תועבה, and זנה is found in parallel to תועבה in Ezek 16:22.

In Ezekiel we frequently encounter the assertion that the worship of the גלולים or שקוצים, which is described as זמה and תועבה, leads to the "pollution"[43] of the Israelites, or of the "women." The Priestly term טמא, "defile oneself," appears most frequently in Leviticus, but it is also used often by Ezekiel, and in all parts of the book. From Ezekiel's call (4:13-14) to the constitutional draft at the end (43:7, 8; 44:23, 25), the word runs like a *cantus firmus* through the book. The Israelites "defile" themselves, for example, by eating unclean bread (4:13), frequently by their behavior with "idols" and "abominations," by disobedience to the law (14:11), or by false sacrifices (20:26, 31). In many places defilement is mentioned in

[40] These (minus זמה I, "plan") include Job 17:11; Prov 24:9, and the personal name in 1 Chr 6:20, 42; 2 Chr 29:12.

[41] For more on the meaning of זמה see above, chapter 7 C; outside the book of Ezekiel זמה appears in the context of the prophetic marriage imagery only in Jer 13:27.

[42] As above in the case of עגב and אהב, so it may also be with זמה and זנה that similarity of sound suggested the use of the terms together.

[43] Behind טמא and טהר are complex OT ideas that, when translated with such modern words as "purity" and "impurity," can only lead to misunderstanding. It is not a question of moral values here. Ina J. Petermann has investigated the "most widely divergent misunderstandings and false interpretations" in the field of anthropology, the legal implications as regards office, and the religious-historical background of these terms ("Machen Geburt und Monatsblutung die Frau 'unrein'? Zur Revisionsbedürftigkeit eines missverstandenen Diktums," in Luise Schottroff and Marie-Theres Wacker, eds., *Von der Wurzel getragen. Christlich-feministische Exegese in Auseinandersetzung mit Antijudaismus* [Leiden and New York: Brill, 1996] 44–45). Regarding this terminology she writes that it "is not about aesthetic or hygienic categories, but rather cultic-ritual concepts (comparable to the contrast between 'sacred' and 'profane'), whose 'Sitz' is in the business of the Temple." This background should be kept in mind when interpreting these texts, especially within the field of sexuality, which in the modern era is also affected by a great variety of "notions about purity": "The priestly strictures regarding the *tum'ah* ['impurity' or 'uncleanness'] of women after delivery (Leviticus 12) and in menstruation (Lev 15:19-30) do not define particular bodily processes, or certainly womanhood itself, as inferior, sick, disgusting, or the like. In spite of the incompatibility of the sexual functions of men and women, the texts make an effort at gender parity: Male emissions are also subject to cultic restrictions (Lev 15:1-18)." This should be noted with particular care in Ezekiel, who associates the sexes with the concepts of "purity" and "impurity" in different ways.

connection with women: sexual congress with the "neighbor's wife" is one of the exemplary "defilements" of the Israelite men (18:6, 11, 15). In addition, sexual intercourse (with or of) a menstruating woman (18:6; 22:10; 36:17), as well as sexual misbehavior with one's own daughter-in-law lead to defilement (22:11).

Only in Ezekiel 23 is טמא used in the context of the prophetic marriage imagery (23:7, 13, 17, 30, 38). The defilement is a direct consequence of "whoring" (זנה: 23:7, 17, 30), both with personified foreign powers (23:7, 13, 17) and through the worship of their gods (23:30). The sisters Samaria and Jerusalem, who now clearly stand for all Israelites, defile YHWH's sanctuary with false sacrifices and nonobservance of the Sabbath (23:38).

This use of the term טמא in Ezekiel in the context of the prophetic marriage imagery is almost unique in the Old Testament. It is true that Hosea uses it in reference to Israel, but not in the marriage-metaphor chapters 1–3; moreover, Israel is here grammatically masculine (Hos 5:3; 6:10). In Jeremiah the "woman" Israel disputes, in 2:23, that she has been defiled. Moreover, it is the Israelites as a whole who, according to Jer 2:7, have defiled YHWH's land. In Isaiah, טמא does not appear in this context at all. It therefore appears to be a special feature of Ezekiel to see the defilement of the "woman" as a consequence of her behavior. This shows how strongly the prophetic marriage imagery, as adapted by Ezekiel, has been colored by his—in this case Priestly—terminology and theology.

It is nevertheless remarkable that in Ezekiel's texts using the marriage imagery the purpose of YHWH's actions is not seen as making the "woman" Jerusalem "clean" again. The contrasting concept to טמא, which is טהר, is used much less frequently throughout Ezekiel than טמא. But it does appear in the context of the marriage imagery in Jeremiah, and precisely with the function we would have expected it to have in Ezekiel. After a summary listing of Jerusalem's crimes and a cry of woe over the city "woman," Jer 13:27 concludes with the question of when she will be "clean" again. One explanation for the absence of the term טהר in Ezekiel's application of the marriage imagery could be that, throughout Ezekiel, טהר is not used in connection with women. While menstruating women are paradigmatically "unclean" (36:17), at no point does the text speak of a "clean" woman. That is probably the obstacle to the use of the word טהר in connection with the marriage imagery. Only in Ezek 24:13 is there mention of the failed "cleansing" of Jerusalem by YHWH. A further reason for the absence of טהר could be that Ezekiel combines two aspects of טמא: on the one hand obvious defilement as a consequence of ethical faults, and on the other hand the defilement or impurity that is unavoidable and not to be atoned for on an ethical level.[44] It seems as if the second element dominates the associated understanding of טמא in Ezekiel. However, we are not compelled to go as far in our interpretation as Julie Galambush does. She finds that YHWH's destruction of the "woman" Jerusalem is especially grounded in the *femaleness* of the metaphor and its implications for Ezekiel:

> Ultimately, the metaphor of Jerusalem as wife is itself a problem, always threatening to transform Yahweh's marriage into a marriage between the Holy and the unclean. Ezekiel therefore depicts Yahweh as ultimately driven to destroy his hopelessly polluted temple. Moreover, just as Yahweh destroys the temple, so also must he preside over the death of his metaphorical wife (16:40), not only to vindicate his dishonored name, but to remove the potential for *future* defilement that the city's feminine persona represents.[45]

If that were so, Ezekiel would have to reject any form of new or rebuilt Temple and set all his hopes on YHWH's purely spiritual presence with his people and in his city. But that is not the case. It seems to me that in Ezekiel the accent is more strongly placed on the idea that *YHWH alone* can remove Jerusalem's uncleanness.

Now once again regarding the behavior of the "women" in Ezek 16 and 23: One special characteristic of the "whoring" of Jerusalem in Ezekiel 16 is that they take no pay for the services. The corresponding term, אתנן, appears four times in Ezekiel, and only in ch. 16: in v. 31 it is first asserted that Jerusalem differs from a normal whore in the fact that she despises money. In vv. 33, 34, and 41 this observation is made still more pointed: Now Jerusalem herself gives her "lovers" money instead of being paid by them. On the historical level this probably represents a reference to tribute, which Ezekiel connects directly with the worship of the major powers' deities; however, it could also refer to gifts made to the deities themselves.[46] In this use of the term אתנן Ezekiel inflates both the absurdity of Jerusalem's behavior and the measure of her crimes. This behavior can no longer be compared to any normal human action. Once again at this point the field of marriage imagery in the narrow sense is abandoned, and the reference is to concrete political or historical circumstances.

[44] On this see Klaus Koch, "Haggais unreines Volk," *ZAW* 79 (1967) 62: "Uncleanness can arise from a sin, a wrong action against God, but need not: consider only the usage in the deuteronomic and priestly writings! To a great extent uncleanness comes to people not because of sin, but as destiny; in everyday life everyone comes somehow into contact with unclean things. The person affected can never escape this sphere by a moral decision."

[45] Galambush, *Jerusalem in the Book of Ezekiel* 88.

[46] There may be a reference here to Deut 23:19, with its prohibition against giving אתנן to the Temple; that would only increase "Jerusalem's" guilt.

The source of this unusually negative behavior on the part of Jerusalem is illustrated in Ezekiel by, among other things, the use of the root עגב and its derivative, עגבה, which only here appear in the context of the marriage imagery. עגב represents an intensive form of desire, being "inflamed." As it is used by Ezekiel, it appears that the focus of the word lies on sexual desire. In Ezek 23:5, 7, 9, 11, 12, 16, 20 עגבה/עגב is said to be the attitude of the "women," Samaria and Jerusalem, toward their lovers. The latter, however, are not described with the plural participle עגבים, as the lovers of Judah/Jerusalem were in Jer 4:30, but as מאהבים (Ezek 23:5, 9) or פלגש (Ezek 23:20).[47] Since עגב and its derivatives do not appear outside the passages cited, in Ezekiel and Jeremiah,[48] it is impossible to give a completely clear explanation of their meaning, as distinct from אהב. We may, however, suspect that these words contain a clearly more dramatic sexual component.

Ezekiel uses the word אהב relatively infrequently. The lovers in Ezek 16:33, 36, 37 and in 23:5, 9, 22 are described with the substantivized participle מאהבים. There is also a single use of the verb אהב in 16:37, here again regarding Jerusalem's lovers. In all the appearances of אהב or מאהבים in Ezekiel it is the "woman" who loves or seeks lovers for herself. Neither the love of Jerusalem or Samaria nor YHWH's love for his people is spoken of in terms of אהב, as is occasionally the case elsewhere in the Old Testament.[49] Different interpretations may be given for this. On the one hand, by this means the marriage between YHWH and his "wives" is more precisely described as a legal relationship and less as an emotional one.[50] This interpretation is strengthened by the historical retrospectives in Ezekiel, which also do not adduce YHWH's love, but instead argue historically. The mention of making the *berit* in this connection in 16:8, 59-61 points in the same direction.[51] It is possible as well that YHWH's loving care for his people, or for the "women," is not to be spoken of in clearly erotic-sexual terms. This could be grounded in the fact that YHWH's "love"

[47] We have already remarked above on this use of פלגש, uniquely for a man (n. 12 above). The other, fairly frequent appearances of the word refer without exception to female "concubines," that is, wives with a less privileged legal position in comparison to the "principal wives."

[48] In Ezek 33:31-32 the form עגבים appears also to describe a way of loving or a love song.

[49] This latter usage is found, for example, in Jer 2:2; 31:2; Hos 3:1; 11:1; 14:5; Mal 1:2; 2:11; Pss 47:5; 78:68; 2 Chr 2:10; 9:8.

[50] In my opinion this is the case despite the fact that אהב is otherwise used also as a legal term, and especially in codes of marital law to describe the principal wife in contrast to a concubine or additional wife, who is described with the verb שׂנא, as for example in Deut 21:15-17.

[51] Besides Prov 2:17, these are the only other passages in the OT in which a woman is the subject of a ברית; cf. Sabine van den Eynde, "Daughters of Abraham?! On 'Covenant,' Women and Gender." LAUD Linguistic Agency, Series A. General and Theoretical. Paper No. 472 (Essen, 1999) 5.

is regarded as something qualitatively different from the love of the "women" and their lovers. The love of the "woman" for her "lovers" is deliberately and emphatically expressed in words that put the accent on sexuality and sexual desire. But it lacks the legal quality that is otherwise also in play in אהב, "love."[52] Julie Galambush offers a third interpretation of this special "love." She points out that it is impossible, within Ezekiel's Jerusalem imagery, for YHWH to approach her in a sexual way.[53]

The only passage in Ezekiel in which we find YHWH saying anything about the attractiveness of Jerusalem can also be integrated within this picture: Ezekiel 16:8 uses the abstract plural דדים, "love," in YHWH's assertion about the maturity of the "woman" for love or sex.[54] It is true that there are some erotic components to this word, as its numerous uses in the Song of Songs attest, but in Ezek 16:8 it is used more as a distanced observation and not so much in the context of God's own desire.

Common to Ezekiel and Jeremiah is the use of the verbs נקע/יקע, "turn away." In Jer 6:8 this does not refer to the "wife," Jerusalem, but to "daughter Zion." However, in Ezek 23:17, 22, 28 it clearly speaks of the separation of the "woman" Jerusalem from her lovers, and vice versa in Ezek 23:18 of YHWH's turning away from Jerusalem. The verbs appear quite seldom in the Old Testament in the *qal;* outside the prophetic marriage imagery they are found only in Gen 32:26 to describe the consequences of YHWH's striking Jacob on the hip. It is difficult to say whether legal connotations also play a part here, but it is clear, from the *hipʿil* and *hopʿal* usage, that the reference is to a drastic kind of capital punishment. The translations suggest "break on the wheel" or "impale."[55] It is probable that at least this brachial-violent aspect of יקע is present in the separation of the "woman" or YHWH. However, differently from Jeremiah, the clearly sexual-lustful term צהל, "whinny," and its derivative מצהלה are not used by Ezekiel, nor does this book employ concepts from the field of "magic" or "sorcery" (כשף; ענן II).

What other evaluations of the conduct of the "women" can be derived from the context? First of all, as in the texts of the prophetic marriage imagery we have already examined, "whoring" (זנה) is connected with "adul-

[52] For אהב see above, Chapter 3 A.

[53] Galambush, *Jerusalem in the Book of Ezekiel* 88 and 104. Apart from that, there is in fact no language to be found anywhere in the OT about sexual activity on the part of YHWH for the purpose of procreation, not even in the context of the marriage imagery, despite the fact that it often contains reference to YHWH's "children" with the "woman/wife" (e.g., Ezek 16:20-21; 23:37).

[54] דדים also appears in the combination משכב דדים in Ezek 23:17, describing Jerusalem's "bed of love."

[55] HAL 412.

tery" (נאף). Although Ezekiel contains the longest texts of the prophetic marriage imagery, the behavior of the "woman" is not very frequently described as נאף. In 16:32 Jerusalem is titled "adulteress," with the feminine *piʿel* participle מנאפת.[56] Forms of נאף and זנה are found together in 23:43, but without an object. This verse uses the abstract plural נאופים, found otherwise only in Jer 13:27.[57] Twice in 23:27 Jerusalem's conduct is described as "adultery," with the verb נאף. We noted above that in this verse the partners of the "women" are the גלולים, the "idols" of Jerusalem/Samaria's foreign allies. The fact that נאף is used only in this connection as a verb with an object can be interpreted as an indication that the "women" do "whore" with the foreign powers, but that a definitive, adulterous offense against marriage with YHWH is only accomplished with other *deities*.[58] A judgment like that for adulteresses and murderesses is pronounced on the "women." This time the adulteresses are described with the feminine of the *qal* participle נאפות. The fact that here adultery and murder are given the same weight and are punished with death corresponds entirely to the view of Israelite legal principles, according to Lev 20:10.

In summary we may say that the prophetic marriage imagery in Ezekiel is differently formulated, at several points and in detail, from that in Hosea and Jeremiah. Apart from the double narrative of the marriage already discussed in the first part, Ezekiel introduces the foreign powers as additional "lovers," with Egypt, Assyria, and Babylon first among them. The "woman" or "women" "whore" with them, while also committing adultery in the narrower sense with deities who are described in pejorative terms. These idols "pollute" the "women"; this semantic field is used only in Ezekiel 23. However, no purification of the "women" is envisaged as the goal of YHWH's punishment; apparently, because of the shaping of Ezekiel's thought by Priestly traditions, that is impossible. Also unique to Ezekiel 23 is the accent on the women's desire, set more strongly in the sexual realm, by use of the verb עגב, than was possible elsewhere with אהב. YHWH's love for the "women," on the other hand, is not expressed. Thus the love between the women and their lovers is the only love expressed in the text, with all its erotic and sexual shadings. Marriage with YHWH acquires

[56] Elsewhere in the OT מנאפת is used only in Hos 3:1 and Prov 30:20.

[57] In this construction the accent appears to lie on habitual behavior; see above on זנונים, Chapter 6 B.

[58] In 16:20; 23:27 the accusation of child sacrifice is also raised; the crimes are summarized by saying that blood is on the hands of the "women." An investigation of this topic cannot be carried out here; moreover, this is a field of research that has received little attention. It is possible that Ezek 16:20-21 is to be regarded as a continuation or a secondary addition; cf. Maier, "Jerusalem als Ehebrecherin," 69–70.

to a still greater degree the character of a relationship that is primarily legal or part of a *berit,* and this is explicitly stated in 16:8, 59-61.

C. Metaphors of violence against the "women" in Ezekiel

Scenes of violence against YHWH's "women/wives" are found in Ezekiel especially in 16:36-42 and 23:10, 24-26, 28-29, 31, 34, 46-47. The focus here is on these passages. In both chapters it is striking that especially here the imagery of sexual violence is formulated with specific reference to the crimes of the "women." This corresponds to the observation already made that there is a close relationship in Ezekiel between the metaphors for guilt and punishment. This is made explicit in 16:43: the "woman's" behavior turns back upon her. In many places this can be demonstrated in detail, while in some the correspondence is more superficial.

Before treating these two chapters with regard to the imagery of violence, we should first point out some differences between them. While the imagery of sexual violence is formulated in parallel over long stretches, the two chapters are clearly different at some points. Ezekiel 23, in contrast to Ezekiel 16, selects the theme of "uncleanness" as an important topos. Moreover, the "women's" "lusting" (עגב) for their "lovers" is only mentioned in Ezekiel 23. Unlike 16:53-63, there is no hint of a restoration of the "women" at the end of ch. 23. Military violence plays a greater role here than in ch. 16. Thus Ezekiel 23 appears to be the chapter in which, on the one hand, the lines begun in ch. 16 are strengthened, and on the other hand new elements are introduced. The purpose is clear: At the end there is no longer any "possibility of improvement" or chance for the "woman" to expiate her behavior.

Ezekiel 16:36-42 begins with a causal backward reference (יען) in v. 36: "Because" the "woman" has uncovered (גלה *pi'el*) her nakedness (ערוה) in "whoring" with her lovers, in v. 37 her nakedness will be uncovered before their eyes by YHWH, and laid open to their eyes. The expression גלה *pi'el* + ערוה does not occur in this literal form in other texts of the prophetic marriage imagery. There either a different object is used (שׁול, מער, or נבלת), or else ערוה appears with the verb חשׂף or with גלה *nip'al.* The expression גלה *pi'el* + ערוה, however, is the term for sexual intercourse in Priestly contexts; it appears in Lev 18:6-19; 20:11, 17-21, and Ezek 22:10.[59] The subjects in each case are men who perform sexual intercourse with women. If this act is done forcibly to a woman, as in Ezek 16:37, we must assume that in our present understanding this represents

[59] On this see above, Chapter 3 C ii.

the rape of the woman, which, to increase the humiliation, is done in the open for all to see. That YHWH's action is not restricted to "uncovering the nakedness," that is, to undressing the woman, can be concluded from the fact that the latter is separately mentioned. On the one hand the "woman" is stripped again by her "lovers" in 16:39. On the other hand, already in v. 37bβ, after the expression גלה ערוה ("uncover the nakedness") the text speaks of "seeing all your nakedness" as an (additional) purpose of the divine action. Since the text here speaks of "all" (כל) her nakedness/shame, it is improbable that ערוה is meant to refer here only to the sexual organs; the reference is rather to something in the sense of "unprotectedness" (Gen 42:9, 12) or "indecency" (Deut 23:14; 24:1). Later, in Ezek 23:29, ערוה appears with a similar meaning, this time in a construct phrase as "nakedness of your whorings . . . your lewdness and your whorings." At this point it does not make much sense, as likewise in Ezek 16:37bβ, to translate ערוה with "pudenda" or "shame" in the sense of genitals.

This showing (ראה) of the ערוה appears in very different contexts. In Gen 9:22, 23 it refers to Noah's nakedness and in Gen 42:9, 12 to the unprotectedness of the land. In Deut 23:14 the Israelites are warned against allowing YHWH to see anything "indecent" in the camp; the reference is to excrement. In Lev 20:17, on the other hand, the expression has a sexual content in the narrow sense: It is parallel to גלה ערוה ("uncover the nakedness") and is thus also an expression for the consummation of sexual intercourse. In the context of the prophetic marriage imagery the scene depicted in Ezek 16:37 is expressed in exactly the same fashion in Lam 1:8. The fallen "woman" Jerusalem is despised by her former admirers because they can now see her "nakedness." Here ערוה could refer both to the sexual organs and to shaming. In Is 47:3aα גלה *nip'al* expresses passively, first of all, the stripping of the ערוה. In v. 3aβ, however, the text speaks of the showing of the "shame" (חרפה). This makes it probable that ראה ערוה in Ezek 16:37 does not mean exactly the same thing as גלה ערוה, but instead that the intent is to express shaming as the purpose of the stripping.

We can observe further analogies between punitive acts and previous actions on the part of the "woman" in the following verses: 16:38 refers to the legal provisions regarding adulteresses and those who shed blood. Thus YHWH's punitive action is legitimated, something that is not so clearly stated in Hosea and Jeremiah. The punishments of the "woman" in 16:39 correspond, even in specific details, to her previous "conduct": She had built a "platform" (גב, 16:24, 31)[60] and "high places" for worship

[60] For the difficult interpretation of this word see above, n. 4.

(16:16, 24-25), donned (colorful)[61] garments (בגד, otherwise in 16:16, and in 16:18 in combination with רקמה, as well as in 23:26 in a context of punishment), and decked herself with ornaments. "Ornaments," תפארת, are given the "woman" by YHWH in 16:12; in 16:17 "she" makes idols out of them, and in 16:39; 23:26 her "lovers" take away not only her ornaments, but everything else as well. The "leaving"[62] of the naked (עירם) and stripped (עריה) woman in v. 39 should be seen as a reference back to the "foundling" story at the beginning of the chapter; in 16:22 YHWH recalls her nakedness before he found her, and her condition in 16:7 before he clothed her in puberty. The same combination of words, עירם ועריה, is found in the same context of punishment in 23:29.[63] עריה as a term for "bare" in Ezek 16:7, 22, 39; 23:29 is semantically very close to ערוה, "nakedness." The relatively rare word (otherwise only in different contexts in Mic 1:11 and Hab 3:9) may have been chosen here to associate nakedness as the original condition of the "woman," and as a punitive consequence, more closely with the clearly sexual connotations of "nakedness" in the sense of genitals.

In 16:40 and 23:47 stoning and death are proposed as punishment for the adulteress(es). The latter corrresponds to the regulations in the Pentateuch: according to Lev 20:10; Deut 22:22 adultery, both by the man (here seen as active) and by the woman, is to be punished with death. Stoning is also envisioned as a punishment within the field of marriage laws, but is expressed with the verb סקל, "stone" and the indirect object אבנים + ב ("with stones").[64] But that is not what is in Ezekiel. Here the text uses רגם with the indirect object (ב)אבן, an expression that otherwise appears primarily in the Pentateuch and is used by Ezekiel only in the context of the marriage imagery in 16:40 and 23:47. According to Lev 20:2, stoning is the punishment for child sacrifice, of which the "women" are also accused in Ezek 16:21; 23:37.[65]

[61] In 16:10, 13, 18 רקמה is used as a term for colored cloth or garments. It otherwise appears only in Judg 5:30; Ezek 26:16; 27:7, 16, 24; Ps 45:25; 1 Chr 29:2. In Ezekiel 26 and 27 it is mentioned in connection with the קינה over the city-state Tyre.

[62] נוח appears otherwise in this context only in 16:42: there, also in the *hipʿil,* YHWH finds rest after having stilled his wrath by punishing Jerusalem. In other contexts, also for the quieting of YHWH's wrath, it appears in Ezek 5:13; 21:22; 24:13.

[63] Another parallel, though in motif rather than terminology, is in Hos 2:3 [MT 5] and the exposure by YHWH of the "woman" who is as naked as when she was born.

[64] This is in Deut 22:21, 24.

[65] If both the mention of child sacrifice and the punishment with stoning are redactional additions, as (for example) Walther Zimmerli supposes (*Ezechiel 1–24* [Neukirchen-Vluyn: Neukirchener Verlag, 1969] 356–57), this supports the link between the two.

Killing with the sword, as a second punishment for the "woman/women," is in fact superfluous in this passage, since stoning already leads to death. Therefore we must suspect that the two punishments were not necessarily chosen on grounds of narrative logic. It may be that here correspondence between crime and punishment plays a greater role, or that this is the culmination of both. The relationship between stoning and child sacrifice has already been clarified. In the case of killing, it is emphasized that this is to be done with the sword. This manner of killing is mentioned by Ezekiel in 5:12; 6:12; 7:15, and 33:27; the sword, together with other verbs that also primarily designate killing, is a word very frequent in Ezekiel. Death by the sword (מות בחרב) is typical for death in war, both for the combatants and for the civilian population. The subject of the punishment also favors the notion that Ezek 16:40; 23:47 refers to the context of war: in Ezekiel קהל describes not only the assembly called together for the purpose of stoning the "woman" (16:40) or "women" (23:46, 47), but also the army. This meaning attaches to קהל especially in the sayings against the foreign nations in chs. 25–32, but also in the context of the prophetic marriage imagery in 23:24.[66] That war is mentioned as background in Ezek 16:40; 23:24, 46, 47 indicates that at this point there is a rupture in the prophetic marriage imagery. Again the stringency of the imagery recedes in favor of its transparency to the historical background. Thomas Krüger also emphasizes this: "The complex of imagery in the texts is completely exploded in the concrete proclamations of punishment. Only the stoning of Jerusalem announced in 16:40 really corresponds to the Old Testament משפטי נאפים (16:38)."[67] The historical background is the conquest and destruction of Jerusalem and Samaria. The burning of the houses in 16:41 points also to this context.

Krüger places the proclamations of judgment in Ezek 16:37-58 and 23:22-49 within a larger context. They "go beyond 5:8ff. in that they include the nations as those who will carry out YHWH's forensic judgments. While 16:37ff. shows a tendency to depict the nations' 'legal forum' as broadly as possible . . . 23:22-23 speaks concretely of the Babylonians/Chaldeans and the Assyrians as Oholibah's 'lovers from whom you turned in disgust.' In the complex of imagery relating to the judicial process both the noun קהל ('judging community'/'military command') and the expression נתן ביד are transparent to the matter designated, Jerusalem's military catastrophe."[68]

[66] Thus in Ezek 26:6; 27:7, 34; 32:3, 22, 23; 38:4, 13, 15.

[67] Krüger, *Geschichtskonzepte im Ezechielbuch* 179.

[68] Ibid.

The quieting of YHWH's wrath is given in Ezekiel 16 as the end and thus the goal of YHWH's actions. He only has rest again (16:42) when Jerusalem becomes ashamed and falls silent.[69] Here her death is not a condition for YHWH's ceasing to rage; instead, the text still speaks of a possible preservation of Jerusalem (16:53-63). In Ezekiel 23 this, and a good deal besides, is different. The remarks in this section are restricted to what was not already said above about ch. 16, and to what is clearly different here.

The war context is much more prominent in Ezekiel 23 than in Ezekiel 16. It is also described in more detail, especially in 23:22-27: for example, the warriors' equipment in 23:24. Krüger has emphasized that here again the imagery is transparent to the historical background: "Something similar is true for the removal of clothing and despoiling of ornaments (16:39; 23:26). According to Hos 2:5 and the ancient Near Eastern parallels this was done by the husband or his children, not by the legal community. Cutting off the nose and ears (23:25) is frequently attested as punishment in ancient Near Eastern law codes (cf. 23:24: מִשְׁפְּטֵיהֶם)—not, however, for adultery and immorality."[70]

Shalom Paul contradicts this last remark, introducing Middle Assyrian legal texts in support of his position. This is especially interesting because Ezek 23:24 explicitly says that the "woman" is to be judged according to the laws of her lovers. Nevertheless, it should be cautioned that the applicable law in that case would not have been Middle Assyrian, but Neo-Assyrian. According to Middle Assyrian law there was drastic punishment for adultery: A woman who left her husband and took refuge with an acquaintance could, for example, have her ears cut off by her husband. The same was true for a woman slave who wore a veil like that of a free woman. There was more severe punishment for adultery if the pair was discovered *in flagrante delicto:* In that case the wronged husband could choose whether or how to punish; the choice of punishments for the woman ranged from cutting off the nose to death.[71] To that extent the imagery of adultery in Ezekiel may admit of concretion through the legal codes of surrounding societies. Nevertheless, Krüger's observation about the text is accurate: "Deportation (23:25), siege (23:24), and 'sword' (16:40; 23:25) ultimately point unmistakably to a military catastrophe."[72]

[69] This is probably to be seen as a redactional addition; cf. Maier, "Jerusalem als Ehebrecherin," 99.

[70] Krüger, *Geschichtskonzepte im Ezechielbuch* 180.

[71] Thus Shalom M. Paul, "Biblical Analogues to Middle Assyrian Law," in Edwin B. Firmage et al., eds., *Religion and Law: Biblical-Judaic and Islamic Perspectives* (Winona Lake: Eisenbrauns, 1990) 344–46, especially 345; for this subject see also above, Chapter 5 B i.

[72] Krüger, *Geschichtskonzepte im Ezechielbuch* 180.

Simply in terms of the length of the text, sexual violence occupies less space in comparison to explicit military violence in Ezekiel 23 than in Ezekiel 16. In 23:10 the "nakedness" of Oholah/Samaria is uncovered. The expressions chosen, as in Ezek 16:37, are גלה *piʿel* ("uncover") and ערוה ("nakedness"); given the parallel to Lev 18:20 described above, we must assume a rape scene here. In this scene YHWH is no longer, as in Ezekiel 16, the one who directly performs the rape, but "only" the judge who passes sentence on the "woman" Jerusalem and leaves the carrying out of the punishment to the ex-lovers or the קהל (see above).

In 23:28 the "woman" Jerusalem is in the power of the ex-lovers from whom she had turned away. They will proceed against her, full of hatred, and take from her everything she has gained. Here again war imagery is visible, but the marriage imagery has not been entirely abandoned.

Ezekiel 23:29 speaks in the most scornful possible tones of the shame or "nakedness" of the "woman." Here, unlike in 16:37 and 23:10, ערוה probably refers to the genitals. The word is more specifically qualified by the substantives for "whoredom" (זנות, זמה, and תזנות) so frequently used by Ezekiel, and indeed is more or less saddled with being the organ in which everything shameful is gathered together and can be looked upon. As a verb or action we find here, with ערוה, not גלה *piʿel,* but גלה *nipʿal.* The expression, as passive, has no explicit subject, but it is clear from the context that it is the ex-lovers who have uncovered the nakedness of the "woman." In the same way, ערוה with גלה *nipʿal* was described as an action of Jerusalem herself; thus here the aspect of backward reference is retained. It is not an issue here of "showing" the shame/nakedness (ראה) or "letting it be seen," probably because the punishment, ultimately, is more drastic than in Ezekiel 16. The goal is killing, and not "merely" humiliation or breaking the spirit. In Ezekiel 23 there is no chance for repentance, but only death and the complete destruction of the "women."

D. Feminist theological interpretation of Ezekiel's marriage imagery

Feminist criticism of the imagery in the book of Ezekiel has been expressed primarily on three points: First, the pornographic depiction of the "women," with its implications for the reception of the text; second, the descriptions of the "women's" biographies; third, the God-image in the book.[73]

[73] There are a number of new feminist publications on Ezekiel 16 and 23 that I could no longer examine; however, I wish to list them here: Peggy L. Day, "Adulterous Jerusalem's Imaged Demise. Death of a Metaphor in Ezekiel XVI," *VT* 50 (2000) 285–309; Erin Runions, "Violence and the Economy of Desire in Ezekiel 16:1-45," in Athalya Brenner, ed., *A Feminist Companion*

The judgment that Ezekiel contains pornographic depictions is based on T. Drorah Setel's thesis, discussed above. Following her, Fokkelien van Dijk-Hemmes was particularly critical; both of their proposals were presented in Chapter One above. According to van Dijk-Hemmes, female sexuality is regarded in Ezekiel as wicked and evil. The descriptions in the text contribute to a portrait of women as "whores," to attaching the guilt for their own wrongful behavior to them, and to punishing them for it. To this is added the supposed "enjoyment" they derive from being abused.[74] Female sexuality is only good when it is under male control: "Both women are degraded and publicly humiliated in order to stress that their sexuality is and ought to be an object of male possession and control."[75] But not only that: Through this pornographic depiction women are reduced to the figures in the text and denied the possibility of other identification. They are not permitted to connect to the figure of the husband.[76]

While van Dijk-Hemmes' interpretation of the text foregrounds the individual activity of the readers, Julie Galambush (whose work is also described in Chapter One) puts the accent more strongly on the imagery within the text. Galambush's basic thesis is that in the metaphor of Jerusalem as a woman the Temple corresponds to the vagina. According to Galambush, "pornography" is present in Ezekiel in two ways: First, in the older sense as the description of a prostitute's life: this applies to the "biographical" passages in Ezek 16:23.[77] Second, we have here a pornographic textual description, as other exegetes have already noted. The purity codes in Ezekiel, affected by Priestly traditions, through the portrayal of Jerusalem as a woman apply in an intensified and double fashion to the Temple—and to the possibilities for its pollution. The goal in Ezekiel 23 is the destruction of the city and thus the legitimizing of divine action. The heavenly Jerusalem presented in Ezekiel 40–48 is not conceived as a textual "woman," but as a city. In this way female imagery in Ezekiel is reduced to negative aspects; there are no positive associations at all.

The origins of the text of Ezekiel 16 are more closely examined by Christl Maier. She sees the metaphors as expanded, and ultimately de-

---

to Prophets and Daniel (Sheffield: Sheffield Academic Press, 2001) 156–69; in the same volume: S. Tamar Kamionkowski, "Gender Reversal in Ezekiel 16," 170–85, and also Mary E. Shields, "Self-Response to 'Multiple Exposures,'" 154–55.

[74] Fokkelien van Dijk-Hemmes, "The Metaphorization of Woman in Prophetic Speech: An Analysis of Ezekiel XXIII," *VT* 43 (1993) 162–70, edited version in eadem and Athalya Brenner, eds., *Reflections on Theology and Gender* (Kampen: Kok Pharos, 1994) 173–74.

[75] Ibid. 175.

[76] Ibid. 176.

[77] Julie Galambush, *Jerusalem in the Book of Ezekiel* 124–25.

stroyed, by redactional additions and reinterpretations. The expansions strengthen the negative portrayal of the "woman" Jerusalem; the background is the historical experience of the destruction of the city. If the portrayal in Ezek 16:1-43* is still creative, in the continuation in 16:44-63 the tension between "woman" and "city" is overdrawn and the metaphors are, in Maier's opinion, destroyed.[78] The result is an androcentric and sexist text. Such an image of women should not be transmitted farther.[79]

The second aspect of feminist critique of the imagery of Jerusalem as "woman" has been developed especially by Elke Seifert. This is the matter of sexual abuse, which can be detected in, or more properly behind the texts. Van Dijk-Hemmes had already mentioned this aspect of Ezekiel 23. Elke Seifert works mainly on the level of imagery and connects Ezekiel's images with contemporary patterns of thought. She points out that the linking of the metaphor of adoption with that of marriage in Ezek 16:1-14 is at least ambiguous. The passivity of the "woman" and her total dependence on the man reflects an androcentric view of women. "From a feminist perspective there arise parallels to the male behavior that is classified under the concept 'sexual abuse of power.' For the relationship between YHWH and the city-'woman' displays a fundamental assymetry that is used by the stronger party for the satisfaction of his sexual desires. . . . Something happens in the images here that can be compared to the sexual abuse of a daughter by her father."[80] The depiction in the text, however, places the accent differently: Here the "father" YHWH continually has a new claim to gratitude from his unworthy "daughter-wife." In Ezekiel 23 another androcentric pattern of thinking asserts itself. "A cliché about 'lusty women' is inserted here that was not in Ezekiel 16: the 'fairy tale of the eternally seductive woman,' the 'Lolita.'"[81] The textual depiction thereby reverses the cause and effect of sexual advances during youth. "Sexual abuse does not lead to a 'basic corruption,' but it can provoke (among other things) serious disturbances in sexual experience and behavior."[82]

Two contributions touch on the third aspect of feminist criticism of the book of Ezekiel, the problem of the image of God. Kathryn Pfisterer Darr primarily summarizes previous feminist critique, but goes further in treating the God-image in Ezekiel. Darr describes as preconditions for understanding Ezekiel an awareness of his God-centered worldview and his

[78] Christl Maier, "Jerusalem als Ehebrecherin in Ezechiel 16," 102.

[79] Ibid. 103.

[80] Elke Seifert, *Tochter und Vater* 262.

[81] Ibid. 271.

[82] Ibid. 272.

effort to see God as the cause of all events and to preserve that image of God through the exile and beyond. It is God who, in Ezekiel's view, brings about Judah's destruction; it is God who does this as a reaction to wrongful human behavior, and the measure of God's punishment, according to Ezekiel, corresponds exactly to the measure of human sin. "His companions might complain that 'the way of the Lord is unfair' (18:25, 29; 33:17, 20), but Ezekiel defended the justice of God's actions."[83]

Mary E. Shields has investigated the different ways of seeing the "male" and "female" body in Ezekiel 16.[84] Her interest is in women,[85] but still more in the God-image in the text. She shows that a variety of rhetorical means are used in the text to divert attention from YHWH as perpetrator of violence. While the "woman" is reduced to her body, which is stripped before the eyes of everyone, YHWH is not visible as a body.[86] YHWH's perspective is presented to the readers in the first person singular. This leads them to adopt YHWH's position as subject and to identify with his perspective: "The story sets up the reader to rationalize the rape and mutilation. Yet what the story obscures is the part of male partners in adultery." In addition, real violence, "gang rape,"[87] is carried out by others. The text's depiction of YHWH is problematic because the question of God's responsibility in the role of a perpetrator of sexual violence is suppressed. Against the background of the fact that even today sexual perpetrators often feel not at all guilty because of their actions this is an especially difficult aspect of the text.[88] Therefore it is necessary to "deconstruct" the text, that is, to point to the gender roles, attributions, and implications hidden in the text, as Shields has done.[89]

[83] Kathryn Pfisterer Darr, "Ezekiel," *WBC* (1992) 185.

[84] Mary E. Shields, "Multiple Exposures. Body Rhetoric and Gender Characterization in Ezekiel 16," *JFSR* 14 (1998) 5–18.

[85] With respect to the image of women her critique corresponds generally to that of Galambush, for example, or van Dijk-Hemmes, as presented in this chapter. Some examples illustrate this: "The body rhetoric, by focusing on nakedness, blood, and the physical attributes of the onset of womanhood, not only objectifies the infant/girl/woman, but also associates the woman with those aspects of the female body which are most problematic in a patriarchal world-view" (ibid. 10). "Woman is written out of the restoration" (ibid. 13).

[86] Ibid. 14: ". . . nowhere is the body of the central male figure described or even mentioned."

[87] Ibid. 6. Elke Seifert's evaluation is similar (*Tochter und Vater* 268): "Male attacks on the metaphorical female persons [in Ezekiel 23—*GB*] are depicted in such a way that the men do not appear as criminals who injure women."

[88] That sexual perpetrators often lack any kind of awareness of having done wrong can be documented through a great many statements collected by Alberto Godenzi. He summarizes (*Bieder, brutal. Frauen und Männer sprechen über sexuelle Gewalt.* [2nd ed. Zürich: Unionsverlag, 1991] 47): "We asked those who called in [i.e., sexual perpetrators!—*GB*] who, in their opinion, is generally responsible for sexual violence. Twenty-five of the thirty-five men agreed: The woman is guilty."

[89] Shields, "Multiple Exposures," 16, 18: "Moreover, the fact that the 'I' figure in the text is God makes the reader even less likely to question the justice or extremity of that figure's action.

In particular the first two aspects of feminist criticism fall strongly on the level of imagery and on the textual depiction of the "woman" and how these can work against our modern background for understanding. Consequently, these criticisms cannot be drained of their power by textual analysis. In the next section the aspects already criticized will be placed again within a larger framework, so that perhaps we may derive a perspective for dealing with them that can be grounded in the book itself and its theology.

E. Marriage metaphors in the context of Ezekiel's religious imagery

The frameworks within which the marriage imagery in Ezekiel must be understood present a series of aspects, some of which were already discussed at the beginning of this chapter: for example, Ezekiel's concept of history and the importance of the idea of purity. Here we will concentrate especially on the female imagery outside Ezekiel 16 and 23, as well as the God-image in the book, and we will link both of these to the special function of marriage imagery in Ezekiel.

The female personifications "Jerusalem" and "Israel" are not the only ones in the book of Ezekiel. In the oracles against the foreign nations (Ezekiel 25–32) there are a number of other cities and countries that are grammatically feminine: Ammon (25:3-4; masculine from v. 6 onward!), Tyre (26:27), and Sidon (28:22). In contrast to these, there are also masculine cities and countries: Moab (25:8-11) and Egypt (29). YHWH does violence against these countries and cities, whatever their grammatical gender, but here more clearly in the form of military force and not in scenes of sexual violence. For Ezekiel the latter appears to be tied to the image of marriage and the punishment of the "whorish wife" Jerusalem.

The sphere of marriage and sexuality also appears outside Ezekiel 16 and 23, namely in 18:6, 11, 18; 22:10-11, and 33:26. In all three places the context is the misbehavior of Israelite men through illicit, polluting (טמא) traffic either with their neighbors' wives, with menstruating women, or with their blood kin. Marriage and sexuality thus serve, by preference, to exemplify Israel's guilt. A positive view of marriage is found nowhere in the book: Even the wife of the prophet is no counterweight. She dies, possibly at YHWH's hand, and as a symbolic action it is forbidden that Ezekiel should mourn for her (24:15-18).

But it is precisely at this point that gender characterization is the most dangerous." "In our culture, where domestic violence is on the rise and where those who participate in it rely on scriptures such as Ezekiel 16 for their warrant, this text is even more problematic. The metaphor, and God's character within it, must be deconstructed, and deconstructed in such a way that it may no longer be used to justify male violence and abuse of any group in our society."

Nowhere are other real women given a positive mention, either: They weep for Tammuz (8:14) or act as prophets and magicians (13:17-18). Paradigmatic for the uncleanness of the nation is the uncleanness of menstruating women (36:17). In addition, certain groups of women are banned from being the wives of priests (44:22)—so that with the priests there can be a special distinction between "clean" and "unclean" and they can teach this to the people (44:23). However, this passage cannot be seen as a positive reference to women. Consequently, it almost appears as if women in the book of Ezekiel and in its imagery are completely saddled with negative connotations.

This impression is strengthened by the fact that the transparency of Ezekiel's marriage imagery toward the realities that lie behind it is deliberately abandoned at one point. In Ezek 23:48 it is expressly emphasized that the punishment of the textual "women" is meant to have a deterrent effect on *all* women. Here the imagery is not, as before, transparent only to the historical situation behind the text; the metaphorical discourse is abandoned at this point. The words in 23:48 are no longer addressed to all Israelites, who previously were included in the notion of Jerusalem/Samaria, and even Sodom. In a certain way this verse confirms the thesis of feminist exegetes who do not reduce the treatment of the "woman" solely to the symbolic or poetic level. Here fantasies of violence against concrete women play their part: These women are promised the same fate as the metaphorical "women." Still more clearly than before, the "shameful deeds" are ascribed to the women in the population, and women are connected to sin and wickedness unless they "take warning" (יסר *hitpaʿel*). Men receive no such warning at any point in the book of Ezekiel.

Finally, what about Ezekiel's picture of God? YHWH is the real subject of the book, so it is important to understand his actions. He is the absolutely powerful figure; he is able to steer his prophet in every way, and even to remove him to distant places, as in Ezek 37:1. To that extent the picture of God in the marriage imagery coincides entirely with the image in the whole of the book of Ezekiel. YHWH leads his people into exile, for good reasons and not as a too-severe punishment for their misdeeds, as Ezekiel shows. God is also brutal in this regard: a God of the sword, one who strikes and devastates. In Ezekiel this picture is not balanced by another side of God, as for example in the picture of the caring parent in Hosea 11. God, as the one in absolute control, creates a new Jerusalem for himself. Here we can draw parallels between Jeremiah 30–31 and Ezekiel. Only God can absolve; only God can give a new neart; only God can circumcise the heart (Ezek 44:7, 9). Human cooperation is not decisive for the success of this project.

There is one tiny crack in this monumental image of God through which female imagery can leak into the divine sphere. One of the most important powers of God, which works on the prophet and on the "dead" Israelites, is the grammatically female power of the רוח, the "spirit."[90] Helen Schüngel-Straumann summarizes: "רוח, which binds together and makes the dead to live again, רוח that gives strength and vitality and sets things right, רוח as source of creativity, רוח as mediating and inspiring power was experienced and described as female."[91] It was possible to integrate female experiences and, within certain limits, female imagery[92] into the image of God as long as it was a question of an entity subordinated to YHWH.

F. Summary

The prophetic marriage imagery, in the form it achieves in Ezekiel, has arrived at a kind of climax: It not only brings the "woman" Jerusalem to a bad end, but with her the marriage imagery itself. The pre-exilic formulation of the warning to the people as "woman" had a positive purpose in using language to shock and disturb in order to bring the people to repentance. The stigma of "harlotry" was attached to worship of deities other than YHWH in order that the people would abandon such worship. Now, however, this "harlotry" or "whoredom" has a different reference: Israel or Jerusalem enters alliances with foreign powers instead of trusting in YHWH alone. If there is meant to be a critique here that aims at repentance and a change in behavior, then it is addressed to a different group than in Hosea or Amos. Political alliances are made by the powerful; this is not like the issue of worship of foreign gods, because individual Israelites have no influence on these treaties. But probably the texts did not have such an impetus at all, for the perspective is not that of future change, but

[90] Helen Schüngel-Straumann, *Rûah bewegt die Welt. Gottes schöpferische Lebenskraft in der Krisenzeit des Exils* (Stuttgart: Katholisches Bibelwerk, 1992) 66–70, has shown that the passages in Ezekiel where רוח is creative and lifegiving are all grammatically feminine in construction. She suggests a background of female experience (pp. 10–11): "Above all, there can be no human experience in which what creates space and is associated with powerful breathing is so intense as in the process of birth. Being able to breathe (again) and to survive (cf. Ps 66:12) and find relief in a critical situation can certainly find an echo in many other situations in both the literal and the broader sense, but these things apply to nothing so precisely as to birth. The audible panting during the birth process and the relieved gasping for breath afterward, which again 'makes space' for the woman in a literal sense, are at the same time creative and life-bringing."

[91] Helen Schüngel-Straumann, "*RÛAH* und Gender-Frage am Beispiel der Visionen beim Propheten Ezechiel," in Bob Becking and Meindert Dijkstra, eds., *On Reading Prophetic Texts. Gender-Specific and Related Studies in Memory of Fokkelien van Dijk-Hemmes* (Leiden and New York: Brill, 1996) 215.

[92] In Ezekiel 37 רוח even shows the beginnings of personification.

rather of looking back on what is past. When the gaze is turned in that direction Ezekiel's imagery serves to demonstrate God's righteousness in his—already accomplished—punishment of his people and his city. The shock effect of the texts is produced by the way in which, very differently from those other books, the prophetic marriage imagery is tied to the reality of the people themselves. They are not to be moved, but only to recognize themselves in the fate of the "women."[93] Whether this in fact succeeded for all parts of the population, men as well as women, may be questioned, as Fokkelien van Dijk-Hemmes has done.[94]

Four reasons appear to me to have been decisive in the handing down of these texts: First, not *in spite of,* but *because of* the fact that they have pornographic features; they operate at a level that gives the addressees very little chance to escape from them. Second, in a certain way they reflect the horrors of war: a way in which (certain) people at that time could recognize their own experiences. Third, they offer a consistent explanatory model for the exilic fate of Israel and of Jerusalem. YHWH is a powerful God, sovereign and exalted, who in the harsh punishment and partial destruction of his people follows a comprehensible logic and legally founded principles. YHWH is not incalculable or arbitrary. A fourth reason we may mention and expand upon is given by Robert P. Carroll, who brings the dimension of religious history into play.[95] In the exilic and post-exilic period YHWH largely succeeded in becoming the only God throughout the Old Testament. Only a few traditions enabled female figures or powers to sustain themselves alongside him. This is the case, as we have shown above, even in Ezekiel in the "spirit," the רוח, as divine force. But nowhere is there a female figure in a position of equal rank. With the metaphorical "killing" of the city "woman" Jerusalem there is no longer any figure present who can appear as a metaphorical counterpart to YHWH, his partner or equal.

[93] Here we would refer to Mary E. Shields' critique of Jer 2:2–4:4 ("Circumcision of the Prostitute: Gender, Sexuality, and the Call to Repentance in Jeremiah 3:1–4:4," *BInt* 3 [1995] 61–74); see Chapter 7 D above.

[94] See Fokkelien van Dijk-Hemmes, "The Metaphorization of Woman" (n. 73 above) 176.

[95] Robert P. Carroll, "Whorusalamin: a Tale of Three Cities as Three Sisters," in Bob Becking and Meindert Dijkstra, eds., *On Reading Prophetic Texts. Gender-Specific and Related Studies in Memory of Fokkelien van Dijk-Hemmes* (Leiden and New York: Brill, 1996) 67–82, especially at 82.

Excursus: Lamentations: Jerusalem Wails

In this study of the prophetic marriage imagery the Lamentations (Threni) also have a place—not as a vote for Lamentations as belonging to the prophetic books of the Old Testament, although there could be a basis for that in the attribution of Lamentations to Jeremiah in the LXX and Vulgate.[1] The reason for discussing the book here is that it also uses terms from the metaphoric complex that we have characterized as "prophetic marriage imagery."

The semantic field of this imagery is touched on, in part, primarily in the first lamentation. Lamentations 1, like the other chapters, is in the form of an alphabetic acrostic; the first consonant of each verse follows the order of the Hebrew alphabet. This poetic form clothes lamentations over the fall of Jerusalem and the suffering of its people. In gripping pictures their misery is placed before our eyes. The text uses elements of the popular lament and of the threnody over a corpse.[2] This is already an initial difference from the use of prophetic marriage imagery in other books: There it mainly appears in the context of judgment, in Isaiah also in announcements of salvation. Here it is found in laments.

[1] Otto Kaiser, "Klagelieder," in Helmer Ringgren, Walther Zimmerli, and Otto Kaiser, *Sprüche. Prediger. Das Hohe Lied. Klagelieder. Das Buch Esther* (3rd ed. Göttingen: Vandenhoeck & Ruprecht, 1981) 295, also votes for regarding 2 Chr 35:25 as a reference to the attribution of Lamentations to Jeremiah; Ivo Meyer, "Die Klagelieder," in Erich Zenger et al., *Einleitung in das Alte Testament* (3rd ed. Stuttgart et al.: Kohlhammer, 1998) 432, sees it differently; he proposes that this is a reference to a work that has been lost.

[2] Hedwig Jahnow, *Das hebräische Leichenlied im Rahmen der Völkerdichtung* (Giessen: A. Töpelmann, 1923) 270, had already pointed accurately to the mixture of genres: "Only in an altered form, then, could the image of the corpse undergo the highly significant *transformation* we find in the Threni: the transformation of what originally was an entirely secular genre into a *religious poem.* In literary-critical terms also we can observe this development, namely as an *influence* from the *genre of the popular psalm of lament,* otherwise strictly distinct from the threnody over a corpse. This influence is especially evident in 1:9c, 11, 20-22; 2:20-22, and is clearest in the appeal to YHWH, whose name never appears in a real threnody." (Emphasis supplied.)

Lamentations 1 focuses on the lament of the city "woman" Jerusalem. Usually called "daughter Zion," the city "woman" also appears in Lamentations 2–4. In the first song this address is used only at 1:6. After an introduction in which the situation of the "woman" Jerusalem is described from a distance, in the third person singular, "she" speaks in Lam 1:9b, 11b-16, 18-22. She herself tells of her hard fate, which historically is most probably to be identified with the conquest of Jerusalem in 586 B.C.E. It is probably also the exilic situation out of which the text, with its drastic and vivid descriptions of great suffering, arises.[3]

The text in Lamentations 1 in which most of the terms from the marriage imagery appear is 1:8, 9a:

> 8 Jerusalem sinned grievously,
> so she has become "uncleanness";[4]
> all who honored you despise you,
> for they have seen your nakedness.
> She herself groaned and turned her face away.
> 9 Her uncleanness is in her skirts;[5]
> she took no thought of her end.
> Her downfall was appalling. There was none to comfort her.**

These two verses immediately preceding Jerusalem's first-person discourse interpret her fate against the background of terms that are other-

[3] Otto Kaiser, "Klagelieder," sees it differently. He points to the parallels in form, structure, motifs, and vocabulary between Lamentations 1 and 2 (p. 312), for which reasons he thinks Lamentations 1 is to be dated simultaneously with the post-exilic text of Lamentations 2 (pp. 301–302). He proposes that Lamentations 1 "originated in the time after the consolidation of the Jewish community around the priesthood of the Second Temple" (p. 313). Ivo Meyer, "Die Klagelieder" 433, takes cautious exception with regard to Lamentations 1: "The text presupposes the destruction of Jerusalem in 586 (cessation of pilgrimages, v. 4; desecration of the Temple, v. 10); it is an open question whether such a text could still be written after Deutero-Isaiah, after the rebuilding of the Temple, and after the permission for the dispersed to return."

[4] At this point Bertil Albrektson, among others, suggests that the otherwise untranslatable *hapax legomenon* לנידה be derived from נדה (*Studies in the Text and Theology of the Book of Lamentations. With a Critical Edition of the Peshitta Text* [Lund: Gleerup, 1963] 64). The expression לנדה is found, with the same reference to Jerusalem, in Lam 1:17. נדה points clearly to the sphere of menstruation and sexuality, which would accord with the reference to ערוה, "shame, nakedness" in the lines that follow. Here we should note that the connotation of the uncleanness of a menstruating woman is to be clearly distinguished from pollution through זמה, "shameful deeds," or תועבה, "abomination." Ethical and biological "pollution" are, indeed, described with the same word, טמא, but the ways of dealing with it are not identical (see above, ch. 8, n. 44). This speaks against the interpretations of, for example, Jacob Milgrom, David P. Wright, and Heinz-Josef Fabry (art. נדה, *niddāh*, *TDOT* 9:234) or Claus Westermann (*Die Klagelieder. Forschungsgeschichte und Auslegung* [Neukirchen-Vluyn: Neukirchener Verlag, 1990] 101).

[5] For שול see above, Chapter 3 C iii; it is not impossible that in this text passage, with its sexual coloring, "genitals" may be intended.

wise used frequently in the prophetic marriage imagery.[6] There are parallels particularly to the scenes and scenery of sexual violence.[7] Here are "admirers," expressed this time with the *pi'el* participle of כבד. In Lam 1:2 (אהבים) and 1:19 (מאהבים) there is also mention of ex-"lovers" who now are no longer the "woman's" comforters; these terms are found a great deal more frequently in the parallel texts. These friends have "dealt treacherously" or "been untrue" (בגד, 1:2). Such a way of speaking is also very common in the context of marriage imagery in Jer 3:7, 8, 11, 12, but there as a predicate or behavior of the "woman." The former admirers' turning away in Lam 1:8-9 is traced to two causes: In the first place, those standing around have seen (ראה *qal*) the "nakedness" or "shame" (ערוה) of the "woman" Jerusalem. The second reason is the "uncleanness" of her skirts or genitals; here, as in other texts of the prophetic marriage imagery, שׁול cannot be reduced to a single meaning. Reading "skirts" recalls what we said about the parallel motif in Jer 2:34; there "Israel" is reproached because the blood of the poor and innocent is found (מצא *nip'al*) on her skirts (כנף). There is thus a clear reference to the Israelites' concrete social misconduct. It is different in Lam 1:8-9: here a double connotation is possible, with reference both to social misdeeds and sexual impurity.[8] In terms of motif both references are possible, but the terminology points rather to the

[6] Therefore in my view Kathleen O'Connor's opinion that Jerusalem's uncleanness in Lam 1:9 results from her adultery is inaccurate ("Lamentations," *WBC* 180).

[7] Ulrike Bail compares the imagery of violence in Lam 1:8b especially with Jer 13:22, 26; Ezek 16:37, and Nah 3:5-7 (*Gegen das Schweigen klagen. Eine intertextuelle Studie zu den Klagepsalmen Ps 6 und Ps 55 und der Erzählung von der Vergewaltigung Tamars* [Gütersloh: Chr. Kaiser/Gütersloher Verlagshaus, 1998] 188–91). On Lamentations 1 she writes (p. 190) that against the background of these texts ". . . and in view of the violent context in Lamentations we may suppose that Lam 1:8b also refers to a rape." There is a connection with sexual violence not only in Lam 1:8-9. In Lamentations 2 as well Elke Seifert discerns imagery of rape: "When God pours his wrath into her tent (2:4) and breaks walls and ramparts (2:8, 9), this awakens associations with the forced penetration of a woman in sexual intercourse" (*Tochter und Vater im Alten Testament. Eine ideologiekritische Untersuchung zur Verfügungsgewalt von Vätern über ihre Töchter* [Neukirchen-Vluyn: Neukirchener Verlag, 1997] 285).

[8] Thus Fokkelien van Dijk-Hemmes (in Athalya Brenner and Fokkelien van Dijk-Hemmes, *On Gendering Texts. Female and Male Voices in the Hebrew Bible* [Leiden and New York: Brill, 1993] 86): "In addition to the isolation menstruation brought with it, this passage also depicts a woman mishandled and rejected by her husband." In contrast, Barbara Bakke Kaiser restricts the meaning of the sexual imagery too severely to menstruation alone ("Poet as 'Female Impersonator': The Image of Daughter Zion as Speaker in Biblical Poems of Suffering," *JR* 67 [1987] 175–76). She does mention that Jerusalem is described as the victim of rape in Lam 1:8 (ibid. 175), but in her interpretation she emphasizes that here the poet is presented as a menstruating woman in order to arouse sympathy on the part of the hearers for Jerusalem's situation, especially her isolation and uncleanness (ibid. 175–76). In my opinion this is overdrawn, also as regards the consequences of menstruation for Israelite women.

latter. Here there is allusion to the scenes of sexual violence in the prophetic marriage imagery (in Hos 2:12; Jer 13:22, 26; Ezek 16:36-37; 23:10, 18, 29; Isa 47:2-3, or Nah 3:5-6). Still more clearly than in those other passages, here the body of the "woman" is the place in which "uncleanness" is made evident. Two expressions for this are placed at the beginning of v. 8 (נ[י]דה) and v. 9 (טמאה). While with נדה the primary thought is probably in the first instance of the "uncleanness" of the menstruating woman, טמאה can also refer to other forms of uncleanness. This word takes up some specific terminology from Ezekiel. The double reference to uncleanness makes it clear that Jerusalem, through both her misdeeds and her punishment, is now quasi-essentially "unclean through and through." The text leaves open the cause of the uncleanness, but the context points to acts of sexual violence. In any case, the consequence of the uncleanness on the metaphorical level will be the isolation of the "woman."[9] Jerusalem here laments the absence of any "consolers."

More problematic is Jerusalem's relationship to YHWH in Lamentations 1, against the background of the marriage imagery. The late parts of the book of Isaiah speak to the same historical situation as Lamentations 1, but there we find no scenes of sexual violence against the textual "woman/wife" of YHWH. If Lamentations 1 is set in the already familiar context of the marriage imagery, no one but YHWH can be the perpetrator of the violence. This is established by the text itself: According to Lam 1:5 the violence clearly comes from YHWH. Against this background the relationship between YHWH and Jerusalem appears as an inscrutable model for a marriage: "She" seeks to renew contact with "him" after "he" has done violence to "her" and "her children," and she herself assumes the guilt for what has happened.

Alongside YHWH the former "lovers" of the "woman" do not play as crucial a role as they do, for example, in Ezekiel. Figures similar to the "lovers" are also mentioned in Lamentations 1, however: In Lam 1:12 they are called "all who pass by" (עברים). These, in turn, play a significant part in Ezekiel 16:[10] In Ezek 16:15, 25 the "lovers," as "passersby," are enticed by "Jerusalem" and invited to engage in intercourse; in v. 37, on the other hand, they are those through whom YHWH carries out his judgment on her. In Lamen-

[9] This aspect of Lam 1:8-9 is pointed out, for example, by Maria Häusl: "When, in vv. 8, 9, the situation of the city is compared to that of a menstruating and therefore unclean woman her isolation in the situation of suffering, her state of being cut off, is especially evident" ("Die Klagelieder. Zions Stimme in der Not," in Luise Schottroff and Marie-Theres Wacker, eds., *Kompendium Feministische Bibelauslegung* [2nd ed. Gütersloh: Gütersloher Verlagshaus, 1999] 271).

[10] As shown in the previous chapter (see Chapter 8 A, at note 8), according to Galambush's model they are also of great significance for the structure of the text.

tations 1 she has already been punished; "all who pass by" are now those to whom Jerusalem calls out her lament, begging them to behold her misery. The role of the "passersby" differs positively from that in Ezekiel.[11]

Besides the parallels, especially in the scenes of punishment, there are also some clear differences from the other texts of the prophetic marriage imagery: Important key words like "whoring" (זנה) or "committing adultery" (נאף) do not appear in Lamentations, and nothing is said about "harlot's wages" (אתנן).[12] It is true that we find גלה, otherwise usually meaning "strip naked" in this imagery (Lam 1:3; 2:14; 4:22), but in a different context and with a different meaning. Otherwise nothing is said in Lamentations about marriage: neither wedding (בעל or לקח) nor betrothal (ארשׂ) is mentioned. Absent also are the words for idols (גלול or שׁקוץ) and for "shame" and the like (זמה, תועבה, or קלון); nothing is said about "being enflamed" (עגב) for lovers or about "lascivious neighing" (צהל). Instead, especially in Lamentations 1 great weight is placed on the absence of "consolers" (מנחם). Their absence yields the basic tone of the text (1:2, 9, 16, 17, 21). The fact that no one is there increases Jerusalem's pain and isolation. The impossibility of finding consolers for one so "devastated" is also emphasized in Nah 3:7 in the case of Nineveh.

Jerusalem's situation as *exiled* is especially obvious here. Differently from Hosea and Jeremiah, there is nothing more said about threats or warnings to repent. It is too late for that: the judgment has been accomplished. But unlike the case in Ezekiel, what is presented to our eyes is not the death of the city, but her terrible punishment. She has suffered severely and still suffers—but she is alive. The fact that, as a person in the text, she can still speak "proves" that she has survived. But she has suffered grave losses. She laments her suffering, and in doing so she acknowledges her guilt.

That the "woman" herself is given a voice is something new in contrast to other texts of the prophetic marriage imagery. "She" herself laments, she gives expression to her suffering, she looks back at the history of her misdeeds. This is an artistic, poetic turn: the created "person" is more than a fiction; through her the suffering of Jerusalem can be more authentically

[11] Bo Johnson sees this differently; he equates the "enemies" in the last two verses of Lamentations 1 with the "lovers" in the first two verses ("Form and Message in Lamentations," *ZAW* 97 [1985] 63). Jerusalem then, in vv. 21-22, wishes on them the same fate that she has suffered. As interesting as Johnson's suggestions for the divisions of the individual chapters of Lamentations are, such an argumentation by itself is not sufficient to identify the two groups with one another.

[12] In my opinion Häusl is wrong ("Die Klagelieder," 276–77) when she says that there is no basis in the text for a marriage between Jerusalem and YHWH. Contrast the different opinion of van Dijk-Hemmes in *On Gendering Texts* 86: "this picture [Lam 1:11b-13, 15b-16] links up with the marriage metaphor developed further in prophetic literature . . . ."

portrayed and her confession of guilt appears more plausible.[13] She is the best witness to what has happened.

This message gives a theological response to Hosea's and Jeremiah's criticism of the people's behavior. Now the "woman" admits her guilt and attests to YHWH that he has imposed a just punishment (Lam 1:18a). In fact it is YHWH, her oppressor, to whom are directed most of the appeals to witness the condition of those who suffer (1:9b, 11, 20). But the text goes still farther: She, who through being "stripped" was so often the humiliated object of observation in the other texts of the prophetic marriage imagery, now begs to be looked at. Not only in this textual depiction do we find the ambivalent echo that has evoked feminist criticism. On the one hand there is the recognition that at last the "woman" is able to speak for herself. To this point she could do so only in a few words in which, for the most part, she accused herself (e.g., in Jer 2:23, 25, 35; Hos 2:5, 7 [MT 9]). Now, finally, she can express her suffering, put her pain into words. Her groaning and sighing are to be heard by all nations (1:18b). YHWH, too, is to hear her suffering (1:21), so that he may see that it is enough. In her disgrace the city "woman" no longer has a single consoler. In light of the reality of concrete women's lives this text has a number of implications. Fokkelien van Dijk-Hemmes emphasizes what it means that and how the "woman" in Lam 1:11b-13, 15b-16 speaks in the first person singular:

> It is the woman's viewpoint which is the focus of the discourse. Therefore, it is quite possible that Goitein is right in his assumption that "words like these were traditional on the lips of the professional lamenting 'wise women'" (Goitein 1988, 27); and that these words echo the lament of women whose individual situation was comparable to that of "Lady Jerusalem."[14]

Women today may be able to associate themselves with the lament of the "woman" in similar situations of suffering, and can draw language from it to express their own pain, as Kathleen O'Connor suggests.[15]

[13] Thus according to William F. Lanahan, "The Speaking Voice in the Book of Lamentations," *JBL* 93 (1974) 41: "The *persona* is not to be thought of as a fiction. It is a creative procedure in the displacement of the poet's imagination beyond the limitations of his single viewpoint so that he may gain a manifold insight into the human experience. The poet's manifold creative insight then becomes the ground by which the reader achieves a more powerful perception of the creative situation."

[14] Fokkelien van Dijk-Hemmes, in *On Gendering Texts* 86.

[15] Kathleen O'Connor, "Lamentations," 181: "Daughter Zion's voice evokes the pain of women who have lost their children, who know sexual abuse, who are victims of war and famine. To pray with daughter Zion is to join with the struggles of women around the globe. It is to reject victimhood by embracing the anger that can provide energy to transform relationships."

On the other hand, Lamentations does present the danger that gender stereotypes that legitimize violence against women may be strengthened and cemented. This may be promoted by four aspects of the text: First, the most intense suffering is portrayed in Lamentations by the use of scenes from the real lives of women.[16] Women are widowed by war (1:2; 5:3); women are raped (5:11). Mothers must witness the death of their children (2:12); in their hunger they even cannibalize them (2:20; 4:10). Here, however, it seems to me that there is not so much an intention to construct a gender stereotype as rather a generally accurate depiction of a real situation: In wartime women, if they survived, have in fact borne the greatest share of the suffering. They had to manage somehow to preserve their lives and those of their children in the rubble, in the midst of starvation and sickness.

A second starting point for feminist criticism is the metaphor of the "uncleanness" of the woman. This is the image by which the consequences of Jerusalem's "sinfulness" are illustrated. This way of thinking is similar to that in Ezek 36:17, where also the ethical impurity of Israel/Jerusalem is confused with the physical uncleanness of women. In this way women become *the* paradigmatically unclean persons.[17]

Still more extensive is a third problem in the text that has been a focus for feminist critics. Kathleen O'Connor points out that the very relationship to God projected in the speech of the textual "woman" Jerusalem in Lamentations 1 contains problematic aspects:

> As daughter Zion gives voice to her sufferings, she describes herself in language that today calls to mind the circumstances of battered women. She is abused, beaten, and tortured by the one whom she trusted. . . . Daughter Zion blames herself for the excesses of her abuser and, like contemporary victims of domestic violence, appears to have no self-esteem left.[18]

A fourth aspect that represents a problematic side of the theology of Lamentations is the passive endurance of suffering, here portrayed as legitimate force exercised by the divine "Lord." It is not clear from the text whether YHWH is more like the "husband" or the father of "daughter Zion." Elke Seifert has said, in the case of the daughter: "The statements [in many passages in Lamentations] can easily be associated with the image of the

[16] Jeremiah chooses a somewhat different focus: Here it is especially the pains of women in childbirth that serve as metaphor for the suffering of the exile.

[17] Feminist critique of this way of thinking and its consequences was presented above, Chapter 8 D.

[18] O'Connor, "Lamentations," 180.

raped daughter. Ultimately the feelings of power and triumph on the part of the man and the humiliation of the woman are essential features of a rape."[19]

Whether it is the "wife" or the "daughter" who must suffer divine violence, in any case these texts are deserving of criticism. This is especially true because here the "woman's voice" is used as a poetic instrument, with the result that they may operate at a level of identification for women that was not possible for the prophetic marriage imagery. The ambivalence of the texts will probably remain. At the same time, we can see here the limited validity of the marriage imagery as an interpretive model, in a case in which the text intends to speak with extreme severity of the horrors of the exile, but also of a new future for YHWH and Israel/Jerusalem. In the exilic situation the prophetic marriage imagery offers two primary possibilities: Either, like Ezekiel 16 and 23, it sees no future because the city is already "dead," or else the marriage imagery must retreat into the background, as here in Lamentations 1. There remains at least some hope that the reality of a marital relationship in Israel was so clearly different from the misery of Israel/Jerusalem in exile that marriage was not an appropriate metaphor for that situation.

[19] Elke Seifert, *Tochter und Vater* 286.

Chapter Nine

Isaiah: Destruction for Babylon, Salvation for Zion

A. Survey of marriage imagery in Isaiah

The beginnings of the book of Isaiah probably extend over a period of about five hundred years.[1] Scholarship distinguishes among three sections of the book with different linguistic, situational, and theological foci: First or Proto-Isaiah, most of which probably stems from the royal period (chs. 1–39*), Second or Deutero-Isaiah, from the exilic period (chs. 40–55*), and Third or Trito-Isaiah (chs. 56–66), whose origins are located in the post-exilic period.[2] The prophetic marriage imagery is used to different extents in the three parts of the book. It scarcely appears at all in Proto-Isaiah, but it is found at a number of important points in Deutero- and Trito-Isaiah.

A rhetorical element that runs through the whole of the book of Isaiah is the figure of "daughter Zion." This personification of the city of Jerusalem or of Zion is found, for example, in Isa 1:8; 10:32; 16:1; 37:22;[3] 52:2; 62:11, thus primarily in the first section of the book.[4] Besides "daughter Zion" there are a number of other "daughter" addressees. At one point, in

[1] This estimation is given by, among others, Hans-Winfried Jüngling ("Das Buch Jesaja," in Erich Zenger et al., *Einleitung in das Alte Testament* [3rd newly revised and expanded ed. Stuttgart et al.: Kohlhammer, 1998] 399), similarly Otto Kaiser, art. "Jesaja/Jesajabuch," *TRE* 16 (1987) 636–37. Further, possibly later changes can be discerned in the Qumran tradition of the book of Isaiah, but these will not be the object of our study.

[2] No overview of the very complex state of Isaiah research can be given here; we will simply refer to the works of Otto Kaiser (see n. 1 above, and the longer works listed in the bibliography).

[3] Here and in the parallel text in 1 Kings 19:21 the title "daughter Zion" is parallel to "daughter Jerusalem."

[4] Beate Schmidtgen has treated all the texts about Jerusalem/Zion as a city-woman in her dissertation (*Die Stadt als Frau im Buch Jesaja*. University of Basel, 2001). She observes that the metaphors of the city as woman in the book of Isaiah fulfill three primary functions: integration, identification, and reassurance. That is, these metaphors integrate different theological concepts, require the readers to identify with the goals of the writers, and offer a model for overcoming the crisis (p. 320).

22:4, the nation or the city is addressed with the title (otherwise typical of Jeremiah) "daughter of my people" (בת עמי).[5] Cities outside Israel, and foreign lands, are so entitled, especially in the first and second sections of the book.[6] However, almost none of the mentions of "daughter Zion" in the book of Isaiah is found explicitly in the context of the marriage imagery. Only in Isaiah 62 is the address "daughter Zion" (v. 11) used in close proximity to expressions from the marriage imagery (vv. 4-5).

It is not specifically a feature of Isaiah that the text speaks of "daughter Zion" without using expressions from marriage imagery in the sense on which this study is based. Jeremiah also mentions "daughter Zion" very frequently, and the expression appears in Mic 1:13; 4:8, 10, 13; Zeph 3:14; Zech 2:10 [MT 14]; 9:9; Lam 1:6; 2:1, 4, 8, 10, 13, 18; 4:22. Except for Lamentations 1, however, the marriage imagery does not furnish the context in these cases. Ezekiel, in contrast, does not speak of "daughter Zion," although he certainly has the idea of Jerusalem as a female personification or "woman." The appearance of the female personification of Zion as "wife" of YHWH in connection with promises of salvation[7] is unique to Deutero- and Trito-Isaiah; otherwise YHWH's "woman/wife" is spoken of in threats and proclamations of judgment, or in Lamentations in the context of laments.

Zion (and so also "daughter Zion") is one of the central figures throughout the book of Isaiah, and this is true even though expressions from the marriage imagery are not used in many places or in central passages. In some texts YHWH's "woman/wife" is not otherwise described. John F. A. Sawyer points out that her identity shifts between city, people, and a "woman/wife" who receives no further description.[8] There is scarcely any possibility that this refers to a figure on the same level as YHWH, and therefore a goddess; the same is true of Hosea, Jeremiah, and Ezekiel.[9]

[5] This address appears in Jer 4:11; 6:26; 8:11, 19, 21, 22, 23; 9:6; 14:17, as well as in Lam 2:11; 3:48; 4:3, 6, 10. In Ezek 13:17 the plural form is used with reference to the concrete "daughters of the people," who in the prophet's opinion are speaking false prophecies.

[6] Here the personification of "daughter Babylon" in Isaiah 47 plays an important part. There are also "daughter Gallim" in 10:30, "daughter Tarshish" in 23:10, and "daughter Sidon" in 23:12. Ulrike Sals is studying the personification of Babylon in the Old and New Testaments. Her dissertation (at the Ruhr-University of Bochum), to be completed in 2003, is entitled *Die Biographie der "Hure Babylon." Studien zur Intertextualität der Babylon-Texte in der Bibel.*

[7] Thus also Odil Hannes Steck, *Gottesknecht und Zion. Gesammelte Aufsätze zu Deuterojesaja* (Tübingen: J.C.B. Mohr [Paul Siebeck] 1992) 144.

[8] John F. A. Sawyer, "Daughter of Zion and Servant of the Lord in Isaiah: A Comparison," *JSOT* 44 (1989) 101–102.

[9] Irmtraud Fischer shows that Zion is not a goddess, an equal partner to YHWH, at any point in Isaiah ("Das Buch Jesaja. Das Buch der weiblichen Metaphern," in Luise Schottroff and Marie

It is true that "daughter Zion" does not appear very often in the context of expressions from the marriage imagery. However, the reverse is not true: When terms from the marriage imagery are used in Isaiah, the reference is usually to Jerusalem/Zion—except in the case of non-Israelite entitites. Here Tyre and Sidon in Isaiah 23 and "daughter Babylon" in Isaiah 47 are prominent. They are threatened, as we will show in section C below, with precisely the same punishments that are announced for YHWH's "whorish wife" in the other prophetic books. To that extent the marriage imagery in the book of Isaiah appears not to be as homogeneous as in the other prophets: The punishment YHWH otherwise imposes on his "wife" is not applied to her in Isaiah. YHWH's "wife," whom he forgives in Isa 54:5-6, can look forward to a happy destiny. After the exile YHWH will no longer leave her side and abandon her to enemies. Deutero-Isaiah's perspective, directed to the salvation and return of the exiled people, apparently explains this emphasis within the marriage imagery. In Trito-Isaiah, in 62:4-5, YHWH is depicted as the one who has forgiven his city—in the hope that, as a result, people will respond with righteous behavior.

The very division of the book of Isaiah into three sections and the absence of a prophetic figure in the second and third sections make it improbable that there is any point of biographical or historical contact for the marriage imagery within it, as seems indicated in Hosea, Jeremiah, and Ezekiel. It is true that the first section of the book tells us that Isaiah had children with a woman prophet (8:3). At YHWH's instruction he—like Hosea—gives these children symbolic names (7:3; 8:3). Apart from these bare notices, however, we know nothing of Isaiah's married life, and so we cannot find a starting point for the development of the prophetic marriage imagery in this area.

B. The use of marriage terms in Isaiah

i. Proto-Isaiah (Isaiah 1–39)

At the very beginning of the book of Isaiah occurs one of the two instances of the word זונה, "whore," with reference to Jerusalem/Israel. In Isa 1:21 it is used to open the passage 1:21-27, couched in the meter of a dirge over Jerusalem.

Theres Wacker, eds., *Kompendium Feministische Bibelauslegung* [2nd ed. Gütersloh: Gütersloher Verlagshaus, 1999] 251, 255), and gives references to other literature. "City" and "woman"—in addition to their grammatical gender in most West Semitic languages—have in common the aspects of giving shelter, nourishing, beauty, complete helplessness (ibid. 252). For "city as woman" see also above, Chapter 5 A.

How the faithful city has become a whore!

The "whore" metaphor is not pursued at this point. Only in 1:29 do we find an expression related to one of the deuteronomistic formulae about "whoring under every green tree": The Israelites have chosen "gardens" (גנות), which are also mentioned as places for illegitimate cultic practices in Isa 65:3; 66:17.[10] In Proto-Isaiah, however, this reproach is not extended or repeated. Hence the titling of *Jerusalem* as a "whore" in 1:21 is a unique instance that can scarcely be understood in this passage apart from the well-known texts from other prophetic books; thus it is probably an allusion to them.

Overall, the passage in 1:21-31, with its emphasis on law, righteousness, and judgment, sounds much like Isaiah 56–66. This is only one of the possible arguments for seeing this chapter, or at least this passage, as one of the redactional insertions in the Proto-Isaianic section by which the book was enhanced at the time of its completion in the post-exilic period.[11] If this is the case, then we may suppose that at the time of the prophet Isaiah the marriage imagery introduced by Hosea was not yet known.

The fact that the image of the "whore" is taken up once more in Proto-Isaiah, in ch. 23, does not contradict this. Chapter 23 is also to be regarded as a later addition to Proto-Isaiah.[12] In 23:15-18 the commercial city of Tyre is called a "whore" (זונה). A "prostitute's song" is sung over her, the "forgotten prostitute."

15 And on that day it will be thus: Tyre will be forgotten for seventy years.
Like the days of another king,[13] at the end of the seventy years,
so it will be for Tyre, as in the song of the whore:
16 Take a harp, go about the city, you forgotten prostitute;
play sweetly, sing many songs, that you may be remembered!
17 And at the end of the seventy years,
YHWH will come down upon Tyre.
And she will return to her prostitute's wages,
and she will whore with all the kingdoms of the world on the
face of the earth.

[10] Interesting in this connection is that the pairing of "trees" and "hills," otherwise characteristic of the deuteronomistic expression about "whoring" under or on them respectively, is given a very positive connotation in Deutero-Isaiah (44:23; 55:12).

[11] On this cf. Otto Kaiser, *Das Buch des Propheten Jesaja. Kapitel 1–12* (5th rev. ed. Göttingen: Vandenhoeck & Ruprecht, 1981) 56, 58.

[12] Otto Kaiser, *Der Prophet Jesaja. Kapitel 13–39* (2nd ed. Göttingen: Vandenhoeck & Ruprecht, 1976) 138–40; likewise idem, "Jesaja/Jesajabuch," 652, with reference to the broad exegetical discussion.

[13] The text is difficult to translate at this point; cf. Kaiser, *Der Prophet Jesaja. Kapitel 13–39,* 137.

18 And her profits and her prostitute's wages will be dedicated to YHWH;
they will not be stored or hoarded,
but her profits will serve those who dwell before YHWH
to eat their fill and dress in fine clothing.**

The fate of Tyre is different from that of the whores in Hosea, Jeremiah, or Ezekiel, and not only because Tyre is not YHWH's "wife." It is not merely that Tyre is negatively judged. After seventy years YHWH will again turn to her, and she will receive her "prostitute's wages." The term אתנן plays a part, especially in Ezekiel, in threats; it serves to mark the absurd attitude of the "woman" Jerusalem. The "woman" pays these wages to her lovers instead of receiving payment from them. In Isa 23:17-18, too, the prostitute's wages are applied in an unusual way: They are given not, as one would expect, to the local gods, but to YHWH as something "dedicated," that is, as a Temple gift. By this use of the wages as a gift to YHWH the negative connotation of the "whore" is somewhat softened here—since it is YHWH who gathers the income[14] and applies it for the benefit of his people.

In the same context there is a remote parallel to the familiar scenes in the prophetic marriage imagery. In 23:11-12 "daughter Sidon," another commercial city on the Near Eastern coast of the Mediterranean, is "treated violently" by YHWH. The verb עשׁק, appearing in 23:12 in the *puʿal* participle, is otherwise used primarily as an expression for the oppression of widows and orphans, foreigners, the sick, the poor, and the lowly. Parallel verbs are גזל, "rob," or רצץ, "oppress." Nowhere is עשׁק found in the context of imagery of sexual violence, and nowhere else in the Old Testament does it appear with a woman as its subject. In the context of threats against a personified city "woman," however, it seems possible that here a connotation of violence directed specifically against women, that is, in the sense of rape, finds an echo. Most German Bible translations tend in this direction as well.[15]

Thus terms from the prophetic marriage imagery are used especially in the chapters in Isaiah 1–39 that in all probability belong to later redactional layers. The instances are restricted to allusions and contain no developed imagery.

[14] Irmtraud Fischer ("Das Buch Jesaja," 252) points out that there YHWH appears in the image of a pimp—something that is not only daring in itself, but also because according to Deut 23:18 "the wages of a prostitute" are not to be brought into the Temple, so that by doing this YHWH in a sense offends against the ordinances he himself has given.

[15] This is true of the Luther Bible (1984), the *Einheitsübersetzung*, and the *Zürcher Bibel*. Translator's note: English Bibles shy away from the stronger language of the German translations. The KJV and almost all modern versions choose the neutral participle "oppressed" (NIV: "crushed").

ii. Deutero-Isaiah (Isaiah 40–55)[16]

In the book of Isaiah "daughter Zion" is presented as a "wife" of YHWH, even though terms from the prophetic marriage imagery are not present in every such passage. In the second and third sections of the book personified Jerusalem is only addressed as "daughter" once in each section, in 52:2 and 62:11.[17] Nevertheless, we will discuss the other passages as well, because they fall within the notion of the city "woman" Jerusalem/Zion, within which there is marriage imagery in Deutero-Isaiah also.

In 40:2, 9, for example, without any use of terms from the marriage imagery, there is the injunction to "speak tenderly" to the city (v. 2),[18] and she is to raise her voice as a messenger of joyful news (v. 9). In 49:14-26 Jerusalem appears as a female personification. At the same time YHWH is compared in v. 15 to a mother: as she cannot forget her children, so YHWH cannot forget Zion. In v. 18, in the context of proclamations of restoration, the city is compared to a bride adorned with jewels. In regard to the bride's adornment, Patricia Tull Willey points to the reception of Jer 2:32 in Isa 49:15, 18.[19] Many children are promised, in Isa 49:20-21, to the formerly

[16] Since this book was completed I have published a more detailed study of this part of the prophetic marriage imagery: Gerlinde Baumann, "Prophetic Objections to YHWH as the Violent Husband of Israel: Reinterpretations of the Prophetic Marriage Metaphor in Second Isaiah (Isaiah 40–55)," in Athalya Brenner, ed., *A Feminist Companion to the Latter Prophets* (Sheffield: Sheffield Academic Press, 2001) 88–120. After an introduction, I begin with a description of the problem, describing in a second section the prophetic marriage imagery in Hosea, Jeremiah, Ezekiel, and Lamentations. In a third section I investigate Deutero-Isaiah's objections to the image of YHWH as a violent husband. First I consider the depiction of YHWH's vengeance on Babylon in Isaiah 47 (especially vv. 2-3); here a kind of composite text is prepared using passages on the punishment of Israel/Jerusalem (Hos 2:12; Jer 13:22, 26; Ezek 16:23; Lam 1:8-9) and applied to Babylon. In a second step I investigate the texts in which YHWH and Zion are depicted as a married couple: Isa 49:14, 17-21; 50:1; 54:1-10. Here again we find, for example, terminological references backward to passages in the text that describe destruction (Isaiah 49; Jeremiah 13), but these are now negated. In a third step I adduce, for a refinement of the God-image, the passages in the text in which YHWH is compared to a woman, or to a mother (41:14; 45:10; 46:3-4; 49:15). Here, from a gender perspective, YHWH's maleness is clearly disrupted. Then, too, the Suffering Servant has to be considered as a counterpart to Zion. In some aspects these two figures are very similar. Zion, as an innocent, suffers for her "children," as the Suffering Servant bears the guilt of the Israelites. In the final section, Part 4, reference is made, in summary, to the elements of Deutero-Isaiah's imagery that require critique: The setting of patriarchal marriage remains determinative for the gender roles.

[17] This was discussed at the beginning of the chapter.

[18] Irmtraud Fischer ("Das Buch Jesaja," 254) points out that this phrase occurs in the OT "as the expression of a man's effort to persuade a woman who has already been injured (cf. Gen 34:3; Judg 19:3; Hos 2:16; Ruth 2:13 . . .)."

[19] Patricia Tull Willey, *Remember the Former Things. The Recollection of Previous Texts in Second Isaiah* (Atlanta: Scholars, 1997) 198–99. In what follows I can only refer in individual instances to Willey's very interesting work.

childless Jerusalem. Thus in this section Jerusalem is personified as a woman in different roles and at different stages of life: she is child, bride, and mother, while YHWH, on the other hand, is not only her husband, but also treats her as if he were her mother.

The otherwise similar metaphors in Isa 51:17-23 also work without terms from the marriage imagery. This text presents a look back at the judgment suffered by the city. YHWH gave Jerusalem the "cup of wrath"; she experienced judgment and harsh punishment. Here there may be references to Jer 25:15-28 or Ezek 23:31-34. Similarly to Isa 49:20, in 51:17-23 the "woman" is also addressed as one who is childless or a widow: According to vv. 18 and 20 her children are fainting or dead. Now, however, the cup of wrath is to be given to her former enemies.

In Isa 52:1-2 "daughter Zion" is called to awaken—her fetters are loosed and she is free to return from her imprisonment.

Now we must consider the passages in which there is frequent use of marriage imagery. First among these is Isaiah 47, which functions within Deutero-Isaiah as a kind of hinge: It clearly marks the division between the first and second parts of that section, characterized respectively by backward looks as the hard fate of Jerusalem/Israel and by a look forward to a happy future.[20] The change of subject to Babylon in ch. 47 marks a caesura. At the same time the two parts of Deutero-Isaiah are linked together by the fact that parallels are drawn to the previous fate of Jerusalem; Babylon and Jerusalem exchange roles. Within Isaiah 47, a pronouncement of judgment or dirge over "daughter Babylon," terms from the marriage imagery are used especially in vv. 2-3:

> 2 Take the millstones and grind meal, remove your veil,
> lift up your "skirt," uncover your legs, pass through the rivers!
> 3 Your nakedness shall be uncovered, and your shame shall be seen.
> I will take vengeance, and no one can stop me.**

In this scenario it is not Jerusalem/Israel who is humiliated, as is otherwise the case in the texts of the prophetic marriage imagery. Here it is the world power Babylon, imaged as a queen cast down from her throne and humbled. In vv. 2-3 the words for public stripping are used, for example, the "uncovering" (גלה) of her "shame" (ערוה).[21] Other terms from the prophetic marriage

[20] This is the thesis of Chris A. Franke ("The Function of the Satiric Lament over Babylon in Second Isaiah [XLVII]," *VT* 41 [1991] 418): "While there is a dramatic change from the misfortunes of Jacob/Israel in the beginning of xl-lv to the fortunes of Zion/Jerusalem in the ending chapters, ch. xlvii can serve not only as a point of division but as a link between the two."

[21] Consequently, this passage will be discussed below in section D.

imagery, such as "whoring" (זנה), "prostitute's wages" (אתנן), "commit adultery" (נאף), or "love" (אהב) are not used in Isaiah 47. The choice of words is easily explained from the context: Babylon has not been YHWH's "woman/wife." There has never been a marital relationship between them that could be destroyed by "whoring" or adultery. Nevertheless, the words of the punishment scene recall the other texts of the prophetic marriage imagery. In addition, vv. 9 and 12 also use "sorcery" (כשף) and other words from the spectrum of terms referring to magic. כשף otherwise appears in the same context only in Nah 3:5, as a reproof against Nineveh—another foreign power to be punished by YHWH. In Isaiah 47 this accusation is to be understood in connection with polemic against foreign gods, which plays a major role in Deutero-Isaiah.[22] Besides the aspect of "sorcery" there are still other parallels between Nah 3:4-5 and Isaiah 47. Babylon and Nineveh are given similar titles of power, though Nineveh's have a negative accent: while Babylon (Isa 47:5) is called "the mistress (גבירה) of kingdoms," Nineveh's title in Nah 3:4 is "mistress of sorcery" (בעלת כשפים).[23] The world powers Assyria and Babylon are thus personified in similar fashion as women, and then in a manner specific to women as persons humiliated and disempowered.

However, it is not only she who suffers this fate in the Old Testament. As Willey has shown, there are parallels even in the choice of words between Isa 47:1-7 and Lam 1:8-10; 2:10:

> The whole first line of 47:1 is composed of words found in Lam 2:10, except for the change in cities. The next line of verse 1 (שׁבי לארץ) and the first line of verse 5 (שׁבי דומם) correspond to the first three words of the verse (ישבו לארץ ידמי). These are the only two instances in the Bible of the idiom ישב לארץ. The combination ישב . . . דמם is likewise quite unusual.
>
> In verses 2-3 Babylon is told to remove her clothing and uncover her legs, so that, like Zion in Lam 1:8 (ראו ערותה), her nakedness is uncovered and her shame is seen (תגל ערותך גם תראה חרפתך). In verse 8 she is told to sit in silence (שׁבי דומם; see Lam 2:10—ישבו לארץ ידמו). In verse 7, Babylon's thoughtless arrogance is described in the same terms in which Zion's was in Lam 1:9 (לא זכרה אחריתה) . . . . This three word idiom concerning failure to remember one's end occurs nowhere else in the Bible.

[22] Chris Franke's article goes in this direction also ("The Function of the Satiric Lament," 418).

[23] There is one figure who combines the features in these two texts (Nah 3:4-5 and Isaiah 47), a royal persona and the accusation of sorcery, as well as that of "whoring," which is in Nah 3:4-5: namely Jezebel, in the first verse of the description of Jehu's murder of Joram in 2 Kings 9:22-26. In a publication that will appear very soon I inquire about the connections among these three texts ("JHWH als vergewaltigender Soldat im Alten Testament?"—see more on this below in Chapter 10, n. 20).

> The only difference between the two instances is in the verb: 3fs in Lamentations ("she did not remember") and 2fs in Isaiah ("you did not remember"). The change of subject from Zion to Babylon hints that the fate Zion already suffered will yet befall her oppressor. This message answers the hope, expressed in Lam 1:21-22, that YHWH punish Zion's enemies as Zion has been punished. Despite her arrogant claim to the contrary (Isa 47:8-9), Babylon is warned that she will be confronted in a single moment by two misfortunes that had once characterized Zion (see Lam 1:1, 20): widowhood (אלמן) and bereavement (שׁכאל).[24]

In this way the wish expressed in Lamentations for the punishment of the enemies is fulfilled—at least on the textual level in Isaiah 47. The choice of words in Deutero-Isaiah makes clear not only the reference to Lamentations, but also the equality of punishment. Jerusalem's (female) enemy encounters a fate as hard as the one she had formerly visited on Jerusalem.

The imagery in Deutero-Isaiah depicting Jerusalem's fate changes from this chapter onward. Henceforth a different tone is sounded. Now expressions from the marriage imagery are applied to Jerusalem/Zion in a positive way. This is especially true of Isa 50:1 and all of ch. 54. In Isa 50:1 YHWH asks rhetorically about a bill of divorce for "your mother":

> Thus says YHWH:
> Where is your mother's bill of divorce with which I have put her away?
> Or which of my creditors (is it) to whom I have sold you?
> Behold: because of your sins you were sold,
> and for your transgressions your mother was put away.**

In Isa 49:20-21; 51:18-20 Jerusalem is personified in the role of mother; as in 50:1, the "children" addressed are the people of Israel. The title "your mother" has other connotations as well: This address is used in Hos 2:4, 7 for Israel. There the Israelites are called upon to accuse their mother for having left YHWH and turned to other "men/husbands." Ezekiel also uses the metaphor of the mother critically. In Ezek 19:2, 10 Israel is the lion "mother" of the kings, and in Ezek 16:3, 44-45; 23:2, in the context of the marriage imagery, non-Israelite lands are called the mother of Jerusalem and Samaria, in order to give reasons for their way of life. Like their mother, so also the daughters do not follow YHWH, but instead turn to their "lovers." Here the mother has less of a caring connotation than she does in Isaiah; instead, she indicates the succession of sinfulness in Israel/Jerusalem. In contrast, especially in the second half-verse in Isa 50:1, the question of guilt is shifted very clearly in the direction of the concrete

[24] Willey, *Remember the Former Things* 168–69.

Israelites: The "mother" has not been punished for her own sins, as in Hosea and Ezekiel, but for the sins of her "children." It is no longer so that the "children," the Israelites, had to suffer exile because of the misdeeds of their "mother," Jerusalem, but rather the reverse.[25]

Another term used in this context also emphasizes that the tendency of Isa 50:1 is different from that of Jeremiah or Ezekiel. YHWH's critical inquiry about a "bill of divorce" (ספר כריתות) in Isa 50:1 has an undertone that is audible when the verse is related to one of the other two Old Testament references to such a document: Jer 3:8.[26] This passage says that YHWH has divorced himself from his "wife," the northern kingdom of Israel, with a bill of divorce. Jeremiah 3:1 ponders the question whether a divorce of YHWH from Israel or Judah can be reversed—by way of a threat intended to bring the inhabitants back to the right path, for the divorce is not yet accomplished. In Isa 50:1, we may suspect, there is an allusion to that context. Here in Deutero-Isaiah YHWH asks ironically whether a genuine document attesting to the divorce of YHWH from Israel, as postulated in Jeremiah, can be presented. The question can only be answered in the negative: First, YHWH's divorce from Israel was, after all, a metaphor. Second, in Jeremiah the divorce from *Israel* had been carried out—but not that from Judah/Jerusalem. In the context of the restoration of Jerusalem, already clearly announced in Deutero-Isaiah, 50:1 is most probably to be understood as a repudiation of the fate of Israel announced in Jer 3:1, 8. From the point of view of Deutero-Isaiah YHWH did not divorce his "wife" Jerusalem, and as a result it is quite possible for him to restore her previous situation, now that her punishment (exile) has been carried out.

The relationship between YHWH and his "wife" Jerusalem is still more clearly thematized in Isa 54:4-6:

> 4 Do not fear, for you will not be ashamed;
> do not be discouraged, for your hope will not be disappointed.
> For you will forget the shame of your youth,
> and the disgrace of your widowhood you will remember no more.
> 5 For your husband[27] is your creator;
> YHWH Sabaoth is his name,
> and your redeemer is the Holy One of Israel; the God of the whole earth he is called.
> 6 For YHWH calls you like a wife forsaken

[25] Similarly ibid. 203.

[26] The third reference is found in the legal ordinances on divorce in Deut 24:1-4; a "bill of divorce" is mentioned in vv. 1 and 3.

[27] HAL (136) also understands this form thus.

7 and grieved in spirit;
and the wife of a man's youth—is she cast off?
says your God.**

Jerusalem bears all the marks of an Israelite woman in deepest misery. She is portrayed as a barren, childless, lonely woman (v. 1) and a widow (v. 4). At the same time, however, YHWH turns her destiny to good: she now has children again (*par* 49:20-21), nor is she any longer a widow; YHWH (v. 5) is her "creator" (עושׂה) and "husband" (בעל),[28] and she is the "wife of his youth" whom he cannot repudiate (v. 6). It is true that in her youth she brought shame upon herself (v. 4b), but that is now forgiven. As "husband" of the "wife" Jerusalem, YHWH is called בעל. Here again there is a link to Jeremiah: In Jer 3:14; 31:32 YHWH calls himself בעל, "lord" of the Israelites. In Hos 2:16 [MT 18], in contrast, the "woman" Israel is expressly told that, after YHWH has renewed his courtship of her, she shall no longer say בעל to him, but instead "husband" (אישׁ). This presumably is to be seen against the background of the circumstance that בעל not only means "husband," but is also the name of the god who in a good many places, at least in the pre-exilic period, was YHWH's principal competitor for Israel's favor. This is how Baal is named, for example, in the broader context of the texts containing the marriage imagery in Jer 2:8 and Hos 2:8 [MT 10]. In the time of Deutero-Isaiah, Baal was no longer important as a primary competitor of YHWH; now Babylonian notions of gods played a much more significant role. Hence YHWH can be connected to the word בעל without any fear of awakening associations with the Canaanite god.

Thus Isa 54:1-6 takes up the older image of YHWH as the marital "lord" of Jerusalem and reshapes it to fit its own perspective. In light of the approaching return from exile, the marriage between YHWH and his "wife" appears in a different light than in the prophecies of disaster in Jeremiah and Hosea. Now YHWH is the husband who looks back at the exile as a time that could only happen because of his absence. As Sawyer emphasizes, YHWH is to be seen now, despite all his world-dominating power, in an astonishing pose of self-renunciation toward his "wife."[29] In Isa 54:7-9 he takes the major responsibility for the previous "crisis in the marriage," and woos her once again.[30] YHWH uses every means to attract "her." The

[28] Marie-Theres Wacker points out that here, differently from Hos 2:18, there is apparently no hesitation in addressing YHWH as בעל, which is both the term for a husband and also for the God who is YHWH's "competition" (Wacker, *Figurationen des Weiblichen im Hosea-Buch* [Freiburg: Herder, 1996] 247).

[29] John F. A. Sawyer, "Daughter of Zion," 94.

[30] Ibid. 95–96.

text does not clearly indicate who the "wife" is. She is only described as the rebuilt city of Jerusalem in 54:11-17.

In summary we may say that Deutero-Isaiah's marriage imagery is dominated by a usage that shows YHWH's partner as a "woman/wife" who may represent a number of concrete things. She can be a city, "daughter Zion," or the mother of the Israelites or of the inhabitants of Jerusalem: Her children are given back to her through the return of the exiles from afar. And she is YHWH's "wife," received back again, who, because she is "the wife of his youth," he cannot reject forever. Here in Deutero-Isaiah, as in the other prophets, the exile is viewed as YHWH's punishment for the pre-exilic sins of the people. But neither the guilt of the people nor the punishments of the "woman/wife" are described in detail. Only the removal and death of the children are mentioned as punishments. Differently from the other prophetic books, here there are no terms of sexual violence to illustrate the punishment of this "woman/wife," although they are used for the humiliation of the enemy, Babylon. Her destruction, a metaphor for the deprivation of political power, makes Jerusalem's return home possible. At the expense of another guilty "woman" the prophetic text can here develop a positive image of Jerusalem as YHWH's "wife." YHWH has forgiven Jerusalem. The "marriage" between the two, after a period of crisis, the time of his absence (54:7), can go forward.

iii. Trito-Isaiah (Isaiah 56–66)

In this section of the book the situation of the exiles, now returned to their homeland, is more central than in the previous chapters. There are no more sayings against foreign powers. Ethics are strongly accented, with emphasis on doing "justice and right."

In Isa 57:3 the Israelites are called "children of a sorceress, offspring of an adulterer and a whore."[31] The term for "sorceress" (from ענן II) is close to כשף, which we mentioned in its context in Isa 47:9, 12. In Isa 2:6 Israel, "the house of Jacob," is described as a place full of diviners (and soothsayers). In addition, "divination" (ענן II) is branded in Deut 18:10 as "abhorrent." In Isa 57:3 the Israelites are accused of a combination of offenses that, taken together, are otherwise only attached to a foreign power: Nineveh in Nah 3:4-5. "She" too, as we will show, is called both "whore" and "mistress of sorcery." In the context in Isaiah this combination represents

[31] The form ותזנה (ו-Perfect *qal,* 3rd singular feminine) lacks an appropriate subject, which is why it makes sense to follow the BHS conjecture for וזנה, resting on the LXX (καὶ πόρνης), and translate "and a whore."

a summary of accusations against YHWH's unfaithful "wife" (1:21) or the "whorish" female personification of Tyre (23:15-18) and "daughter Babylon," each of them called "sorceress" (47:9, 12). Since Trito-Isaiah contains no threats against foreign peoples this adjustment of imagery can be understood to mean that the "evil" of familiar foreign and domestic entities is ascribed to Jerusalem in 57:6-13—perhaps as a reflection of religious practices "brought along" from Babylon?

One thing that is especially new in contrast to Deutero-Isaiah is that here the Israelites are not addressed as children of the "woman" Jerusalem/Zion. Now they have two parents. This mention of such a pair is unique in the Old Testament, since otherwise in the context of the prophetic marriage imagery it is usually only the mother who is mentioned, and she is called an adulteress.[32] Thus in Isa 57:3 the Israelites who do not do justice and right are (dis)qualified as children of parents who practice sorcery and adultery. The "succession of sin" thus does not run, as was especially the case in Hosea or Ezekiel, through the mother alone, but through both parents; it is not only the "woman/wife" who is responsible for the misbehavior of the "children."

Immediately after this accusation against the Israelites the (again personified) "woman" Jerusalem is confronted with one of the typical reproaches of the prophetic marriage imagery, not found in Isaiah to this point: She has set her bed on the mountains—there are associations here with the deuteronomic expression about "whoring under every green tree and on every high hill"[33]—and has purchased partners for her nightly couch (57:6-8). Here there is an echo both of acts of adultery and of the payment of "prostitute's wages," used by Ezekiel to show the absurdity of Jerusalem's lascivious behavior: The "woman" buys lovers for herself instead of being paid for her services (Ezek 16:34, 41). We are also familiar, from the context of Ezekiel, with the accusation of child sacrifice, raised against the Israelites immediately before the beginning of this speech to personified Jerusalem, in 57:5b. In addition, Jerusalem has "freed" herself from YHWH, a reproach expressed in 57:8 with גלה *piʿel*. Elsewhere this word in this context always describes the uncovering of nakedness as a

[32] Thus, e.g., in Hosea and Jeremiah, but somewhat differently in Ezekiel, where in 16:3, 45 powers outside Israel are called the parents: the mother a Hittite, the father an Amorite, in each case *pars pro toto* for the whole nation. Here, of course, the naming of the parents does not yet have an explicit connotation of adultery or "whoring," but that the "negative" association with worship of foreign gods is thus handed on to the daughters certainly lends such a meaning to the passage.

[33] There is an echo of this expression, as mentioned above in section A, in Proto-Isaiah in 1:29, which is probably late.

symbol of sexual intercourse. Here it is used with a different meaning, but it still establishes a connection to the other passages of the prophetic marriage imagery.

Thus parts of Isaiah 57, expecially vv. 3-13, appear as references to older theologoumena that are now taken up again in order to call to mind "Jerusalem's" inescapable sinfulness.

This image of Jerusalem, as well as its relationship to YHWH, is revised, at the latest, in Isaiah 60: Here, again in the tone of Deutero-Isaiah, a vision is projected of a righteous Jerusalem that stands altogether in a healthy relationship to YHWH. Without using words from the prophetic marriage imagery the text addresses Jerusalem directly as a "woman," in the second person singular. She again has children; they had been thought to be lost, but now they return to her (v. 4). In another passage (v. 16) she herself is again a nursling at the kings' breasts.[34]

A marriage metaphor is also used in the next chapter, at Isa 61:10, where the text speaks of being decked like a bridegroom or bride in the first person singular. We can think of this as a speech by Jerusalem, giving expression to her joy over YHWH's righteousness.

At two other places in the third section of the book personified "Jerusalem" is again addressed by YHWH. Isaiah 62:1-8 sounds much like ch. 60. Both of these chapters begin with a metaphor of light. At 62:4-5 the text speaks of a (re?)marriage of YHWH and Jerusalem:

> 4 You shall no more be termed Forsaken,
> and your land shall no more be termed Desolate;
> but you shall be called My Delight Is in Her,[35]
> and your land Married;
> for YHWH delights in you,
> and your land shall be married.
> 5 For as a young man marries a young woman,
> so shall your builder marry you,
> and as the bridegroom rejoices over the bride,
> so shall your God rejoice over you.

In 62:4 the textual "woman" first receives new titles: instead of negatives, she now has names that sound positive. In 48:8, in Deutero-Isaiah, Jerusalem had a negative name. Trito-Isaiah, in contrast, chooses designa-

[34] Irmtraud Fischer points out ("Das Buch Jesaja," 254) that the attribution of YHWH's motherly care to the most powerful rulers in the world is very daring.

[35] Thus HAL 327. This symbolic name is identical with the personal name of the mother of Manasseh and the wife of Hezekiah in 2 Kings 21:1.

tions for the city that are clearly more positive, as in 60:14 and 62:12. Here in 62:4 the title is "My Delight Is in Her," and her land is called "Married" (בעולה); YHWH rejoices over the city, and her land will be married (בעל *nipʿal*); the only plausible construction in the context is that it will be married to YHWH. In the following verse the image of the marriage is more colorfully painted: As a young man marries a young woman (בעל *qal*), so YHWH, the builder, will marry his city Jerusalem (בעל *qal*); both weddings are accompanied by joy, expressed here from the male perspective of the bridegroom speaking about the bride. The verb בעל is used four times in these two verses. It is one of the few Old Testament words that mean "marry" in most contexts. The heaping up of this verb, which otherwise occurs very seldom, in Isa 62:4-5 is unique in the Old Testament. Since the verb has the same sound as the noun בעל we can say again here what we said above regarding Isa 54:5: Apparently in the time of Deutero- and Trito-Isaiah it was no longer necessary to set YHWH and everything that could refer to his former competitor בעל in such crass opposition. In Isa 62:4-5 YHWH's delight (חפץ) in Israel and closeness to it are very clearly expressed in terms of marriage. The marital image is strongly accented again, as in Isa 54:1-6, but there is a difference between the texts inasmuch as in Isaiah 62 Jerusalem's children no longer play a part.

These children are important again in the last chapter of the book. In Isa 66:7-13 Jerusalem is once again shown in the image of a "woman," this time set in the foreground of the imagery in her role as a mother in childbirth. She is scarcely in labor before she gives birth. YHWH is the midwife. All her children, the inhabitants of the city, are to suck at Jerusalem's breast like nurslings (66:11). In connection with these motherly images of Jerusalem, YHWH is also drawn more powerfully into the picture: In Isa 66:13 YHWH will comfort the Israelites, through Jerusalem, as a mother comforts her child.

In summary we may say of the marriage imagery in Trito-Isaiah that it offers a kind of cross-section of the expressions from marriage imagery found in the first two sections of the book. The third section of the book of Isaiah contains a loose collection of harsh critique of Jerusalem alongside promises of joy and images of her marriage with YHWH. In the special sequence of themes in Trito-Isaiah we can read this as a "history of Jerusalem": from sinfulness through marriage with YHWH to wealth of children.

iv. Observations on the book of Isaiah as a whole

It is characteristic of the use of marriage imagery in the book of Isaiah that only a very limited spectrum of the corresponding terminology appears. For example, the terms favored by Ezekiel, such as גלול and שקוץ

("idols"), תועבה ("abomination"), טהר and טמא ("pure" and "impure"), and עגב ("be enflamed"), do not appear in the context of marriage imagery. The typical terms of that imagery, such as זנה ("whore," "play the harlot"), נאף ("commit adultery"), or "uncovering" (גלה) the "shame" or "nakedness" (ערוה) are seldom used by Isaiah. Moreover, the majority of these terms are not used with reference to Israel/Jerusalem, but in connection with foreign powers; thus the accusation of practicing "sorcery" (כשף) in Isa 47:9, 12 is directed at Babylon, and the reference to "prostitute's wages" (אתנן) in 23:17-18 has to do with what the city of Tyre, called a "prostitute" in 23:15-17, has "earned."

A third selection of words from the field of marriage imagery is used in Isaiah with different connotation than in the other passages. In Jeremiah, צהל is primarily a term for "whinnying" with sexual lust; in Isa 12:6; 24:14; 54:1 it expresses jubilation or joy. זמה, which in Ezekiel is a term frequently used for sexually-flavored "shameful deeds," does not appear with that meaning, but instead in Isa 32:7 is used with the sense of a (criminal) "plan."[36]

Only a few late examples reveal the use of marriage imagery in the same vein as in the prophets we have previously considered: the naming of the city of Jerusalem as a "whore" (זונה), for example, in 1:21, or the address to part of the Israelites as children of an adulterer (מנאף) in 57:3. This same context (57:8-11) contains the sole instance of the "lovers" of Israel/Jerusalem. Differently from the other prophets, here it is not Zion herself who is called to account for her pre-exilic bad behavior: "The fate of violence and humiliation is never tied directly to her own behavior."[37]

The development of the "woman" with her various concretions proceeds in the book of Isaiah like the course of a woman's life in ancient Israel. As Irmtraud Fischer observes, the dominant image of "daughter Zion" in the first part of the book shifts, from Isaiah 40 onward, to the image of the "woman" Zion, YHWH's "wife" and the mother of the inhabitants.[38] The third part of the book presents a third journey through this biography.

Thus the book of Isaiah makes use of a highly varied female imagery whose focus is clearly more positive than that in Hosea, Jeremiah, and Ezekiel. This is also evident in the use of the prophetic marriage imagery, which takes its place in the second and third parts of the book, in an exilic and post-exilic perspective, in a context of restoration and new beginnings.

[36] Thus, e.g., Sigurdur Ö. Steingrimsson, art. זמם, *zmm*, *TDOT* 4:89.

[37] Irmtraud Fischer, "Das Buch Jesaja," 253.

[38] Ibid. 254.

C. Metaphors of sexual violence in Isaiah

The book of Isaiah refers to sexual violence against real persons in only two passages. Both are in military contexts: In the vision of the conquest of Babylon in Isaiah 13, vv. 13-18 describe excesses that were probably typical of wars in that period. Verse 15 first portrays people being slain by the sword; vv. 16 and 18 give a vivid depiction of children being smashed before their mothers' eyes (v. 16) or killed in other ways (v. 18); houses are plundered and women raped. The verb שׁגל is used in this passage, as in Deut 28:3; Jer 3:2, and Zech 14:2; in all these places it refers to the rape of women as one of many gruesome deeds associated with conquest.

Isaiah 20:4 depicts the sexual humiliation of prisoners of war. Egyptians and Kushites are told that they will be led away by the king of Assyria, with their buttocks bared (חשׂופי שׁת) as an act of shaming. Immediately following this expression ערוה, "shame," is used in a construct phrase with "Egypt," and thus apparently serves more to describe the "shaming" than to designate the sexual organs. There is a material parallel to this verse in 2 Sam 10:4, where David's messengers, sent in friendship, are seized by the Ammonite king Hanun, their beards half shaved, and their garments cut off up to their "buttocks" (שׁת). They had to return home thus bared. Both these passages make it clear that public stripping of opponents was not restricted in ancient Israel or the Near East to women; men could also suffer that fate. As indicated above (Chapter 5 B iii), there are also pictorial representations of such scenes. However, women were also frequently raped as well as being shamed through stripping, which had far more severe consequences than mere humiliation. It is probable that the depiction of the punishment of the textual "women" also rests on experiences and images from wartime.

Much more frequently and in a more developed manner than in the passages referring to actual persons, metaphors of sexual violence are used in the book of Isaiah in association with metaphorical "women." One text in which the "daughter of my people" suffers sexual violence stands alongside a number of others in which the victims are personified foreign cities or nations. The address "daughter of my people," frequently found in Jeremiah and Lamentations, is also used in Isa 22:4 for Jerusalem or Israel. In this context the personified "woman" suffers "mistreatment" (שׁד). The associated verb שׁדד otherwise describes "devastation" or "laying waste," but it can also have sexual connotations, as in its reference to Nineveh in Nah 3:7. There it is used in the sense of a description by observers of the situation of the textual "woman" Nineveh. Sexual violence has been done to her, and now she is "laid waste." Differently from the case of Nineveh, however, in Isa 22:4 there is no soberly distant observation; this verse expresses the prophet's unconsolability over this mistreatment, because of which he weeps.

In two places in Isaiah metaphors of violence that can also have sexual connotations are applied to female personifications of foreign powers: In Isa 23:12 "daughter Sidon" is addressed as an "oppressed" (עשׁק) young woman. It is not clear from other usages or from the surrounding context of this verse whether the reference is to sexual or other forms of violence, but given the reference to a female personification and the very specific acts of sexual violence that are otherwise done to her, it cannot be excluded.

In contrast, that context is clearly present in Isaiah 47. "Daughter Babylon," who is here the center of interest as regards punishment, is developed in Deutero-Isaiah as a contrast figure to "daughter Zion." There was already a depiction of Babylon as a hostile power in Isaiah 13–14 and 21:1-10.[39] In Isaiah 47, by contrast, the focus is, on the one hand, on the personification of this world power, and on the other hand on the changed political situation: Babylon is no longer the great threat to tiny Israel/Judah, but is itself a power on the verge of toppling. Its fall, and the humiliations and disempowerments associated with it, are illustrated in Isaiah 47 with the image of a queen dragged down from her throne.

Throughout the whole of ch. 47 the textual "woman" Babylon is threatened with violence; images of sexual violence occur primarily at the beginning of the text in vv. 2-3.[40] In v. 2 "daughter Babylon" is commanded, in a manner we are familiar with from the prophetic marriage imagery, to remove (גלה *piʿel*) her veil (צמה) and also to strip off (חשׂף) her "robe" (שׁבל), so that her legs (שׁוק) are uncovered (גלה *piʿel*) and she can walk through the rivers. In v. 3 it is then announced that her "nakedness" (ערוה) is to be "uncovered" (גלה *nipʿal*), and her "shame" (חרפה) will be seen (ראה *nipʿal*). The whole passage—except for the beginning in v. 2 and the "passing through the rivers"—reminds one strongly of the scenes depicted in Jer 13:22, 26; Ezek 16:36-37; 23:10, 18, 29; Nah 3:5; Lam 1:7-9, pictures of humiliation through public stripping and with it, quite possibly, sexual violence. The choice of words is not completely identical with any of these passages, but all the words used in Isaiah 47 appear in at least one of the other texts. The special feature of Isaiah 47, as mentioned above,[41] is that here a fairly broad description of violence appears, using the familiar vocabulary—but the reference is different, since the threat is directed not at

[39] On this cf. Otto Kaiser, "Jesaja/Jesajabuch," 638.

[40] A translation and remarks on these verses can be found above.

[41] See above at B i.

Israel or Jerusalem, but at the personification of a foreign power. The only Old Testament parallel to this reference of imagery of sexual violence to a non-Israelite "woman" is in Nah 3:4-7.[42] Here the violence is directed against the female personification "Nineveh," standing for the world power Assyria, which according to Nahum's depiction is also about to topple.

The judgment against "daughter Babylon" in Isaiah 47—differently from the other prophetic books that use daughter-imagery for foreign nations—is couched in the same words used in those other prophetic books for the judgment against Jerusalem/Israel: namely, in imagery of sexual violence. In contrast to other allusions to metaphors of sexual violence, here the context of marriage is abandoned because the proclamation of sexual violence is directed against a foreign power, with which YHWH does not have a marital tie. There is an intensification with respect to the other imagery of violence insofar as here there is also a clear alteration in the status of the "woman." In Mesopotamian legal texts, covering with a veil (here as צמה in 47:2) marks a woman's social position. The removal of the veil, at least at certain periods and in certain places, was to be seen as social degradation or loss of status.[43]

In summary of this section we may say that imagery of sexual violence appears at a number of points in the book of Isaiah in a less well-developed form, and in one passage in more detailed fashion. There is no such imagery in Trito-Isaiah. The sole well-developed text containing imagery of sexual violence is Isaiah 47, with the threat of humiliation and destruction directed at "daughter Babylon." With the vocabulary otherwise applied to Israel/Jerusalem, here the text depicts violence directed at a foreign power. This is otherwise found in the Old Testament only in Nah 3:4-7. Deutero-Isaiah, in ch. 47, contrasts "daughter Zion" and "daughter Babylon" within the framework of daughter-imagery. According to my thesis female imagery is used to place the sayings against foreign nations and threats against foreign peoples that are so frequent in Proto-Isaiah in

[42] For this text, see Chapter 10 C below.

[43] Here Shalom Paul refers to Middle Assyrian legal texts: "Though no mention of the practice of veiling is found in Babylonian texts, it is the subject of MAL A:40, marking the distinction of different social classes of women. Married women and women of the upper classes must be veiled in public (lines 42-57), for veiling is the privilege of the respectable and distinguished lady. . . . [A] common prostitute, *ḫarimtu* (lines 66-76), and an ordinary slave girl, *amtu* (lines 88-93), are not permitted to be veiled under any circumstances. If they do veil themselves, they are severely punished" ("Biblical Analogues to Middle Assyrian Law," in Edwin B. Firmage et al., eds., *Religion and Law: Biblical-Judaic and Islamic Perspectives* [Winona Lake: Eisenbrauns, 1990] 341–42]). The various methodological problems in comparing ancient Near Eastern parallel texts were discussed above, in Chapter 5.

contrast to the promise of salvation to Israel/Jerusalem: While the one "woman," Jerusalem, is promised a happy future, the other can expect only judgment and destruction. Thus the past suffering of the one stands in the scales against the predicted suffering of the other.

D. Feminist theological interpretation of Isaiah's marriage imagery

For some time now the descriptions of scenes from women's lives or the female imagery of "daughter Zion" in the book of Isaiah have been the subject of feminist-theological interest. The marriage imagery, however, has not been at the center of that interest. In Renita Weems's work, which interprets the problematic texts containing marriage imagery in a general overview, Isaiah does not appear at all. This lack of interest can be explained by the fact that the marriage imagery in Isaiah is by no means so broadly developed as in Hosea, Jeremiah, or Ezekiel, but also by the circumstance that it is not used here to such an extent in a way that demands criticism. "Whoredom" and "adultery" are mentioned only very marginally; in the second and third parts of the book the relationship of YHWH to his "wife" is depicted in tones of forgiveness and reconciliation, and the sole act of sexual violence on YHWH's part is directed not against his (ex)-"wife," but against Babylon, a foreign power.

Feminist critique has now begun to be applied to Isaiah 47. Elke Seifert considers "daughter Babylon" alongside other "daughters," and writes:

> The behavior of the "daughters," in which form foreign cities or countries are personified in this imagery, always requires punishment. Violence is done to them. They appear as stereotypes of "ruined" women in a patriarchal society that demands subordination of women, condemns sexual promiscuity, and permits men the right to sexually subject women and do violence against them. In this way their situation is like that of women who, in war, fall into the hands of the enemy: They are regarded as "whores" whom a man, according to an androcentric system of values, may put to shame without burdening his sense of what is right (cf. Nah 3:6; Lam 4:22). The loss of their honor makes women silent and frequently leads to their rejection (cf. Isa 47:5). Damaged and even ruined, they are forced to flee (cf. Isa 23:12; Jer 49:19). Often nothing remains to them except weeping before the altars (cf. Isa 15:2).[44]

This already gives us some indication of the original context of this imagery and its special problems. Part of the gruesome reality of war is the

[44] Elke Seifert, *Tochter und Vater im Alten Testament. Eine ideologiekritische Untersuchung zur Verfügungsgewalt von Vätern über ihre Töchter* (Neukirchen-Vluyn: Neukirchener Verlag, 1997) 298.

rape of the female inhabitants of conquered cities or countries by the troops on the winning side. As early as Isa 13:16 the prospect of their rape is presented to the eyes of the Babylonian women, and this proclamation is repeated to personified Babylon in Isaiah 47.

This text is especially problematic because here YHWH appears as the rapist. It is true that the concrete act of violence is expressed in passive form (Isa 47:3a), but in v. 3b YHWH is clearly the initiator of the act. Therefore YHWH's role here, and still more clearly in Nah 3:4-7, is that of a rapist. As Majella Franzmann notes, most interpreters eliminate the problem of this facet of the God-image at the primary level of the text itself, or in the translation,[45] or else they trivialize the rape in various ways.[46] The image of YHWH as rapist can be explained from the context in which the texts originated, as she writes:

> Violence done to women is a normal part of everyday life in a patriarchal society, and members are not socialized to feel sympathy for the victims of such violence. When people in such a society describe God by using male metaphors, then the danger is inevitable that "he" will not be able to escape what is regarded as normal behaviour for men in this context. To use the image of Yahweh as a warrior is to make possible Yahweh's acting as a soldier rapist.[47]

This kind of male God-as-rapist image has been handed down for thousands of years without being subjected to any kind of fundamental critique. This is not without consequences:

> In a reverse or circular process, men will be supported in their behaviour by the authority of the metaphor. It is never really the case that "it's just a metaphor." The long history of Hebrew and Christian communities dealing with God via male metaphors has made it well-nigh impossible for these

[45] Majella Franzmann, "The City as Woman: The Case of Babylon in Isaiah 47," *ABR* 43 (1995) 17: "The easiest solution taken to the problem of this metaphor by many commentaries and studies is to ignore the fact of the rape or to play it down to such an extent that it virtually disappears. Other scholars appear to believe that they will unduly offend readers' sensibilities if they speak plainly about the action."

[46] Here Franzmann quotes a passage from Robert Martin-Achard ("Esaïe 47 et la tradition prophétique sur Babylone," in John A. Emerton, ed., *Prophecy. Essays Presented to Georg Fohrer on his sixty-fifth birthday, 6 September 1980* [Berlin and New York: Walter de Gruyter, 1980] 92–93), here reproduced in context: ". . . she is to be reduced to being the least of slaves, the kind almost interchangeable with beasts (Exod 11:5), her work is to be hard and humiliating, even to being forced to turn the mill, her veil stripped off, her skirts tucked up, her thighs uncovered, and her femininity at the mercy of her masters (vv. 2-3). An inhuman labor with incessant insults, a degrading situation—this is what YHWH's vengeance has reserved for Nebuchadnezzar's capital (v. 3b), while at the same moment Second Isaiah invites Jerusalem to lift herself up, to cast off the yoke, and to put on once more her magnificent garments (Isa 52:1-2)!"

[47] Franzmann, "The City as Woman," 18.

> communities to differentiate the metaphors and the reality to which they refer. This is quite clear from the long list of religious and social ideologies, concepts, behaviours, regulations, and so on which are dependent on God's seemingly inherent maleness for their justification.[48]

These sorts of notions of omnipotence and violence shape images of the male even today, as illustrated, for example, by the quotations assembled by Alberto Godenzi.[49]

Beyond the necessity of dealing critically with such an image of God, we must point to the problem that what is here described is divine sexual violence not only against a female personification, but also against one who is ethnically other, a "foreign woman." The image of God that is otherwise developed "inwardly," in reference to reconciliation with Jerusalem/Israel, apparently has no contact with violence directed "outward," against "the others." Or can internal harmony be purchased only at the price of a redirection of violence against outsiders, foreigners?

E. Marriage metaphors in the context of Isaiah's religious imagery

This section will primarily sketch the overall context of the prophetic marriage imagery, both with a view to female imagery and also to the image of God in Isaiah and in its several parts. The material will be arranged thematically, and within the various themes the sequence in which the several aspects are treated will generally follow the order of the book itself.

i. The use of feminine imagery in the book of Isaiah

In the first part of the book the sufferings of the people Israel are illustrated primarily through examples of women or of experiences drawn from the context of women's lives. Isaiah mentions "widows" as well as orphans as *the* socially powerless, whose oppression represents an especially egregious injustice (1:17, 23; 9:16; 10:2). The "daughters of Zion" will be robbed at a minimum[50] of their beauty and their ornaments (3:16-24). Ac-

[48] Ibid.

[49] Alberto Godenzi, *Bieder, brutal. Frauen und Männer sprechen über sexuelle Gewalt* (2nd ed. Zürich: Unionsverlag, 1991), especially 38–59 ("'Any man who's halfway normal'—Confessions of Non-Indicted Perpetrators"); cf. also Elke Seifert, *Tochter und Vater* 308–309 and the literature she mentions. She also makes frequent reference to Godenzi's telephone interviews, conducted in Switzerland.

[50] F. Rachel Magdalene, "Ancient Near-Eastern Treaty-Curses and the Ultimate Texts of Terror: A Study of the Language of Divine Sexual Abuse in the Prophetic Corpus," in Athalya Brenner, ed., *A Feminist Companion to the Latter Prophets* (Sheffield: Sheffield Academic Press, 1995) 332–33, sees references also in vv. 17 and 26 to rape of the "daughters of Zion."

cording to 4:1, because of the shortage of marriageable men resulting from war, seven women will beg a single man that they be allowed at least to bear his name, in order that they may not be forced to live in shame, that is, without support. Isaiah 32:9-12 announces to the carefree and self-assured daughters of Jerusalem that they will soon be performing the rituals of mourning. Parallel to these examples from women's lives, Isaiah illustrates the consequences of war primarily through examples drawn from the lives of men. In contrast to Jeremiah, it is not the case in Isaiah that female imagery is preferred for the portrayal of suffering. Female imagery can also express Israel's self-confidence: In 37:22 "daughter Zion/Jerusalem" mocks the powerful Neo-Assyrian king Sennacherib—in a woman's voice![51]

In some passages female imagery, again in the first part of the book, is used in deprecatory fashion: The fact that "women" rule the people in Jerusalem (3:12) is not to be seen as a complimentary reference to queens or other women in high political office; it is meant to categorize the exercise of office by those in power as inadequate—for which reason fundamental rights are being violated.[52] A similar effect is intended by the attribution of "womanliness" to the Egyptians in Isa 19:16: They will be (weak) like women; "feminization" is intended as a depreciation of the strength and power of the Egyptians.

In contrast to Jeremiah and Ezekiel, in the book of Isaiah we can observe a different way of YHWH's dealing with his prophets. One difference is that the prophet Isaiah himself desires to prophesy (6:8). Isaiah is not a prophet "enticed" or "seduced" by YHWH, like Jeremiah, nor is he a prophet like Ezekiel who is totally at YHWH's command. Isaiah is much less pressured by YHWH, and consequently the office of prophet is not nearly so much portrayed as laden with pain in Proto-Isaiah as in the other two great prophetic books. As a consequence of this image of the prophet in Isaiah, YHWH also appears as the sender and most important conversation partner of the prophet, thus in a much different light than in Jeremiah and Ezekiel: he applies much less force against his prophet. From Isaiah 40 onward we cannot even perceive a prophetic figure at all: YHWH speaks much more "directly" to human beings, mediated only by the text itself.[53]

[51] Fokkelien van Dijk-Hemmes uses Isa 37:22 as an example of a mocking song sung by women. According to her thesis this can be regarded as an indication that F-voices (i.e., female) are behind this text (in Fokkelien van Dijk-Hemmes and Athalya Brenner, *On Gendering Texts. Female and Male Voices in the Hebrew Bible* [Leiden and New York: Brill, 1993] 44).

[52] Thus Irmtraud Fischer, "Das Buch Jesaja," 250, against Susan Ackerman, "Isaiah," *WBC* (1992) 164.

[53] Even though the figure of the Servant has many of the features of a prophet, he cannot be identified unmistakably and exclusively as a prophet.

Birth imagery is used especially in the first part of the book of Isaiah, and in an ambivalent manner.[54] On the one hand giving birth or being in labor is used as an image for the pains and/or the disempowerment to be suffered at YHWH's judgment, for example in 13:8; 21:3; 26:17. This third passage, as also 33:11, according to Irmtraud Fischer, has miscarriage as its background.[55] In any case, in both these passages one must note critically from a feminist perspective, as regards the use of imagery, that here birth represents only the crisis, guilt, or failure of the people; the fact that it can reflect an experience of strength and female potency plays no role here. On the other hand, birth can also be an image of the inbreaking of the salvation bestowed by YHWH, as in 7:14 with the birth of the "Immanuel." Fischer points out in this connection that with the exception of 33:11 "the image of giving birth in divine discourse is always seen from a female perspective and internalized appropriation, and therefore positively."[56]

In the second part of the book of Isaiah the imagery of being "woven" or "chosen" by YHWH "in the mother's womb" before birth is employed several times.[57] It appears elsewhere in the Old Testament in a number of places, especially in hymnic and Wisdom texts, regarding the creation of the individual.[58]

A striking feature of Deutero-Isaiah is the sometimes inclusive language used in referring to particular groups of persons. In 40:6 both sons and daughters are named as those who are to be brought back from exile. Isaiah 45:10 speaks of both fathers and mothers as those who beget offspring, something that is by no means frequent in the Old Testament. Still more unusual is the naming of Sarah alongside Abraham as ancestors of Israel in 51:2; this is also unique within the book of Isaiah.[59] In Isa 14:2 and 49:23 men and women are also presented in the references to foreign peoples. However, this language, inclusive of both sexes, is not consistently used in Deutero-Isaiah.[60]

[54] For more on this see Irmtraud Fischer, "Das Buch Jesaja," 248–49.

[55] Ibid.

[56] Ibid. 249.

[57] Isaiah 44:2 and 49:1 refer to YHWH's actions for the *ʿebed* before his birth; 44:24 speaks of Israel formed in the mother's womb, and 46:3-4—similarly to Moses' task in Num 11:12—emphasizes YHWH's care for Israel before it was born, something that will not end even when it is old.

[58] Peter Doll (*Menschenschöpfung und Weltschöpfung in der alttestamentlichen Weisheit* [Stuttgart: Katholisches Bibelwerk, 1985] 165) sees the texts in Deutero-Isaiah as determinative for other OT texts using this imagery of the creation of human beings.

[59] Fischer, "Das Buch Jesaja," 247, also points this out. Otherwise Abraham is named alone, that is, without Sarah.

[60] Fischer also indicates (ibid.) that the "children" mentioned in Isaiah 7, 9, and 11 are without exception sons; daughters in Isaiah have no significant names and exercise no function in the scheme of salvation.

Alongside this, in Deutero-Isaiah both a female and a male figure each play an important role. The "servant of God," addressed as male, and Zion/Jerusalem, personified as female, are set over against one another in important theological functions. To this point only a first beginning has been made in investigating the significance of this duality.[61] It is certainly worth asking whether "(daughter) Zion" is a figure on a theologically equal footing with the *'ebed*. Is it possible that she reflects the realities of women's lives, realities that, as sources of imagery, dare not and cannot any longer be further neglected? A second question in this connection is whether, perhaps, the *'ebed* and "Zion" are deliberately conceived as a male-female "pair" in order to underline the complementarity in their relationship to YHWH. Does the *'ebed* substitute in bearing the guilt of the people, which in Deutero-Isaiah, differently from Hosea, Jeremiah, and Ezekiel, the "woman" does not bear?[62]

In the second part of the book of Isaiah "daughter Zion" has another counterpart besides the *'ebed*. As already shown above in section B ii, Isaiah 47 paints a broad picture of the destruction of "daughter Babylon." What Hosea, Jeremiah, and Ezekiel threaten as the fate of the "whorish wife" Israel/Jerusalem is now to fall upon the foreign power. YHWH, as avenger and initiator of this punishment, is here clearly described in different terms from those used elsewhere in the second part of the book of Isaiah. There is a tension between this picture and the otherwise restorative, healing, and forgiving God. In Isaiah 47 it is the foreign "woman/wife" toward whom YHWH exercises violence. While he bestows salvation on "his" "woman/wife," he brings destruction and evil on the other.

Thus female imagery is used in the book of Isaiah with widely different significance and in very different contexts. Many areas of life are given voice, and many connotations enter into the picture. The imagery functions both to appreciate and to deprecate, and it appears both in a prominent position (for "daughter Zion") and in a marginal stance. This very

[61] For this cf. Marjo C. A. Korpel, "The Female Servant of the Lord in Isaiah 54," in Bob Becking and Meindert Dijkstra, eds., *On Reading Prophetic Texts. Gender-Specific and Related Studies in Memory of Fokkelien van Dijk-Hemmes* (Leiden and New York: Brill, 1996) 153–67, with references to W.A.M. Beuken, "Isaiah LIV: The Multiple Identity of the Person Addressed," *OTS* 19 (1974) 29–70; L.E. Wilshire, "The Servant-City: A New Interpretation of the 'Servant of the Lord' in the Servant Songs of Deutero-Isaiah," *JBL* 94 (1975) 356–67; Tryggve N.D. Mettinger, *A Farewell to the Servant Songs. A Critical Examination of an Exegetical Axiom* (Lund: Gleerup, 1983); and John F.A. Sawyer, "Daughter of Zion," 89–107.

[62] In the framework of Israelite thought, within the relationship between an action and its consequences, it would, at any rate, be plausible that sin can be forgiven but still must be atoned for. On this cf., for example (for Isa 52:13–53:12) Bernd Janowski, *Stellvertretung. Alttestamentliche Studien zu einem Theologischen Grundbegriff* (Stuttgart: Katholisches Bibelwerk, 1997) 90–92.

multiplicity and plurality distinguish its usage in Isaiah from that in the other prophetic books.

ii. The image of God in the book of Isaiah[63]

The image of YHWH in the book of Isaiah is shaped differently in the several parts of the book, and is in tension between them. On the one hand YHWH, as we have already said above, appears not to be as controlling and encroaching toward his prophet(s) as he is in Jeremiah or Ezekiel. Also in contrast to those two prophetic books, in Isaiah YHWH is clearly more caring and forgiving toward "his" "daughter Zion" or "wife" Jerusalem. However, there are also scenes such as Isaiah 47 in which YHWH is a rapist. In Isa 63:1-6, in a blatantly bloodthirsty image, YHWH appears in the role of one who treats the nations as someone treading a winepress treats the grapes, or as a war god treats the defeated. Irmtraud Fischer makes an important observation about YHWH's violent aspects in the book of Isaiah: "YHWH in the image of a woman is never violent, but in the male image he is."[64] We should point out another violent aspect of the God-image in Proto-Isaiah: In the passage about "daughter Tyre" and her status as a "prostitute" in 23:15-18 YHWH is portrayed in the role of the one who collects her "prostitute's wages" and uses them himself—in other words, he appears here as a pimp.[65]

One special feature of the imagery, especially in the first part of the book of Isaiah, is that marriage metaphors are not dominant or without competition in illustrating YHWH's actions. Isaiah, in painting the punishment of the nation or the city metaphorically, does not resort to (sexual) metaphors of violence within the framework of marriage imagery in reference to Israel; other metaphors are chosen instead. Here we may mention examples from the realm of plant imagery, as well as the vineyard metaphors in Isaiah 5; 16:8-9 (Moab); 27:2-5; 24:7-11. Even birth can be imaged in plant metaphors (11:1, 10).

In Deutero- and Trito-Isaiah the God-image is given a different focus. Here God is more clearly depicted as a lover: God *loves* Israel/Jacob (43:3) as well as Cyrus (48:14). YHWH is even described in the image of a woman—a marginal appearance in the Old Testament, especially in the prophetic books. In Isa 42:14b YHWH struggles and suffers like a woman in labor. In 46:3-4 YHWH appears in the role of a mother: She carries Israel from the womb onward. This imagery is more strongly developed in

[63] On this see also Baumann, "Prophetic Objections," 110–14.
[64] Fischer, "Das Buch Jesaja," 257.
[65] Elke Seifert, *Tochter und Vater* 309–10; Fischer, "Das Buch Jesaja," 252.

49:15: As it is impossible for a mother to abandon her child, so would it be impossible for YHWH to abandon Zion.

However, there is a problem with this female image of God when the prophetic marriage imagery is interpreted within this framework. If YHWH is also a mother, how can she at the same time be Zion's "husband"? This tension in the God-image can be partly explained, I think, by the fact that the authors of Isaiah 40–66 were very interested in depicting YHWH in female imagery, but at the same time wanted to connect with the imagery of YHWH as husband of his people or his city that had been handed down to them. So it happens that the "new" female God-imagery comes to stand alongside of and in tension with the "old" marriage imagery. Something similar is the case with YHWH's attitude toward Israel/Jerusalem in the different parts of the book of Isaiah. If the book is read as a whole, judgment stands alongside salvation, and threats beside promises. The origin of such tensions or contradictions can be explained by the fact that the texts come out of different times and situations.

In addition to this reference to the tension between the YHWH-image in the prophetic marriage imagery and the female God-imagery we should not forget that YHWH as "husband/lord" is depicted in Isaiah 40–66 in a different fashion than in the other prophetic books. "The husband/lord is . . . not depicted in the image of a disappointed lover who makes a new effort, but as an insightful husband who recognizes the full extent of the misery of his wife, left without resources, and therefore patiently attempts to persuade her that his love has not been lost (54:6-8)."[66] YHWH continuously appears as forgiving, caring, and consoling toward his textual "wife" Jerusalem, but he is violent against her female enemy.

We can sketch a general line of development within the God-image in the book of Isaiah: From a rather controlling God, depicted among other things as a pimp-God, runs a line to the "treader of the winepress" and rapist in the later parts of the book. But within this, YHWH can also be portrayed in entirely different images, as a thoughtful husband, a midwife, a mother. This development has also influenced the use of the prophetic marriage imagery: That imagery is only taken up in the later parts of the book, and it has been clearly reshaped in contrast to its usage in the earlier prophets. The imagery has experienced a deep shattering through the circumstance that God can also be seen in female images. We can only surmise that different experiences by and with women or marital relationships played a role in these alterations.

[66] Fischer, "Das Buch Jesaja," 255.

F. Summary

The prophetic marriage imagery in the book of Isaiah is embedded within a vast panoply of other metaphors. YHWH is "husband" and Jerusalem is "wife," but the two are also frequently presented in different and more striking ways. In the later parts of the book YHWH also displays feminine and motherly traits. We can observe here a dissolution of the boundaries of the marriage imagery with its necessarily fixed roles. However, the God-image is by no means blurred as regards the fullness of its power: YHWH is here, as never before, thought of as the universal ruler, the one God. Did this "strong" framework make it possible to admit, within it, more images from spheres of life that are not primarily directed to the demonstration of power? Favoring this is that in Isaiah 47 YHWH still makes use of his "old" role as a sexual perpetrator, but now in altered form, as the rapist of a foreign power. In any case it is clear in the texts of Deutero- and Trito-Isaiah that YHWH can use his enormous power *whenever he wants to.*

"Daughter Zion" is one of the two important partner figures with YHWH, no longer merely as his "wife," but also as his "daughter." The "Suffering Servant" is the other important theological metaphor of a partner to YHWH. As John F. A. Sawyer has emphasized, neither has a completely fixed identity; with certain reservations both can be interpreted as "corporate personalities."[67] They represent individuals, but also the collective Israel. Here we find the beginnings also of a change in the prophetic marriage imagery. A development is beginning in which individual people are regarded as YHWH's partners. No longer is it "only" metaphorical figures whom YHWH binds closely to himself; in some places these are collectivities of people. As we will show in the next chapter, the process that begins here moves still farther at the end of the canon of prophetic writings.

[67] John F. A. Sawyer, "Daughter of Zion," 101; for the concept of a "corporate personality" and its application to the Suffering Servant cf. Herbert Haag, *Der Gottesknecht bei Deuterojesaja* (2nd ed. Darmstadt: Wissenschaftliche Buchgesellschaft, 1993) 134–38, 153–56.

Chapter Ten

The Twelve Prophets: The Marriage Imagery Completed

Unlike Isaiah, Jeremiah, and Ezekiel, the Book of the Twelve Prophets reveals the long history of its development. The individual parts of the book, which will be called "writings" in what follows,[1] have superscriptions that indicate their authorship and time of writing, even though these are sometimes more fictional than historical.

In this chapter our consideration of the Book of the Twelve will exclude Hosea, since we have already devoted an entire chapter to that writing. Outside Hosea, prophetic marriage imagery is only used in a few places in the Book of the Twelve. These few passages are brief and unconnected. Hence we will use a different structure in this chapter than in the chapters on the major prophets and Hosea: First we will offer an overview of the terms from the prophetic marriage imagery in the Book of the Twelve. In this process a few texts in which the imagery forms a focus will crystallize out of the whole. These will be discussed in the canonical order of the writings, integrating the portions using imagery of sexual violence. The chapter will close with some overarching considerations and an evaluation of religious imagery and the Book of the Twelve as a whole.

A. The use of marriage terms in the Twelve Prophets

One of the central words in the prophetic marriage imagery is גלה, "uncover" or "lead away." It appears 19x in the Book of the Twelve. However,

[1] In this I follow Aaron Schart, *Die Entstehung des Zwölfprophetenbuchs. Neubearbeitungen von Amos im Rahmen schriftübergreifender Redaktionsprozesse* (Berlin: Walter de Gruyter, 1998) v, with reference to James D. Nogalski, *Literary Precursors to the Book of the Twelve* (Berlin and New York: Walter de Gruyter, 1993), and idem, *Redactional Processes in the Book of the Twelve* (Berlin and New York: Walter de Gruyter, 1993).

the overwhelming number of occurrences, especially in Amos, fall within the second meaning and therefore outside the context of the marriage imagery (Hos 7:1; 10:5; Amos 1:5, 6; 3:7; 5:5, 27; 6:7; 7:11, 17; Mic 1:16). In almost all the instances in Amos גלה is the classic word for leading away/being led away into exile. In the context of the prophetic marriage imagery גלה appears three times, and only in the *piʿel* and *puʿal*. Hosea 2:10 [MT 12] and Nah 2:7 [MT 8]; 3:5 refer to scenes employing imagery of sexual violence. In Mic 1:6 the case is more complicated: here it is a question of the "foundations of Samaria." We will have more to say on this below.

The occurrences of זנה, "whore, play the harlot" in the Book of the Twelve also point toward two of the texts just mentioned. The overwhelming majority of these occurrences are in Hosea. It is striking that in many places זנה refers to the behavior of concrete Israelites,[2] and not to YHWH's "whorish wife." The latter, however, is intended in Hos 1:2 (4x); 2:2, 4, 5 [MT 4, 6, 7]; 3:3; Mic 1:7 (2x) and Nah 3:4 (3x).

Closely associated with זנה is the "harlot's wages," אתנן. In the Book of the Twelve it appears in Hos 2:12 [MT 14]; 9:1, and in Mic 1:7, there in reference to the "woman" Samaria. Samaria has bought her idols with her "harlot's wages."

"Idols" or false gods are not called גלולים, as in Ezekiel, nor is שקוץ the word for them in the Book of the Twelve. The latter word, שקוץ, should rather be translated as "abomination" or "filth/dung." In Mic 1:7 the idols are פסל, "image of a god"; this word is not otherwise used in the context of the prophetic marriage imagery. Two other words from this field also appear, but only once each: תועבה—otherwise appearing primarily in Ezekiel, and quite frequently, for the "abominable deeds" done by Israel/Jerusalem—is selected only in Mal 2:11, there for the misdeeds of "faithless" (בגדה) Judah.[3]

While גלה and זנה are the focal terms in Hosea, Micah, and Nahum, the case is different with אהב, "love," and its derivatives. It is true that this term is found primarily in Hosea, as well as in Amos (4:5; 5:15) and Micah (3:2; 6:8), but it appears also near the end of the Book of the Twelve, in Zech 8:17, 19; 13:6, and in Mal 1:2; 2:11. While in Hosea the reference is often to the "lovers" (מאהבים), in Amos 5:15; Mic 3:2; 6:8; Zech 8:17, 19 the term refers to the ethically-colored "loving" of good or evil. YHWH is at no point the object of loving, but is frequently its subject: in Hos 3:1; 11:1; 9:15

[2] Thus in Hos 4:10, 11, 12, 13, 14, 18; 5:4; also with reference to Israel, personified as masculine, in Hos 4:15; 9:1, or to Ephraim, also masculine, in Hos 5:3; 6:10.

[3] In this group we should also mention זמה, but it appears in the Book of the Twelve only in Hos 6:9, for the deeds of the priests.

(negated); 14:4; Zeph 3:17, and clearly in Mal 1:2 and 2:11. We can already ask the question at this point: does the pointed placement of "loving" in Hosea and Malachi, with its framing function, perhaps permit some conclusions about the development of the Book of the Twelve?

The more sexually colored term עגב, so frequent in Ezekiel, is not used in the Twelve Prophets.

Otherwise interesting is the use of בגד, "be faithless/unfaithful," in Malachi. In the context of the marriage imagery it appears as a title, "faithless one," with reference to the "woman/wife" Judah, in Jer 3:7, 8, 10, 11, and in other contexts primarily referring to the Israelites, male and female. The same is true in the Book of the Twelve. While it is not used in a context thoroughly marked by marriage imagery, it does appear in a context in which it is possible that YHWH's marriage to Israel is in the background of the discourse about marriage: Mal 2:10-16. We will examine this passage more thoroughly below.

The accusation of adultery is more severe than that of infidelity. The legal term נאף, an important indicator of a text containing marriage imagery, is used in the Book of the Twelve, apart from Hosea, only in Mal 3:5. In the latter, the concrete Israelites are called "adulterers" and "sorcerers" (מכשפים). Elsewhere in the Book of the Twelve the accusation of sorcery is raised only in Nah 3:5, against the personified city of Nineveh; it is one of the charges that justify her being treated as a "prostitute" (זונה). We will also take a closer look at Nah 3:4-7 below.

"Betrothal" (ארש), as an act preliminary to marriage, is spoken of in the Book of the Twelve only in Hos 2:19, 20 [MT 21, 22],[4] but בעל appears in the *Dodekapropheton* not only in Hosea, but also in Nah 3:4-7 and in the passage in Malachi.[5] The appearance of בעל as (marital) "lord," or as the verb "to marry" is one of the surest indications of the word-field "marriage." In Joel 1:8 it is part of a comparison, the point of which is that here the joy that ordinarily characterizes the situation of bride and bridegroom (בעל) is absent. Similarly, Joel 2:16 is not about marriage as such, but rather asserts that the bride and bridegroom are exempted from the fulfillment of certain commandments. In Nah 3:4 we have one of the few Old Testament examples of "mistress" (בעלה), when Nineveh is called the "mistress" of sorcery. By contrast, the verb בעל in the sense of "marry" appears in Mal 2:11b: Judah, now as masculine, has married the daughter of a foreign god. Here the marriage imagery is reversed. Now-masculine

[4] Otherwise ארש is found in Exod 22:15; Deut 20:7; 22:23, 25, 27, 28; 28:30, in legal texts.

[5] The address to Baal as a deity in Zeph 1:4 will not be investigated here.

Judah is subjected to the accusation otherwise hurled at "woman" Judah: that of joining himself to foreign gods. Within the ancient Israelite context this is not a charge of adultery, since, after all, a man could have more than one wife.

We must still consider the words for "nakedness" or "shame." Derivatives of ערה appear (apart from Hosea) in the Book of the Twelve in the context of marriage imagery only as מער in Nah 3:5: After her stripping, the nations will be able to see the "nakedness" or "shame" of the "woman," Nineveh. The two other occurrences of the verb ערה *pi'el* in Hab 3:13 and Zeph 2:14 are in completely different contexts.

Parallel to מער in Nah 3:5 is קלון, again meaning "nakedness, shame"; the קלון of Nineveh will be visible to the kingdoms after her stripping. In the Book of the Twelve קלון is used elsewhere with a clearly sexual connotation only in Hab 2:16: Here there is a sexual allusion to the disrobing of the neighbor who, to her shame, has been made drunk (v. 15) and to the (uncircumcised) foreskins of the Babylonians (v. 16). In this context, as in Nah 3:4-7, connotations of sexuality and nakedness/shame overlap.

The terms טהר, "pure, clean" and טמא, "impure, unclean," so central in Ezekiel, are not used in the Book of the Twelve in the context of marriage imagery. It is true that they are mentioned in Amos 7:17 when it is predicted that the priest Amaziah will suffer death in an "unclean" (טמא) land and his wife will be subjected to the fate of a prostitute (זונה), after Amaziah has been driven out of the land along with Israel (*figura etymologica* with גלה *qal*). Here, then, terms from the prophetic marriage imagery are used together, but the context is different: a pronouncement of judgment on the priest, his family, and the whole people Israel.

We may conclude that terms from the prophetic marriage imagery pile up in certain passages in the Book of the Twelve; among these are (apart from Hosea), especially[6] Mic 1:5-7; Nah 3:4-7; Mal 2:10-16. In what follows we will examine each of these texts more closely.

B. Micah

The bridge constructed by Micah to represent Israel's (or Jerusalem's) fate stretches from proclamations of destruction to announcements of salvation. However, as regards YHWH's "wives" we should add that salvation

[6] Amos 5:2 can be excluded here, because there is no use of marriage imagery; the same is true of the texts about "daughter Zion." The metaphor "city as daughter" has implications different from those of the prophetic marriage imagery and is to be distinguished from them in most cases. There are OT exceptions in Deutero-Isaiah and Trito-Isaiah, where the metaphors overlap.

is given to Jerusalem, "daughter Zion," while the fate of Israel/Samaria is sealed from the first verses of the book. This very passage makes use also of prophetic marriage imagery to express its charges and pronouncements of judgment on (feminine) Israel/Samaria (Mic 1:6-7):

> 6 Therefore I will make Samaria a heap of ruins in the open country,[7]
> a place for planting vineyards.
> I will pour down her stones into the valley,
> and uncover her foundations.
> 7 All her images shall be beaten to pieces,
> all her prostitute's wages shall be burned with fire,
> and all her idols I will lay waste;
> for as a prostitute's wages the prostitute (she) gathered them,
> and as the prostitute's wages of a prostitute they shall again be used.**

Especially in v. 7 Samaria is clearly and dramatically called a prostitute.[8] In the context of the prophetic marriage imagery אתנן as "prostitute's wages" is used especially often by Ezekiel (16:31, 34, 41), but there the emphasis is not, as it is in Micah, on the purchase of idols with prostitute's wages. Instead, the focus is on a very different statement: Here the "prostitute" Jerusalem, in her great "lust," even gives wages to her "lovers" instead of receiving from them. Micah wants to express something different. What is striking in the phrasing of v. 7 is that אתנן appears three times: In v. 7a it stands by itself, parallel to "images." The linking in *parallelismus membrorum,* each time with a preceding כל, points to a close relationship: The images have been acquired by means of the prostitute's wages. In v. 7b אתנן is set in a construct phrase with זונה. Occasionally אתנן suffices, without further qualification, to express unequivocally what is meant (Hos 9:1; Ezek 16:31, 34, 41). In Deut 23:19 and Isa 23:17-18 זונה is added. The reference to the prohibition on donating אתנן זונה to the Temple emphasizes the especially reprehensible nature of Samaria's actions on the religious level.[9] It is possible that this mode of expression also serves to describe Samaria once again, and unmistakably, as a "prostitute." She has not been so entitled by Micah before. Moreover, Samaria is by this means personified, something that would not otherwise be apparent in the text at

[7] The translation of עי השדה is unclear; cf. Ges[17] 779.

[8] Sophia Bietenhard ("Das Buch Micha. Ruf nach Gerechtigkeit—Hoffnung für alle," in Luise Schottroff and Marie-Theres Wacker, eds., *Kompendium Feministische Bibelauslegung* [2nd ed. Gütersloh: Gütersloher Verlagshaus, 1999] 341) disputes this, but without giving reasons.

[9] For discussion of the location of this verse within Micah's theology cf. Rainer Kessler, *Micha* (Freiburg: Herder, 1999) 89: "It is not the images as such that are the objects of the critique of Samaria, but what they symbolize, namely the practical rejection of YHWH, who is not trusted to

first glance. Probably this is meant to set up Samaria as a counter-figure to "daughter Zion," who plays an important role from Mic 1:13 onward.

This way of using prophetic marriage imagery continues the discourse about the "prostitute" Israel in Hosea 1–3* and at the same time takes up Hos 9:1, the only passage before Micah in the Book of the Twelve that spoke of prostitute's wages, which Israel loved to receive on all the threshing-floors—a clear reference to her sins. Micah 1:7 reads, against this background, like a continuation of the story of the textual "woman" Israel begun in Hosea: In the present order of the Book of the Twelve, Hosea is followed by Amos, with the "fall" of "virgin Israel" in 5:2. Here again she appears as a personification, and also, it seems, as a city.[10] No one helps her up again. In Mic 1:7, then, her fate is finally sealed: she is never again referred to as a "woman" in the Book of the Twelve.

A further indication that the city of Samaria is to be regarded as a "prostitute" appears to be the use of גלה in Mic 1:6. As indicated above,[11] this verb otherwise refers, for the most part, to the "laying bare" of the textual "nakedness" (ערוה) of the textual "woman." In Mic 1:6, as in the other passages, it is in the *piʿel*. But now the object is the foundations (יסודים) of Samaria. Foundations are generally designated by derivatives of יסד, and גלה can stand in the same context, but this is the only passage with גלה *piʿel:* a further indication that here the text speaks quite plainly of the city of Samaria as "woman" and prostitute.

Samaria/Israel as a "prostitute" whose end has already come: that is the perspective Micah presents, continuing Hosea's image. In the rest of the Book of the Twelve nothing more is said of Israel as YHWH's "wife," nor is there any further allusion to her. Jerusalem, or "daughter Zion," is now in the foreground; she appears in Mic 1:13; 4:8, 10, 13; Zeph 3:14; Zech 2:10 [MT 2:14]; 9:9. The ending of the "life story" of the textual "wife" Israel/Samaria in the Book of the Twelve resembles the view presented in Ezekiel.

---

preserve the gifts of the land and external security. One may thus speak of a shift in accent with respect to Micah's social-critical message, but scarcely of a 'distortion'. . ." (here Kessler refers to Volkmar Fritz, "Das Wort gegen Samaria Mi 1,2-7," in idem, *Studien zu Literatur und Geschichte des Alten Israel* [Stuttgart: Katholisches Bibelwerk, 1997] 139): "Cultic circumstances also reflect economic, social, and political attitudes."

[10] Thus John J. Schmitt, "The Virgin of Israel: Referent and Use of the Phrase in Amos and Jeremiah," *CBQ* 53 (1991) 387, on בתולת ישׂראיל ("virgin Israel"): ". . . in its four prophetic occurrences, [it] is the capital of the country—either of the northern kingdom or of the southern kingdom. The idea connected with the cities, beyond their feminine status, seems to be their divine protection, whether it is about to cease or even to be assured. The books of both Amos and Jeremiah use the phrase as part of the traditional Israelite language about cities. With this phrase, they refer to capitals in which prophets had preached, Samaria and Jerusalem."

[11] See Chapter 3 C ii.

C. Nahum

Nahum is one of two writings in the Book of the Twelve that centers on Nineveh. Differently from Jonah and his repentant Nineveh, in Nahum the military conflict with the capital of the Neo-Assyrian empire is in the foreground. Descriptions of martial violence give an impression of how it will be when righteous and powerful YHWH avenges the wounding of his little Judah by destroying Nineveh.[12]

Terms from the prophetic marriage imagery are used in this context—that of the punishment of Nineveh[13]—in Nah 3:4-7:

> 4 Because of the countless whorings of the whore, of the beauty (with) allure, of the mistress of sorcery,
> who bought nations with her whoring and tribes with her magic arts!
> 5 See, I will (come) upon you, says YHWH of hosts:
> I will lift up your "skirts"[14] over your face.
> I will let (the) nations look on your nakedness
> and (the) kingdoms on your shame.
> 6 I will throw filth at you, and I will defile you;[15]
> and I will make you a spectacle.

[12] I have written elsewhere about this book and the problems with its God-imagery: Gerlinde Baumann, "Das Buch Nahum. Der gerechte Gott als sexueller Gewalttäter," in Luise Schottroff and Marie-Theres Wacker, eds., *Kompendium Feministische Bibelauslegung* (2nd ed. Gütersloh: Gütersloher Verlagshaus, 1999) 347–53. Another article forthcoming concerns Nah 3:4-7 in connection with Isa 47:2-3: "Gott als vergewaltigender Soldat im Alten Testament?" See below, n. 20.

[13] Nah 2:6-7 (MT 7-8) is also an interesting text in this regard:

> 6(7) The river gates are opened,
> the palace trembles.
> 7(8) It is decreed: she has been stripped naked (גלה *puʿal*),
> she will be led away.
> And her slave women sob like doves (doves' voices);
> they beat their breasts.**

Here there is no use of marriage imagery, but the depiction of the conquest of Nineveh certainly contains metaphors of sexual violence, as F. Rachel Magdalene has emphasized ("Ancient Near-Eastern Treaty-Curses and the Ultimate Texts of Terror: A Study of the Language of Divine Sexual Abuse in the Prophetic Corpus," in Athalya Brenner, ed., *A Feminist Companion to the Latter Prophets* [Sheffield: Sheffield Academic Press, 1995] 333): "Here, wet gates are opened and captured, [the] stripped woman is carried off for rape, while those who serve her suffer over her fate."

[14] For the translation of שׁול in this passage see above, Chapter 3 C iii.

[15] נבל *piʿel* ("treat with contempt") appears with עשׂה ("do, make") as an evaluation in other contexts that are about rape, as in Gen 34:7; Judges 19–20; 2 Sam 13:12 (cf. Johannes Marböck, art. "נבל, *nāḇāl*," *TDOT* 9:161. In any case it represents a serious "destruction of communal bonds" (ibid. 162). The same characters are found in the hard-to-translate נבלות in Hos 2:12; on this see above, Chapter 6 C.

7 Then all who see you will shrink from you and say:
"Nineveh is devastated;[16] who will show sympathy[17] for her?
Where shall I seek comforters for you?"**

The violence done to Nineveh here by YHWH is certainly to be understood as sexual: Nineveh's nakedness (מער) or shame (קלון) is laid bare (גלה *pi'el*) so that all the world can see it (ראה *hip'il*). Filth or dung are thrown at her; here שקוץ, frequently used by Ezekiel to refer to the "idols," appears in its other meaning. By means of all this Nineveh is very explicitly made a spectacle (ראי). She is so destroyed that all spectators flee in disgust, and no one is prepared to comfort her.

This divine action is justified by the many and great "whorings" of Nineveh. Nahum 3:4 three times uses words from the root זנה: two of these are forms of the abstract plural זנונים, which emphasizes the habitual aspect of "whoring" or "prostitution."[18] In the context of the prophetic marriage imagery it is otherwise found, in a prominent position, in Hos 1:2. The Book of the Twelve begins with the command to Hosea to "take a wife of whoredom and have children of whoredom." The expression also appears in the context of the prophetic marriage imagery in Hos 2:2, 4 [MT 4, 6]; 4:12; Ezek 23:11, 29. It repeatedly summarizes the accusations against YHWH's "wife," usually involving the worship of foreign gods.

This accusation cannot be raised here, since Nineveh is not in a marital relationship with YHWH. This has led to efforts at explanation: it is said that this passage may originally have been directed at Jerusalem. According to Jörg Jeremias the circumstance of adultery in Nah 3:4-5 appears

> . . . to be emphasized in such a way that it can reasonably refer only to Israel's defection from YHWH. In any case, however, this proclamation of punishment appears to be dependent on the Hoseanic material (cf. Hosea 2:5, 12 [English 2:3, 10]), so that from that very fact an interpretation of the city addressed as Jerusalem seems completely unforced. Such a proclamation of judgment against a foreign nation is found only once, at a later period.[19]

[16] שדד ("devastate") in the *pu'al* is frequently associated with personified lands or cities: cf. Isa 23:1, 14; Jer 48:20; Zech 11:2. They are to lament after their (usually complete) destruction. In the *Dodekapropheton* שדד appears in Hos 10:2, 14; Joel 1:10; Obadiah 5; Mic 2:4; Nah 3:7; Zech 11:2, 3; it always means destruction or devastation. Micah 2:4 introduces a jeering song against the rich: On the Day of YHWH they themselves will sing: "We are ruined, utterly ruined." On the metaphorical level, as applied to the wealthy land of Assyria, this proclamation is also fulfilled in Nah 3:7.

[17] This expression is intended to hint at the meaning of the verb נוד, "bow the head as a sign of sympathy," which is not completely obvious in our context.

[18] On this see above, Chapter 6 B.

[19] Jörg Jeremias, *Kultprophetie und Gerichtsverkündigung in der späten Königszeit Israels* (Neukirchen-Vluyn: Neukirchener Verlag, 1970) 37.

Jeremias refers here to the parallel in Isa 47:3. In fact, that is the Old Testament text most closely related to Nah 3:4-7. There, as we have pointed out in several connections,[20] a scene of sexual violence against a personified foreign nation is presented in familiar terms from the prophetic marriage imagery. Parallel to Nahum, Isa 47:9, 12 also presents the accusation of "sorcery" (כשׁפים) against the "woman" Babylon/Nineveh. But the justification in terms of "whoring," which seems out of place in Nahum, is not mentioned in Isaiah. To that extent Isaiah 47 is more plausible than Nah 3:4-7, where, apart from all possible considerations about the origins of the text, we must ask what sense the text yields, in its present form, with reference to Nineveh.

Nahum 3:4-7 and its attribution of "whoredom" to Nineveh is understandable if we suppose a broader application of זנה here. Similarly to the usage of זנה in Ezekiel, what is described here is not merely sexually deviant behavior by concrete persons. As in Ezekiel, so also in Nah 3:4 "whoring" and "buying nations" allude to alliances with other countries, but here from the opposite point of view: Here we have in view vassals rather than major powers. The metaphor of the "whorish woman/wife" not only makes use of the language and existing connotations of זנה, but also takes control of it to create new undertones and shades of meaning. Now these metaphorical applications work backward on the usage of זנה. In Nahum we find a use of זנה that places the weight on the pejorative aspect. The "woman" Nineveh is verbally made a "whore." This evokes agreement among the readers or hearers, enabling them to follow the intent of the text and welcome the punishment that is described next.[21] This attribution prepares for the later dubbing of a hostile and oppressive major power as a "whore," as found in the New Testament in the "whore" (πορνή) Babylon in Rev 17:18. Here again the removal of her clothing and

[20] See above, Chapter 9 B, C, and D. In another article ("Gott als vergewaltigender Soldat im Alten Testament?") I propose that Nah 3:4-7 should probably be read, on the one hand, on the basis of the prophetic marriage imagery in Hosea 1–3*, and on the other hand against the background of the negative deuteronomistic *typos* of a powerful, sorcery-practicing female figure (according to the model of Jezebel in 2 Kings 9:22, here discredited as a whore). Isaiah 47:2-3 takes up this image anew and transfers it to Babylon, augmenting further contacts with the marriage imagery in other texts.

[21] This presupposes a late dating of Nahum in the post-exilic, or at least the post-Ezekiel period. An indication that the text is not pre-exilic could be, for example, the remarkably uncritical posture of Nahum toward Israel/Judah and its "sins." In addition, the question of the dating of the book of Nahum has become more fluid at present because of newer theses on the origins of the Book of the Twelve: cf., for example, Aaron Schart, "Zur Redaktionsgeschichte des Zwölfprophetenbuchs," *VF* 43 (1998), 25–26; cf. also James D. Nogalski, *Literary Precursors to the Book of the Twelve* (Berlin and New York: Walter de Gruyter, 1993) 87–88, with notes.

the consequent baring of her nakedness are proclaimed as a kind of sexual violence as punishment (Rev 17:16).[22] Here, then, we have "pornography" in the literal sense: Through titling and poetic adornment a female personification is "written into whoredom,"[23] so that all the hatred of the readers can be directed at her. Nahum 3:4-7 can be seen as the beginning of this process.

Elke Seifert has summarized the implications of the imagery in Nahum's context from a feminist perspective:

> Before the city of Nineveh is here personified and sexualized as a metaphorical female figure, the prophet tells how her enemies attack her with the crack of whip, the rumble of wheel, the galloping horses (Nah 3:2). They force their way into her with glittering swords and flashing spears and kill countless people (Nah 3:3). Here already, violence is "lustfully" described; the victorious enemies of the city seem to be caught up in "blood lust." Thus we are not surprised that after this, from the masculine-military-victor perspective, the violence exercised against the city is expressed in erotic imagery (Nah 3:5-6). The authors no longer present the Medes and Babylonians, but rather YHWH himself as the destroyer and "disgracer" of Nineveh. After her inhabitants have been killed, the city-woman herself is destroyed by him. Her "rape" expresses ultimate triumph. In all this, the sexual cruelties serve both to satisfy aggression and to abase and irretrievably devalue the woman.[24]

Thus here scenes of punishment are detached from the prophetic marriage imagery and applied in another context, that of the destruction of the city "woman" Nineveh. Her status is first reduced, in that she is made a whore, and then she is "physically" raped. In this text we can see evidence that what is behind the punishment scenes in the prophetic marriage imagery really *is* sexual violence. Its embedding in military violence in Nahum and the consistent image of God both point to this. YHWH dominates his male enemies as military commander and avenger, his female foe Nineveh as rapist.

[22] There is a whole series of content parallels between Revelation 17–18 and Nahum that has scarcely been developed. Adela Yarbro Collins has made a beginning ("Feminine Symbolism in the Book of Revelation," *BInt* 1 [1993] 20–33). Ulrike Sals is currently working on the image of the "woman" Babylon (*Die Biographie der "Hure Babylon." Studien zur Intertextualität der Babylon-Texte in der Bibel.* Dissertation, Ruhr-Universität Bochum).

[23] Adela Yarbro Collins ("Feminine Symbolism," 30) gives a different interpretation of the Greek word "pornography" in connection with Revelation 17: "Revelation 17 is 'pornographic' in the etymological sense; it draws a picture (γράφειν) of a prostitute (πόρνη)."

[24] Elke Seifert, *Tochter und Vater im Alten Testament. Eine ideologiekritische Untersuchung zur Verfügungsgewalt von Vätern über ihre Töchter* (Neukirchen-Vluyn: Neukirchener Verlag, 1997) 308.

Such a text alerts us in shocking fashion to the close ties between metaphors of war and rape.[25] The reason is that rape was and is part of the reality of war for women, so that one can stand for the other. The biblical imagery in Nahum, which approaches the limits of what can be said, does not hesitate to show YHWH as a raging, vindictive man and therefore a rapist.[26] Here we have a kind of "continuation" of the marriage imagery that demands, even more than the other texts, that we engage the whole complex of imagery in critical fashion.

D. Malachi

With Malachi we reach the end of the Book of the Twelve and of the "Prophets" (נביאים) portion of the canon. Probably this part of the *Dodekapropheton* was in writing from the outset, perhaps even as a conclusion to this book, or even to this part of the canon.[27] As a result it assumes an especially important role for, among other things, the formulation of the prophetic marriage imagery: Malachi has, so to speak, the last word.

Terms from the prophetic marriage imagery appear especially in 1:2 and 2:10-16. At the very beginning of the book, Mal 1:2a speaks of YHWH's love for the Israelites:

> I have loved you, says YHWH. But you say, How have you loved us?

God's love is onesidedly stated here: it is YHWH who loves. The Israelites are given the role of asking for concrete examples of this love. As the book continues, it works toward changing this perspective on the part of the readers. The accent is more strongly on the kinds of religious and ethical praxis on the human side that can correspond to this love of YHWH. The same is true in Mal 2:10-16, where, at least at first glance, the subject is love between human beings in the form of a marital relationship:

> 10 Have we not all one father? Has not one God created us?
> Why then is a man faithless to his brother, profaning the *berit*
> of our ancestors?

[25] Pamela Gordon and Harold C. Washington ("Rape as a Military Metaphor in the Hebrew Bible," in Athalya Brenner, ed., *A Feminist Companion to the Latter Prophets* [Sheffield: Sheffield Academic Press, 1995] 309) point this out not only as regards OT texts, but also in reference to the American military at the present time.

[26] I have already pointed out the implications of such a God-image above, Chapter 9 D.

[27] These are the theses recently under discussion, e.g., in Erich Bosshard and Reinhard Gregor Kratz, "Maleachi im Zwölfprophetenbuch," *BN* 52 (1990) 46, or Odil Hannes Steck, *Der Abschluss der Prophetie im Alten Testament. Ein Versuch zur Frage der Vorgeschichte des Kanons* (Neukirchen-Vluyn: Neukirchener Verlag, 1991) passim.

11 Judah (fem.) has been faithless, and abomination has been committed in Israel and Jerusalem;
for Judah (masc.) has profaned the sanctuary of YHWH, which he loves,[28]
and has married the daughter of a foreign god.
12 YHWH has cut off the one who does this,
the witness and the one who answers in the tents of Jacob,
who brings an offering for YHWH of hosts.
13 And this, the second thing, you do as well: You cover YHWH's altar with tears,
(with) weeping and groaning because there is no longer regard for the offering,
to accept it with favor from your hands.
14 But you have said: Why?
For this reason: because YHWH was a witness
between you and the wife of your youth,
to whom you have been faithless;
but she is your companion and your wife of your *berit.*
15 And has he not made (them) (as) one,[29] as flesh and spirit in him?
And what is the One? Seeking offspring of God.
(Therefore) guard yourselves, as regards your spirit,
and as regards the wife of your youth: Be not faithless!
16 For (I) "hate"[30] divorce (of a wife),
says YHWH, the God of Israel,
and covering one's garment with violence, says YHWH of hosts.
Guard yourselves, as regards your spirit, and be not faithless!**

[28] Julia M. O'Brien ("Judah as Wife and Husband: Deconstructing Gender in Malachi," *JBL* 115 [1996] 247–48) points out the change of gender for Judah in this verse and discusses the different ways of dealing with it: avoidance through conjecture or trivialization on the basis of a supposed preference for the masculine in Hebrew.

[29] This is the reasoned translation also of Wilhelm Rudolph, "Zu Mal 2,10-16," *ZAW* 93 (1981) 86; differently Henning Graf von Reventlow, *Die Propheten Haggai, Sacharja und Maleachi* (Göttingen: Vandenhoeck & Ruprecht, 1993) 146: "And no one does this if there is a remnant of spirit in him. And what is with the one?" He apparently chooses this translation in agreement with Stefan Schreiner, "Mischehen—Ehebruch—Ehescheidung. Betrachtungen zu Mal 2,10-16," *ZAW* 91 (1979) 217. That article was the occasion of a contentious discussion of the passage: as reactions cf. Rudolph's article, and Clemens Locher, "Altes und Neues zu Maleachi 2,10-16," in Pierre Casetti, Othmar Keel, and Adrian Schenker, eds., *Mélanges Dominique Barthélemy. Études bibliques offertes à l'occasion de son 60e anniversaire* (Fribourg: Éditions universitaires; Göttingen: Vandenhoeck & Ruprecht, 1981) 241–71.

[30] "Hate" (שׂנא) is here to be understood as a term from marital law indicating a husband's turning away from his wife; cf. Édouard Lipiński, art. "שׂנא, *śāneʾ*," *ThWAT* 7:833.

In this passage, the text of which is not easy,[31] the first subject is the interlocking themes of the marriage of Israelite men to non-Israelite women and divorce. As in other parts of Malachi, so also in 2:10-16 a complex theme is presented as a conversation between quoted positions of the Israelites and that of the writing prophets. One such position is presented in v. 14 in the form of a question.

At the very beginning of the text the divine Father is interwoven with human "fathers." Infidelity to the *berit* of the human fathers and brothers is a denial of our common origin in the fatherhood of God. In v. 11 Judah is introduced as an example of infidelity: it has become "faithless" (בגד). Infidelity on the part of the Israelites toward YHWH is not only asserted in Hos 5:7; 6:7; at the beginning of the book of Jeremiah בגד is predicated (Jer 3:7, 8, 11, 12) of the "unfaithful one," the "wife," Judah, who has turned away from YHWH. It seems entirely possible that Mal 2:11 contains a reference to Jeremiah, and this could represent an allusion to the prophetic marriage imagery. The connection is extended in the second half-verse, but with a clear shift: "Judah" is now addressed as a masculine entity. "He" has married (בעל) the daughter of a foreign god. This statement is interpreted either as the marriage of concrete Israelite men with women of non-Israelite descent,[32] or as the worship of foreign gods.[33] The theme of infidelity and marriage to a non-Israelite partner could also be an allusion to the Hosean marriage between YHWH and Israel and her "whoring" with other gods. The text does not take a clear position on this question. It seems to me worthwhile, though, to keep in mind the implications of an allusion to the prophetic marriage imagery.[34] In Malachi the gender of the actors has changed: Now it is the male Judah who enters into a marriage with another woman. In this way, on the level of gender roles, the prophetic marriage imagery has been altered by its reception in Malachi: Now it is the male partner, not the female, who has worshiped foreign gods.[35] Abel Isaksson has formulated the consequences of the imagery for the picture of God, starting from vv. 14-15:

[31] Many commentators have addressed the problems in the textual tradition, with very different results. This is not the place to present the extensive discussion of the text and its problems. Overall, the position of Stefan Schreiner ("Mischehen," 208–14) is persuasive. He proceeds on the assumption that the MT is on the whole "lexicographically correct" and therefore translatable. As regards the disputed v. 16, I prefer the suggestion by Rudolph, "Zu Mal 2,10-16," 86–87, against Schreiner; Rudolph's argument, with textual logic and reference to the context, seems convincing here.

[32] Thus, e.g., by Reventlow, *Haggai, Sacharja und Maleachi* 148.

[33] See, e.g., the examples in Julia M. O'Brien, *Priest and Levite in Malachi* (Atlanta: Scholars, 1992) 67–69.

[34] O'Brien has done something similar in her "Judah as Wife and Husband," 248.

[35] In the familiar terminology of the marriage imagery this was called "whoring" or "prostitution" (זנה). But Malachi does not go that far. Beth Glazier-McDonald, however (*Malachi, the Divine*

> However, the expressions "the wife of your youth" and "the wife of your covenant" [in vv. 14-15] need not be reduced to meaning the worship of Yahweh or belief in Yahweh. It is really Yahweh himself who is given these designations. And the reason why he, who is otherwise represented as the husband in the marriage between Yahweh and Israel, is mentioned in this verse quite unexpectedly as the wife is simply that the prophet is continuing to use the same image as in v. 11. There Judah is mentioned as the man who has married the daughter of a foreign god. This marriage means treachery towards Yahweh, the wife of his youth and the wife of his covenant. In order to enable the author to carry on using the image from v. 11, Yahweh must be represented as the wife.[36]

At least as far as v. 11 is concerned, Isaksson's observation seems to me altogether accurate. From that starting-point Mal 2:10-16 can be understood as a text working on several levels:[37] On the one hand it concerns the male Israelites, who are to be warned against marriages with women of non-Israelite descent.[38] In this connection it is made clear in the remainder of the text that divorce from the "wife of one's youth" is not an escape that will obtain YHWH's favor. What is addressed here is an ethical conflict. On the other hand, building on the parallel drawn at the beginning of the section (v. 10) between the divine Father and the ancestors of Israel, there is reference to a solution based on YHWH's past marital relationship: YHWH, too, had a "wife" who had turned to other gods, but—and here Malachi follows the late Isaianic line of interpretation—he did not abandon or reject her for all time. YHWH's marriage, which in this case stands as a model, was not dissolved; YHWH did not become "faithless" (v. 16), even though his "wife" had been so before. On still a third level, if we follow Isaksson's line of thinking, YHWH is even imagined as a wife. In this way the perspective of the addressees, probably for the most part men, is clearly shifted toward the fate of the affected women: the imagery links

---

Messenger [Atlanta: Scholars, 1987] 98), makes the suggestion that we read Mal 2:12 differently: "In view of the sexual connotations of both עוֹר and ענה, it is conceivable that the qal participles used in Mal 2:12 have such overtones and may be translated, 'the one who is aroused (from sexual inactivity, i.e., the aroused one) and the lover.' Such a translation suits the context of the oracle unit. Indeed, both עֵר and עֹנֶה may here be veiled synonyms of זָנָה, 'to play the harlot, commit fornication.'"

[36] Abel Isaksson, *Marriage and Ministry in the New Temple. A Study with Special Reference to Mt. 19.3-12 and 1. Cor. 11.3-16* (Lund: Gleerup, 1965) 33.

[37] An insight into the history of scholarship on the question whether Mal 2:10-16 must be understood in "symbolic" or "literal" fashion is offered by Gordon Paul Hugenberger, *Marriage as Covenant. A Study of Biblical Law and Ethics Governing Marriage, Developed from the Perspective of Malachi* (Leiden: Brill, 1994) 7–8, n. 51.

[38] For the background of this problem see, for example, Locher, "Altes und Neues," 259.

YHWH to the women, thus focusing attention more sharply on them and how they are affected by decisions regarding divorce.

Thus in Malachi ethics and theology are tightly interwoven. There is a warning against the danger of worshiping foreign gods, brought about by marriages between Israelite men and non-Israelite women. At the same time, the book takes a position on the subject of divorce that is in opposition to the "hard line" of the Ezra-Nehemiah texts. Malachi's position is supported by reference to the prophetic marriage imagery that, after all, opened the Book of the Twelve, in Hosea 1–3.[39] But in Malachi this imagery is not merely received; it is also interpreted in a particular way: Malachi does not adopt Ezekiel's version, in which the marriage imagery ends in the death of the "woman/wife." Instead, he continues the late-Isaian line in which the divine and human spheres are more directly connected. Thus at the conclusion of the Book of the Twelve the prophetic marriage imagery is once again taken up and altered. In the post-exilic period the marriage imagery was no longer so necessary for dealing with the situation. Previously it had offered the opportunity to warn against the horrors of exile and to move Israel/Jerusalem to return to YHWH, or else to interpret the exile during the exilic or early post-exilic period. In Malachi it is again adduced, this time to give an example of the theme of human marriage and expand its perspective. The theme of the love of YHWH for his "wife" Israel/Judah is abandoned or transformed; now the theme is love on two different levels, and these are especially emphasized in Malachi: love between human beings and the loving relationship between YHWH and individual Israelites (Mal 1:2a).

The shift in Judah's gender and the "reversed metaphor" with YHWH in the female role can be evaluated in different ways. Julia M. O'Brien sees here the product of a writing prophet who gets tied up in his own gender constructs and cannot find an escape.[40] But, on the contrary, we can equally well surmise awareness and deliberation behind the imagery in this text:

[39] The connection between Hosea and Malachi has been frequently pointed out: e.g., by Terence Collins (*The Mantle of Elijah. The Redaction Criticism of the Prophetical Books* [Sheffield: JSOT Press, 1993] 81): ". . . Malachi also brings us back to the themes and language which were dominant at the very start of The Twelve. This is evident in the use of the father-son relationship as an image of the relationship between God and Israel (Mal. 1.6-7 and Hos. 11.1-2), and in the fact that both appeal to the need for covenant faithfulness in marriage, though in slightly different ways (Mal. 2.13-16 and Hos. 2.14-19)." However, we have given reasons above why the differences between the views of marriage in Hosea and Malachi are anything but slight.

[40] O'Brien, "Judah as Wife and Husband," 249: "Malachi draws upon both images—Judah as wife *and* husband—but in so doing undermines the hierarchical/gender-scripted basis of its own argument. Having called in the authoritative voices of the prophetic and legal fathers, Malachi cannot control their influence. Whatever actual practice the book is decrying, the prophetic discourse of idolatry has overwritten his own argument."

Behind the exchange of gender roles there emerges even more than a new, closer definition of relationships between the divine and human ethos. Malachi not only concludes the prophetic marriage imagery in such a way that the relationship between God and individuals is the one to which henceforth marriage imagery should apply. By the textually-created confusion of genders he also destroys any further "normal" application of the marriage imagery. Through this opening to other gender-attributions for YHWH and Judah the metaphor *as metaphor* emerges more clearly; through its alteration it is unmasked, revealed as a human construction. There is a measure of travesty of the prophetic marriage imagery in this text: At the end of the Book of the Twelve Prophets the thing that had its origin at the beginning, with Hosea, is taken up in such a way that the metaphor is broken apart.

E. Summary

The marriage imagery in the Book of the Twelve as a whole is distinguished by its completeness: No other prophetic book contains the entire spectrum of motifs of the prophetic marriage imagery. First the complete history of YHWH's "love" for Israel is narrated (Hosea 1–3*), including the prehistory in the wilderness, the "whoring" of the "woman/wife," and the threat of punishment. This last is reported in Amos 5:2 and especially in Mic 1:7-8. Also to be found here is the "whoring" of a "strange woman," i.e., a foreigner, in personified Nineveh in Nah 3:4-7.[41] The same fate that befell Samaria/Israel later falls upon Jerusalem; but to her, as his "daughter Zion," YHWH turns more deeply after the exile: her restitution constitutes a preliminary end-point (Zeph 3:14-17; Zech 2:10 [MT 2:14]; 9:9).[42] Here, however, the prophetic marriage imagery has already been abandoned: as we observed in the later chapters of Hosea, it is surrendered in favor of the parent-child metaphor. At the end of the Book of the Twelve, as we saw in the case of Mal 2:10-16, the "love of God" is elevated to a different level. Now the text does not speak about love between two metaphorical marriage partners (YHWH and Israel/Jerusalem), but rather of YHWH's love for individual Israelites, female and male. At the same time a closing strophe to the prophetic marriage imagery is sung: Through the

[41] In addition, the "woman in a basket" (Zech 5:8) brought to Babylon may possibly be put in this context. Cf. Ulrike Sals, "Reading Zechariah 5:5-11: Prophecy, Gender and (Ap)Perception," in Athalya Brenner, ed., *A Feminist Companion to the Latter Prophets* (Sheffield: Sheffield Academic Press, 2001) 186–205.

[42] These texts are mentioned at this point although they are not part of the prophetic marriage imagery in the proper sense; however, in "daughter Zion" they adopt a related metaphor.

shift in the gender of the "partners," from this point on it is no longer clear which is to take what part: the marriage imagery has been dissolved by its own travesty.[43]

[43] In another article soon to appear I have shown (among other things), alongside the reading of the marriage imagery in canonical sequence of the books in the *Dodekapropheton*, the line that results if one orders the texts according to their probable sequence of composition. There are no serious differences between the two: the early texts of the prophetic marriage imagery tend to stand at the beginning of a book, the later ones near the book's conclusion. At any rate, the marriage-imagery focus of the Book of the Twelve clearly lies in the first half of the book. (Cf. Gerlinde Baumann, "Die prophetische Ehemetaphorik und die Bewertung der Prophetie im Zwölfprophetenbuch. Eine synchrone und diachrone Rekonstruktion zweier thematischer Fäden," in Paul Redditt and Aaron Schart, eds., *Thematic Threads in the Book of the Twelve* (Berlin and New York: Walter de Gruyter, 2003).

Part III

Summary and Conclusion

The question that began this book was whether the aspect of sexual violence is inextricably bound up with the prophetic marriage imagery. In answering this question one must review the results of the study on the two levels that are distinguished in the discussion of the concept of metaphor given above (Chapter 2 H). In what follows we will first (in Chapter 11) review the results of our investigation of the texts, looking at the marriage imagery in these texts once again in context. YHWH, we may say in advance, is in fact shown as a sexual perpetrator in some passages (see Chapter 11 C below). Another question is how sexual violence against women was perceived in Old Testament times, and how it was classified. Here—presumably—there are clear differences from present-day feminist interpretations; these will be reviewed in Chapter 12. Given such differences, how can we interpret the texts? We will pursue this issue in Chapter 13, with our focus placed especially on the problem of the God-image. Finally, in Chapter 14, we will offer a look ahead.

This evaluation cannot produce satisfactory answers in all cases. There is a significant need for research, and not only in the realm of the study of ancient Near Eastern parallel ideas. There is also a lack of hermeneutical projects that know how to deal with the violent aspect of the biblical image of God. Thus the following reflections are meant to be understood as steps along the way toward an adequate understanding, one that will include both explanation and interpretation. It is possible that such understanding will remain unattainable. It is the task of every time and context to seek anew for some answers to the question of how to approach biblical traditions. Since in this process the readers must render an account of themselves, engagement with biblical texts always produces a profitable outcome.

Chapter Eleven

The Marriage Imagery in the Individual Prophetic Books

A. Summary of the results of the textual studies

Where, in each of the biblical books we have considered, is the key statement and the "point" of the prophetic marriage imagery? What follows is a review of the prophetic writings for purposes of clarification.

Hosea introduces the imagery of a marriage between YHWH and Israel as a theological *topos* in the prophetic writings. Here for the first time a parallel is drawn between land and "woman/wife" in order to denounce the "whorish" behavior of both. Divine punishment of "woman" Israel follows, stated in images of sexual violence, but also in metaphors applying to the land and its fertility. At the end of Hosea this imagery of punishment is set in contrast with an imagery of parenthood and creation that is full of solicitous concern.

The parts of the book of Jeremiah containing marriage imagery were probably composed in light of an awareness of the shaping of the fundamental features of the imagery in Hosea. Now it is the two "women," Israel and Judah, with whom YHWH has an unhealthy marriage. "He" considers whether to obtain a divorce. The guilt of the "women" in the text is strongly emphasized; they refuse to abandon their "whorish" behavior, which primarily represents the social sins of the people and the worship of foreign gods. The fall of the Northern Kingdom of Israel and the impending end of the Southern Kingdom as well are the background for this imagery. The suffering of the people, interpreted as YHWH's punishment, is illustrated above all in images drawn from women's lives. Female imagery in Jeremiah is overwhelmingly applied in contexts that have a negative tinge. The depiction of YHWH in Jer 13:22, 26 is unmistakable: he acts against Jerusalem in the role of a perpetrator of sexual violence.

Ezekiel expands the negative possibilities of the prophetic marriage imagery still further. In this book the imagery serves to explain the utterly violent end of the "women," Samaria and Jerusalem, and to legitimate it. For this purpose the author chooses the form of two different narratives presenting model "biographies" of the "women." The marriage imagery is expanded by the use of other metaphors from the realm of family life. Samaria's and Jerusalem's "lovers" in these texts are primarily the cities' political "partners." The end of the "women" is brought on by sexual violence, initiated by YHWH. Above all, the imagery is shattered by the descriptions of violence and the murder of the women; the reality of war and deportation, as depicted in images, forces itself into the foreground. In Ezekiel there is scarcely any room for a positive female imagery: the new Jerusalem is not presented metaphorically as a "woman." The text offers a God-image characterized by a combination of power and righteousness. In the situation of exile such an image can only be maintained at a price: that YHWH is seen as the author of the most horrible acts of violence against his people and his land.

Also from the situation of exile, Lamentations has the raped "woman" Jerusalem speak. Once again it was YHWH who had done violence to her. In her utmost suffering and complete isolation, nothing remains for the "woman" but lament and appeal to YHWH in which she takes upon herself the guilt for what has happened.

Most of the texts of the prophetic marriage imagery in Isaiah also derive from the exilic and post-exilic period. Here YHWH shows a number of different faces: On the one hand "he" is the husband who has abandoned his wife because of her wicked behavior. Hence the "wife/woman" was handed over, defenseless, to her enemies. But then YHWH returns and desires to continue the "marriage." On the other hand, though, YHWH is a perpetrator of sexual violence against the enemy "woman," Babylon. Despite the positive marital images and the feminine side of the God-image that is also present here, YHWH's omnipotence is preserved at every moment. YHWH is absolutely free in his actions; abandonment and destruction are in his hands, and restoration as well.

The presentation of the prophetic marriage imagery in the Book of the Twelve Prophets is marked by a retrospective character. The whole sum of the motifs encountered thus far (see the next chapter) is gathered here; thus the marriage imagery runs throughout the whole time of Israel's history covered by the Book of the Twelve, including the restoration of Zion, but this last is no longer expressed in terms that are clearly part of the marriage imagery. After the beginning of the book and Hosea's introduction of the marriage imagery, "whoring," the separation and reconciliation of YHWH and Israel, and also divine violence against the enemy "woman" Nineveh, at the end of the book, in Malachi, reference is made to marriage one more time. Here the use of the marriage imagery reaches its end: In an exchange of roles, YHWH now takes the female and Judah the male part. This travesty of the prophetic marriage imagery leads to a shift in reference points: Now YHWH's most important partner is no longer his land (Hosea), his people, or his city (Jeremiah, Ezekiel, Isaiah, Lamentations), but, much as in Trito-Isaiah, each individual Israelite, male and female.

B. Systematic view of the results

In simplified terms, there are five motifs in the prophetic marriage imagery that can be organized into two major lines of interpretation.[1] The dominant motifs are: "the "whoring/prostitution" of the "woman" Israel, the "whoring/prostitution" of the "woman" Jerusalem, YHWH's punishment of Israel, YHWH's punishment of Jerusalem, and YHWH's restoration of the "woman," who for the most part is no longer given a name.[2]

The first line of interpretation is indebted to the deuteronomic-deuteronomistic pattern for interpreting the exile, which is regarded as punishment for the "iniquities" of the "woman." Here YHWH is both accuser and judge, and in most of the texts also the one who carries out the sentence. The "I"-lament of the "woman," who in Lamentations speaks of her guilt and sinfulness, but also of the suffering YHWH has brought upon her, can be seen as an associated motif.

The second line, because it appears primarily in the book of Isaiah, can be called the Isaian pattern of interpretation. Here the exile is interpreted in such a way that YHWH, the "husband," has abandoned his "wife" because of her iniquities. "She" is thus delivered, defenseless, into the hands of her enemies, who have done violence to her. The Isaian line is thus closely associated with a motif that, because of the choice of words in the imagery, is to be included within a marginal field of the prophetic marriage imagery: namely, the motif of the rape of the female personification of a foreign power (Isaiah 47: Babylon; Nahum 3: Nineveh).

[1] These two lines of interpretation (deuteronomic-deuteronomistic and Isaian) were also detected by Marie-Theres Wacker (*Figurationen des Weiblichen im Hosea-Buch* [Freiburg: Herder, 1996] 230, 247) in the related texts in Hosea.

[2] I have described this division elsewhere in more detail (Gerlinde Baumann, "Connected by Marriage, Adultery and Violence: The Prophetic Marriage Metaphor in the Book of the Twelve and in the Major Prophets," *SBL Seminar Papers* [Atlanta: Scholars, 1999] 552–69).

The overwhelming majority of the texts reveal the deuteronomic-deuteronomistic pattern. Here are the scenes of sexual violence against YHWH's "wives," but texts belonging to the Isaian pattern are not without incidence of violence by YHWH against a "woman," if we consider the whole context of each book. While in these texts the marriage imagery does not project any direct violence of YHWH against his "wife," violence is nevertheless practiced against a "foreign woman." Perhaps these can be interpreted as examples of how one aspect of the prophetic marriage imagery had come to seem self-evident, or else we can say that here we see the emergence of role-patterns that are very closely associated with metaphors of marriage or war: the role of the violent husband or of the conquering, rapist soldier. In the case of זנה, "to whore, prostitute oneself" we observe that the image of the "whore" has shifted among the different texts and as the result of different interweavings of metaphor and reality.[3] Did something similar happen to the God-image? Did the image of YHWH as a perpetrator of sexual violence become so matter-of-fact that even a complex of imagery that no longer attributes this trait to him in his role as "husband" can still not do without it?

In most of the texts the prophetic marriage imagery is not the only image-complex for expressing the relationship between YHWH and Israel/Jerusalem. Especially in Hosea, Isaiah, and the Book of the Twelve there are "counter-metaphors" that can be seen as correctives to or relativizing of the marriage imagery and that at least insert a contrary accent. More rare, in contrast, are metaphors offering alternatives to the relationships between the sexes projected in the marriage imagery. Here we could mention, for example, the passage in Jer 31:22bβ, "the 'woman' will encompass the 'man,'" the meaning of which remains quite open to interpretation. As alternative God-images that do not permit a description of YHWH as a rapist, we may mention the female images of God in the second half of the book of Isaiah.[4] Whether such images could really serve as "alternatives" to the problematic aspects of the God-imagery in the interpretation of these texts is something we must discuss further below, in Chapter 14.

C. Metaphors of sexual violence in the texts?

After this summary, we return to the question that began this study: is imagery of violent sexual abuse an essential element in marriage imagery?

[3] See above, Chapter 10 C.

[4] See above, Chapter 9 E ii.

Do these texts really contain metaphors of sexual violence, or are they only interpreted as such from a contemporary feminist perspective?

In most, although not all of the texts of the prophetic marriage imagery YHWH's violence against his "wife" is described in such a way that—within the framework of Old Testament and ancient Near Eastern language and its world of images—it must be interpreted as sexual abuse. This is not an observation that emerges solely from a feminist interpretation of the text; it can be philologically and historically verified. However, what—for the moment—must remain open is the connotations such images and actions had in ancient Israel. It seems to me rather improbable that a God-image like that of YHWH in the marriage imagery was experienced, in that context, as offensive or scandalous to the extent that is reflected in many current interpretations. Certainly the images were meant to cause offense, but the offense was coupled with positive recognition of YHWH's powerful actions: At no point are those actions represented as illegitimate. On the contrary: they are legitimated by the marriage imagery itself.

That this perspective was valid for all the people in ancient Israel, however, is questionable. Athalya Brenner and Fokkelien van Dijk-Hemmes[5] have discussed whether women participated directly in the composition of texts in Israel. While they deny this, they do admit that the realities of women's lives found entry into the traditions in indirect fashion. However, in the case of the problematic texts of the prophetic marriage imagery they have serious doubts about this.[6]

We may therefore start with the assumption that even in Israel's time the imagery of punishment of "woman/women" was perceived as a scenario of sexual violence. The next question would be: Is it impossible to conceive the prophetic marriage imagery without this particular form of violence? Central to the marriage imagery, as a way of interpreting Israel's experience of exile, is the accusation of "whoring/prostitution" against the "woman" Israel/Jerusalem. In all the texts this "whoring" is regarded as the reason for YHWH's violence as experienced in the exile—directly or indirectly. This model is also found in the Isaian line, where YHWH is reconciled with his "wife"; YHWH can practice violence against the "woman/wife," or he can renounce it and simply leave the "woman/wife" defenseless until, after a time, he returns to her. Thus two elements are central to the imagery's statement: YHWH's adherence to his tie to Israel/Jerusalem and his punishing acts against "her." To that extent the question

[5] *On Gendering Texts. Female and Male Voices in the Hebrew Bible* (Leiden and New York: Brill, 1993) 1–10 (Brenner); 25–32 (van Dijk-Hemmes).

[6] *On Gendering Texts* 12–13 (Brenner); 176 (van Dijk-Hemmes).

whether YHWH's punishing violence is a necessary element in the prophetic marriage imagery can only be answered with a "yes."[7] The purpose of the marriage imagery in the prophetic texts of the Old Testament—namely, to interpret the experience of exile—could not be fulfilled without YHWH's violent acts. This necessity does not exist solely as regards the choice of images. The imagery can, as the Isaian line of interpretation shows, exist without scenes of sexual violence against the "wife." The choice of images is probably explained by the fact that violent sexual abuse represented reality, both in the sphere of what was to be depicted (war) and in the realm from which the metaphors were drawn (marriage).

[7] Purely hypothetically, of course, we could imagine a marriage imagery in which there were no scenes of punishment or violence, but there are none such in these texts.

Chapter Twelve

Dealing With the Texts of the Prophetic Marriage Imagery: Critical Reading

As is evident from the feminist theological interpretation of the prophetic marriage imagery, serious problems arise when one attempts to interpret the texts against a present-day background of understanding. This is true both of the representation of women, men, and their relationships, and of the God-image. The hermeneutic point of this critique can be formulated this way: Explanations of the text against their own background yield a different result from that achieved when this imagery is read against the background of today's (modern Western) images and experiences of marriage.[1] The overlap between Old Testament and present-day understandings of marriage and the relationship of the sexes is too narrow to permit an uncritical and hermeneutically unreflective reading that will not lead to false conclusions. An interpretation of these biblical texts against a present-day background of understanding neglects the changes in contexts of life and of interpretation that have taken place in the intervening time.

The message of the text is also changed when the distinction between past and present eras and circumstances is not made. Here, in connection with the feminist critique presented in Part 2, I want to mention the dangers that threaten in three areas:

With regard to the image of women, or for women readers, there is the danger of reading the texts in such a way that women identify with the biblical view of Israel/Jerusalem, assume the guilt for the violence that was suffered, and accept the role of victims of violence.[2] One consequence can

[1] This was explained above, in the considerations on understanding the imagery in Chapter 2 G.

[2] Cf. Susan Thistlethwaite, "Every Two Minutes: Abused Women and Feminist Biblical Interpretation," in Letty M. Russell, ed., *Feminist Interpretation* (Philadelphia: Westminster, 1985)

be a damaged view of the self: namely, seeing oneself not as a person with freedom of action and decision, but rather as someone burdened with an "ontological handicap" and therefore inclined to "whoring." To that extent the image of women is damaged by the texts. In addition, because of God's involvement in the abusive actions, women who have suffered domestic violence in this case no longer even have God to turn to in their misery.[3]

In the texts of the prophetic marriage imagery, marriage is first of all an unsuccessful form of relationship. The marriage that is presented there offers no positive image for the mutual life of a woman and a man. In many aspects it is a failed relationship. Male violence and female infidelity are both presented here as "the normal state of things."

As regards the image of men, and for male readers, I see the danger at a different level. There is a threat to male humanity when men identify too strongly with the dominant God-images, formulated in male terms. Exegetical commentaries serve to illustrate the less harmful variants of this identification. Most exegetes adopt the perspective of God or the prophet, wholeheartedly agree with the divine critique of Israel's sinful behavior, and attempt to apply it. Only in very exceptional cases are the scenes of sexual violence named as such[4] or regarded as offensive. The connection between gender and social role, as can be demonstrated, makes such an identification easy. That identification is dangerous when no critique can be offered against a God, as imaged in the biblical texts, who exercises violence against women. If there is an uncritical and unreflective reception of these texts, men may see themselves as "justly violent."[5] A divine perpetrator, with all the authority that belongs to such a one, demonstrates such behavior to them and receives no negative judgment. At this point the role of God also becomes problematic: "His" behavior is taken by many people to be a moral example, but in these texts that would be fatal. The function of a moral authority—to which a God-image cannot be reduced,

---

96–97. Later in the essay she includes an account of a woman's experience that is surely not unique, in which a pastor points out to a woman that the Bible requires her to obey her husband.

[3] Hedwig-Jahnow-Forschungsprojekt, "Feministische Hermeneutik und Erstes Testament," in Hedwig Jahnow et al., *Feministische Hermeneutik und Erstes Testament. Analysen und Interpretationen* (Stuttgart: Kohlhammer, 1994) 10: "'God is the father, powerful, a protector and provider. My father was sort of God. He read from the Bible and said what was good and what was bad. I was his little girl, whom he used and misused. My father had God, and so there was no God for me.'" Quoted from "Statement of a woman in a workshop on sexual abuse."

[4] One positive exception that may be mentioned is the work of William Holladay, *Jeremiah 1. A Commentary on the Book of the Prophet Jeremiah, Chapter 1–25* (Philadelphia: Fortress, 1986) 414, for example, on Jer 13:22: ". . . it is clearly sexual violence that is meant . . . ."

[5] See the statement of an abusive husband quoted above in Chapter 1, n. 88.

but which it does possess—is, when God is imaged as a violent husband and a rapist, nothing short of devastating.

This brings us to the third danger I see in the realm of the God-image. Seeing God as a righteous perpetrator of violence and a "legitimator" of male violence does damage to the image of God. A God who so obviously performs actions that in our context are punishable offenses in law discredits himself and his authority. Here we must pose broader questions and open wider horizons within which the image of God is to be found.

Chapter Thirteen

The Problem of the God-Image

The problem of violence in the God-image is not confined to the prophetic marriage imagery. It appears (with different implications, but with parallels also) whenever violence experienced by people is traced to God as its cause. In the world of the Ancient Near East, and especially in Israel, a tiny land surrounded by larger nations that were in part hostile, the experience of war's violence was much closer to people's lives than is the case for most Europeans or North Americans today. Thus from this point of view as well the originating context of the prophetic marriage imagery is different. Therefore it makes sense to consider the God-image in the various biblical texts against their own particular cultural and contextual—historical and literary—backgrounds, as, for example, Walter Dietrich and Christian Link have begun to do.[1] This work shows, incidentally, that the problem of a violent God arises in a good many other texts; it is not only the texts of the prophetic marriage imagery, which were first reintroduced into the discussion by feminist critics, that are problematic. Other contemporary questions also raise problems with respect to the violent aspects of the God-image. For example, in 1980, in the context of the peace movement, YHWH's role as a God of war was sharply called into question.[2]

[1] *Die dunklen Seiten Gottes. Willkür und Gewalt* (Neukirchen-Vluyn: Neukirchener Verlag, 1995). God's arbitrariness and violence are here addressed as problems. The latter include God's jealousy, revenge, wrath, and militancy, which are generally discussed in terms of the historical contexts in which the texts originated.

[2] Here we will mention only a few works with this question as background: Norbert Lohfink, "'Gewalt' als Thema alttestamentlicher Forschung," in idem, ed., *Gewalt und Gewaltlosigkeit im Alten Testament* (Freiburg: Herder, 1983) 15–50; idem, "Der gewalttätige Gott des Alten Testaments und die Suche nach einer gewaltfreien Gesellschaft," in Ingo Baldermann et al., eds., *Der eine Gott der beiden Testamente* (Neukirchen-Vluyn: Neukirchener Verlag, 1987) 106–36; Jürgen Ebach, *Das Erbe der Gewalt. Eine biblische Realität und ihre Wirkungsgeschichte* (Gütersloh: Gerd Mohn, 1980).

However, a historical embedding in the biblical texts or a contemporary questioning is not adequate, because the hermeneutical problem of the texts remains: How can we deal with such a biblical God-image if the Bible is to remain relevant and a positive guide for us today? The scandal of some texts endures and cannot be historically "explained away."[3] The problem field of the violent God has not yet been adequately measured either by exegesis or by systematic theology; there is still need for research. Even though no satisfactory answer can be given at this point, we may at least point out that in the future the broad horizon of this question must be kept in view when the texts of the prophetic marriage imagery are interpreted.

[3] See, similarly, Manfred Görg, *Der un-heile Gott. Die Bibel im Bann der Gewalt* (Düsseldorf: Patmos, 1995); at the end of his examination of violent narratives about YHWH he calls for maintaining the tension within the God-image (pp. 173–82).

Chapter Fourteen

A Look Ahead

While I was working on this book I repeatedly wrestled with the question of what one might set over against the metaphors for God and the images of the textual "woman." There must surely be texts in which we could find other images of God and of women, images with which I could contradict these biblical texts, perhaps even "neutralize" the prophetic marriage imagery! For example, as regards the image of women one could hold up texts that depict independent, strong women. There are such narratives: about Hagar in Gen 16:21, Deborah in Judges 4–5, Hannah in 1 Samuel 1–2, and still more.[1] However, the cultural framework within which these stories describe the actions of the women severely restricts liberation and escape. In addition, in the Old Testament women are almost entirely viewed from a male perspective; women's own language, perspective, and view of the world appear in the texts only in a very filtered form.[2] It seems as if the search for positive biblical traditions for women can only represent an attempt to make "women's voices" again audible in a male world.

What about the search for "equalizing metaphors" in regard to the image of YHWH as the rapist of his "wife"? In the immediate textual field there are other images that can be set against this one, as I have described above in the course of studying the texts. But if we are to uncover true alternatives, the field of metaphors drawn from human social life must be abandoned. There are no non-hierarchical, egalitarian images for God to

[1] Annie Imbens-Fransen, *Befreiende Gottesbilder für Frauen. Damit frühe Wunden heilen* (Munich: Kösel, 1997) has collected such images precisely on behalf of women who have suffered violence.

[2] On this see Fokkelien van Dijk-Hemmes in eadem and Athalya Brenner, *On Gendering Texts. Female and Male Voices in the Hebrew Bible* (Leiden and New York: Brill, 1993) 25–32; see also Chapter 11, nn. 6-7.

be found in that field. Non-personal God-images can point the way here, or poetic God-images arising out of an appeal to God.[3] In the book of Job, God is called upon as a helper against violence that is experienced as something caused by God: That could offer a biblical-theological solution.

All the same, such texts cannot be regarded as "equalizers" against the problematic God-images in the prophetic marriage imagery, for hermeneutical reasons: Images of God as the rapist or abuser of his daughter cannot be "neutralized" even by the most positive "counter-images." Their scandalousness cannot and should not be softened by counter-texts. Only permanent outrage is an adequate response to an outrageous image of God. There is no biblical "medicine" that can help the story of God as the abusive husband of his "wife" Israel to come to a happier end. There have been attempts to reinterpret this violent story, as a look at the second half of the book of Isaiah shows. But even these texts, because they make another woman the victim of divine violence, are anything but unproblematic. And all the offense that these Isaianic texts may have taken at the God-image in Hosea, Jeremiah, and Ezekiel did not lead to any questioning of the canonicity of the texts themselves. Thus they can only stand as a warning from a phase of Israel's history shaped by violence and interpreted by certain groups with certain particular interests, a warning and a reminder of the story of a textual "woman" whose divine husband made use of violent and abusive means to bring her back to the "right way," a warning and a reminder of many women who have suffered from the violent abuse of their very real husbands and partners, and still do—and an encouragement to the detection and naming of violence, in Scripture and in life.

Constant engagement with violence against women and violence in the image of God requires a lot of energy. Anyone who feels bound to religious traditions and biblical images, and yet often finds herself incapable of relating to them otherwise than critically, is engaged in a demanding and exhausting task. Therefore at this point I would like to point to some sources from which, perhaps, such energy can be drawn. Little by little, feminist theological proposals are being formulated, beyond criticism, to project some positive images of God.[4] Here God is not only depicted in

[3] Ulrike Bail points such a way (*Gegen das Schweigen klagen. Eine intertextuelle Studie zu den Klagepsalmen Ps 6 und Ps 55 und der Erzählung von der Vergewaltigung Tamars* [Gütersloh: Chr. Kaiser/Gütersloher Verlagshaus, 1998]) when, with the aid of other texts, including passages from Pss 6 and 55, she gives a voice to the raped and silenced Tamar from 2 Samuel 13. However, this approach seems to me not so promising when, as in the case of the prophetic marriage imagery, God is the rapist.

[4] There is an overview, for example, in Monika Jakobs, *Frauen auf der Suche nach dem Göttlichen. Die Gottesfrage in der feministischen Theologie* (Münster: Morgana Frauenbuchverlag,

images drawn from Nature, but can be addressed as a person. For the most part these God-images deliberately avoid the hierarchies that are inherent in the previous images of God, hierarchies that enable violence. God accompanies people throughout their lives and even through suffering. God is thought of as "power in relationship,"[5] as a (female) friend, or (male or female) lover,[6] in the image of a self-transforming clown.[7] May God, and these images of God, give us the strength to be able to struggle with the other images.

1993). Another very inspiring publication is Elizabeth Johnson, *She Who Is. The Mystery of God in Feminist Theological Discourse* (New York: Crossroad, 1992).

[5] I. Carter Heyward, *The Redemption of God: A Theology of Mutual Relation* (Washington, D.C.: University Press of America, 1982).

[6] Sallie McFague, *Models of God. Theology for an Ecological, Nuclear Age* (Philadelphia: Fortress, 1987), especially 78–180.

[7] Gisela Matthiae, *Clownin Gott. Eine feministische Dekonstrution des Göttlichen* (Stuttgart et al.: Kohlhammer, 1999).

Abbreviations

Abbreviations in general follow Siegfried M. Schwertner, *Internationales Abkürzungsverzeichnis für Theologie und Grenzgebiete. Zeitschriften, Serien, Lexika, Quellenverzeichnisse mit bibliographischen Angaben.* 2nd rev. ed. Berlin and New York: Walter de Gruyter, 1994. Other abbreviations not in Schwertner's list include:

*	Texts to which the author refers in general, without including the whole text in detail.
**	English translations based on the author's German version.
AHw	Wolfram von Soden, *Akkadisches Handwörterbuch.* 3 vols. Wiesbaden: Harrassowitz, 1965–1981.
ANEP	James B. Pritchard, *The Ancient Near East in Pictures Relating to the Old Testament.* 2nd ed. Princeton: Princeton University Press, 1969.
BibIS	Biblical Interpretation Series. Leiden and New York, 1993–.
BInt	*Biblical Interpretation. A Journal of Contemporary Approaches.* Leiden, 1993–.
FemCB	*The Feminist Companion to the Bible.* Sheffield: Sheffield Academic Press, 1993–.
Ges^{17}	Wilhelm Gesenius, *Hebräisches und aramäisches Handwörterbuch über das Alte Testament, bearbeitet von Frants Buhl, unveränderter Neudruck der 17. Auflage 1915.* Berlin and New York: Springer, 1962.
Ges^{18}	Wilhelm Gesenius, *Hebräisches und aramäisches Handwörterbuch über das Alte Testament; unter verantwortlicher Mitarbeit von Udo Rütersworden; bearbeitet und herausgegeben von Rudolf Meyer und Herbert Donner.* 2 vols. 18th ed. Berlin and New York: Springer, 1987–1995.
GK	Emil Kautzsch, *Wilhelm Gesenius' hebräische Grammatik.* 28th rev. ed. Leipzig: Vogel, 1909; reprint Hildesheim: G. Olms, 1962.
HAL	Ludwig Köhler and Walter Baumgartner, *Hebräisches und Aramäisches Lexikon zum Alten Testament.* 3rd ed. Leiden: Brill, 1968–1990.
HBS	Herders Biblische Studien. Freiburg: Herder, 1994–.
HThKAT	Herders Theologischer Kommentar zum Alten Testament. Freiburg: Herder, 1999–.

TDOT G. Johannes Botterweck, Helmer Ringgren, and Heinz-Josef Fabry, eds., *Theological Dictionary of the Old Testament.* Grand Rapids and Cambridge: Eerdmans, 1974– .

TUAT Otto Kaiser, ed., *Texte aus der Umwelt des Alten Testaments.* 3 vols. Gütersloh: Gerd Mohn, 1982–1997.

WBC Carol A. Newsom and Sharon Ringe, eds., *The Women's Bible Commentary.* Louisville: Westminster John Knox, 1992; expanded ed. 1998.

Bibliography

Ackerman, Susan. "Isaiah," *WBC* (1992) 161–68.

Adler, Elaine June. *The Background for the Metaphor of Covenant as Marriage in the Hebrew Bible.* Dissertation, University of California, Berkeley. Ann Arbor: University Microfilms, 1989.

Albrektson, Bertil. *Studies in the Text and Theology of the Book of Lamentations. With a Critical Edition of the Peshitta Text.* STL 21. Lund: Gleerup, 1963.

André, Gunnel. art. "כָּשַׁף, *kāšap̱*," *ThWAT* 4:375–81 (*TDOT* 7:360–66).

Backhaus, Franz-Josef, and Ivo Meyer. "Das Buch Jeremia," in Erich Zenger et al., *Einleitung in das Alte Testament.* Kohlhammer-Studienbücher Theologie 1,1. 3rd newly revised and expanded ed. Stuttgart et al.: Kohlhammer, 1998, 405–30.

Bail, Ulrike. *Gegen das Schweigen klagen. Eine intertextuelle Studie zu den Klagepsalmen Ps 6 und Ps 55 und der Erzählung von der Vergewaltigung Tamars.* Gütersloh: Chr. Kaiser/Gütersloher Verlagshaus, 1998.

Bal, Mieke. "Metaphors He Lives By," *Semeia* 61 (1993) 185–207.

Barth, Karl. *Die Kirchliche Dogmatik..* 4 vols. in 13 [Zollikon/Zürich: Evangelischer Verlag, 1939–67]. III/2: *Die Lehre von der Schöpfung.* English: *Church Dogmatics.* 4 vols. in 12. Authorized translation by G. T. Thompson. [London] T & T Clark, 1936–63.

Bauer, Angela (1999a). "Das Buch Jeremia. Wenn kluge Klagefrauen und prophetische Pornographie den Weg ins Exil weisen," in Luise Schottroff and Marie-Theres Wacker, eds., *Kompendium Feministische Bibelauslegung.* 2nd ed. Gütersloh: Gütersloher Verlagshaus, 1999, 258–69.

_____. (1999b). *Gender in the Book of Jeremiah. A Feminist-Literary Reading.* Studies in Biblical Literature 5. New York: Peter Lang, 1999.

Bauer, Hans, and Pontus Leander. *Historische Grammatik der hebräischen Sprache des Alten Testaments.* Halle a.S.: Max Niemeyer, 1922; repr. Hildesheim: G. Olms, 1965.

Baumann, Gerlinde (1999a). "Das Buch Nahum. Der gerechte Gott als sexueller Gewalttäter," in Luise Schottroff and Marie-Theres Wacker, eds., *Kompendium Feministische Bibelauslegung.* 2nd ed. Gütersloh: Gütersloher Verlagshaus, 1999, 347–53.

_____. (1999b). "Connected by Marriage, Adultery and Violence: The Prophetic Marriage Metaphor in the Book of the Twelve and in the Major Prophets," *SBL Seminar Papers* (Atlanta: Scholars, 1999) 552–69.

_____. "Prophetic Objections to YHWH as the Violent Husband of Israel: Reinterpretations of the Prophetic Marriage Metaphor in Second Isaiah (Isaiah 40–55)," in Athalya Brenner, ed., *A Feminist Companion to the Latter Prophets. FemCB* Second Series 8. Sheffield: Sheffield Academic Press, 2001, 88–120.

_____. "Die prophetische Ehemetaphorik und die Bewertung der Prophetie im Zwölfprophetenbuch. Eine synchrone und diachrone Rekonstruktion zweier thematischer Fäden," in Paul Redditt and Aaron Schart, eds., *Thematic Threads in the Book of the Twelve*. BZAW 325. Berlin and New York: Walter de Gruyter, 2003.

Beeston, A.F.L. "Hebrew *Šibbolet* and *Šobel*," *JSS* 24 (1979) 175–77.

Bergman, Jan, Alfred Haldar, and Gerhard Wallis. art. "אהב, *ʾāhab̲*," *ThWAT* 1:105–28 (*TDOT* 1:99–118).

Beuken, W.A.M. "Isaiah LIV: The Multiple Identity of the Person Addressed," *OTS* 19 (1974) 29–70.

Biddle, Mark E. "The Figure of Lady Jerusalem: Identification, Deification and Personification of Cities in the Ancient Near East," in K. Lawson Younger, Jr., William W. Hallo, and Bernard F. Batto, eds., *The Biblical Canon in Comparative Perspective*. Scripture in Context IV; Ancient Near Eastern Texts and Studies 11. Lewiston, N.Y.: Edwin Mellen, 1991, 173–94.

Bietenhard, Sophia. "Das Buch Micha. Ruf nach Gerechtigkeit—Hoffnung für alle," in Luise Schottroff and Marie-Theres Wacker, eds., *Kompendium Feministische Bibelauslegung*. 2nd ed. Gütersloh: Gütersloher Verlagshaus, 1999, 338–46.

Bigger, Stephen Frank. *Hebrew Marriage and Family in the Old Testament Period. A Perspective from the Standpoint of Social History and Social Anthropology*. Dissertation in typescript, Manchester, 1974.

Bird, Phyllis (1989a). "The Harlot as Heroine: Narrative Art and Social Presupposition in Three Old Testament Texts," *Semeia* 46 (1989) 119–39 (reprinted in eadem, *Missing Persons and Mistaken Identities*, 197–218).

_____. (1989b). "'To Play the Harlot': An Inquiry into an Old Testament Metaphor," in Peggy L. Day, ed., *Gender and Difference in Ancient Israel*. Minneapolis: Fortress, 1989, 75–94 (reprinted in Bird, *Missing Persons and Mistaken Identities*, 219–36).

_____. *Missing Persons and Mistaken Identities. Women and Gender in Ancient Israel*. Minneapolis: Fortress, 1997.

Bitter, Stephan. *Die Ehe des Propheten Hosea. Eine auslegungsgeschichtliche Untersuchung*. GTA 3. Göttingen: Vandenhoeck & Ruprecht, 1975.

Black, Max. *Models and Metaphors*. Ithaca, N.Y.: Cornell University Press, 1962.

Blumenberg, Hans. *Paradigmen zu einer Metaphorologie*. stw 1301. Frankfurt: Suhrkamp, 1998.

Böhler, Dieter. "Geschlechterdifferenz und Landbesitz. Strukturuntersuchungen zu Jer 2,2–4,2," in Walter Groß, ed., *Jeremia und die "deuteronomistische Bewegung."* BBB 98. Weinheim: Beltz Athenäum,1995, 91–127.

Borger, Rykle. "Akkadische Rechtsbücher," *TUAT* I/1. *Rechtsbücher* (1982) 32–95.

_____. "Assyrische Staatsverträge," *TUAT* I/2. *Staatsverträge* (1983) 155–76.

Bosshard(-Nepustil), Erich. "Beobachtungen zum Zwölfprophetenbuch," *BN* 40 (1987) 30–62.

_____. *Rezeptionen von Jesaja 1–39 im Zwölfprophetenbuch. Untersuchungen zur literarischen Verbindung von Prophetenbüchern in babylonischer und persischer Zeit.* OBO 154. Fribourg: Universitätsverlag; Göttingen: Vandenhoeck & Ruprecht, 1997.

Bosshard, Erich, and Reinhard Gregor Kratz. "Maleachi im Zwölfprophetenbuch," *BN* 52 (1990) 27–46.

Bowen, Nancy R. "Can God Be Trusted? Confronting the Deceptive God," in Athalya Brenner, ed., *A Feminist Companion to the Latter Prophets. FemCB* 8. Sheffield: Sheffield Academic Press, 1995, 354–65.

Bozak, Barbara A. *Life "Anew." A Literary-Theological Study of Jer. 30–31.* AnBib 122. Rome: Biblical Institute Press, 1991.

Brenner, Athalya. "On Incest," in eadem, ed., *A Feminist Companion to Exodus to Deuteronomy. FemCB* 6. Sheffield: Sheffield Academic Press, 1994, 113–38.

_____. "On Prophetic Propaganda and the Politics of 'Love': The Case of Jeremiah," in eadem, ed., *A Feminist Companion to the Latter Prophets. FemCB* 8. Sheffield: Sheffield Academic Press, 1995, 256–74.

_____. "Pornoprophetics Revisited: Some Additional Reflexions," *JSOT* 70 (1996) 63–86.

_____. (1997a). "Identifying the Speaker-in-the-Text and the Reader's Location in Prophetic Texts: The Case of Isaiah 50," in Athalya Brenner and Carol R. Fontaine, eds., *A Feminist Companion to the Bible. Approaches, Methods and Strategies.* Sheffield: Sheffield Academic Press, 1997, 138–50.

_____. (1997b). *The Intercourse of Knowledge. On Gendering Desire and 'Sexuality' in the Hebrew Bible.* BibIS 26. Leiden and New York: Brill, 1997.

Brenner, Athalya, and Fokkelien van Dijk-Hemmes. *On Gendering Texts. Female and Male Voices in the Hebrew Bible.* BibIS 1. Leiden and New York: Brill, 1993.

Brockhaus. *Die Enzyklopädie in vierundzwanzig Bänden.* 20th ed. Leipzig and Mannheim: F. A. Brockhaus, 1996– . Volume 17 (1998).

Brockhaus, Ulrike, and Maren Kolshorn. *Sexuelle Gewalt gegen Mädchen und Jungen: Fakten, Theorien.* Frankfurt: Campus, 1993.

Brongers, Hendrik A. "Die metaphorische Verwendung von Termini für die Kleidung von Göttern und Menschen in der Bibel und im Alten Orient," in W. C. Delsman et al., eds., *Von Kanaan bis Kerala. Festschrift für J.P.M. van der Ploeg.* AOAT 211. Neukirchen-Vluyn: Neukirchener Verlag, 1982, 61–74.

Brueggemann, Walter. "At the Mercy of Babylon: A Subversive Reading of the Empire," *JBL* 100 (1991) 3–22.

Caird, George B. *The Language and Imagery of the Bible.* London: Duckworth; Philadelphia: Westminster, 1980.

Camp, Claudia V. "Metaphor in Feminist Biblical Interpretation: Theoretical Perspectives," *Semeia* 61 (1993) 3–36.

Carroll, Robert P. "Whorusalamin: A Tale of Three Cities as Three Sisters," in Bob Becking and Meindert Dijkstra, eds., *On Reading Prophetic Texts. Gender-Specific and Related Studies in Memory of Fokkelien van Dijk-Hemmes.* BibIS 18. Leiden and New York: Brill, 1996, 67–82.

Cassin, Elena. "Pouvoirs de la femme et structures familiales," *RA* 63 (1969) 121–48.

Collins, Adela Yarbro. "Feminine Symbolism in the Book of Revelation," *BInt* 1 (1993) 20–33.

Collins, Terence. *The Mantle of Elijah. The Redaction Criticism of the Prophetical Books.* The Biblical Seminar 20. Sheffield: JSOT Press, 1993.

Conrad, Joachim. art. "פלא, *pl'*," *ThWAT* 6:569–83 (*TDOT* 11:533–46).

Curtis, Adrian H. W., and Thomas Römer, eds. *The Book of Jeremiah and Its Reception.* BETHL 128. Louvain: Leuven University Press, 1997.

Darr, Katheryn Pfisterer (1992a). "Ezekiel," *WBC* (1992) 183–202.

_____. (1992b). "Ezekiel's Justifications of God: Teaching Troubling Texts," *JSOT* 55 (1992) 97–117.

Diamond, A. R. Pete, and Kathleen O'Connor. "Unfaithful Passions: Coding Women Coding Men in Jeremiah 2–3 (4:2)," *BInt* 4 (1996) 288–310.

Dietrich, Walter, and Christian Link. *Die dunklen Seiten Gottes.* Vol. 1: *Willkür und Gewalt.* Vol. 2: *Allmacht und Ohnmacht.* Neukirchen-Vluyn: Neukirchener Verlag, 1995/2000.

Dijk-Hemmes, Fokkelien van. "The Imagination of Power and the Power of Imagination. An Intertextual Analysis of Two Biblical Love Songs: The Song of Songs and Hosea 2," *JSOT* 44 (1989) 75–88.

_____. "The Metaphorization of Woman in Prophetic Speech: An Analysis of Ezekiel XXIII," *VT* 43 (1993) 162–70.

Dijk-Hemmes, Fokkelien van, and Athalya Brenner, eds. *Reflections on Theology and Gender.* Kampen: Kok Pharos, 1994.

Doll, Peter. *Menschenschöpfung und Weltschöpfung in der alttestamentlichen Weisheit.* SBS 117. Stuttgart: Katholisches Bibelwerk, 1985.

Dommershausen, Werner. art. "כנף, *kānāp*," *ThWAT* 4:243–46 (*TDOT* 7:229–31).

Driver, Godfrey R. "Isaiah 6:1 'His Train Filled the Temple,'" in Hans Goedicke, ed., *Near Eastern Studies in Honor of William Foxwell Albright.* Baltimore and London: Johns Hopkins University Press, 1971, 87–96.

Dupont-Sommer, André. *Les Inscriptions araméennes de Sfiré (Stèles I et II). Extrait des Memoires présentés par divers savants à l'Academie des Inscriptions et Belles Lettres* XV. Paris: Impr. nationale, 1958.

Ebach, Jürgen. *Das Erbe der Gewalt. Eine biblische Realität und ihre Wirkungsgeschichte.* GTBS 378. Gütersloh: Gerd Mohn, 1980.

Elliger, Karl. "Das Gesetz in Leviticus 18," *ZAW* 67 (1955) 1–25.

_____. *Leviticus*. HAT 4. Tübingen: J.C.B. Mohr, 1966.

Elliger, Karl, and Wilhelm Rudolph, eds. *Biblia Hebraica Stuttgartensia*. 4th improved ed. Stuttgart: Deutsche Bibelgesellschaft, 1990 (= *BHS*).

Emerton, John A. "The Meaning of the Verb *ḥāmās* in Jeremiah 13,22," in Volkmar Fritz et al., eds., *Prophet und Prophetenbuch. Festschrift für Otto Kaiser zum 65. Geburtstag*. BZAW 185. Berlin and New York: Walter de Gruyter, 1989, 19–28.

Engelmann, Angelika. "Deuteronomium. Recht und Gerechtigkeit für Frauen im Gesetz," in Luise Schottroff and Marie-Theres Wacker, eds., *Kompendium Feministische Bibelauslegung*. 2nd ed. Gütersloh: Gütersloher Verlagshaus, 1999, 67–79.

Erlandsson, Seth. art. "זנה, *zānāh*," *ThWAT* 2:612–21 (*TDOT* 4:99–104).

Eslinger, Lyle. "The Infinite in a Finite Organical Perception (Isaiah VI 1-5)," *VT* 45 (1995) 145–73.

Even-Shoshan, Avraham. *A New Concordance of the Bible. Thesaurus of the Language of the Bible. Hebrew and Aramaic. Roots, Words, Proper Names, Phrases and Synonyms*. Jerusalem: Kiryat Sefer, 1989.

Exum, J. Cheryl. "The Ethics of Biblical Violence against Women," in John W. Rogerson et al., eds., *The Bible in Ethics*. JSOT.S 207. Sheffield: Sheffield Academic Press, 1995, 248–71.

_____. "Prophetic Pornography," in eadem, *Plotted, Shot, and Painted. Cultural Representations of Biblical Women*. Gender, Culture, Theory 3. JSOT.S 215. Sheffield: Sheffield Academic Press, 1996, 101–108.

Eynde, Sabine van den. "Daughters of Abraham!? On 'Covenant,' Women and Gender." LAUD Linguistic Agency, Series A. General and Theoretical. Paper No. 472. Essen, 1999.

Fensham, F. Charles. "The Marriage Metaphor in Hosea for the Covenant Relationship between the Lord and His People (Hos 1:2-9)," in idem, ed., *Northwest Semitic Studies in Honor of Adrianus van Selms*. *JNWSL* 12 (1984) 71–78.

Fischer, Irmtraud. "Das Buch Jesaja. Das Buch der weiblichen Metaphern," in Luise Schottroff and Marie-Theres Wacker, eds., *Kompendium Feministische Bibelauslegung*. 2nd ed. Gütersloh: Gütersloher Verlagshaus, 1999, 246–57.

Fitzgerald, Aloysius. "The Mythological Background for the Presentation of Jerusalem as a Queen and False Worship as Adultery in the OT," *CBQ* 34 (1972) 403–16.

_____. "*BTWLT* and *BT* as Titles for Capital Cities," *CBQ* 37 (1975) 167–83.

Franke, Chris A. "The Function of the Satiric Lament over Babylon in Second Isaiah (XLVII)," *VT* 41 (1991) 408–18.

Franzmann, Majella. "The City as Woman: The Case of Babylon in Isaiah 47," *ABR* 43 (1995) 1–19.

Freedman, David Noel, and John W. Welch. art. "שדד, *šaḏāḏ*," *ThWAT* 7:1072–1078.

Freedman, David Noel, and B. E. Willoughby. art. "נאף, *nā'ap*," *ThWAT* 5:123–29 (*TDOT* 9:113–18).

Friedman, Mordechai A. "Israel's Response in Hosea 2:17b: 'You are my Husband,'" *JBL* 99 (1980) 199–204.

Fritz, Volkmar. "Das Wort gegen Samaria Mi 1,2-7," in idem, *Studien zu Literatur und Geschichte des Alten Israel*. SBAB 22. Stuttgart: Katholisches Bibelwerk, 1997, 125–40.

Fuhs, H. F. art. "עבר, *ʿāḇar*," *ThWAT* 5:1015–1033 (*TDOT* 10:408–25).

Galambush, Julie. *Jerusalem in the Book of Ezekiel. The City as Yahweh's Wife*. SBL.DS 130. Atlanta: Scholars, 1992.

Gerstenberger, Erhard S. art. "ענה, *ʿānāh*," *ThWAT* 6:247–70 (*TDOT* 11:230–52).

_____. *Das dritte Buch Mose. Leviticus*. ATD 6. 6th fully rev. ed. Göttingen: Vandenhoeck & Ruprecht, 1993.

Gildemeister, Regine. "Die soziale Konstruktion von Geschlechtlichkeit," in Ilona Ostner and Klaus Lichtblau, eds., *Feministische Vernunftkritik. Ansätze und Traditionen*. Frankfurt and New York: Campus, 1992, 200–39.

Glazier-McDonald, Beth. *Malachi, the Divine Messenger.* SBL.DS 98. Atlanta: Scholars, 1987.

_____. (1992a). "Haggai," *WBC* (1992) 228–29.

_____. (1992b). "Joel," *SBC* (1992) 204–205.

_____. (1992c). "Malachi," *WBC* (1992) 232–34.

_____. (1992d). "Obadiah," *WBC* (1992) 210–11.

_____. (1992e). "Zechariah," *WBC* (1992) 230–31.

Godenzi, Alberto. *Bieder, brutal. Frauen und Männer sprechen über sexuelle Gewalt*. 2nd ed. Zürich: Unionsverlag, 1991.

Gordis, Robert. "Hosea's Marriage and Message: A New Approach," *HUCA* 25 (1954) 9–35.

Gordon, Cyrus H. "Hos 2:4-5 in the Light of New Semitic Inscriptions," *ZAW* 54 (1936) 277–80.

Gordon, Pamela, and Harold C. Washington. "Rape as a Military Metaphor in the Hebrew Bible," in Athalya Brenner, ed., *A Feminist Companion to the Latter Prophets. FemCB* 8. Sheffield: Sheffield Academic Press, 1995, 308–25.

Görg, Manfred. *Der un-heile Gott. Die Bibel im Bann der Gewalt*. Düsseldorf: Patmos, 1995.

Greenberg, Moshe. "Ezekiel 16: A Panorama of Passion," in John H. Marks and Robert M. Good, eds., *Love & Death in the Ancient Near East. Essays in Honor of Marvin H. Pope*. Guilford, Conn.: Four Quarters, 1987, 143–50.

_____. *Ezekiel 1–20. A New Translation with Introduction and Commentary.* AB 22. Garden City, N. Y.: Doubleday, 1983.

_____. *Ezekiel 21–37. A New Translation with Introduction and Commentary.* AB 22a. New York: Doubleday, 1997.

Greengus, Samuel, "A Textbook Case of Adultery in Ancient Mesopotamia," *HUCA* 40/41 (1969–70) 33–44, at 34–35.

Gross, Walter. *Zukunft für Israel. Alttestamentliche Bundeskonzepte und die aktuelle Debatte um den Neuen Bund*. SBS 176. Stuttgart: Katholisches Bibelwerk, 1998.

Haag, Herbert. art. "חמס, *ḥāmās*," *ThWAT* 2:1050–1061 (*TDOT* 4:478–87).

_____. *Der Gottesknecht bei Deuterojesaja*. EdF 233. 2nd ed. Darmstadt: Wissenschaftliche Buchgesellschaft, 1993.

Hall, Gary H. *The Marriage Metaphor of Jeremiah 2 and 3: A Study of Antecedents and Innovations in a Prophetic Metaphor.* Dissertation, Union Theological Seminary of Virginia, 1980.

_____. "Origin of the Marriage Metaphor," *HebStud* 23 (1982) 169–71.

Hasel, G. F. art. "כרת, *kārat*," *ThWAT* 4:355–67 (*TDOT* 7:339–52).

Häusl, Maria. "Die Klagelieder. Zions Stimme in der Not," in Luise Schottroff and Marie-Theres Wacker, eds., *Kompendium Feministische Bibelauslegung*. 2nd ed. Gütersloh: Gütersloher Verlagshaus, 1999, 270–77.

Hedwig-Jahnow-Forschungsprojekt. "Feministische Hermeneutik und Erstes Testament," in Hedwig Jahnow et al., *Feministische Hermeneutik und Erstes Testament. Analysen und Interpretationen*. Stuttgart: Kohlhammer, 1994, 9–25.

_____. "Möglichkeiten befreiender Lektüre von alttestamentlichen Texten über Gewalt gegen Frauen," *epd-Dokumentation* 17 (1997) 71–73.

Herrmann, Siegfried. art. "Jeremia/Jeremiabuch," *TRE* 16 (1987) 568–86.

Heyward, I. Carter. *The Redemption of God: A Theology of Mutual Relation*. Washington, D.C.: University Press of America, 1982. German: *Und sie rührte sein Kleid an. Eine feministische Theologie der Beziehung*. Stuttgart: Kreuz, 1986.

Hillers, Delbert R. *Treaty-Curses and the Old Testament Prophets*. BibOr 16. Rome: Pontifical Biblical Institute, 1964.

_____. "Rite: Ceremonies of Law and Treaty in the Ancient Near East," in Edwin B. Firmage et al., eds., *Religion and Law: Biblical-Judaic and Islamic Perspectives*. Winona Lake: Eisenbrauns, 1990, 351–64.

Hobbs, T. Raymond. "Jeremiah 3,1-5 and Deuteronomy 24,1-4," *ZAW* 86 (1974) 23–29.

Holladay, William L. "'On every high hill and under every green tree,'" *VT* 11 (1961) 170–75.

_____. *Jeremiah 1. A Commentary on the Book of the Prophet Jeremiah, Chapters 1–25*. Hermeneia. Philadelphia: Fortress, 1986.

_____. *Jeremiah 2. A Commentary on the Book of the Prophet Jeremiah, Chapters 26–52*. Hermeneia. Philadelphia: Fortress, 1989.

Hossfeld, Frank-Lothar. "Das Buch Ezechiel," in Erich Zenger et al., *Einleitung in das Alte Testament*. Kohlhammer-Studienbücher Theologie 1,1. 3rd newly revised and expanded ed. Stuttgart et al.: Kohlhammer, 1998, 440–57.

Hossfeld, Frank-Lothar, et al. art. "שׁלח, *šālaḥ*," *ThWAT* 8:46–70.

Huehnergard, John. "Biblical Notes on Some New Akkadian Texts from Emar (Syria)," *CBQ* 47 (1985) 428–34.

Hugenberger, Gordon Paul. *Marriage as Covenant. A Study of Biblical Law and Ethics Governing Marriage, Developed from the Perspective of Malachi*. VT.S 52. Leiden: Brill, 1994.

Hunter, Jannie. *Faces of a Lamenting City. The Development and Coherence of the Book of Lamentations*. BEAT 39. Frankfurt: Peter Lang, 1996.

Imbens-Fransen, Annie. *Befreiende Gottesbilder für Frauen. Damit frühe Wunden heilen*. Munich: Kösel, 1997.

Isaksson, Abel. *Marriage and Ministry in the New Temple. A Study with Special Reference to Mt. 19.3-12 and 1. Cor. 11.3-16*. ASNU 24. Lund: Gleerup, 1965.

Jahnow, Hedwig. *Das hebräische Leichenlied im Rahmen der Völkerdichtung*. BZAW 36. Giessen: A. Töpelmann, 1923.

Jakobs, Monika. *Frauen auf der Suche nach dem Göttlichen. Die Gottesfrage in der feministischen Theologie*. FrauenForschung 1. Münster: Morgana Frauenbuchverlag, 1993.

Janowski, Bernd. *Stellvertretung. Alttestamentliche Studien zu einem Theologischen Grundbegriff*. SBS 165. Stuttgart: Katholisches Bibelwerk, 1997.

Janowski, J. Christine. "Zur paradigmatischen Bedeutung der Geschlechterdifferenz in K. Barths 'Kirchlicher Dogmatik,'" in Helga Kuhlmann, ed., *Und drinnen waltet die züchtige Hausfrau. Zur Ethik der Geschlechterdifferenz*. Gütersloh: Chr. Kaiser, 1995, 140–86.

Jenni, Ernst. *Das hebräische Piʿel. Syntaktisch-semasiologische Untersuchung einer Verbalform im Alten Testament*. Zürich: EVZ-Verlag, 1968.

_____. *Die hebräischen Präpositionen*. Vol. 1: *Die Präposition Beth*. Stuttgart: Kohlhammer, 1992.

Jeremias, Alfred. *Das Alte Testament im Lichte des Alten Orients. Handbuch zur biblisch-orientalischen Altertumskunde*. 3rd ed. Leipzig, 1916.

Jeremias, Jörg. *Kultprophetie und Gerichtsverkündigung in der späten Königszeit Israels*. WMANT 35. Neukirchen-Vluyn: Neukirchener Verlag, 1970.

_____. *Der Prophet Hosea*. ATD 24/1. Göttingen: Vandenhoeck & Ruprecht, 1983.

_____. art. "Hosea/Hoseabuch," *TRE* 15 (1986) 568–98.

Johnson, Bo. "Form and Message in Lamentations," *ZAW* 97 (1985) 58–73.

Johnson, Elizabeth. *She Who Is. The Mystery of God in Feminist Theological Discourse*. New York: Crossroad, 1992.

Jones, Barry Alan. *The Formation of the Book of the Twelve: A Study in Text and Canon*. SBL.DS 149. Atlanta: Scholars, 1995.

Jost, Renate. "Von 'Huren' und 'Heiligen.' Ein sozialgeschichtlicher Beitrag," in Hedwig Jahnow et al., *Feministische Hermeneutik und Erstes Testament. Analysen und Interpretationen*. Stuttgart: Kohlhammer, 1994, 126–37.

_____. *Frauen, Männer und die Himmelskönigin. Exegetische Studien*. Gütersloh: Chr. Kaiser, 1995.

Jost, Renate, and Elke Seifert. "Das Buch Ezechiel," in Luise Schottroff and Marie-Theres Wacker, eds., *Kompendium Feministische Bibelauslegung*. 2nd ed. Gütersloh: Gütersloher Verlagshaus, 1999, 278–90.

Jüngel, Eberhard. "Metaphorische Wahrheit. Erwägungen zur theologischen Relevanz der Metapher als Beitrag zur Hermeneutik einer narrativen Theologie," in Paul Ricoeur and Eberhard Jüngel, *Metapher. Zur Hermeneutik religiöser Sprache*. EvTh Sonderheft. Munich: Kaiser, 1974, 71–122.

Jüngling, Hans-Winfried. "Das Buch Jesaja," in Erich Zenger et al., *Einleitung in das Alte Testament.* Kohlhammer-Studienbücher Theologie 1,1. 3rd newly revised and expanded ed. Stuttgart et al.: Kohlhammer, 1998, 381–404.

Kaiser, Barbara Bakke. "Poet as 'Female Impersonator': The Image of Daughter Zion as Speaker in Biblical Poems of Suffering," *JR* 67 (1987) 164–82.

Kaiser, Otto. *Der Prophet Jesaja. Kapitel 13–39.* ATD 18. 2nd ed. Göttingen: Vandenhoeck & Ruprecht, 1976.

_____. "Klagelieder," in Helmer Ringgren, Walther Zimmerli, and Otto Kaiser, *Sprüche. Prediger. Das Hohe Lied. Klagelieder. Das Buch Esther.* ATD 16. 3rd ed. Göttingen: Vandenhoeck & Ruprecht, 1981, 291–386.

_____. *Das Buch des Propheten Jesaja. Kapitel 1–12.* ATD 17. 5th rev. ed. Göttingen: Vandenhoeck & Ruprecht, 1981.

_____. art. "Jesaja/Jesajabuch," *TRE* 16 (1987) 636–58.

Keefe, Alice A. "Rapes of Women/Wars of Men," *Semeia* 61 (1993) 79–97.

Keel, Othmar. *Goddesses and Trees, New Moon and Yahweh. Ancient Near Eastern Art in the Hebrew Bible.* JSOT.S 261. Sheffield: Sheffield Academic Press, 1998.

Keel, Othmar, and Christoph Uehlinger. *Göttinnen, Götter und Gottessymbole. Neue Erkenntnisse zur Religionsgeschichte Kanaans und Israels aufgrund bislang unerschlossener ikonographischer Quellen.* 4th ed. Freiburg, Basel, and Vienna: Herder, 1998. English: *Gods, Goddesses, and Images of God in Ancient Israel.* Translated by Thomas H. Trapp. Minneapolis: Fortress, 1998.

Kessler, Rainer. *Micha.* HThKAT. Freiburg: Herder, 1999.

Kittel, Rudolf, ed. *Biblia Hebraica.* 16th rev. ed. Stuttgart: Württembergische Bibelanstalt, 1973 (= *BHK*).

Koch, Klaus. "Haggais unreines Volk," *ZAW* 79 (1967) 52–66.

_____. *Die Profeten II. Babylonisch-persische Zeit.* UTB 281. 2nd ed. Stuttgart et al.: Kohlhammer, 1988.

_____. *Die Profeten I. Assyrische Zeit.* UTB 280. 3rd ed. Stuttgart et al.: Kohlhammer, 1995.

Köhler, Ludwig. "Alttestamentliche Theologie," *ThR* 7 (1935) 255–76.

Köhler, Ludwig, and Walter Baumgartner. *Lexicon in Veteris Testamenti Libros.* 2nd ed. Leiden: Brill, 1958 (= KBL^2).

Korpel, Marjo Christina Annette. *A Rift in the Clouds. Ugaritic and Hebrew Descriptions of the Divine.* UBL 8. Münster: Ugarit-Verlag, 1990.

_____. "The Female Servant of the Lord in Isaiah 54," in Bob Becking and Meindert Dijkstra, eds., *On Reading Prophetic Texts. Gender-Specific and Related Studies in Memory of Fokkelien van Dijk-Hemmes.* BibIS 18. Leiden and New York: Brill, 1996, 153–67.

Krieg, Matthias. *Mutmassungen über Maleachi.* AThANT 80. Zürich: Theologischer Verlag, 1993.

Kruger, Paul A. "The Hem of the Garment in Marriage. The Meaning of the Symbolic Gesture in Ruth 3:9 and Ezek 16:8," *JNWSL* 12 (1984) 79–86.

_____. "The Symbolic Significance of the Hem *(kanaf)* in 1 Samuel 15.27," in Walter T. Claassen, ed., *Text and Context. Old Testament and Semitic Studies for F. C. Fensham*. JSOT.S 48. Sheffield: JSOT Press, 1988, 105–16.

_____. "Rites of Passage Relating to Marriage and Divorce in the Hebrew Bible," *JNWSL* 21 (1995) 69–81.

_____. "'I will hedge her way with thornbushes' (Hosea 2,8): Another Example of Literary Multiplicity?" *BZ* 43 (1999) 92–99.

Krüger, Thomas. *Geschichtskonzepte im Ezechielbuch*. BZAW 180. Berlin and New York: Walter de Gruyter, 1989.

Kuhl, Curt. "Neue Dokumente zum Verständnis von Hosea 2,14-15," *ZAW* 52 (1934) 102–109.

Kurz, Gerhard. *Metapher, Allegorie, Symbol*. KVR 1486. 4th ed. Göttingen: Vandenhoeck & Ruprecht, 1997.

Kutsch, Ernst. *Verheissung und Gesetz. Untersuchungen zum sogenannten "Bund" im Alten Testament*. BZAW 131. Berlin and New York: Walter de Gruyter, 1973.

_____. *Neues Testament—neuer Bund? Eine Fehlübersetzung wird korrigiert*. Neukirchen-Vluyn: Neukirchener Verlag, 1978.

_____. art. "Bund I. Altes Testament," *TRE* 7 (1981) 397–403.

Lakoff, George, and Mark Johnson. *Metaphors We Live By*. Chicago: University of Chicago Press, 1980. German: *Leben in Metaphern. Konstruktionen und Gebrauch von Sprachbildern*. Heidelberg: Carl-Auer-Systeme, 1998.

Lanahan, William F. "The Speaking Voice in the Book of Lamentations," *JBL* 93 (1974) 41–49.

Lang, Bernhard. *Ezechiel. Der Prophet und das Buch*. EdF 153. Darmstadt: Wissenschaftliche Buchgesellschaft, 1981.

_____. art. "Ehe I. Altes Testament," *NBL* 1 (Zürich, 1991) 475–78.

Lipiński, Édouard. art. "מכר, *mkr*," *ThWAT* 4:869–75 (*TDOT* 8:291–96).

_____. art. "שׂנא, *śāneʾ*," *ThWAT* 7:828–39.

Lisowsky, Gerhard. *Konkordanz zum hebräischen Alten Testament nach dem von Paul Kahle in der Biblia Hebraica edidit Rudolf Kittel besorgten Masoretischen Text*. With the collaboration of Leonhard Rost. 2nd ed. Stuttgart: Württembergische Bibelanstalt, 1958.

Locher, Clemens. "Altes und Neues zu Maleachi 2,10-16," in Pierre Casetti, Othmar Keel, and Adrian Schenker, eds., *Mélanges Dominique Barthélemy. Études bibliques offertes à l'occasion de son 60e anniversaire*. OBO 38. Fribourg: Éditions universitaires; Göttingen: Vandenhoeck & Ruprecht, 1981, 241–71.

Lohfink, Norbert. "'Gewalt' als Thema alttestamentlicher Forschung," in idem, ed., *Gewalt und Gewaltlosigkeit im Alten Testament*. QD 96. Freiburg: Herder, 1983, 15–50.

_____. "Der gewalttätige Gott des Alten Testaments und die Suche nach einer gewaltfreien Gesellschaft," in Ingo Baldermann et al., eds., *Der eine Gott der beiden Testamente*. JBTh 2. Neukirchen-Vluyn: Neukirchener Verlag, 1987, 106–36.

_____. art. "Bund," *NBL* 1 (Zürich, 1991) 344–48.

Long, Burke O. "The Stylistic Components of Jeremiah 3,1-5," *ZAW* 88 (1976) 386–90.

Lutzmann, Heiner. "Aus den Gesetzen des Königs Lipit Eschtar von Isin," *TUAT* I/1. *Rechtsbücher.* Gütersloh: Gerd Mohn, 1982, 23–31.

Lutzmann, Heiner, and Willem H. P. Römer. "Sumerische Dokumente," *TUAT* I/3. *Dokumente zum Rechts- und Wirtschaftsleben.* Gütersloh: Gerd Mohn, 1983, 32–95.

Magdalene, F. Rachel. "Ancient Near-Eastern Treaty-Curses and the Ultimate Texts of Terror: A Study of the Language of Divine Sexual Abuse in the Prophetic Corpus," in Athalya Brenner, ed., *A Feminist Companion to the Latter Prophets. FemCB* 8. Sheffield: Sheffield Academic Press, 1995, 326–52.

Maier, Christl. "Jerusalem als Ehebrecherin in Ezechiel 16. Zur Verwendung und Funktion einer biblischen Metapher," in Hedwig Jahnow et al., *Feministische Hermeneutik und Erstes Testament. Analysen und Interpretationen.* Stuttgart et al.: Kohlhammer, 1994, 85–105.

_____. "Die Klage der Tochter Zion. Ein Beitrag zur Weiblichkeitsmetaphorik im Jeremiabuch," *BThZ* 15 (1998) 176–89.

Marböck, Johannes. art. "נבל, *nāḇāl,*" *ThWAT* 5:171–85 (*TDOT* 9:157–71).

_____. art. "קלה, *qlh* II," *ThWAT* 7:34–40.

Martin, James D. "Forensic Background to Jeremiah III 1," *VT* 19 (1969) 82–92.

Martin-Achard, Robert. "Esaïe 47 et la tradition prophétique sur Babylone," in John A. Emerton, ed., *Prophecy. Essays Presented to Georg Fohrer on his sixty-fifth birthday, 6 September 1980.* BZAW 150. Berlin and New York: Walter de Gruyter, 1980, 83–105.

Matthiae, Gisela. *Clownin Gott. Eine feministische Dekonstrution des Göttlichen.* PTHe 45. Stuttgart et al.: Kohlhammer, 1999.

McFague, Sallie. *Models of God. Theology for an Ecological, Nuclear Age.* Philadelphia: Fortress, 1987.

McKane, William. *Jeremiah.* ICC 1: *Introduction and Commentary on Jeremiah I–XXV.* Edinburgh: T & T Clark, 1986.

McKeating, Henry. "Sanctions Against Adultery in Ancient Israelite Society. With Some Reflections on Methodology in the Study of OT Ethics," *JSOT* 11 (1979) 57–72.

Mettinger, Tryggve N. D. *A Farewell to the Servant Songs. A Critical Examination of an Exegetical Axiom.* SMHVL 1982–1983 (3). Lund: Gleerup, 1983.

Meyer, Ivo. "Die Klagelieder," in Erich Zenger et al., *Einleitung in das Alte Testament.* Kohlhammer-Studienbücher Theologie 1,1. 3rd newly revised and expanded ed. Stuttgart et al.: Kohlhammer, 1998, 430–35.

Meyers, Carol L. "Everyday Life. Women in the Period of the Hebrew Bible," *WBC* (1992) 244–51.

Milgrom, Jacob, David P. Wright, and Heinz-Josef Fabry, art. "נדה, *niddāh,*" *ThWAT* 5:250–53 (*TDOT* 9:232–35).

Moran, William L. "The Ancient Near Eastern Background of the Love of God in Deuteronomy," *CBQ* 25 (1963) 77–87.

Mosis, Rudolf. art. "פתה, *pth*," *ThWAT* 6:820–31 (*TDOT* 12:162–72).

Müller, Hans-Peter. *Vergleich und Metapher im Hohenlied.* OBO 56. Fribourg: Universitätsverlag; Göttingen: Vandenhoeck & Ruprecht, 1984.

Müllner, Ilse. *Gewalt im Hause Davids: Die Erzählung von Tamar und Amnon (2 Sam 13,1-22).* HBS 13. Freiburg: Herder, 1997.

_____. "Sexuelle Gewalt im Alten Testament," in Ulrike Eichler and Ilse Müllner, eds., *Sexuelle Gewalt gegen Mädchen und Frauen als Thema der feministischen Theologie.* Gütersloh: Chr. Kaiser, 1999, 40–75.

Neufeld, Ephraim. *Ancient Hebrew Marriage Laws, With Special References to General Semitic Laws and Customs.* London and New York: Longmans, Green, & Co., 1944.

Newsom, Carol A. "A Maker of Metaphors: Ezekiel's Oracles against Tyre," in James L. Mays and Paul J. Achtemeier, eds., *Interpreting the Prophets.* Philadelphia: Fortress, 1987, 188–99.

Niehr, Herbert. art. "ערה, *ʿārāh*," *ThWAT* 6:369–75 (*TDOT* 11:335–41).

Nielsen, Kirsten. *There is Hope for a Tree. The Tree as Metaphor in Isaiah.* Translated by Christine and Frederick Crowley. JSOT.S 65. Sheffield: JSOT Press, 1989.

Nissinen, Martti. *Prophetie, Redaktion und Fortschreibung im Hoseabuch. Studien zum Werdegang eines Prophetenbuches im Lichte von Hos 4 und 11.* AOAT 231. Neukirchen-Vluyn: Neukirchener Verlag; Kevelaer: Butzon & Bercker, 1991.

Nogalski, James D. (1993a). *Literary Precursors to the Book of the Twelve.* BZAW 217. Berlin and New York: Walter de Gruyter, 1993.

_____. (1993b). *Redactional Processes in the Book of the Twelve.* BZAW 218. Berlin and New York: Walter de Gruyter, 1993.

_____. "Intertextuality and the Twelve," in James W. Watts and Paul R. House, eds., *Forming Prophetic Literature. Essays on Isaiah and the Twelve in Honor of John D. W. Watts.* JSOT.S 235. Sheffield: Sheffield Academic Press, 1996, 102–24.

O'Brien, Julia M. *Priest and Levite in Malachi.* SBL.DS 121. Atlanta: Scholars, 1992.

_____. "Judah as Wife and Husband: Deconstructing Gender in Malachi," *JBL* 115 (1996) 241–50.

O'Connor, Kathleen M. (1992a). "Jeremiah," *WBC* (1992) 169–77.

_____ (1992b). "Lamentations," *WBC* (1992) 178–82.

Olyan, Saul M. "'In the Sight of Her Lovers': On the Interpretation of *nablut* in Hos 2,12," *BZ* 36 (1992) 255–61.

_____. "Honor, Shame, and Covenant Relations in Ancient Israel and Its Environment," *JBL* 115 (1996) 201–18.

Ortlund, Raymond C., Jr. *Whoredom. God's Unfaithful Wife in Biblical Theology.* New Studies in Biblical Theology. Grand Rapids: Eerdmans, 1996.

Paul, Shalom M. "Biblical Analogues to Middle Assyrian Law," in Edwin B. Firmage et al., eds., *Religion and Law: Biblical-Judaic and Islamic Perspectives.* Winona Lake: Eisenbrauns, 1990, 333–50.

Petermann (Batmartha), Ina Johanne. "Machen Geburt und Monatsblutung die Frau 'unrein'? Zur Revisionsbedürftigkeit eines missverstandenen Diktums," in Luise Schottroff and Marie-Theres Wacker, eds., *Von der Wurzel getragen. Christlich-feministische Exegese in Auseinandersetzung mit Antijudaismus.* BibIS 17. Leiden and New York: Brill, 1996, 43–60.

Phillips, Anthony. "Another Look at Adultery," *JSOT* 20 (1981) 3–25.

Podella, Thomas. *Das Lichtkleid JHWHs. Untersuchungen zur Gestalthaftigkeit Gottes im Alten Testament und seiner altorientalischen Umwelt.* FAT 15. Tübingen: J.C.B. Mohr (Paul Siebeck), 1996.

Pope, Marvin H. "Mixed Marriage Metaphor in Ez 16," in Astrid Beck et al., eds., *Fortunate the Eyes that See.* Grand Rapids: Eerdmans, 1995, 384–99.

Pressler, Carolyn. "Sexual Violence and Deuteronomic Law," in Athalya Brenner, ed., *A Feminist Companion to Exodus to Deuteronomy. FemCB* 6. Sheffield: Sheffield Academic Press, 1994, 102–12.

Preuss, Horst-Dietrich. art. "תועבה, *toʿeḇāh,*" *ThWAT* 8:580–92.

Redditt, Paul L. "Zechariah 9–14, Malachi, and the Redaction of the Book of the Twelve," in James W. Watts and Paul R. House, eds., *Forming Prophetic Literature. Essays on Isaiah and the Twelve in Honor of John D. W. Watts.* JSOT.S 235. Sheffield: Sheffield Academic Press, 1996, 245–68.

Rendtorff, Rolf. *Die "Bundesformel": Eine exegetisch-theologische Untersuchung.* SBS 160. Stuttgart: Katholisches Bibelwerk, 1995.

Reventlow, Henning Graf von. *Die Propheten Haggai, Sacharja und Maleachi.* ATD 25/2. Göttingen: Vandenhoeck & Ruprecht, 1993.

Ricoeur, Paul. "Stellung und Funktion der Metapher in der biblischen Sprache," in Paul Ricoeur and Eberhard Jüngel, *Metapher. Zur Hermeneutik religiöser Sprache.* EvTh Sonderheft. Munich: Kaiser, 1974, 45–70.

_____. "The Metaphorical Process as Cognition, Imagination, and Feeling," *Critical Inquiry* 5 (1978) 143–59.

_____. *Die lebendige Metapher.* Texte und Studien zu Handlung, Sprache und Lebenswelt 12. 2nd ed. Munich: Fink, 1991. French original: *La metaphore vive.* Paris: Seuil, 1975. English: *The Rule of Metaphor: Multi-Disciplinary Studies of the Creation of Meaning in Language.* London: Routledge and Kegan Paul, 1978.

_____. "Die Metapher und das Hauptproblem der Hermeneutik," in Anselm Haverkamp, ed., *Theorie der Metapher.* 2nd ed. Darmstadt: Wissenschaftliche Buchgesellschaft, 1996.

Ringgren, Helmer. art. "טהר, *ṭāhar,*" *ThWAT* 3:306–15 (*TDOT* 5:287–96).

Ringgren, Helmer, Klaus Seybold, and Heinz-Josef Fabry. art. "מלך/מלך, *meleḵ/mālaḵ,*" *ThWAT* 4:926–57 (*TDOT* 8:346–75).

Roche, Michael de. "Israel's 'Two Evils' in Jeremiah II 13," *VT* 31 (1981) 369–71.

Rogerson, John William. art. "Dodekapropheton," *TRE* 9 (1982) 18–20.

Rozelaar, Marc. "An Unrecognized Part of the Human Anatomy," *Jdm* 37 (1988) 97–101.

Rudolph, Wilhelm. "Zu Mal 2,10-16," *ZAW* 93 (1981) 85–90.

Russell, Letty M., ed. *Feminist Interpretation of the Bible*. Philadelphia: Westminster, 1985.

Ryken, Leland, et al., eds. *Dictionary of Biblical Imagery*. Downers Grove, Ill.: InterVarsity, 1998.

Sals, Ulrike. "Reading Zechariah 5:5-11: Prophecy, Gender and (Ap)Perception," in Athalya Brenner, ed., *A Feminist Companion to the Latter Prophets. FemCB* Second Series 8. Sheffield: Sheffield Academic Press, 2001, 186–205.

Sanderson, Judith E. (1992a). "Amos," *WBC* (1992) 205–209.

_____. (1992b). "Habakkuk," *WBC* (1992) 222–24.

_____. (1992c). "Micah," *WBC* (1992) 215–16.

_____. (1992d). "Nahum," *WBC* (1992) 217–21.

_____. (1992e). "Zephaniah," *WBC* (1992) 225–27.

Sawyer, John F. A. "Daughter of Zion and Servant of the Lord in Isaiah: A Comparison," *JSOT* 44 (1989) 89–107.

Scharbert, Josef. "Ehe und Eheschliessung in der Rechtssprache des Pentateuch und beim Chronisten," in Georg Braulik, ed., *Studien zum Pentateuch. Walter Kornfeld zum 60. Geburtstag*. Vienna, Freiburg, Basel: Herder, 1977, 213–25.

_____. art. "Ehe/Eherecht/Ehescheidung II. Altes Testament," *TRE* 9 (1982) 311–13.

Schart, Aaron (1998a). *Die Entstehung des Zwölfprophetenbuchs. Neubearbeitungen von Amos im Rahmen schriftübergreifender Redaktionsprozesse*. BZAW 260. Berlin: Walter de Gruyter, 1998.

_____ (1998b). "Zur Redaktionsgeschichte des Zwölfprophetenbuchs," *VF* 43 (1998) 13–33.

Schmid, Konrad. *Buchgestalten des Jeremiabuches. Untersuchungen zur Redaktions- und Rezeptionsgeschichte von Jer 30–33 im Kontext des Buches*. WMANT 72. Neukirchen-Vluyn: Neukirchener Verlag, 1996.

Schmidt, Werner H. *Alttestamentlicher Glaube*. 8th ed. Neukirchen-Vluyn: Neukirchener Verlag, 1996.

Schmidtgen, Beate. *Die Stadt als Frau im Buch Jesaja*. Dissertation, Universität Basel, 2001.

Schmitt, John J. "The Motherhood of God and Zion as Mother," *RB* 92 (1985) 557–69.

_____. "The Virgin of Israel: Referent and Use of the Phrase in Amos and Jeremiah," *CBQ* 53 (1991) 365–87.

Schmoldt, Hans. art. "פשט, *pāšaṭ*," *ThWAT* 6:787–91 (*TDOT* 12:129–32).

Schreiner, Stefan. "Mischehen—Ehebruch—Ehescheidung. Betrachtungen zu Mal 2,10-16," *ZAW* 91 (1979) 207–28.

Schroer, Silvia. *In Israel gab es Bilder. Nachrichten von darstellender Kunst im Alten Testament*. OBO 74. Fribourg: Universitätsverlag; Göttingen: Vandenhoeck & Ruprecht, 1987.

_____. "Die Zweiggöttin in Palästina/Israel. Von der Mittelbronze II B-Zeit bis zu Jesus Sirach," in Max Küchler and Christoph Uehlinger, eds., *Jerusalem.*

Texte–Bilder–Steine. Zum 100. Geburtstag von Hildi und Othmar Keel-Leu. NTOA 6. Fribourg: Universitätsverlag; Göttingen: Vandenhoeck & Ruprecht, 1987, 201–25.

Schulte, Hannelies. "Beobachtungen zum Begriff der Zônâ im Alten Testament," *ZAW* 104 (1992) 255–62.

Schulz-Rauch, Martin. *Hosea und Jeremia. Zur Wirkungsgeschichte des Hoseabuches.* CThM 16. Stuttgart: Calwer, 1996.

Schüngel-Straumann, Helen. "God as Mother in Hos 11," in Athalya Brenner, ed., *A Feminist Companion to the Latter Prophets. FemCB* 8. Sheffield: Sheffield Academic Press, 1995, 194–218.

_____. *Rûah bewegt die Welt. Gottes schöpferische Lebenskraft in der Krisenzeit des Exils.* SBS 151. Stuttgart: Katholisches Bibelwerk, 1992.

_____. "Mutter Zion im Alten Testament," in Theodor Schneider and Helen Schüngel-Straumann, eds., *Theologie zwischen Zeiten und Kontinenten. Für Elisabeth Gössmann.* Freiburg: Herder, 1993, 19–30.

_____. "*RÛAH* und Gender-Frage am Beispiel der Visionen beim Propheten Ezechiel," in Bob Becking and Meindert Dijkstra, eds., *On Reading Prophetic Texts. Gender-Specific and Related Studies in Memory of Fokkelien van Dijk-Hemmes.* BibIS 18. Leiden and New York: Brill, 1996, 201–15.

Seebass, Horst. art. "לקח, *lāqaḥ,*" *ThWAT* 4:588–94 (*TDOT* 8:16–21).

_____. (1986a). art. "נפל, *nāpal,*" *ThWAT* 5:521–31 (*TDOT* 9:488–97).

_____. (1986b). art. "נפשׁ, *nepeš,*" *ThWAT* 5:531–55 (*TDOT* 9:497–519).

Seifert, Brigitte. *Metaphorisches Reden von Gott im Hoseabuch.* FRLANT 166. Göttingen: Vandenhoeck & Ruprecht, 1996.

Seifert, Elke. *Tochter und Vater im Alten Testament. Eine ideologiekritische Untersuchung zur Verfügungsgewalt von Vätern über ihre Töchter.* Neukirchener Theologische Dissertationen und Habilitationen 9. Neukirchen-Vluyn: Neukirchener Verlag, 1997.

_____. "Tochter und Vater im Alten Testament oder: Die Notwendigkeit einer Ideologiekritik an patriarchalen Rollenklischees im Ersten Testament," in Ulrike Eichler and Ilse Müllner, eds., *Sexuelle Gewalt gegen Mädchen und Frauen als Thema der feministischen Theologie.* Gütersloh: Chr. Kaiser, 1999, 76–98.

Setel, T. Drorah. "Prophets and Pornography: Female Sexual Imagery in Hosea," in Letty M. Russell, ed., *Feminist Interpretation of the Bible.* Philadelphia: Westminster, 1985, 86–95.

Sherwood, Yvonne. *The Prostitute and the Prophet. Hosea's Marriage in Literary-Theoretical Perspective.* JSOT.S 212. Gender, Culture, Theory 2. Sheffield: Sheffield Academic Press, 1996.

Shields, Mary E. "Circumcision of the Prostitute: Gender, Sexuality, and the Call to Repentance in Jeremiah 3:1–4:4," *BInt* 3 (1995) 61–74; reprinted in Athalya Brenner, ed., *A Feminist Companion to the Latter Prophets. FemCB* Second Series 8. Sheffield: Sheffield Academic Press, 2001, 121–33, with a Self-Response: 134–36.

_____. “Multiple Exposures. Body Rhetoric and Gender Characterization in Ezekiel 16,” *JFSR* 14 (1998) 5–18; reprinted in Athalya Brenner, ed., *A Feminist Companion to the Latter Prophets. FemCB* Second Series 8. Sheffield: Sheffield Academic Press, 2001, 137–52, with a Self-Response: 154–55.

Simian-Yofre, Horacio. art. “פנים, *pānîm,*” *ThWAT* 6:629–59 (*TDOT* 11:589–615).

Sölle, Dorothee. *Es muss doch mehr als alles geben. Nachdenken über Gott.* Hamburg: Hoffmann und Campe, 1992.

Soskice, Janet Martin. *Metaphor and Religious Language.* New York: Oxford University Press, 1985.

Steck, Odil Hannes. “Zion als Gelände und Gestalt. Überlegungen zur Wahrnehmung Jerusalems als Stadt und Frau im Alten Testament,” *ZThK* 86 (1989) 261–81; reprinted in idem, *Gottesknecht und Zion,* 126–45.

_____. *Der Abschluss der Prophetie im Alten Testament. Ein Versuch zur Frage der Vorgeschichte des Kanons.* BThSt 17. Neukirchen-Vluyn: Neukirchener Verlag, 1991.

_____. *Gottesknecht und Zion. Gesammelte Aufsätze zu Deuterojesaja.* FAT 4. Tübingen: J.C.B. Mohr (Paul Siebeck), 1992.

_____. *Die Prophetenbücher und ihr theologisches Zeugnis. Wege der Nachfrage und Fährten zur Antwort.* Tübingen: J.C.B. Mohr (Paul Siebeck), 1996.

Steingrimsson, Sigurdur Ö. art. “זמם, *zmm,*” *ThWAT* 2:599–603 (*TDOT* 4:87–90).

Steymans, Hans Ulrich. *Deuteronomium 28 und die adê zur Thronfolgeregelung Asarhaddons. Segen und Fluch im Alten Orient und in Israel.* OBO 145. Fribourg: Universitätsverlag; Göttingen: Vandenhoeck & Ruprecht, 1995.

Stienstra, Nelly. *YHWH is the Husband of His People. Analysis of a Biblical Metaphor with Special Reference to Translation.* Kampen: Pharos, 1993.

Swanepol, M. G. “Ezekiel 16: Abandoned Child, Bride Adorned or Unfaithful Wife?” in Philip R. Davies and David J. A. Clines, eds., *Among the Prophets: Language, Image, and Structure in the Prophetic Writings.* JSOT.S 144. Sheffield: JSOT Press, 1993, 84–104.

Theweleit, Klaus. *Männerphantasien.* Vol. 1: *Frauen, Fluten, Körper, Geschichte.* Vol. 2: *Männerkörper. Zur Psychoanalyse des weissen Terrors.* Frankfurt: Roter Stern, 1977–1978 (rpt. Munich, 1995). English: *Male Fantasies.* Vol. 1: *Women, Floods, Bodies, History.* Vol. 2: *Male Bodies, Psychoanalyzing the White Terror.* Minneapolis: University of Minnesota Press, 1987–1989.

Thistlethwaite, Susan Brooks. “Every Two Minutes: Abused Women and Feminist Biblical Interpretation,” in Letty M. Russell, ed., *Feminist Interpretation.* Philadelphia: Westminster, 1985, 96–110.

Thomas, D. Winton. “The Root אהב, ‘love,’ in Hebrew,” *ZAW* 57 (1939) 57–64.

Torczyner, Harry (= Tur-Sinai, Naphtali H.). “Nachträge und Berichtigungen zu meinen Proverbia-Studien,” *ZDMG* 72 (1918) 154–56.

Törnkvist, Rut. *The Use and Abuse of Female Sexual Imagery in the Book of Hosea. A Feminist Critical Approach to Hos 1–3.* AUU, Uppsala Women's Studies, A. Women in Religion 7. Uppsala: Academia Ubsaliensis, 1998.

Vieweger, Dieter. *Die literarischen Bezüge zwischen den Büchern Jeremia und Ezechiel*. BEAT 26. Frankfurt and New York: Peter Lang, 1993.

Vogelzang, Marianna E., and Wout J. van Bekkum. "Meaning and Symbolism of Clothing in Ancient Near Eastern Texts," in Herman L. J. Vanstiphout et al., eds., *Scripta Signa Vocis. Studies about Scripts, Scriptures, Scribes and Languages in the Near East, Presented to J. H. Hospers by his Pupils, Colleagues, and Friends*. Groningen: E. Forsten, 1986, 265–84.

Volz, Paul. *Der Prophet Jeremia*. KAT X. Leipzig: J. C. Hinrichs, 1922.

_____. *Der Prophet Jeremiah*. KAT X, unaltered reprint of the 2nd Leipzig ed. of 1928. Hildesheim, et al.: G. Olms, 1983.

Wacker, Marie-Theres. "Traces of the Goddess in the Book of Hosea," in Athalya Brenner, ed., *A Feminist Companion to the Latter Prophets*. *FemCB* 8. Sheffield: Sheffield Academic Press, 1995, 219–41.

_____. *Figurationen des Weiblichen im Hosea-Buch*. HBS 8. Freiburg: Herder, 1996.

_____. "Das Buch Hosea. Der gott-identifizierte Mann und die Frau(en) Israel(s)," in Luise Schottroff and Marie-Theres Wacker, eds., *Kompendium Feministische Bibelauslegung*. 2nd ed. Gütersloh: Gütersloher Verlagshaus, 1999, 299–311.

Waltke, Bruce K., and Michael P. O'Connor. *An Introduction to Biblical Hebrew Syntax*. Winona Lake: Eisenbrauns, 1990.

Wanke, Gunther. *Jeremia 1,1–25,14*. ZBK 20/1. Zürich: Theologischer Verlag, 1995.

Washington, Harold C. "Violence and the Construction of Gender in the Hebrew Bible: A New Historicist Approach," *BInt* 5 (1997) 324–63.

Weems, Renita J. "Gomer: Victim of Violence or Victim of Metaphor?" *Semeia* 47 (1989) 87–104.

_____. *Battered Love. Marriage, Sex, and Violence in the Hebrew Prophets*. Minneapolis: Fortress, 1995.

Weider, Andreas. *Ehemetaphorik in prophetischer Verkündigung. Hos 1–3 und seine Wirkungsgeschichte im Jeremiabuch. Ein Beitrag zum alttestamentlichen Gottes-Bild*. FzB 71. Würzburg: Echter, 1993.

Weinfeld, Moshe. *Deuteronomy and the Deuteronomic School*. Oxford: Clarendon Press, 1972.

_____. art. "בְּרִית, *bᵉrît*," *ThWAT* 1:781–808 (*TDOT* 2:253–79).

Weippert, Helga. "Textilproduktion und Kleidung im vorhellenistischen Palästina," in Gisela Völger et al., eds., *Pracht und Geheimnis. Kleidung und Schmuck aus Palästina und Jordanien*. Köln: Rautenstrauch-Joest-Museum der Stadt Köln, 1987, 136–42.

Westbrook, Raymond. "Adultery in Ancient Near Eastern Law," *RB* 97 (1990) 542–80.

_____. "Punishment and Crimes," *ABD* 5 (1992) 546–56.

Westermann, Claus. *Das Buch Jesaja. Kapitel 40–66*. ATD 19. 4th ed. Göttingen: Vandenhoeck & Ruprecht, 1981.

_____. *Die Klagelieder. Forschungsgeschichte und Auslegung.* Neukirchen-Vluyn: Neukirchener Verlag, 1990.

Westermann, Claus, and Rainer Albertz. art. "גלה, *glh,* aufdecken," *THAT* I^4 (1984) 418–26.

White, Marsha C. "Jonah," *WBC* (1992) 212–14.

Whitt, William D. "The Divorce of Yahweh and Asherah in Hos 2,4-7.12ff.," *SJOT* 6 (1992) 31–67.

Willey, Patricia Tull. *Remember the Former Things. The Recollection of Previous Texts in Second Isaiah.* SBL.DS 161. Atlanta: Scholars, 1997.

Wilshire, L. E. "The Servant-City: A New Interpretation of the 'Servant of the Lord' in the Servant Songs of Deutero-Isaiah," *JBL* 94 (1975) 356–67.

Winter, Urs. *Frau und Göttin. Exegetische und ikonographische Studien zum weiblichen Gottesbild im Alten Israel und dessen Umwelt.* OBO 53. Fribourg: Universitätsverlag; Göttingen: Vandenhoeck & Ruprecht, 1983.

Wiseman, Donald J. *The Vassal Treaties of Esarhaddon.* London: British School of Archaeology in Iraq, 1958.

Wolff, Hans Walter. *Dodekapropheton I. Hosea.* BK.AT XIV/1. 3rd ed. Neukirchen-Vluyn: Neukirchener Verlag, 1976.

Woude, A. S. van der (1984a). art. "כנף, *kānāp,* Flügel," *THAT* I^4 (1984) 833–36.

_____. (1984b). art. "פנים, *pānīm,* Angesicht," *THAT* II^3 (1984) 432–60.

Yee, Gale A. "Hosea," *WBC* (1992) 195–202.

Zenger, Erich. "Das Zwölfprophetenbuch," in idem, et al., *Einleitung in das Alte Testament.* Kohlhammer-Studienbücher Theologie 1,1. 3rd newly revised and expanded ed. Stuttgart et al.: Kohlhammer, 1998, 467–533.

Ziegler, Joseph. *Die Liebe Gottes bei den Propheten. Ein Beitrag zur alttestamentlichen Theologie.* ATA XI/3. Münster: Aschendorffsche Verlagsbuchhandlung, 1930.

Zimmerli, Walther. *Ezechiel 1–24.* BK.AT XIII/1. Neukirchen-Vluyn: Neukirchener Verlag, 1969.

_____. art. "Ezechiel/Ezechielbuch," *TRE* X (1982) 766–81.

Zipor, Moshe A. "'Scenes from a Marriage'—According to Jeremiah," *JSOT* 65 (1995) 83–91.

Zobel, Hans-Jürgen. art. "גלה, *gālāh,*" *ThWAT* 1:1018–1031 (*TDOT* 2:476–88).

_____. art. "עקב, *ʿqb,*" *ThWAT* 6:338–43 (*TDOT* 11:315–20).

Scripture Index